Financial Modelling in
Corporate Management

Financial Modelling in Corporate Management

Edited by
JAMES W. BRYANT
Department of Mathematics, Statistics, and Operational Research
Sheffield City Polytechnic
Pond Street
Sheffield
S1 1WB

1807 1982

JOHN WILEY & SONS
Chichester · New York · Brisbane · Toronto

Library of Congress Cataloging in Publication Data:
Main entry under title:

Financial modelling in corporate management.

   Bibliography: p.
   Includes index.
   1. Corporations—Finance—Mathematical models—
Addresses, essays, lectures. I. Bryant, James, W., Ph. D.

HG4012.F54   658.1'5'0724   81–13059

ISBN 0 471 10021 8   AACR2

British Library Cataloguing in Publication Data

Financial modelling in corporate management.
   1. Corporations—Finance—Mathematical
   models
   I. Bryant, James W.
   658.1'5'0724   HG4026

ISBN 0 471 10021 8

Typeset by Activity, Salisbury, Wilts
and printed in the United States of America by
Vail-Ballou Press, Inc., Binghamton, N.Y.

HG
4012
. F54

List of Contributors

ANTHONY BAKER, formerly Group Head in the Operational Research Executive of the National Coal Board, is now Head of the Economic Assessment Service at IEA Coal Research

LEO BRESSMAN, formerly a Management Engineer at the Port Authority of New York and New Jersey, is now with the Irving Trust Company

JAMES BROWNE is Supervisor of Management Engineering Services for the Port Authority of New York and New Jersey

JAMES BRYANT, formerly lecturer in Operational Research at the University of Sussex, is now Principal Lecturer in Systems Modelling at Sheffield City Polytechnic

DAVID CHAMBERS is Professor of Operational Research at the London Business School

JOHN COLEMAN, formerly Associate Professor of Public Administration and Director of the Center for Health Systems Analysis at the University of New Haven, is now Associate Professor in the College of Health Related Professions at Wichita State University

LEWIS CORNER is Lecturer in Operational Research at the University of Sussex

IAN CRAWFORD is Management Accountant for TAC Construction Materials Ltd.

JOHN DOLBEAR is Operational Research Group Leader at Blue Circle Industries Ltd

JOHN DROBNY is a Management Engineer with the Port Authority of New York and New Jersey

JOHN GRINYER, is Professor of Accounting at the University of Dundee

PETER GRINYER, formerly Professor of Business Strategy at City University Business School, is now Esmee Fairbairn Professor of Economics (Finance and Investment) at the Univesity of St. Andrews

BRIAN HARRISON, formerly Deputy Managing Director of NCB (Coal Products) Ltd, is now Board Member for Finance on the National Coal Board and Chairman of NCB (Coal Products) Ltd.

ROBERT HILL is Assistant Professor in the College of Business Administration at Texas A & M University

JOHN HOLLAND is Lecturer in Accounting at the University of Glasgow

BARBARA JACKSON is Associate Professor of Business Administration at Harvard Business School

FRANK KAMINSKY is Professor in the Department of Industrial Engineering and Operations Research at the University of Massachusetts

STEPHEN LYUS is Operational Research Consultant in Group Management Services at the Imperial Group Ltd.

JOHN MACGREGOR is a Consultant with EPS Consultants Ltd. and a Lecturer at the Polytechnic of North London

JOHN PRECIOUS is Group Financial Controller for the Tioxide Group Ltd.

TONY RANDS is a Fellow at the Oxford Centre for Management Studies

ALFRED RAPPAPORT is Leonard Spacek Professor of Accounting and Information Systems in the J. R. Kellogg Graduate School of Management at Northwestern University

BENSON SHAPIRO is Associate Professor of Business Administration at Harvard Business School

BOB VAUSE is Dean of the Oxford Centre for Management Studies

BAL WAGLE is Development Planner in the D.P. Product Group of International Business Machines Corporation

GEOFFREY WELLS is Operational Research Manager in Group Management Services of the Imperial Group Ltd.

PETER WHYTE is a Management Accountant with the Treasurer's Department at Imperial Chemical Industries Ltd.

Contents

Preface   xiv

PART 1 FUNDAMENTALS

1. Corporate Financial Management   3
James Bryant
1.1   Corporate Financial Objectives.   3
1.2   Financial Aspects of Corporate Activity.   4
1.3   Financial Decision-making   5

2. Techniques in Financial Management   9
James Bryant
2.1   Management Accounting Activity.   9
2.2   Financial Reports   10
2.3   Evaluating Alternatives.   13
2.4   Monitoring Performance   17

3. Concepts of Financial Modelling.   23
James Bryant
3.1   Nature of Financial Modelling   23
3.2   Types of Model.   26
3.3   Options in Financial Model Building   30
3.4   Use of Financial Models   32

4. Techniques of Financial Modelling   35
James Bryant
4.1   Forecasting   35
4.2   Risk Analysis   40
4.3   Optimization   45

5. A Simple Financial Planning Model.   47
James Bryant
5.1   Model Specifications   47

5.2   Structure of the Model   48
5.3   Programming the Model   55

PART 2 OPERATIONAL PLANNING MODELS

6. **A Computer Model for Aiding Product-line Decisions** **69**
    Barbara Jackson and Benson Shapiro
    6.1   Introduction   69
    6.2   Product-line Policy in the Paper Industry   69
    6.3   Computerized Alternative for Product-line Management   70
    6.4   Making a Product Map   71
    6.5   Designing the Model   73
    6.6   Using the Model   73
    6.7   Implementing the Model   76
    6.8   Conclusions   77

7. **Plant Planning Models in the Coal Industry** **81**
    Brian Harrison and Anthony Baker
    7.1   Introduction   81
    7.2   Coal Products Division   81
    7.3   Why Think of Using Models?   82
    7.4   The Range of Models Developed   84
    7.5   Financial Model for Coking-plant Budgets   86
    7.6   Corporate Model for Production Policy Planning   89
    7.7   Provision of Data for the Models   92
    7.8   Use of the Models and their Value   92
    7.9   Conclusions   94

8. **Pricing Models in the Imperial Group** **97**
    Stephen Lyus and Geoffrey Wells
    8.1   Introduction   97
    8.2   Imported Cigar and Cardboard Box Models   98
    8.3   Beer Costing Model   104
    8.4   Smedley–HP Foods Pricing Model   111

9. **The Use of Computers in Cash Management for the Small Company** . .   **121**
    Tony Rands and Bob Vause
    9.1   Introduction   121
    9.2   Cash-flow Problems and Models   122
    9.3   A Computer Modelling Method for Managing Cash-flows in
           Small Companies   125
    9.4   An Example of the Application of the Method   129
    9.5   The Value of a Model   135
    9.6   Conclusions   139

10. **Linear Programming in Cash Management: A Technical Note** 141
    Robert Hill
    10.1   Introduction. 141
    10.2   Common Approaches to Solving the Cash-management
            Problem 142
    10.3   An Example of the Linear-programming Approach to
            Cash Management 143
    10.4   Shortcomings of these Cash Management Tools. 147

11. **Budget Modelling in the Construction Materials Industry** 149
    Ian Crawford
    11.1   Introduction. 149
    11.2   Model Development. 150
    11.3   The Budget Model. 151
    11.4   Use of Model in Planning Process 163
    11.5   Future Developments. 172
    11.6   Conclusion. 173

12. **Comparison of Alternative Financing Methods** 175
    Lewis Corner
    12.1   Introduction. 175
    12.2   Financing Methods 176
    12.3   DCF Appraisal of Financing Terms 178
    12.4   An Illustrative Example 179
    12.5   Discussion 180

PART 3 STRATEGIC PLANNING MODELS

13. **Financial Models for Industrial Development Strategy** 185
    Leo Bressman, James Browne and John Drobny
    13.1   Introduction. 185
    13.2   Industrial Park Model. 187
    13.3   Applications of Industrial Park Model 191
    13.4   Background on Resource Recovery 194
    13.5   Resource Recovery Model. 195
    13.6   Applications of Resource Recovery Model 198
    13.7   Appraisal of the Simulation Approach. 199
    13.8   Conclusions 201

14. **Blue Circle's Investment-Planning Models.** 203
    John Dolbear
    14.1   Introduction. 203
    14.2   Model Development. 204
    14.3   Model Structure 205

14.4   Use of the Model.   226
14.5   Conclusions   229

15. Developing Dividend and Financing Policies Using a Computer.   231
David Chambers
15.1   Introduction.   231
15.2   Policies Identified   232
15.3   Some Numerical Examples   235
15.4   Use of the Program   240
15.5   Relation to Optimization Methods   243

16. Financial Planning Models Including Dividend Growth   245
John Grinyer
16.1   Introduction.   245
16.2   Shareholder Wealth and Financial Management   245
16.3   Dividend Growth Simulation Models.   250
16.4   Conclusion.   259

17. Strategic Analysis for More Profitable Acquisitions   261
Alfred Rappaport
17.1   Introduction.   261
17.2   Steps in the Analysis   262
17.3   Case of Alcar Corporation.   266
17.4   Conclusion.   280

PART 4 MODELS IN CORPORATE PLANNING

**18. A Computerized Financial Planning Model for Health Maintenance
Organizations 285**
John Coleman and Frank Kaminsky
18.1   Introduction.   285
18.2   Planning in HMOs   290
18.3   Financial Planning Models for HMOs.   294
18.4   Implementation of the FPM in Different HMO Planning
       Settings.   311
18.5   Summary and Conclusions   314

19. Corporate Planning in Local Authorities   317
Bal Wagle
19.1   Introduction.   317
19.2   Local Government Reorganization   318
19.3   The Corporate Planning Process   319
19.4   Planning System Requirements   321
19.5   Background to Development of the Modelling System   322

19.6	Structure of the Modelling System	323
19.7	Enhancements to the Basic Modelling System	332
19.8	Use of the System	335
19.9	Role of the Modelling System in Clwyd County Council's Corporate Planning	336
19.10	Conclusion.	339

PART 5 FINANCIAL MODELLING CASE HISTORIES

20.	**Financial Modelling on an In-House Mini-computer**	**345**
	John Macgregor and Peter Whyte	
20.1	Introduction.	345
20.2	Applications and Problems	345
20.3	Move to 'In-House'	347
20.4	In-House Model Developments.	348
20.5	The FCS–EPS System.	349
20.6	Application A: Long-term Cash Forecast Models.	353
20.7	Application B: The Suite of ICI Tax Models	357
20.8	Application C: Quarterly Profit and Sales Reports	361
20.9	Application D: Corporate Report to Board.	362
20.10	Hardware.	362
20.11	Graphical Output	367
20.12	Conclusion.	367
21.	**An Experience of Corporate Modelling**	**371**
	John Precious	
21.1	Introduction.	371
21.2	When Success can be a Long-term Forecast.	371
21.3	. . . But Long-term Forecasts are Usually Wrong	388
21.4	The Years in Retrospect	393
22.	**A Model Development and Evolution Strategy: A Case Study**	**401**
	John Holland	
22.1	Introduction.	401
22.2	Financial Modelling	401
22.3	A Managerial Strategy for Financial Model Development.	404
22.4	A Case Study of Model Development and Evolution.	407
22.5	Appraisal of the Methodology	422

PART 6 THE PRACTICE OF FINANCIAL MODELLING

23. The Historical Development and Current Practice of Corporate Modelling in the U.K..	**427**
Peter Grinyer	

23.1   The Growth of Modelling   427
23.2   Reasons for Growth.   428
23.3   Types of Model in Use   429
23.4   Changing Applications   435
23.5   A Prognostication   437

24. Future Developments in Financial Modelling **441**
James Bryant
24.1   Introduction.   441
24.2   New Requirements   441
24.3   New Methodologies   443
24.4   New Facilities.   444

Additional Bibliography **447**

Index **451**

Preface

Despite more than a decade of financial modelling activity in organizations of all types and sizes, descriptions of the work which has been carried out is confined in the main to the occasional article in a specialist journal or to a passing reference in a computer-software consultant's sales pitch. The intention of this book is to bring together within a structured framework a collection of articles which represent the ranges of applications of financial modelling in practice.

A basic aim in gathering material for this text has been to include descriptions of modelling projects by those who have been involved with them at first hand. It is to be hoped that their accounts of practical modelling work will do something to dispel the mystique which regrettably still surrounds the use of modelling methods in financial decision-making. However, for obvious reasons, the articles are not intended to be blueprints for future modelling activity, although the basic principles which they demonstrate and some of the structures created should be of value to anyone contemplating or continuing their own work in this area.

The book is addressed to a number of audiences. Firstly, it should provide a broad introduction to the field of financial modelling for the non-specialist manager or accountant. Secondly, it should help to widen the perspective of those already engaged in modelling work, both in financial and other contexts, and suggest potential fields of application within their own organizations. And thirdly, it should be of educative value to students in accounting, business management and related subjects by introducing them to one of the most rapidly growing practical areas of contemporary organizational control.

The structure which has been adopted for the text is extremely simple. In Part 1, after a brief consideration of the demands of modern financial management, the concepts of financial modelling are explained and some of the most important techniques used are outlined. Parts 2 and 3 give illustrations of models which have been developed to aid in operational and strategic planning applications respectively, the timescale and financial implications of the latter generally being greater. Part 4 sets financial modelling activity within a wider corporate-planning context, the two examples given emphasizing the planning systems rather than the model structures employed. The case histories in Part 5 each describe the development of financial-modelling activity within a particular organization and pay special attention to the

xiii

subject of implementation, drawing out salient lessons for the newcomer to modelling. Finally, Part 6 traces the historical development of financial modelling since its inception and gives some suggestions as to the direction of future work.

Acknowledgement by name of all those who contributed, often unknowingly, to the shaping of this book is an impossible task. Its origins may be traced back to a seminar on financial modelling which I organized at the University of Sussex and indeed several of the contributors also gave presentations on that occasion. However, the seminar in turn would not have taken place without the encouragement of Pat Rivett, who also provided me with an ideal setting in which to complete the book. Nor would the seminar have occurred had I not been thrown in at the deep end of financial modelling by Dave Wilkinson and Frank Wolstenholme at TAC, my former employers. At many times since then during the preparation of course materials and later during the compilation of this book, I have had encouragement and advice from friends in consultancies, universities and businesses, for which I thank them. I must also acknowledge the help given to me when seeking information by several libraries, notably that of the Institute of Chartered Accountants. More specifically, the work carried out by Sheila Ridgwell provided me with a useful review of current financial modelling activity.

Finally, I must express my gratitude to my contributors for their cooperation, and for their success in meeting deadlines; to Pauline for all her encouragement in the earliest and most precarious stages of planning this book; to my parents for immersing me in accounting in a way from which I have never recovered; and to Hazel without whose interest and hard work as editorial assistant and typist this book might never have seen the light of day.

PART 1 FUNDAMENTALS

In the parable attributed to Budda, a group of blind men, who have never encountered an elephant before, are asked to describe one which is brought before them. In turn they move forward and touch the great animal, and later discuss their impressions. The first, who has felt one of the creature's legs, says that an elephant is like a huge living pillar. The second man is surprised by this description: he feels the animal's trunk and to him an elephant is just like a giant snake. A third man disagrees; surely an elephant is like a broom—he touches the tuft of the beast's tail. Another man, who feels one of the tusks interposes that *his* impression is that an elephant is like a ploughshare: and as the opinions are added, so argument and contradiction rage. But the Raja, who has created the dissension by asking the blind men to give their descriptions, sits quietly to one side laughing at the absurdity of the situation which has arisen. So it is with financial modelling, that there is no general agreement as to the meaning of the term, although the activity itself flourishes!

To illustrate a few of its many facets, consider the following examples:

(1) In a multi-product food company, management wish to examine the financial impact of changes in commodity prices and labour costs, and of alternative marketing and distribution policies.

(2) A shipping company requires a procedure to ease the preparation of budgets so that changes in cargo flows and fleet movements can rapidly be re-evaluated, and reports on ships, routes and on-shore facilities can be generated.

(3) The economics of oil exploration and production for a company operating in the North Sea must be assessed, and a system is therefore needed which will be capable of handling the complex financing arrangements involved and the taxation implications of alternative strategies.

(4) An international hotel group seeks to investigate manning requirements in the event of changes in activity levels, and to calculate the financial consequences of currency movements between its constituent nationally-based companies.

(5) Head office management of a multinational conglomerate wish to consolidate the regional business plans of its industrial products division so as to investigate product-planning options regarding plant capacity and product allocations.

1

In each of these situations a financial model might be used to aid and inform managerial decision-making.

The basis of all financial modelling is the representation of the relationships among financial variables, and between these variables and other measures of corporate activity. The models which enshrine these relationships are then used to assist decision-makers, being structured so as to generate reports and analyses relating to the alternatives between which a choice is to be made. This role in decision-making is a key feature which distinguishes financial modelling from other forms of financial analysis.

Frequently, although not inevitably, financial models today are computer-based. Thus a model structure appropriate to a given problem is set up within a computer and is then used to test the effects of the alternatives being considered. This structure is usually in a generalized form, specific numerical values to be tested being input as the need arises, rather in the way that a fixed balance-sheet format may be used by a firm in its annual reports even though different figures appear from year to year. This computerization of model structures has developed rapidly in recent years, and is now an essential feature of financial modelling work.

In this first Part of this book, the fundamentals of financial modelling are described at some length, so that the concepts and terminology used in the case histories, which constitute the bulk of the remainder of the text, may be made clear. Chapter 1 provides a context for this exposition by outlining a few of the features of modern financial management which have stimulated the development of modelling methods in the finance area. Some of the techniques which have been developed in recent years to cope with an increasingly complex managerial situation are described in Chapter 2, which should be helpful for those readers who are less familiar with modern finance methodologies. In Chapter 3 the basic concepts of financial modelling are presented using simple examples, and the computerization of models is explained in a way that should aid readers who are unfamiliar with computer-based modelling techniques. Chapter 4 deals with some specific modelling techniques which are of particular relevance to financial model building, some of which, though under-used today, may be more important in the future. Chapter 5 contains an extremely detailed illustration of a financial model structure, which is intended to demonstrate how the relationships between financial and other variables in a generalized manufacturing setting might be depicted, and how the principal standard financial reports could be generated.

Financial Modelling in Corporate Management
Edited by J. W. Bryant
© 1982 John Wiley & Sons Ltd.

1

Corporate Financial Management

JAMES BRYANT

1.1 Corporate Financial Objectives

The subject of corporate objectives has attracted much attention in recent years as
the importance of an organization's interactions with its environment and of the
welfare of the individuals and groups of which it is composed have been more
generally recognized. This has meant that the historical tendency to consider
corporate objectives in purely monetary terms has been supplemented by the use
of broader goals including measures of social welfare. One of the principal features
of this change of emphasis has been a widening of the working definition of the
boundaries of corporate responsibility. For example, in the opening of a new
factory not only must its potential as a revenue-generating unit providing financial
benefits for employees and shareholders be examined, but the impact it will have
on the locality in which it is to be sited has also to be considered; this may include
the physical effects of manufacturing processes on the natural environment, the
economic effects of the additional wealth created on the local business community,
and the social effects of migration and housing development on the character of
a neighbourhood. This new perception of the role of corporate management brings
with it more and conflicting demands on an organization's resources and new
constraints on the deployment of those resources and so makes the process of
management more complex.

Despite the broader view of corporate objectives now held in many organizations,
the financial objectives of most continue to be stated implicitly if not explicitly in
terms of relatively unsophisticated measures. The assertion, to be found with slight
variants in most texts on financial management, that the purpose of financial
control is to direct an organization towards such traditional targets as profit
maximization has only recently been challenged. Indeed much of accounting
methodology is concerned with the creation of conventions to provide unambiguous

3

statements of corporate profitability. The cynical may argue that the provision of good working conditions, community benefits or efficient product servicing are simply means to the ultimate end of organizational economic growth through the generation of profits, but this is too superficial and one-sided a view for the management of business enterprises in contemporary conditions. At the very least, recent worldwide economic instability and the accompanying inflationary tendencies have led to a shift in emphasis for many firms from profit to related metrics such as economic value, reflecting a greater concern for the long-term net benefits of financial policies for the ownership interests of the corporation. In other firms the narrowness of the shareholder benefit criterion of financial performance has been challenged by the 'stakeholder theory' of corporate objectives which reflects the responsibility, mentioned earlier, of an organization towards all those 'stakeholders' with which it significantly interacts; these include not only shareholders but also moneylenders, suppliers, debtors, customers, employees and the general public. This view leads to the alternative financial objective of maximizing net social consumption, where this is defined as the value of the total consumption that an organization makes possible less its own consumption. Social disbenefits resulting from an organization's activities have a negative effect on such a measure while other cash flows such as wages paid to employees have a positive effect. A broader measure of this sort has the advantage of embracing the system-wide effects of management decisions, but unfortunately the methodology and databases required for its use remain to be fully developed. Financial management today is therefore in the uneasy position of continuing to work with measures that are exact but which are recognized as being inadequate for corporate decision-making, while the new broader measures have still to be soundly defined and practically established.

1.2 Financial Aspects of Corporate Activity

Despite the uncertainties which have been stated about the choice of appropriate financial objectives, the management of corporate activity cannot be 'put on ice' until this issue has been resolved. How then do corporations operate to achieve their financial targets? Organizations function in financial terms by using long-term funds to support activities which will generate short-term gains. Financial management therefore involves the control of two interacting cash-flow cycles as illustrated in Figure 1.1. Cash is raised from capital markets and is invested in assets required for operations; these facilities are used for the production of goods and services and the products traded to provide a cash flow for future organizational growth as well as to repay market liabilities. The capital cash-flow cycle has an enabling function and involves interchanges between the organization, sources of funds such as moneylenders and shareholders, and investment opportunities such as debtors. The trading cash-flow cycle made possible by the capital base involves the organization in transmitting earnings from product sales to employees as wages, to suppliers for purchases and to the government for the provision of a wider

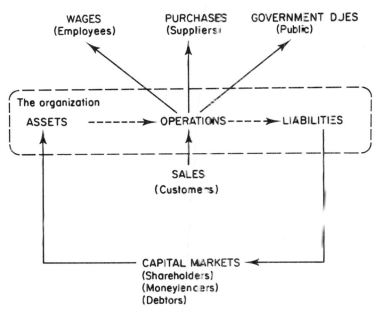

Figure 1.1 Organization cash-flow cycles

economic infrastructure. The stakeholders referred to earlier have been explicitly indicated in these cycles which identify their roles.

Despite the strong interaction between the capital and trading cycles, these two aspects of financial management are conventionally held apart and may even be the responsibilities of two separate functional elements within the finance department of an organization. Thus a financial controller may be primarily concerned with the trading cash flows, while a corporate treasurer handles the financing of operations by dealing with external sources of capital. The central problem of purposeful financial management is the provision of integrated control for the two cash-flow cycles, in order to achieve overall corporate goals.

1.3 Financial Decision-making

The process of financial management involves the direction of a corporation towards its financial objectives but within the constraints imposed by other corporate aims. This process involves the taking of decisions which have financial implications for the organization. Decision-making can only properly be regarded as a cyclical process which can be considered to have a number of interacting elements. A variety of questions are raised by different parts of this process and these can be more clearly related by using the representation of the decision-making cycle given in Figure 1.2. The four elements included, here entitled concept, value, inquiry and design, combine in different ways to perform the two principal decision-making functions: problem identification and solution implementation.

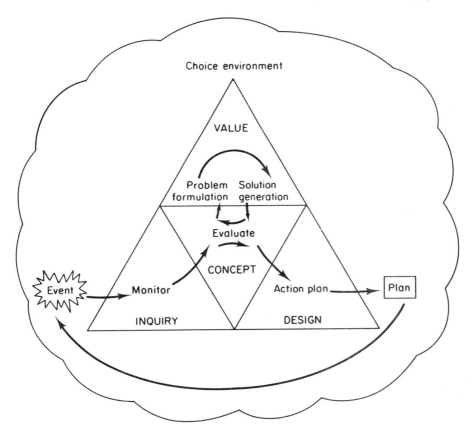

Figure 1.2 Decision-making cycle

Financial decision-making arises when events occur in the choice environment; these may be either internal or external to the corporation. Examples might be a change in bank rate or the compilation of monthly product sales statistics. Detection of such events depends crucially on the monitoring capabilities of the finance function which in turn depends on what features of the environment are regarded as important and on the availability of information relating to these features. Thus it is only in recent years that the energy budgets of organizations have received much attention as the cost of energy has become an increasingly important debit item. Incoming information is evaluated in accordance with a concept or model of the perceived situation. If a substantial mismatch with what is expected is present the information may either be rejected or supplementary evidence sought before the process proceeds further. If a substantial mismatch with what is desired is present then a problem has been formally recognized. This may occur because of a change in the choice environment resulting from earlier decisions or external forces; for example, a change in pricing policy or exchange-rate fluctuations may have had a harmful effect on sales. Alternatively the desired state may be modified because of changes in corporate objectives or perceptions: a target level of profitability might, for instance, no longer be regarded as adequate. A variety of solutions to a problem is usually generated, although this may include a 'no action' option. These solutions are attempts to reduce the mismatches detected and are most likely to involve changes in the perceived situation, although it is possible that the financial goals may be altered instead. For instance a corporation which discovers that it has inadequate funds to finance a new development may issue shares or debentures, raise loans or bank overdrafts or discontinue existing un-profitable activities; alternatively the new development plans may be modified or abandoned so that the funds are no longer required. Problems range from those which are repetitive and familiar to the novel and unique, and the effort involved in solution generation varies accordingly, possibly involving problem re-formulation in an iterative manner. Additionally, solutions may be suggested at a number of levels and the choice of an appropriate level may be at least as difficult as the selection of a particular solution at that level. Thus a high level of debtors in a particular market may be tackled by introducing a tighter debt-monitoring policy to pressure customers, by using a factor to handle debt-collection activities, or by moving out of that particular market; within each of these levels several options may exist. The next stage in the decision-making process is the evaluative comparison of alternative solutions so that a selection can be made. This evaluation involves again the use of models which predict the outcomes of the options under consideration. Such models may be complex mathematical formulations or simple rules of thumb. Consider the example of anticipating dividend levels for property and mining shares over the next five years; this may interest a portfolio analyst. At one extreme detailed mathematical models relating dividend policies to macro- and micro-economic factors may be developed; at the other extreme it may be assumed that dividend levels in one sector would be double those in the other. Both of these predictive methods involve models, although the level of explanation offered in very different. Provided that a uniform set of measurement scales is available for comparison of the predicted outcomes and provided that a procedure for selection based on these scales can be arrived at, choice of a course of action is possible. Common measurement scales employed for investment appraisal include payback period and rate of return and the corresponding selection procedure is simply the choice of the option giving the minimum or maximum value respectively. However, selection of a solution is rarely such a straightforward matter, as a multiplicity of scales is normally involved in each assessment. Thus in addition to the criteria for capital budgeting suggested above, non-monetary considerations such as the creation of goodwill with a particular supplier may come into play. When a choice of solution has finally been made it is expressed in the form of an action-plan and implemented. The consequences of this choice are then subjected to the normal monitoring procedure so that further corrective action can be taken if necessary.

The decision-making process poses a variety of problems for financial management and some of these have been suggested above. Further difficulties are associated with the tradeoffs that have to be made between incommensurable variables in the evaluation of existing or proposed policies, the handling of uncertainty in projected outcomes and the presence of time lags in cash flows which can have a great impact on the levels of balances held. Constraints on the choice of solutions considered range from those imposed by legal or economic conditions, to those based on humanitarian or ethical grounds, or to others resulting from internal or external political wrangling. It is the handling of these and other features which forms the substantive subject matter of the practice of accountancy.

Bibliography

Ackoff, R. L. (1974). *Redesigning the Future,* Wiley, New York.

Franks, J. R., and Broyles, J. E. (1979). *Modern Managerial Finance,* Wiley, London.

Myers, S. C. (1976). *Modern Developments in Financial Management,* Dryden, Hinsdale, Illinois.

Financial Modelling in Corporate Management
Edited by J. W. Bryant
© 1982 John Wiley & Sons Ltd.

2

Techniques in Financial Management

JAMES BRYANT

2.1 Management Accounting Activity

The process of financial management and control has greatly increased in complexity as the social and technological context in which organizations operate has become more dynamic. In many cases too the sheer size of organizations has posed new problems of internal control, and the development of management information systems has been of paramount importance in coming to terms with these difficulties. Nevertheless the basic concern of the finance function remains the monitoring and recording of financial transactions, the analysis and forecasting associated with financial decision-making and the management of cash flows on a continuing basis.

Financial accounting, the stewardship of a business involving the maintenance and interpretation of historical financial records, remains a major part of the accounting function. In recent years, the advent of computer-based book-keeping and auditing systems has released management time for the less mundane aspects of financial accounting. In particular, it has led to a concern with the principles of financial record maintenance rather than exclusively with the techniques involved. Thus, with the additional stimulus of world economic conditions, inflation accounting has been a topic of widespread interest involving the formulation of new conventions for financial reporting.

The developments in decision accounting have been no less marked. A range of analytical techniques has been developed and now forms part of the corpus of knowledge expected of the qualified practitioner. Advances in the general area of business forecasting as well as in the more specialized areas of operational research methodology have provided an input that is increasingly valued in financial analysis. In addition, new measurement concepts such as discounting procedures have lent precision to the comparison of alternatives. Largely because of these innovations, it has been possible to push planning horizons forward into the future in accordance with the contemporary need for adequate lead times for effective management decision-making.

The purpose of control accounting is the short-term guidance of an organization to achieve performance in line with planning targets. Here too there has been a twofold impetus given by advances in technology and methodology. The former has made it possible to obtain rapid feedback of information about the consequences of operating decisions and gives potential access to instantly updated databases reflecting the current financial situation at any time. The latter has introduced a number of new measures for performance monitoring in the form of control ratios ultimately derived from the science of cybernetics.

Overall, financial management is concerned with the provision and interpretation of information about business performance and with the use of financial projections to guide future actions. The methodologies used have developed rapidly in recent years and an even greater subtlety of representation is likely to be achieved in future as the more mechanistic aspects of accounting practice are taken over by electronic information-handling systems. A range of widely accepted techniques and methodologies has evolved to deal with the more common accounting problems, several of which have been mentioned above, and these will be considered in more detail in the remainder of this section. However, before this is done, it will be helpful to provide a context for the discussion.

At any time, a corporation may be characterized by a number of state variables. These variables are selected features which are considered to be of importance both in describing its current position and also in understanding its behaviour through time. Financial management is primarily concerned with state variables such as those that appear as balance-sheet items like asset valuations or bank overdrafts. Corporate activity changes the values of these variables with time. It follows that the financial development of an organization can be represented by a record of the changes in the values of its financial state variables. As an example, consider just two financial variables, loan capital and ordinary shareholders' funds. Then changes in the financial situation can be represented by the graph in Figure 2.1 which shows the values of these two state variables over a period of ten years for a major U.K. conglomerate. The path traced out by joining the points corresponding to successive annual values of the variables is called the trajectory of the corporation in the state space defined by the two chosen financial characteristics. In practice a large number of financial state variables would be considered, but the concept of a trajectory in a state space is one which can usefully be generalized to such cases even if a diagrammatic representation is no longer possible.

2.2 Financial Reports

Accounting reports, which summarize the activities of a corporation over a period of time and which provide statements of the financial situation at particular dates,

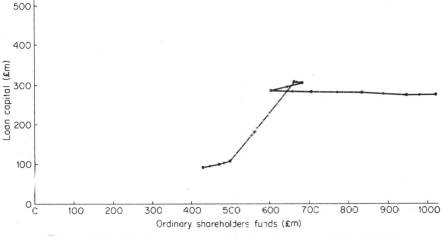

Figure 2.1 System trajectory for Imperial Group Ltd. (1969–78)

are routinely used for management purposes, as well as being required by external agencies. The three most familiar, which will be discussed here, are the balance sheet, flow of funds statement and profit and loss account.

The balance sheet presents a 'snapshot' of a corporation at a given date and therefore corresponds to a single point on the corporate trajectory. This snapshot includes as variables the deployment of funds within a company and the amounts of those funds derived from different sources. The former are the assets of the organization, the latter are the liabilities and net worth. Assets are conventionally sub-divided into categories such as fixed and current assets, stocks and debtors; liabilities into loans, creditors and taxation due; and net worth into share capital and reserves. Thus the balance sheet may be expressed concisely by the identity:

assets = liabilities + net worth.

Since all funds deployed must necessarily have been obtained from somewhere, the balance sheet inevitably balances.

Movement along the corporate trajectory is explained by the flow of funds statement which describes changes in balance-sheet items. Net changes in the application of funds, again normally sub-divided into different asset groups, are balanced by changes in the sources of funds detailed as in the balance sheet into liability, share capital and reserve items. The identity for a flow of funds statement is:

Δassets = Δ liabilities + Δ net worth

where Δ stands for 'net change (during a specified period) in' the term it precedes.

The profit and loss account is a more detailed report that explains changes in just one of the balance-sheet items, the retained profit, which forms part of the company's reserves. This account is therefore an expansion of part of the flow of

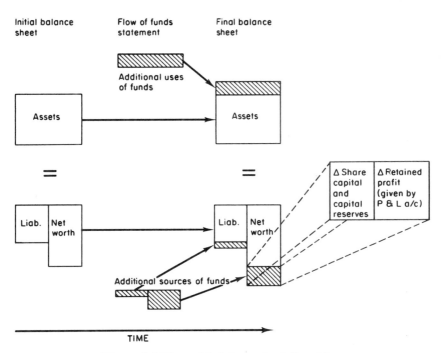

Figure 2.2 Financial statement relationships

funds statement, and describes changes over a period of time arising from profits or losses arising from corporate activity. The following identity explains this relationship:

$$\Delta \text{ net worth} = \Delta \text{ share capital and capital reserves} + \Delta \text{ retained profit,}$$

where

$$\Delta \text{ retained profit} = \text{revenue} - \text{expenses} - \text{net interest} - \text{taxation} - \text{dividends.}$$

These relationships between the three financial statements are illustrated in Figure 2.2.

The double-entry system which underlies conventional accounting practice ensures that all sources and applications of funds are separately recorded and thereby provides a sound basis for auditing. In this system, each transaction is recorded as a credit entry in the giving account and as a debit entry in the receiving account. Thus if an asset is acquired for cash, the cash account contains a credit entry of the amount paid while an asset account contains a debit entry of the same value. Double-entry methods also make possible the detailed analysis of the interests of the owners in a business and so facilitate evaluation of past policies.

It is principally because of the double-entry system that an historical cost convention has been adopted, and this has been found to have severe deficiencies in times of high inflation. The recording of assets at acquisition cost and the application of depreciation to this figure means that adequate provision is not made for their replacement if inflationary tendencies have pushed up the cost of such replacements. Addtionally, profits will be overstated on an historical cost basis if inflated revenues are matched against the corresponding expenses which generated them. That is, there will be a difference between the actual costs incurred on goods sold and the costs of replacing those goods at the time of sale. For these reasons, new conventions have recently been suggested which attempt to present a more helpful picture of the financial position of an organization than traditional reports can give.

Currently, inflation accounting information is presented in the form of reports which supplement rather than replace the historical accounts. Adjustments are made to depreciation and cost of sale figures to reflect current costs, and a proportion which reflects the ownership share of these adjustments is then deducted from the historically calculated profit to produce the profit figure under the current cost convention. The adjustments themselves are generally based on price indices, supplemented by other valuations as necessary.

Financial reports either express the position of an organization in a financial state space or the movement of the organisation along its trajectory in this space during some period of time. However, because of the nature of accounting conventions the state variables are not always the most appropriate ones to be used as a basis for policy-making. For example, the concept of a business as a going concern means that asset valuations do not usually correspond to the amount that they would realize on sale. Again, conservative conventions are used whereby stocks are valued at the lower of cost or net realizable value. Additional problems are posed by the inclusion in financial reports of cash flows taking place in different time periods, and the way in which current and non-current items are handled, especially in relation to corporate taxation, presents further problems for analysis. These features make it important to expose with the utmost clarity the methodology and conventions which have been used to prepare financial statements.

2.3 Evaluating Alternatives

One of the central problems of decision-making in any context is the selection of a method for the evaluation of the various options which may be available. In general, as was pointed out in the earlier discussion of the decision-making cycle, a multiplicity of measurement scales is needed to define the state space used to assess each option. However, the choice is not between one point and another in this space but rather between one trajectory and another. If, for instance, a share issue is being contemplated, this does not only have implications for a corporation at the time when the issue is actually made, but by altering the capital structure it will affect the course of corporate development thereafter. In financial management it is therefore necessary to compare the paths taken through time under alternative policies in terms of selected financial variables.

Adequate quantitative techniques have not yet been devised in any area of decision-making to deal with the evaluative comparison of alternative state-space trajectories. In general, two procedures are applied to simplify the comparison process. One is to reduce the state space to a single dimension, commonly by working with a weighted combination of the various measures. To take a simple example, if broad policy issues are being considered, the total turnover of a product group may be considered rather than the sales volumes of individual product lines: turnover is in fact the sum of the sales volumes weighted by the product-line prices (i.e. Σ (price $\times$ volume) over all lines). The second procedure is to eliminate the time dimension by performing a weighted summation over successive points on the trajectory. Frequently, this summation takes the form of a discounting routine which systematically reduces the weight given to values more distant in the future. These two procedures may be carried out in either order, but if both are used they result in the options being reduced to single points on a scale from which a choice may be made directly.

The use of a single, composite financial measure to characterize alternative policies is common. For instance, projects involving an initial capital investment which generates revenue in later time periods can be described in terms of the cash outflows and inflows which are expected to take place. The use of measures of this sort is in principle straightforward, although there may be considerable scope for professional argument in estimating individual figures. However, such analyses are not intended to, and cannot, take account of aspects of a policy which cannot be expressed in monetary terms. While it may legitimately be argued that this is inevitable, as accounting is only concerned with events that can be measured in monetary terms, it can lead to an appraisal being conducted exclusively using these variables and ignoring other features which are more difficult to measure. The application of a more broadly based single measure along the lines of cost–benefit analysis is a possible solution to this difficulty.

Condensation of a set of figures on one or more financial variables measured through time, to a single point, commonly invokes the concept of the time value of money. This principle is a recognition of the fact that the basic monetary unit is not a homogeneous one; £1 today is not equivalent to £1 at some past or future date. This is because today's £1 could be invested to yield a larger sum in the future, and so its worth is not only its current face value but also the future flows which it can generate. Inflation reinforces this tendency, since £1 can be used to buy more today than £1 will do in the future. Conventionally, values n years in the future are translated into today's terms by dividing them by a discount factor,

$$(1 + r)^n,$$

where r is the discount rate used. Using discounting methods a project history can be represented by a single figure and thus easily compared with other options.

A number of criteria have been developed for financial appraisal of alternatives, mainly in the context of capital budgeting studies. To illustrate these criteria, consider a project which is expected to produce the cash-flow pattern shown in Figure 2.3(a). After an initial outlay, the project generates a growing cash inflow which rises to a peak and then slowly declines up to the time horizon of the appraisal, A. This pattern may be discounted at some chosen rate to reflect the time value of money, and the corresponding discounted cash flow is also shown in the figure. The basic cash flow (CF) and discounted cash flow (DCF) patterns are not a convenient form for appraisal purposes, and it is usual to work instead with the cumulative cash flow (CCF) and cumulative discounted cash flow (CDCF) respectively. The graphs of these two series, illustrated in Figure 2.3(b), plot the total CF and DCF up to the corresponding point in time since the initiation of the project. The simplest and one of the most commonly used appraisal criteria, the payback period, defined as the time required for a project to generate sufficient cash inflows to cover the initial investment, is simply point B in Figure 2.3(b), since it corresponds to the time when the CCF reaches zero. Unfortunately payback period does not provide a measure of profitability, but rather indicates a project's liquidity: it also has the limitation that cash flows after time B are ignored. For these and other reasons the rate of return is frequently employed. Basically this is the average earnings from a project expressed as a fraction of the average capital employed. If, in the example, it is assumed that the initial cash outflow represents the capital investment in the project, then the rate of return corresponds to the ratio of the area under the cash-flow graph between C and A in Figure 2.3(a) (which is the total cash inflow from the project), to the area above the cash-flow graph between O and C (which is the capital investment in the project), and multiplied by $(2/T)$, where T is the life of the project, OA (to perform the necessary averaging). The rate of return ignores the timing of cash flows, a disadvantage which is overcome by the use of discounting methods. Straightforward application of a discount factor produces the net present value (NPV), defined as the present value of a project's net cash flows, discounted at a chosen rate, r, to the start of the project. This corresponds to the terminal value of the CDCF as illustrated in Figure 2.3(b). While there may be some difficulty in selecting an appropriate value of r to calculate the NPV, there is much to be said in favour of the calculation of an absolute monetary value as a measure of project worth. The alternative discounting criterion is the internal rate of return (IRR) defined as that rate, r, which will make the NPV of a project zero: the CDCF at the IRR is also shown in Figure 2.3(b). The IRR is probably the most widely used appraisal criterion today, and it certainly provides in a single figure a measure of profitability which takes account of the cash-flow pattern in time, but it can produce problems when more than one value of r makes the NPV zero. A further measure intended to overcome the shortcomings of other discounting methods is the profitability index, defined as the ratio of the present value of the cash inflows divided by the present value of the cash outflows. The abundance of assessment measures demonstrates the lack of agreement about the most critical features of investment alternatives. More generally it illustrates the difficulties of reducing a

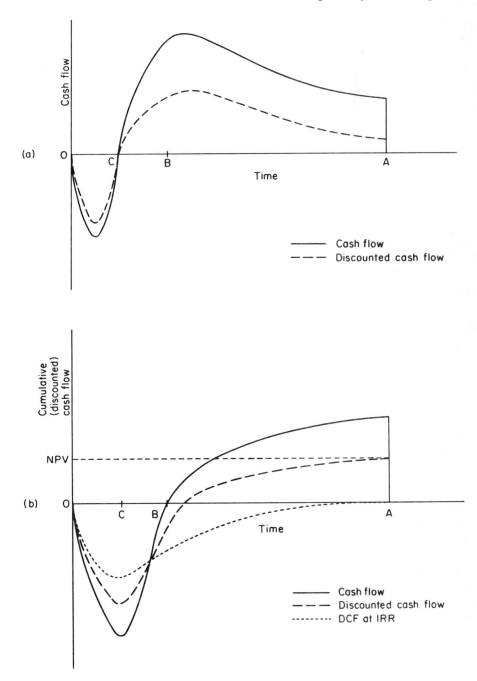

Figure 2.3 Discounted cash-flow concepts

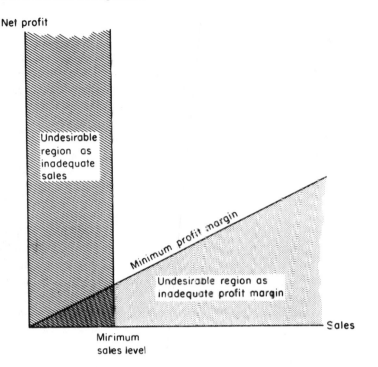

Figure 2.4 Financial objectives in a state space

complex, dynamic, multidimensional situation to a single figure and the problems
of interpretation that arise.

2.4 Monitoring Performance

The essence of management is control. Financial managers attempt to direct an
organization towards its financial objectives. That is, they attempt to steer along a
desirable corporate trajectory in their chosen state space towards some identified
goal. More realistically, the goal is unlikely to be so precisely defined as to be a
specific point in the state space. For instance, there will not be a unique combination
of asset value, sales turnover and distributed profit that is considered satisfactory.
Instead there will be certain regions that are regarded as being desirable and others
that are regarded as being undesirable ones to enter. Taking profit margin as an
example, where this is defined by the net profit as a proportion of sales,
the undesirable region may be described by a target ratio below which the value
should not fall. If there is also a minimum level of sales turnover required, then the
two regions in the relevant state space could appear as in Figure 2.4, where the
unshaded area is considered as desirable in terms of the two stated requirements;
of course, much of this area may be unattainable in practice for other reasons.

This concept of regions in a state space is realized in practice by two common accounting devices, budgets and control ratios.

Budgets are used mainly in short-term planning and specify a point in a financial state space which has been chosen through a comprehensive forward-planning exercise as representative of the desired target region. The variables used to define the state space are the expenditures and incomes anticipated under each of a large number of budget heads. Thus, based on assumptions about future economic and trading conditions, sales forecasts are made and from these the associated costs of production, selling and administration are found. Taken in conjunction with capital budgets relating to fixed assets, inventories, debtors and creditors, these are then used to obtain an overall cash flow budget which is usually expressed in standard financial report format.

The use of a budget as a control device is normally achieved by the analysis of the variances or divergences found between the actual and the budgeted figures under each budget head. Now each budget item is a monetary amount based upon two components: a quantity and a valuation. The quantity, often physically measurable, is the level of the variable measured and the valuation is an economic statement of the worth or cost of the variable being set at this level. For example, a budgeted labour cost is based upon a number of man-hours worked and an hourly wage rate; a budgeted sales revenue is based upon a sales volume and a unit price; and a budgeted overdraft charge is based upon an overdraft level and a bank interest rate. Variances for a budget item can stem from one or both of variances in quantity or value. Thus if a budgeted quantity, q, and value, v, are used to derive a budget item, $q.v$, and if individual variances of Δq and Δv occur for quantity and value respectively, then as the actual amount observed is,

$$(q + \Delta q)(v + \Delta v) = q.v + \Delta q.v + q.\Delta v + \Delta q.\Delta v$$

the divergence from the budgeted value is $(\Delta q.v + q.\Delta v + \Delta q.\Delta v)$. Conventionally the first term is called the quantity or volume variance and the remaining two terms are referred to as the value, price or cost variance depending on the context. Once variances have been calculated, it remains to determine if they are important and whether they indicate that control action should be taken. It would obviously be laborious to investigate the causes of every variance and so it is usual to employ a screening criterion to highlight the most significant items. This may take the simple form of a fixed percentage divergence from the budgeted value for any item. For instance, if an actual amount is ±5% from the budget amount it may be separated out for further study. Alternatively, more technically complex methods may be used based upon the use of statistical control charts. In this approach, the historical fluctuations of the variable concerned about its average level are used to define limits beyond which any variations should be investigated. A control chart to monitor a particular budget item could appear as in Figure 2.5, where the limits indicated are values that will be transgressed by chance on the percentage of occasions stated: that is there is only a 5% or 1 in 20 chance of obtaining a value

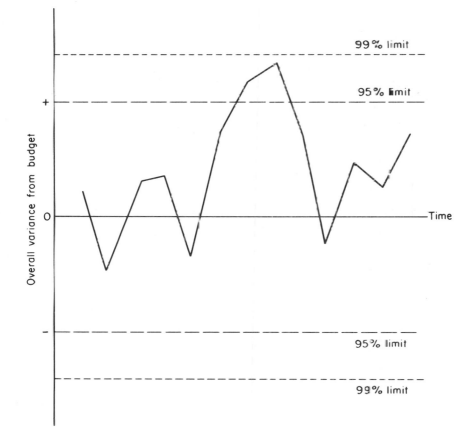

Figure 2.5 Variance control chart

beyond the 95% limits and this may suggest that any such instances should be investigated. Finally, it is necessary to determine what action, if any, should be taken as a result of any significant variances detected. Generally the variances themselves will suggest the nature of any remedial activity, but if they are due in large degree to changes in external circumstances beyond managerial control no action may be required except perhaps the preparation of a revised budget. This is a restatement of the methods of dealing with identified mismatches in the decision-making cycle described in the last chapter.

The discussion of budgets has suggested the use of variances or differences as control measures. However, there are some circumstances in which budget/actual ratios can be more powerful. Ratios have the advantage of being independent of the original units of measurement and this can be helpful for comparison purposes. Such comparisons can be extended beyond the scope of budgetary control to the assessment of wider financial structuring by the use of control ratios. These ratios,

Table 2.1 Control ratios for Cadbury-Schweppes Ltd. (1970–78)

Measure and control ratio		1970	1971	1972	1973	1974	1975	1976	1977	1978
Profitability										
Return on capital	$\dfrac{\text{Operating profit}}{\text{Assets employed}}$ (%)	13.2	15.2	16.8	15.5	15.0	15.1	15.1	15.1	15.2
Capital turnover	$\dfrac{\text{Sales}}{\text{Assets employed}}$	1.78	1.90	1.95	1.87	2.20	2.07	2.16	2.25	2.49
Profit margin	$\dfrac{\text{Operating profit}}{\text{Sales}}$ (%)	7.4	8.0	8.6	8.3	6.8	7.3	7.0	6.7	6.1
Managerial performance										
Credit policy	$\dfrac{\text{Sales}}{\text{Debtors}}$	5.08	5.48	5.17	5.24	6.10	7.10	6.16	6.81	7.40
Inventory policy	$\dfrac{\text{Sales}}{\text{Inventory}}$	4.00	4.51	5.11	5.40	4.19	4.74	4.62	4.49	5.26
Structural policy	$\dfrac{\text{Current assets}}{\text{Fixed assets}}$	1.14	1.12	1.36	1.02	1.19	1.28	1.42	1.60	1.54
Solvency										
Short-term	$\dfrac{\text{Current assets}}{\text{Current liabilities}}$	1.53	1.58	1.61	1.43	1.35	1.73	1.80	1.90	1.87
Gearing	$\dfrac{\text{Loan capital}}{\text{Ordinary share capital}}$	0.28	0.29	0.52	0.39	0.55	0.70	0.94	1.08	1.35

which are extensively used in long-term planning, trace the relationships between different financial variables rather than between intended and observed values of a single variable.

Various hierarchies of control ratios have been developed which may be used to explore different aspects of an organization's financial performance. However, the ratios that have been found of practical benefit are fewer in number than the multitude that have been advocated by theoretical texts, and fall into three main subject areas: profitability, managerial performance and solvency. The first group relates the profit achieved to the sales turnover and assets employed and also indicate the return obtained by shareholders. The second group measures aspects of management control including the outcome of credit and inventory policies and the cost-effectiveness of administrative activity. The final group of ratios indicates the short-term liquidity and the long-term solvency of an organization. Examples of some of these measures and their behaviour over a period of time is given in Table 2.1. Immediately apparent for the figures given are the gradual decline in profit margin despite improved managerial performance, and a change towards a more highly geared structure brought about by attractive long-term loans. To emphasize the relationship between these ratios and the concept of the corporate financial trajectory it may be pointed out that the final ratio in Table 2.1 is equivalent to the slope of a line drawn from the origin to a point plotted in the coordinate system of Figure 2.1, which was also based upon loan and ordinary share capital. The actual tabulated figures thus correspond to a trajectory which would gradually curve upwards if graphically displayed in this manner. As in budgetary control, decisions about the nature of any action suggested by changes in the values of control ratios depends upon the threshold level of change considered as significant and upon the interpretation of reasons for movements in the state space.

Bibliography

Bird, P. (1979). *Understanding Company Accounts*, Pitman, London.

Courtis, J. K. (1978). 'Modelling a Financial Ratios Categoric Framework', *J. Bus. Finance & Acct.* 5, 371–86.

Eilon, S. (1978). 'Some Useful Ratios in Evaluating Performance', *Omega*, 7(2), 166–8.

Parker, R. H. (1972). *Understanding Company Financial Statements*, Penguin, Harmondsworth, Middlesex.

Sizer, J. (1975). *An Insight into Management Accounting*, Penguin, Harmondsworth, Middlesex.

Taylor, A. H. and Palmer, R. E. (1980). *Financial Planning for Managers*, Pan, London.

Financial Modelling in Corporate Management
Edited by J. W. Bryant
© 1982 John Wiley & Sons Ltd.

3

Concepts of Financial Modelling

JAMES BRYANT

3.1 Nature of Financial Modelling

The concept of a financial state space, which was introduced earlier, can be used to describe concisely the principal activities of management accounting. Briefly these are to identify where an organization is in the state space at any time, to record how it reached that point, to predict in which direction it will move under the various options available, and, when action has been taken, to monitor subsequent progress and to explain any divergencies from the forecasted path. That is, management accounting is concerned with the historical and possible future trajectories of an organization in a financial state space, as seen from the particular point on that trajectory corresponding to the present time.

The three main aspects of management accounting, financial accounting, decision accounting and control accounting, which have already been discussed, are intended to deal respectively with the past trajectory, the future trajectory and the monitoring of the present position in the state space. In principle the mechanics of these three functions is not difficult, and simply demands record-keeping procedures coupled with some kind of predictive capability. However, the practical requirements in an organization of even modest size are usually considerable, and it is only in recent years with the development of computerized accounting procedures that such functions as the keeping of ledgers, the preparation of invoices and the handling of the payroll have ceased to absorb an inordinate amount of company time. Such applications of the ability of computers to perform mundane repetitive tasks following simple rules have gained wide acceptance, but it has taken rather longer for activities involving more than basic record keeping to be dealt with in a similar way. It is however in such areas that computerized methods have the greatest potential benefit, since while it is of considerable value if invoices can be despatched swiftly or the manpower used to prepare wage slips can be reduced, it is

23

likely to be of even greater long-term value if strategic or tactical decisions influencing future prospects can be better informed. This latter role is one which financial modelling methods are intended to fulfil.

The idea of a financial model can best be introduced by considering an example from one of the established areas of computer application mentioned above; the payroll. The net salary which an employee receives is based upon a gross figure which is adjusted downwards by various deductions and upwards by various allowances in any period. Considered from the employee's point of view the net salary is therefore related to the gross salary by the following identity:

net salary = gross salary − deductions + allowances.

This simple statement relates a number of financial variables to one another. It does this without reference to any specific numerical values which net salary, gross salary and the other variables may take, but expresses the general structure of the relationship between these four elements. Thus, given particular figures for the gross salary, deductions and allowances, the net salary could be calculated according to the rule which the identity above provides. A statement of this sort which embodies the relationship between financial variables may be called a financial model.

In practice, of course, the relationships between financial variables of interest to management, and indeed even those of interest to people as individuals, are usually far more complex than those given in the last example. The example itself is a gross simplification, since several highly aggregated variables have been included. For instance, the deductions from salary probably comprise income tax, health insurance and pension fund contributions. In turn, the tax figure involves all the intricacies of current government revenue regulations in its calculation. Now these further details could also be expressed in the form of identities. A model which explains the calculation of deductions might therefore appear as follows:

deductions = income tax + health insurance + pension contribution.

It would obviously be possible to continue in this manner, setting down further equations which described the calculation of the variables on the right-hand side of this equation from other more fundamental variables. Thus the deduction for pension contributions might be simply a percentage of the gross salary. However, it can become rather difficult to handle a set of interrelated models or equations of this type when the level of detail increases. This is where the use of a computer which can be programmed to hold such sets of relationships in its memory is advisable.

Essentially, computers are machines in which sets of instructions can be stored and used to manipulate incoming information to produce an output information stream. The means by which this is achieved, involving as it does the alteration of the electrical state of component parts, is of little concern to most users, and these so-called hardware aspects will not be discussed here. On the other hand, it is helpful to have some appreciation of the nature of software, the conceptual as opposed to the physical means by which information manipulations are carried out.

Most computers are built as general-purpose machines without any particular application in mind. That is, they simply have the general ability to manipulate data in accordance with a set of instructions, but specific instructions to be used are not present. The general ability is provided by the hardware through appropriate electronic circuit design, while the sets of instructions have to be provided by the user as software whenever the machine is employed. The software is in the form of computer programs; sets of instructions written in a highly stylized form which are simultaneously intelligible to user and computer. The stylized nature of these programs, which are written in languages having their own strictly defined grammar, is necessary because computers can in fact only carry out a very limited range of operations and the user's intentions have to be translated unambiguously and rapidly into an appropriate form for these operations to be executed. Once a program has been provided, a computer can then be used to carry out the manipulations which the program dictates, on any data which the user may care to input, and to produce the results of these calculations as an output stream.

How might a simple financial model be handled by computer? Reverting to the salary calculation example above, it is apparent that the first equation given constitutes an instruction for the calculation of the net salary from the other variables. If suitable translation facilities were available within a computer for this equation as it stands to be acceptable as a valid set of instructions, then it would suffice as a computer program to carry out the desired calculation. All that would then remain would be to inform the computer of the values taken on any particular occasion by the variables gross salary, deductions and allowances, and to request it to output the calculated value of the net salary. If the more detailed version of the example, in which the deductions are split down into three components, is considered, then the program comprises the two equations given, and input values are now required for the following variables: gross salary, income tax, health insurance, pension contributions and allowances. Very crudely, this is the basis of computerized financial modelling.

Practical financial models are not necessarily confined, as is the example chosen above, to variables relating to a single time period. Frequently the values of a financial variable in one period are related to the values of other variables in later periods. For instance, credit-card purchases made by an individual in one month may be invoiced in the next and any balance remaining unpaid at the end of that period will be charged with interest. In general such inter-period transfers occur with any variables where a balance is passed on from one period to the next.

Even if models are being handled by computer, they still have to be constructed or defined by the user first, and it is helpful here to have a form of representation that is more immediately comprehensible than a vast set of identities. The most commonly used representation, and one which is visually appealing, is the so-called operations tree diagram. In such a diagram the arithmetic relationships between

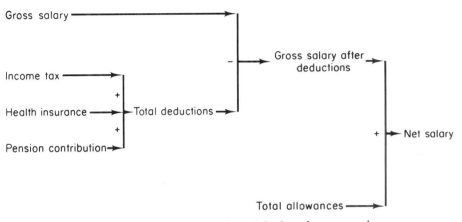

Figure 3.1 Simple financial model: the salary example

financial variables are expressed by symbols used in conjunction with a tree-like structure which links the individual variables. The idea of an operations tree is best illustrated by example, and so Figure 3.1 gives the tree corresponding to the salary example which has been discussed in this section. The compact form of the representation makes it ideal for handling large models and it is also useful as a device for communicating models to new users. Some conventions which may be used in drawing up diagrams are given in Table 3.1.

It is useful to have a means of representing the broad structure of very large operations tree diagrams. For this purpose a flow diagram can be used which illustrates the relationship between sub-models or modules, each of which contains a large number of calculations and each of which corresponds to a section of the overall operations tree. An example of such a flow diagram which illustrates a model used for corporate planning purposes in the Cunard Steam Ship Company is given in Figure 3.2. Thus, for instance, one sub-model in the flow diagram is concerned with the calculation of interest charges from details of debt capital and interest rates. In such diagrams, arrows represent the flow of information from one module to another without specifically indicating any algebraic relationships involved.

3.2 Types of Model

Financial modelling is conceptually a very simple process. However, the fundamentals discussed in the last section have been elaborated upon in practical studies so as to provide models that more faithfully reflect financial structures, and which are more flexible and efficient in use than would otherwise be the case. Some of these elaborations relate to the structuring of models while others relate to their content, and these two areas will now be considered in turn.

Two aspects of model structure can be identified which will be termed here microstructure and macrostructure. The former refers to the nature of the relation-

Table 3.1 Basic operations tree conventions

Operations tree	Equivalent identity
Arithmetic	$C = A + B$ Also equivalent forms for subtraction $(-)$, multiplication $(*)$ and division $(\div)$
Inverse operation	$C = B - A$ (i.e. variables are read upwards) Also equivalent form for division $(\ominus)$
Constant term	$C = A + (2 * B)$ Also equivalent forms for other arithmetic operations
Time shift	$C_t = A_{t-1} + B_t$ Also equivalent forms for positive time shifts
Summation $A \xrightarrow{\Sigma} C$	$C = \sum_i A_i$ (i.e. summation over all A_i) $\sum_t$ denotes summation over time periods
Change $A \xrightarrow{\Delta} C$	$C = A_t - A_{t-1}$ (i.e. change in A between times t and $t-1$)
Discounting $A - \boxed{D} \longrightarrow C$	$C_t = \dfrac{A_{t+t'}}{(1+r)^t}$ (i.e. discounted at rate r to time t)

ship between financial variables and is depicted by the operations tree: the latter refers to the relationships between modules and is depicted by the flow diagram. To a large extent it is possible to discuss developments of these two aspects independently, despite their obvious interrelationship.

The operations tree diagram was introduced as an attractive way of showing the form of what are essentially arithmetic relationships between financial variables.

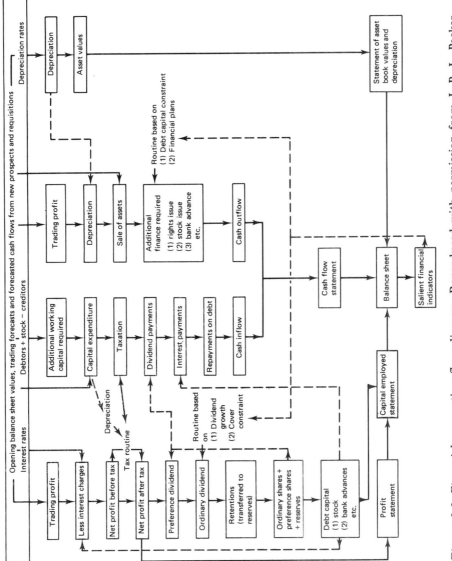

Figure 3.2 *Financial accounting flow diagram*. Reproduced with permission from J. P. L. Packer 'The Projection of Financial Results' in B. Taylor, *Long Range Planning*, Pergamon Press, April 1971, pp. 49–53

These range from simple addition and subtraction to the use of discount factors. However, quite commonly there are also logical relationships between variables. For example, dividend restraint regulations may limit the increase paid over a previous year's level. Other logical functions may involve the use of conditional statements; for instance, if cash balances fall below a certain level, then new loans may be raised. Such logical statements can often be attached as appropriate to an operations tree diagram and illustrations of this procedure will be found in later sections.

The other aspect of microstructure which needs to be further examined is concerned with the evaluation of variables in an operations tree. In the examples given so far the process of evaluation is straightforwardly a matter of moving progressively through a tree from the 'roots' to the 'trunk' calculating successive variables. However, there are many instances where this is not possible. Taking the simple salary example of Figure 3.1, how can the calculation be carried out if pension contributions are not as suggested earlier a proportion of gross salary, but instead a proportion of net salary? This would mean that net salary would have to be found for the pension contribution to be calculated, but that the former could not be evaluated until the latter was known. The solution to this apparent impasse lies in the simultaneous evaluation of both variables, which can be carried out by trial-and-error methods or, more rigorously, by the use of mathematical techniques to solve the implied set of simultaneous equations. This form of interdependence between variables is called recursion and is commonly found in the finance sector, for instance in the relationship between the demand for loans and loan interest rates. The presence of recursive relationships is apparent from an operations tree diagram, as completed loops will be observed.

Turning next to the macrostructure of models, elaborations here are concerned mainly with the efficient functioning of a model, rather than with any features that are mandatory for logical reasons. It may be useful to be able to recalculate or modify portions of a model while leaving the remainder as it is These portions may correspond to the modules identified in a flow diagram, or they may be at an even higher level of aggregation. Thus, if the method of calculation of depreciation in Figure 3.2 were to be altered, it would be desirable not to recalculate those parts of the flow diagram which are unaffected by the change. This intention can be achieved by the division of the model into self-contained elements. Such modularization of a model is largely dependent on the software available, an aspect of modelling that will be discussed in later sections of this chapter.

The content of the models which have so far been presented is of the simplest kind, being both deterministic and non-optimizing in character. By deterministic is meant that they have the property that all the variables included are precisely specified by a single value. In practice, input variables in particular may only be available in the form of uncertain estimates, and it is important that this uncertainty is preserved in the calculation of any later dependent variables. The use of probabilistic estimates of this kind is the subject of risk analysis, a technique which is expounded further in the next chapter, where the concept of optimization is also outlined. Briefly, optimization is an essential feature of financial modelling when the achievement of pre-determined targets, possibly within constraints on the values of certain variables, is required. This may, for instance, be found in models where a specified rate of dividend growth is sought within a context which restricts the capital structure of an organization. By the inclusion of probabilistic values a model becomes non-deterministic or stochastic, while the provision of target-seeking capabilities makes it an optimizing model. Either or both of these extensions of the basic model content described before may be needed in an application. However, as a footnote it may be added that currently the majority of practical models still do not incorporate these extensions.

3.3 Options in Financial Model Building

The financial model-building concept involves more than the abstract formulation of the models themselves. Equally important, and stemming from the almost invariable use of computers as the basis for the calculations, is the context for model building in the form of the software and hardware used. The options available in this area complicate considerably the simplistic picture drawn earlier, in which it was glibly stated that models written in equation form using conversational English might be 'understood' as instructions by a computer. Furthermore no limits on the scale of calculations carried out and no constraints on the effort involved in model building were suggested: indeed these factors were not even indicated as worthy of consideration.

As soon as the decision has been taken to proceed with a financial modelling exercise in some area, management is confronted by a number of subsidiary choices which must be made before the actual model-building process begins. These choices, which relate to the mode of implementation of the proposed model in terms of computer-based resources, affect the form of subsequent developments and are also important constraining factors when the system has been completed and is in everyday use. Essentially, the choices concern the logistics of model development and the qualities of the modelling medium used.

Models can be 'custom-built' or bought 'off-the-shelf'. Any model-building activity makes manpower demands in terms both of time and expertise, and choices depend on the resources available. Ready-made models require the least manpower investment, but their general nature means that any deviations from the standard form can be difficult if not impossible to handle. Such models, in the form of complete computer programs, are of value to small firms who lack software development personnel but their inflexibility has caused many users to turn to custom-built modelling, increasingly as the modelling systems available have become more readily comprehensible without specialist training being required. Modelling systems are 'high-level' languages which permit the user to construct a model to desired specifications ('high level' means that sophisticated translation facilities exist which allow the user to address the computer in a close approximation to normal English, whereas 'lower-level' languages are more formal and mathematical in nature, closer to the machine code with which the computer actually works). A wide range of modelling systems are marketed, some being available for internal company development, others only through the use of external consultancy services. As an alternative method of producing custom-built systems, standard, general-purpose, computer-programming languages not specifically intended for financial modelling can be used, but these normally require the use of specialist staff which can be a handicap when it comes to implementation. Whichever option is taken up as the means of developing a model, it can be seen that the logistic support required and the properties of the model constructed are intimately inter-related, and trade-offs between the various benefits provided have to be made. These trade-offs have been much debated elsewhere, but perhaps the best approach for the intending user is to discuss the particular application with as many users and representatives of the different options as possible.

Their very nature implies that the development of financial models necessitates the involvement of personnel who understand the financial structures being described. The translation of these structures into computer programs of any sort requires mastery of the syntax involved in the particular programming medium chosen and so may often be carried out by specialists with operational research or data-processing training. However, as only a capacity for the logical application of clearly stated rules is needed, such a background is by no means mandatory, and recently developed modelling systems are intended to dispel the mystique often introduced through the use of programming experts, by permitting financial managers without previous programming experience to construct their own models without difficulty. Model construction today may be time-consuming or tedious but it is unlikely to pose severe intellectual problems.

Different modelling media have different potentialities and shortcomings depending on features which they offer the user. Model structure and model content are both constrained by the quality of the software used. The importance of being able to use a modular structure has already been mentioned and related to this is the ability to link otherwise separate models. Such linking is often achieved by the use of intermediate files of data held on electronic disc. The ability to access disc files may also facilitate linking a financial model with a generalized management-information system. It is of evident value if data input values for a financial model, for instance sales forecasts projected from historical values taken from the sales ledger, can be obtained directly. Model linking for the consolidation of company accounts into group financial statements or for consolidation at other levels is also a frequently desired feature. Considering next the content of models, this is evidently limited by the presence or absence of facilities for carrying out dis-counting, forecasting, tax calculations, risk analysis, simulation and other operations which may be required. However, it is also limited in a far more fundamental sense by such factors as the size of model which can be handled in terms of the number of variables and time periods used. Attractive output facilities like the drawing of histograms or graphs can do much to make results more immediate for a user, and even the ease with which tabular output in varying formats can be produced may be of critical importance in a particular application. In finding a way through the bewildering range of features offered by competing financial modelling systems it is probably helpful to employ one of the many checklists which have been published on this subject.

3.4 Use of Financial Models

Applications of financial modelling are as diverse as the range of financial decisions with which managements are faced. Models to aid in the construction of corporate budgets and for subsequent use in budgetary control are one of the most common points of entry of an organization into the financial modelling field. Experience with these models may then lead into the development of longer-term corporate planning models, typically looking about three years ahead at broader issues of company policy. Investment appraisals and financial analyses carried out as an adjunct to production and marketing planning are other common areas of application. Surveys suggest that a wide range of organizations, both public and private, have found models useful in each of these fields of application.

Depending on the purpose of a model, the level of detail in its structure varies. Models may be characterized as being 'bottom up', 'top down' or 'middle up' models. The first type was historically the earliest developed, and typically may be used to calculate cash-flow statements from fundamental information at a very high level of detail. Some applications of this sort in manufacturing industry have taken as input data basic production details and the models have depicted the physical flows of materials which are then converted into monetary units and used to prepare financial reports. 'Top down' models in contrast operate at a high level of data aggregation and may be used in long-term corporate planning exercises. They are usually closely related to existing financial reporting systems, and generate information for strategic decision-making. Both 'bottom up' and 'top down' models have been found wanting in practical studies because of difficulties in integrating them into the decision-making process. Recent innovations in computing have made feasible the development of 'middle up' models by managers themselves, which operate at an intermediate level of detail and to some extent get over the deficiencies of earlier model types.

The purpose of financial modelling has been stated as being to provide information support for tactical and strategic financial decision-making. Perhaps the main advantage of using this methodology is that it enables management to explore a larger number of alternatives than would otherwise be possible. The implications of these alternatives can then be calculated in detail, allowing full account to be taken of interrelationships between variables, and showing at any desired time intervals the position attained on the trajectory through the selected financial state space. The 'middle up' model has developed as an approach to modelling which makes the maximum use of the educative potential of models. By interacting with and evolving their own models, managers enter into a symbiotic relationship with the computer, which enhances by an order of magnitude their capabilities in financial decision-making.

Bibliography

Bhaskar, K. (1978). *Building Financial Models: A Simulation Approach*, Associated Book Publishers, London.

Boulden, J. B. (1971). 'Computerized Corporate Planning', *Long Range Planning*, 3(4), 2–9.

Grinyer, P. H. and Wooler, J. (1975). *Corporate Models Today*, Institute of Chartered Accountants in England and Wales, London.

Meyer, H. I. (1977). *Corporate Financial Planning Models*, Wiley, New York.

Naylor, T. H. (1979). *Corporate Planning Models*, Addison-Wesley, New York.

Power, P. D. (1975). 'Computers and Financial Planning', *Long Range Planning*, 8(6), 53–59.

Financial Modelling in Corporate Management
Edited by J. W. Bryant
© 1982 John Wiley & Sons Ltd.

4

Techniques of Financial Modelling

JAMES BRYANT

4.1 Forecasting

Financial models describe the relationships between financial variables, so that the changing values through time of these variables can be traced. A model only represents the structure of financial relationships and to 'bring it to life' it must be supplied with numerical values, in much the same way that a geographical map needs a scale if it is to be used to measure real distances. These input values determine the usefulness of a model since the old computing maxim 'garbage in—garbage out' obviously applies.

Depending on the structure of a model, input numerical values may have to be supplied for the whole period of the time path of interest, or they may only be required initially to give the starting position of the financial trajectory. The former type of model can be termed the open-loop type since the output values do not influence the inputs, which may be estimated externally to the model before it is used. Consider as an illustration the model in Figure 4.1(a) which calculates the trading profit on a product for successive time periods. As it stands this is of the open-loop type with values of such variables as unit price, advertising and unit costs being provided as management estimates for each period. By contrast a closed-loop model requires variable values only for initialization purposes. Thus in the example, the unit price might for instance be found as a fixed proportional increase on the corresponding figure for the previous time period, as shown in Figure 4.1(b), so that once the value for the first period has been stated, the others follow directly. In more complex closed-loop models the value of a variable in one period may depend on the values of a number of variables in earlier periods. Using the same illustration again, the unit price might then be modelled as dependent on not only previous prices but also on the level of sales achieved or profits made in earlier periods. These three types of model, open-loop, single-variable closed-loop,

35

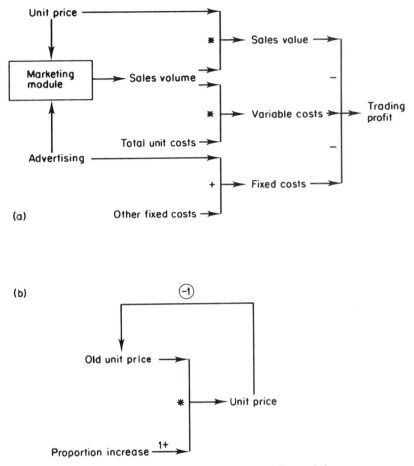

Figure 4.1 Simplified trading profit model

and many-variable closed-loop, require different approaches when numerical values are introduced and these will be dealt with in turn below.

Any procedure used to provide predetermined data values for input to an open-loop type of financial model can be described verbally, even if this description consists of no more than stating that values are random guesses made by the company finance director. On closer inspection it is usually found that such subjective estimates for a variable in successive time periods are not independent values, but that some rough rule is being used to relate the values to each other. Thus estimated raw-material prices may actually be based on a notion that a fixed compound rate of increase will occur over the period concerned. If such calculations were to be made explicit they could be incorporated in the model itself, being calculated in each time period from previous values, and the model would then be a closed-loop one for this variable. Open-loop structure is therefore associated with those variables for which no such relationships are made explicit. In particular it is associated with those input data values derived from external sources where the estimates given are trusted, but where the quantitative justification for them is not known or is irrelevant to the purposes of the model in hand. An example of this kind of data might be government estimates for future interest rates, which could be used as direct model input. Direct data input also occurs importantly when a model is being used interactively by a decision-maker who wishes to explore the effects of alternative future values of a particular variable. In this case values tested relate to some hypothesized future scenario and need have no further formalized justification. However, in a sense this is really a closed-loop example, with the user closing the loop, since interactive use implies that output values influence the values of input variables tested later.

Turning next to models with an implicit closed-loop form, a wide range of techniques can be employed to generate a series of forecasted values for a particular variable. These techniques may as suggested above, either be incorporated in the model itself, or else be used externally to provide an input data sequence for the variables concerned. However the range of methods which can be used within a model is naturally restricted by the facilities of the modelling system being used, and so external calculation may sometimes be unavoidable.

The simplest forecasting technique, subjective estimation, has already been mentioned. Management may postulate, for example, a fixed linear growth rate for a variable on the basis of past experience and expert knowledge of future trading conditions. If y_t represents the value of the variable to be forecasted at period t, then this can be formalized as the model,

$$y_t = y_0 + at,$$

where y_0 is the initial value of the variable and a is the growth expected in each period. A second example is provided by the compound growth of the price model of Figure 4.1(b), where if y_t now represents the price at time t and a is the proportional increase each period,

$$y_t = y_0(1 + a)^t$$

or equivalently,

$$y_t = y_{t-1}(1 + a).$$

The latter expression is in a so-called recursive form, each value in the series being related to the corresponding value for the previous period. What is subjective about the method of forecasting being discussed is the estimation of the growth rates, a, in the above models. However, there exist more sophisticated techniques for estimating such model parameters.

Statistical methods can be used to find model parameters which provide a 'best fit' to historical data for a variable. These same parameter values are assumed to hold good in the future and so the models can be used to make forecasts for any coming period. Obviously trial and error methods could be used to find suitable parameter values for a specific model, but statistical results produce immediately the best-fit values and so are preferable. The range of models which can be treated in this way extends far beyond the simple examples given so far, to those incorporating powers of the forecasted variable such as the quadratic model,

$$y_t = y_0 + at + bt^2,$$

and others incorporating decay factors such as the sigmoid form,

$$y_t = \frac{a}{1 + be^{-ct}}$$

where *a, b,* and *c* are all parameters to be estimated. This curve-fitting approach as outlined assumes that a suitable model can be found and that the series of values is likely to continue to follow a well-behaved mathematical function. Consideration of many series encountered in practice shows that such behaviour is exceptional.

An alternative type of forecasting model formulation is provided by the range of time series smoothing techniques. These consist of a variety of models which relate, using functional forms of varying complexity, the value of a variable to earlier values on the assumption that an underlying pattern exists and will persist into the future. Linear weighting models are the simplest in this class of techniques and are typified by the relationship,

$$y_t = \sum_{i=1}^{T} w_i y_{t-i},$$

where the w_i are parameters which given different weights to the T historical data values considered relevant to the forecast for period t. If these weights are all identical, then a moving average is effectively being calculated, while a commonly used model in which the weights are related to each other in a geometric manner is termed exponential smoothing. More complex models must be used if a series exhibits any trend or cyclical fluctuations over time but the principle remains the same. The weights to be used, which are the parameters of this type of model, are again calculated to provide the best fit to a set of historical data.

A possible objection to the models so far presented is that they incorporate fixed parameter values and so are inflexible in their behaviour over time. Adaptive forecasting models surmount this limitation by incorporating parameter values which alter as a data series develops. For instance, the method called adaptive filtering uses a linear weighting model as described above, but systematically recalculates the w_i after each new forecasted value is found in the light of any discrepancies from the actual values recorded. The subsidiary model for recalculating the w_i is fitted from historical data and can then be used for predictive purposes. This self-correcting feature enables adaptive models to perform well in tracking data values and in generating future estimates.

One of the inevitable problems of statistical forecasting concerns the choice of a good model to use. This choice has to be made by examining the ability of the alternatives to fit historical data and also by considering the plausibility of the models' form. The fit is usually measured by summing either the absolute or the squared values of the discrepancies between the actual values and those produced by the model over the period for which historical figures are available. A best-fit model can then be found by trying a variety of forms. As an alternative to this rather haphazard approach, so-called Box–Jenkins methods provide a structured rationale for selecting a suitable model from a large family of generalized formulations. The question of plausibility is a largely subjective one but, for instance, it would be nonsensical to adopt a model incorporating long-term exponential sales growth in a market where a limit on potential sales was considered to exist.

Many-variable models take the discussion into the arena of explanatory or causal modelling. In the present context these are usually econometric in character, relating the values of economic variables to each other through mathematical functions. Such models attempt to explain changes in one variable in terms of changes in variables that are believed to have contributed to those changes. The structuring of explanatory models requires an intimate knowledge of the processes being described, but can give far more satisfactory results than the consideration of an isolated time series. The financial model of Figure 4.1(a) needs a causal model in the box labelled 'marketing module', which predicts sales from the unit price and level of advertising used. This model may be of the simple linear form:

$$s_t = a_0 + a_1 p_t + a_2 A_t$$

where the sales in period t, s_t, is related to the price p_t, and advertising expenditure, A_t, using three constant parameters a_0, a_1 and a_2: a_1 is probably negative, the others positive. Values for the parameters could be estimated as usual by finding a good fit to historical data. Such a crude model would probably be a poor predictor of sales and in practice non-linear functions recognizing the possibility of saturation advertising, of consumer's memory of past advertising, and of varying demand elasticities, might be required.

Attractive as the prospect is of developing detailed models that really explain changes in the value of a variable some notes of caution must be made. Firstly, the presence of an apparent association between variables does not imply any causal link. For instance, sales may be related to advertising not because the latter causes the former but because advertising budgets may be set on the basis of earlier sales, thus giving rise to a self-perpetuating relationship. Secondly, it is easy to allow enthusiasm in model-building to get out of control, thereby creating enormously complicated structures. The purpose of modelling must continually be borne in mind and models based on a principle of parsimony, new explanatory variables being added only if they provide better explanatory power. Finally, caution must be exercised if predicted values lie at or near the extreme historical data values used to fit the model parameters. In explanatory modelling, as indeed in any of the other approaches mentioned above, it is useful to provide a quantitative measure of the uncertainty associated with any predicted values. This is a point that will be taken up in some detail in Section 4.2.

It is apparent that a wide range of forecasting techniques is available and this range can bewilder the intending modeller. The choice of approach depends on the nature of the forecast required. Key features to be considered in providing forecasts for financial models are the time horizon, level of detail, desired accuracy and ease of calculation. For example, curve-fitting methods are seldom appropriate for long-term forecasting, for which explanatory models are likely to be more successful. There is often a trade-off to be made between accuracy and detail in calculation, and the uncertainty associated with data input to the forecasting procedure chosen may render complex modelling irrelevant. Perhaps the most important feature of any technique of forecasting is that the user has confidence in it; without this, the predictions of the financial model with which it is employed will always be regarded with scepticism.

4.2 Risk Analysis

The fact that models need not be deterministic was mentioned in the last chapter when the content of models was being discussed. It seems eminently sensible to recognize that the future is uncertain by building stochastic models. However, the incorporation of uncertainty can be positively misleading if care is not taken in model formulation, and so this section aims not only to outline the principles of risk analysis but also to point out the hazards that await the unwary modeller.

Predictions of the values of any financial variables will normally be uncertain, and this uncertainty can conveniently and conventionally be represented using a probability density function. Such a function is illustrated in Figure 4.2(a) and indicates the uncertainty associated with an estimate of the sales of some product during a specified period of time. The probability of the sales level falling within a given range of values is indicated by the area under the curve between the corresponding points on the horizontal sales axis. Thus the hatched area is the probability of achieving sales between A and B in amount. This probability, p, is a number between zero and one (the total area under the curve is unity), and can be thought of as the proportion of times in a large number of realizations that values between A and B would occur. Alternatively or additionally it can be thought of as indicating the strength of belief an assessor has of obtaining values in this range, given that zero on the probability scale represents impossibility and one represents certainty. A probability density function can be specified for a variable by stating its functional form and the values of its parameters. For instance, the familiar bell-shaped curve of the Normal distribution may often be considered appropriate to represent the uncertainty in financial variables. If it is chosen, then the precise form is given by stating its two parameters, the mean and variance, which

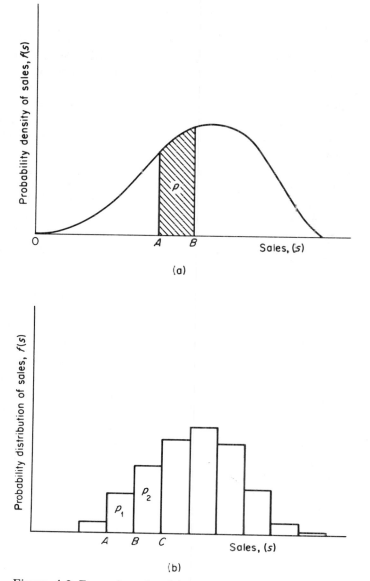

Figure 4.2 Examples of : (a) probability density function; (b) probability distribution

respectively indicate the average level of the variable and its spread about this average value. The large range of statistical distribution models available can represent almost any desired form of probability function.

Values of financial variables following standard distribution models will usually be produced by the more formal forecasting techniques discussed earlier. Thus causal regression models will probably generate a series of forecasted values each of which is taken as the mean of a Normal distribution whose variance is also given. However, the more subjective methods of producing forecasts are likely to express uncertainty in a less mathematical manner as a so-called probability distribution. Here, rather than the variable concerned being regarded as continuously variable, ranges are considered and estimates are then attached to these ranges which indicate the probability of occurrence of the corresponding values. Figure 4.2(b) gives an illustration of a probability distribution: here p_1 is the probability of sales falling between A and B, p_2 of their lying between B and C. Estimates which can be depicted as probability distributions can be elicited from managerial decision-makers provided that it is made quite clear what the probabilities represent. Difficulties in understanding the concept of probabilities in this connection and of interpreting the distributions are the main reasons why the risk analysis approach has not been more successful or more widely used.

Uncertainty, however it is expressed in the data input to a financial model, is transmitted through the model structure to the other variables. If a single uncertain variable were involved in a model while all the other variables could be specified exactly, then it would be quite easy to calculate the effect of the uncertainty at any subsequent stage of calculation. For instance, uncertainty in the 'other fixed costs' variable of the model in Figure 4.1 gives rise to the same level of uncertainty in the trading profit figure to which it is related by simple arithmetic. If, however, a number of variables are uncertain, then the evaluation of later variables becomes very difficult. Figure 4.3 gives a slightly simplified version of the previous model in which not only fixed costs but also sales volume and unit costs are expressed in probabilistic terms as shown by the corresponding distributions. Sales value will have a distribution identical with that of sales volume, since the former is simply the latter multiplied by the constant unit price. By contrast, the distribution of variable costs is complex as both sales volume and unit costs are uncertain. The complications which develop in more extensive models can easily be appreciated.

How can the distributions of variables which are dependent on uncertain input values be found? It is theoretically possible to use advanced statistical methods to derive the distribution of a variable which is a simple arithmetic function of two or more other variables whose distributions are known. However, in any but the simplest examples this is a very difficult procedure, and so a quite different approach using so-called Monte Carlo methods is invariably used. This approach can best be understood by remembering that one interpretation of probability density functions or distributions is that they indicate the proportion of times that an event will occur in a large number of repetitions of the variable concerned. That is, if it were possible to run repeatedly through the single time period, whose sales volume distribution is as shown in Figure 4.3, then this distribution would be built up from the frequency of occurrence of different sales volumes observed. Conversely, the distribution can be used to mimic or simulate the possible sales volumes that would occur in repeated realizations of a time period. A simulation of this sort uses a

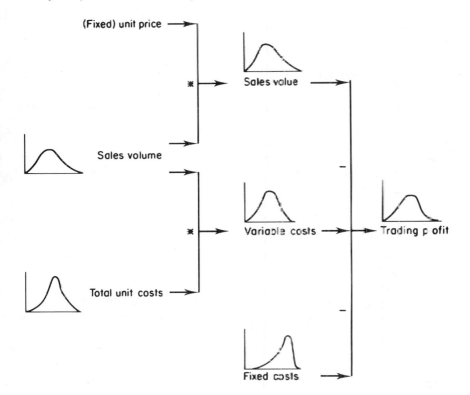

Figure 4.3 Trading profit model with uncertainty

structured procedure to select random values from the distribution, and as the selection is purely random, over a large number of such selections the distribution of occurrence of the different values corresponds to the distribution from which this random sample of values is being taken.

This process of random selection can be carried out for each input variable in a model and for each set of variable values on a particular realization the values of dependent variables can be found. Thus a randomly selected sales volume and a randomly selected unit cost from the respective distributions could be used to calculate a sales value and variable costs value for the model in Figure 4.3. Taken with a fixed-cost figure also selected by a similar randomizing method, these will yield a trading-profit value for this particular realization or run of the model. Repetition of this process gives different sales volume, unit cost and fixed-cost figures from the input distributions and a different trading-profit figure. In a large number of such repetitions, the full spread and shape of the input distributions is represented and a distribution is also generated for the calculated variables; sales value, variable costs and trading profit. In this way distributions can be found for any variables output from a financial model.

The method of simulation which has been described so far could produce results that are seriously in error. This is because it has been assumed that the selection of random values for different input variables is carried out quite independently. In practice, variables are likely to be strongly inter-related. Thus in the model of Figure 4.3, there may be a relationship between sales volume and costs, since higher sales levels may make possible longer production runs with lower associated costs. It would therefore be quite inappropriate if a randomly selected sales volume at the upper end of the distribution were coupled with a cost figure also at the upper end of the distribution. The presence of such correlations between variables must always be taken into account and explicitly used to constrain the values of related variables selected in each simulation run. Not all financial modelling systems have a facility to make the modelling of such dependency relationships straightforward. A distinct but similar note of caution must be made if autocorrelations are likely to be present for any variable. Autocorrelations are relationships between the value of a variable in one time period and the values it held in earlier periods. It is easy to see that, for instance, a simulation in which prices oscillated violently up and down from period to period might not be at all realistic, and changes that involve 'set up' or 'break down' charges would probably also be avoided. A satisfactory simulation model must be able to incorporate such temporal interrelationships if it is to produce sensible results.

Interpretation of the output of a model when it is in the form of probability distributions can be problematic. The distribution tells the user the chances of output variables falling in any range of values of interest. It is then a question of managerial judgment to select, as a basis for action or further analysis, a value that is regarded as satisfactory, given the level of risk or uncertainty calculated as associated with this value. For example, a trading-profit value from the model of Figure 4.3 might be used as the basis of a new product-development decision. It could be that management would not be willing to take the risk of the project yielding profits at the lower end of this distribution with the probability calculated. Considerable expertise may be required in the interpretation of the output of risk analyses and in deciding where it should be employed, and this can be a barrier to its use.

Much has been written, a lot of it critical, about the use and advantages of risk analysis. The benefits are that it allows explicit consideration to be taken of uncertainty in the predicted values of input variables. It avoids the rather crude assumptions often made when traditional contingency provisions are used to indicate variability in estimates. And it can be more accurate than simply using average values for all variables without taking account of the probable asymmetry of errors about the mean. However, the concepts underlying it have seldom been clearly understood by managers, and so the advantages are not seen to outweigh the additional computing costs that stem from running a model one hundred or more times. Despite this, risk analysis is being used increasingly in capital investment appraisal studies and it is likely to gain acceptance in other fields as familiarity with the method develops.

4.3 Optimization

Financial managers may be content to use financial models as a convenient way of calculating the consequences of alternative scenarios. It is undoubtedly the case that used in this way models can save much time and effort and enable a wider range of alternatives to be explored. However, often little thought is given to the selection of the scenarios to be investigated. Further, the alternatives chosen in this fairly arbitrary manner usually differ mainly in terms of low-level policy variables such as product prices or sales forecasts, rather than in terms of the higher-level variables such as dividend rates or liquidity ratios with which management might more properly be concerned. What is needed is a structured approach to the selection of scenarios for financial model evaluation, and this is what optimization methods can offer.

In an earlier chapter, when the monitoring of performance was being discussed, the idea that organizations attempt to remain within a region in a financial state space, bounded by limits corresponding to their financial goals, was suggested. At the level of strategic decision-making, these goals might relate to capital structure or shareholder policy. Conventional, non-optimizing financial models trace out the trajectories that would be obtained in scenarios which differ mainly in the values of low-level decision variables, and these paths are then examined to see how well they lie within the pre-designated desirable region. Such models usually incorporate very simple rules of thumb so that, for instance, in any run of the model the changes in loan capital from one period to the next may match the change in financial requirements, rather than the loan capital changes more realistically being a definite part of management policy, which will instead constrain and modify the requirements themselves. In an optimizing model, corporate goals, usually expressed as high-level control variables, are given as constraints on the trajectory which must always be recognized, and the best trajectory which fulfils these conditions is then calculated. Financial policies are therefore input directly as constraints in this form of modelling, rather than the results of a model being examined retrospectively to see how well financial goals are satisfied.

Selection of a 'best' trajectory which satisfies financial goals has been stated as the objective of an optimizing model, but the criterion to be used has not been considered. In a sense this question returns the discussion to the opening remarks in this book about corporate objectives, although in those optimizing models which have been developed the maximization of the present value of the shareholders' equity has been used as the objective function. However, it is unwise to allow discussion of optimizing models to become dominated by the choice of an objective function, since a model of this sort may best be used by testing different objective functions and seeing how sensitive results are to such changes.

Now that the purpose and broad approach of optimizing models have been discussed it is appropriate to outline the way in which they can be used. Most optimizing models take as input, policy constraints over the period of interest together with forecasts of exogenous variables such as interest or tax rates. An optimal financial plan is developed, normally using the technique of mathematical programming, and is presented in the form of standard financial reports which indicate the values required of key financial variables such as dividend payments and working capital levels. Further 'what if' runs of the model may then be carried out with different policy constraints; for instance, the minimum working capital ratio may be raised. The net effect is a series of financial plans each of which represents the best possible strategy in terms of the selected objective function, rather than the set of haphazardly chosen plans, which might be produced by a non-optimizing model, with trajectories wandering in and out of the region delimited by corporate goals.

It would be misleading to end here without mentioning that optimizing models have so far failed to obtain wide acceptance among financial managers. Instead their main uses have been in the more limited areas of production and marketing planning. Indeed many financial modelling systems have no optimization facilities in any case. Nevertheless optimization does appear to be a technique which can beneficially direct the focus of management attention to issues of strategic importance instead of allowing it to become attracted by minor problems of a tactical nature, and it is likely that wider use will be made of it as these benefits are more generally recognized.

Bibliography

Firth, M. (1977). *Forecasting Methods in Business and Management,* Arnold, London.

Hertz, D. B. (1979). 'Risk Analysis in Capital Investment', *Harvard Business Review,* 57(5), 169–81.

Higgins, J. C. (1980). *Strategic and Operational Planning Systems,* Prentice-Hall, London.

Mallinson, A. H. (1974). 'A Risk Analysis Approach to Profits Forecasts', *Accounting & Business Research* (14), 83–95.

Myers, S. C. (1976). *Modern Developments in Financial Management,* Dryden, Hinsdale, Illinois.

Financial Modelling in Corporate Management
Edited by J. W. Bryant
© 1982 John Wiley & Sons Ltd.

5

A Simple Financial Planning Model

JAMES BRYANT

5.1 Model Specifications

The financial planning model which is described in this chapter is intended purely as an illustrative example with a number of aims in mind. Firstly, it provides a demonstration of the model-building process and shows the way in which a model develops once the initial specifications have been laid down. This process involves two elements, the elucidation of the model structure and the translation of this structure into a computer program, and both aspects require discussion. Secondly, it illustrates many of the concepts which have been introduced in previous chapters in a slightly more elaborate and realistic context than was desirable there. Thirdly, it serves as a manageable specimen model through which the novice to the field can clarify his understanding of the principal issues. Taken as the basis for an implemented version on the user's chosen modelling system, it provides tuition through active experience of a working model. And finally within this book it acts as a bridge between the rather theoretical material so far provided and the reports of actual case histories to which the remainder of the text is devoted. These aims in fact constitute the preliminary specifications of the model since they define its general character.

As the principal use of financial models still appears to be in medium-term financial planning on a company-wide basis, the model presented here is a highly stylized example of this general type. It produces these basic financial reports, the balance sheet, the flow of funds statement, and the profit and loss account, from input data relating to trading activity and information regarding asset investments and divestments. Additional reports produced include the increasingly popular value-added statement, and current cost accounts in accordance with modern conventions. Trading activity is simply represented by the sale of products which are manufactured by the blending of a number of purchased raw materials, although the interpretation of these entities could obviously be quite broad. Balance-sheet items are grouped into a small number of distinct categories and treated too in a strictly limited way. This paring away of complicating details may suggest that the model is far removed from reality, but planning models can usually benefit from an economical approach in their construction, and so ideally may not appear very different from that discussed here.

An interactive mode of use has been chosen for the model, as it is felt that this can be of the greatest benefit to the user who quickly acquires a 'feel' for the properties of the modelled system. The time scale selected takes the year as the basic unit, and, once the model has been initiated, the user has to supply as input, decisions for successive years of the simulated time period, thereby steering the organization along a particular trajectory in the financial state space. The model is therefore not an optimizing one, and may be concisely described as a financial report simulator. For simplicity too the use of risk analysis has been omitted.

The purpose of the model described can be thought of as being to enable the user to explore the effects of alternative policies, relating both to capital and trading cash-flow cycles, on the financial trajectory. 'What if?' questions may be asked about, for example, the implications of changed values or timings of investment decisions, financing methods or inventory policies. What the model does not do is to provide a detailed picture of company operations, and the adoption of the year as the basic time increment makes it impossible to retain any fine structure in the temporal dimension such as would be needed, for instance, to describe seasonal patterns. No particular forecasting routine has been suggested for the provision of future values of those variables which must be directly input, since this must depend on data availability. Indeed the whole question of linking the model to existing corporate databases has been avoided, even though in a practical implementation this would need to be considered, and might substantially influence the eventual model structure. Nevertheless, given the caveats which have been made, the model does bear a strong similarity in structure and purpose to many working models being used for corporate financial planning.

5.2 Structure of the Model

Since a financial model describes the relationships between financial variables, the first stage of model-building must be to identify the relevant variables and to establish the nature of the interactions between them. In this section this process will be carried out first for the trading cycle and then for the capital cycle. In conclusion, the way in which these two elements are brought together in the summary financial statements will be considered.

For present purposes, trading is seen as the sale of products manufactured by company employees from basic purchased raw materials. It is assumed that the cost of products is made up of a fixed and variable component, the former due to wages and services and the latter due to the cost of the constituent materials. The profit contribution made by a product is the sales turnover less the cost of the goods sold and selling costs, where the latter are assumed to be a proportion of turnover. The major complicating feature of trading activity is the existence of stocks of materials, work-in-progress and finished goods. In the present model only raw material and finished goods stocks are considered, and the usual convention is adopted whereby these are valued at the lower of cost and net realizable value. This convention has been handled in the model by keeping separate account in each time period of the depletion of the initial stocks in the period and the use of new additions to stock, assuming a first-in—first-out policy. The logic of these calculations for raw materials and for finished goods is very similar and is shown in Figures 5.1 and 5.2 respectively. In these and later figures, each module is given a code letter and this is used to label the links between modules which are indicated by numbered circles: for instance, the unit product cost calculated in the raw material module is passed across to the finished products module through link M3.

Turning next to the capital cycle, five separate categories are included in the model: fixed assets, investments, current assets, share capital and loans. The cash movements associated with fixed assets relate to acquisitions, sales or revaluations of items in the asset portfolio. In addition, assets will be depreciated over their lifetimes and there may also be related allowances against the total tax liability which can be claimed. The interactions between the variables concerned are shown in Figure 5.3, where the bulk of the complexity results from the calculation of tax allowances on a straight-line or reducing-balance basis. By contrast the investments and loans modules illustrated in Figure 5.4(a) and (d) share a common simple structure, the only cash flows involved being interest payments and charges, in addition to purchase, sale and revaluation figures. Current assets, represented by debtors and creditors totals are also described in the most economical terms as Figure 5.4(b) shows. Share capital gives rise to cash flows when new stock is issued and when dividends are paid. Because of the importance of the timing of dividend payments with respect to taxation and related considerations, interim and final dividends are handled quite separately in the share capital sector module which is illustrated in Figure 5.4(c). These five capital sector modules are quite straightforward in structure, yet still accommodate most of the policy decisions that are likely to be of interest.

It is common in non-optimizing models designed to be used in an exploratory 'what if?' manner, to use the level of cash at the bank as the means of balancing the cash flows in any year. Thus the difference between the sources and applications of funds is taken as the change in the bank balance over the corresponding year. This practice, which is adopted here, can lead to modelling difficulties since recursive relationships are introduced as Figure 5.5(a) demonstrates. The changes in the bank balance determine the average balance during a year and thence the interest paid or charged, which in turn is a source of funds affecting the bank balance. An exact solution to this dilemma can be found algebraically as Figure 5.5(b) shows, and this is the basis of calculation used in the present model. Thus, the pre-tax profit and

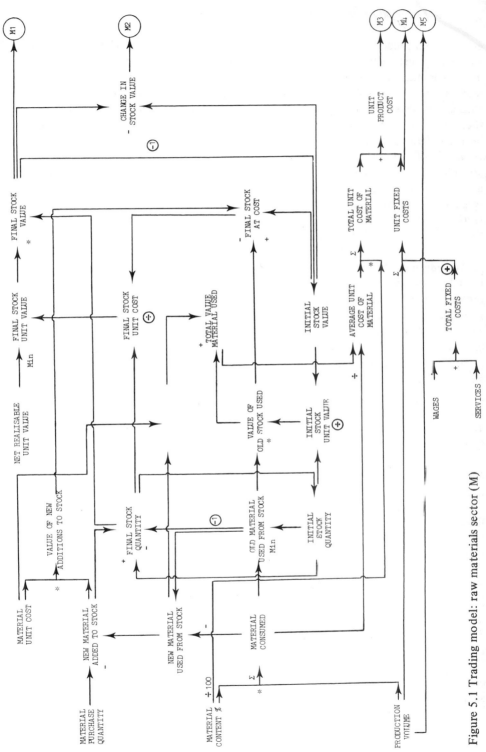

Figure 5.1 Trading model: raw materials sector (M)

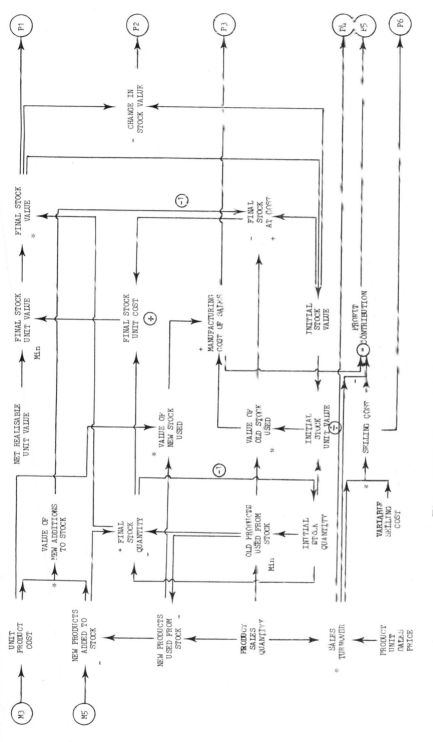

Figure 5.2 Trading model: finished products sector (P)

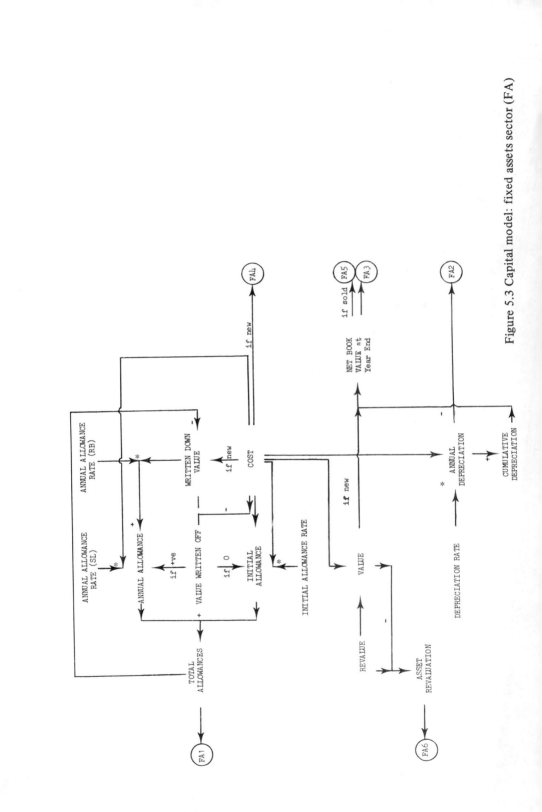

Figure 5.3 Capital model: fixed assets sector (FA)

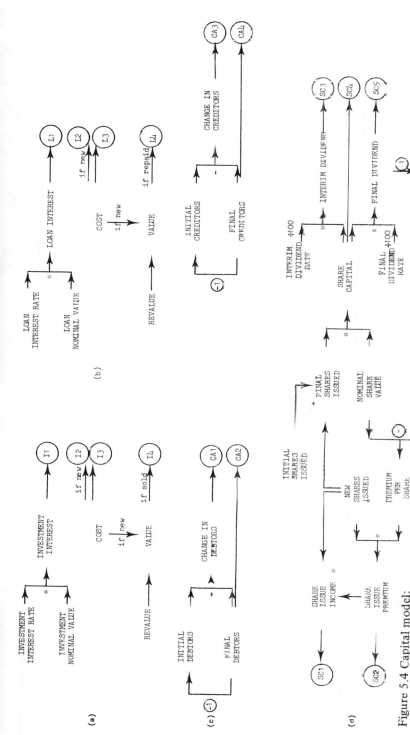

Figure 5.4 Capital model:
(a) investments sector (I);
(b) loans sector (L);
(c) current assets sector (CA);
(d) share capital sector (SC)

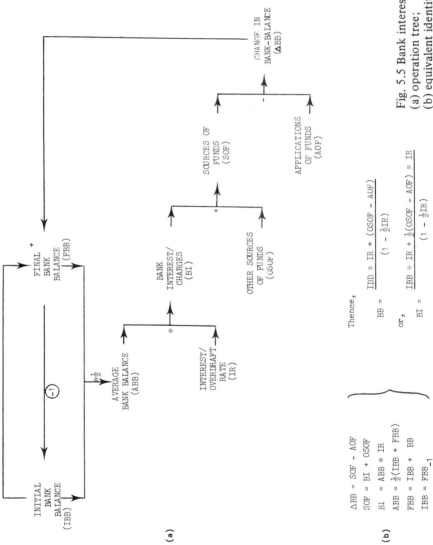

(a)

Thence,

$$BB = \frac{IBB * IR + (OSOF - AUF)}{(1 - \tfrac{1}{2}IR)}$$

or,

$$BI = \frac{IBB * IR + \tfrac{1}{2}(OSOF - AOF) * IR}{(1 - \tfrac{1}{2}IR)}$$

$\Delta BB = SOF - AOF$
$SOF = BI + OSOF$
$BI = ABB * IR$
$ABB = \tfrac{1}{2}(IBB + FBB)$
$FBB = IBB + BB$
$IBB = FBB_{-1}$

(b)

Fig. 5.5 Bank interest recursion loop:
(a) operation tree;
(b) equivalent identities and solution

consequent flow of funds statement for the year is obtained, omitting the bank interest item. Taking this together with the initial bank balance and interest rate and using the results of Figure 5.5(b), the complete profit and loss account and flow of funds statement can be obtained. The module used to obtain the profit and loss account is shown in Figure 5.6, and apart from a section included to permit changes in corporation tax rate to be described, simply brings together results calculated elsewhere. The flow of funds module of Figure 5.7 similarly performs an aggregating function. One of the inputs of the flow of funds module is from a part of the model not yet mentioned which performs the tax calculations. This tax module which is shown in Figure 5.8 calculates the tax payments, as opposed to the tax payable, on profits under the current U.K. system, but making simplifying assumptions about the dates of dividend payments and omitting consideration of tax on capital items. U.K. companies paying dividends to shareholders pay tax in two instalments; advance corporation tax (ACT) which is effectively a payment at source on dividends received by shareholders and is paid in the quarter following the dividend payment; and mainstream corporation tax which accounts for the balance of tax due and which is paid in the financial year following that on which it is calculated. In the model it is assumed that interim dividends are paid in the current financial year and final dividends during the first nine months of the next year.

All the calculations relating to financial activities during a year have now been covered and it remains to describe the modules which produce the end of year statements. These are shown in Figures 5.9 and 5.10 which depict respectively the derivation of the balance sheet and value-added reports. In each case the function of the report is to draw together values from other modules in a standardized format.

Some additional modules are required to produce inflation accounting reports. Firstly the three adjustments conventionally used must be calculated. The cost of sales adjustment is the difference between the current cost of stock as it is consumed and the amount charged in calculating the historical trading profit. The depreciation adjustment is based on indices of asset costs and results from charging depreciation on the current cost rather than the historical costs of assets. Finally the gearing adjustment eliminates that proportion of the inflation adjustments which is borne by the providers of long-term borrowing. The calculation of these adjustments is shown in Figure 5.11. Once computed they can be used to obtain the current cost-accounting reports, one example of which is the profit and loss account using the current cost convention shown in Figure 5.12. This concludes the review of calculations required to produce reports for any financial year.

5.3 Programming the Model

Translation of the structure which has been derived into a computer program is naturally influenced by the modelling system being used. However, the logic of the computer model, as opposed to its actual form, is largely independent of the mode of implementation and so can usefully be discussed in a general manner.

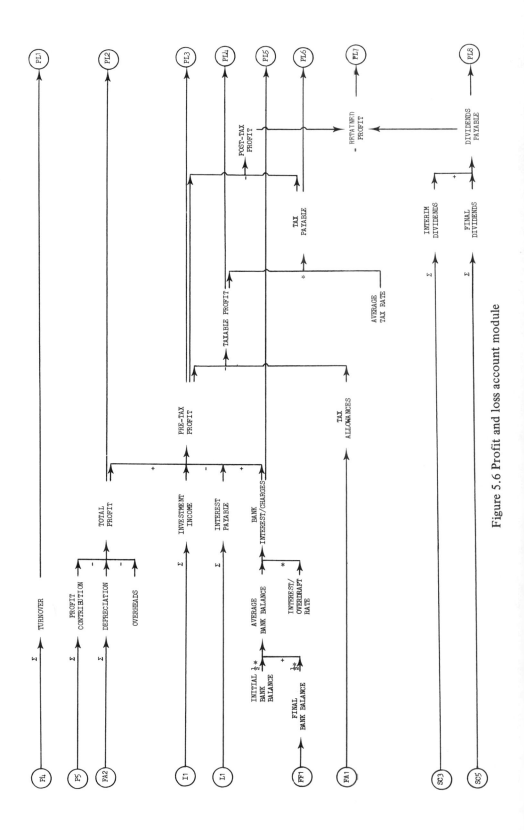

Figure 5.6 Profit and loss account module

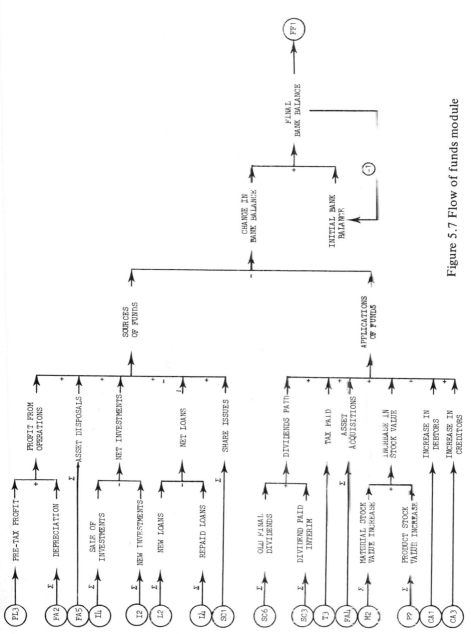

Figure 5.7 Flow of funds module

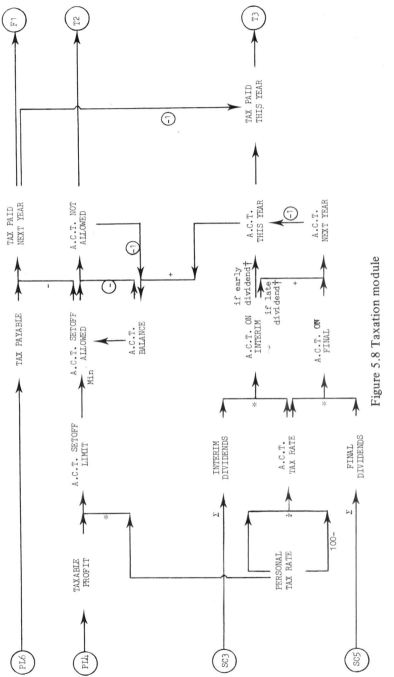

Figure 5.8 Taxation module

† Late dividend is one paid during last 3 months of financial year; early dividend the one paid before this.

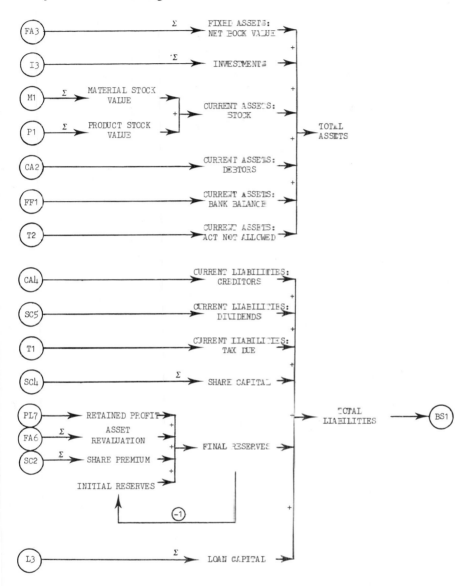

Figure 5.9 Balance sheet module

It is instructive to begin by drawing together the various elements of the model which have been discussed above, so that the overall structure can be appreciated. This is depicted in Figure 5.13 which shows the links between the modules that have been constructed. Each link has been labelled at exit from its source module using the same numerical code as was employed earlier. The table accompanying

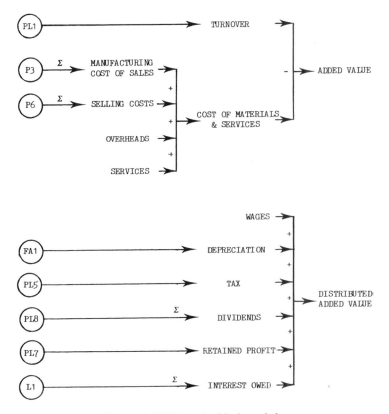

Figure 5.10 Valued added module

the diagram shows the dependencies between modules in another way, and gives a guide to the ordering of calculations within a program. Those modules which have no prerequisites for their evaluation may be dealt with first, and the table then shows the succession which later modules must follow. This order is broadly that in which the modules were introduced and described in the last section.

How then might a program be organized to perform the calculations which have been defined, and to produce the output reports stipulated in response to user inputs at the beginning of each year of the simulation? A possible program structure is shown in Figure 5.14. The first stage must be to input all the invariable data relating to the model in an initialization module. Details included here might be the name of the organization and the date when its financial year begins. Also input at this stage would be the initial balances and variable values obtaining at the commencement of the simulated time period. It would probably be advisable to output a trial balance sheet at this stage to verify the correctness of the data input. Following this, the details of all transactions in both the trading and the

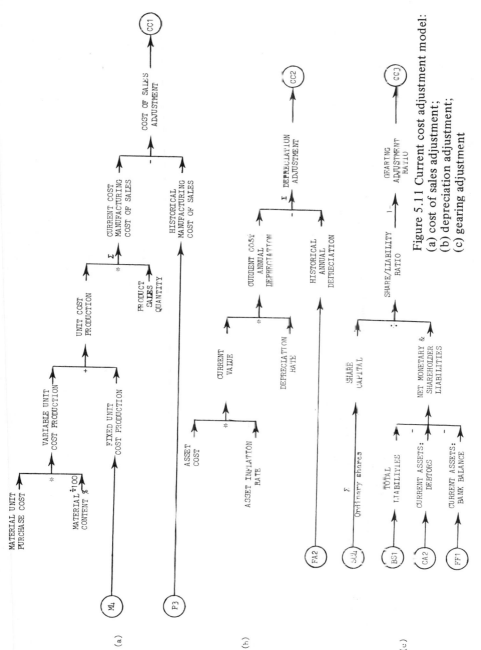

Figure 5.11 Current cost adjustment model:
(a) cost of sales adjustment;
(b) depreciation adjustment;
(c) gearing adjustment

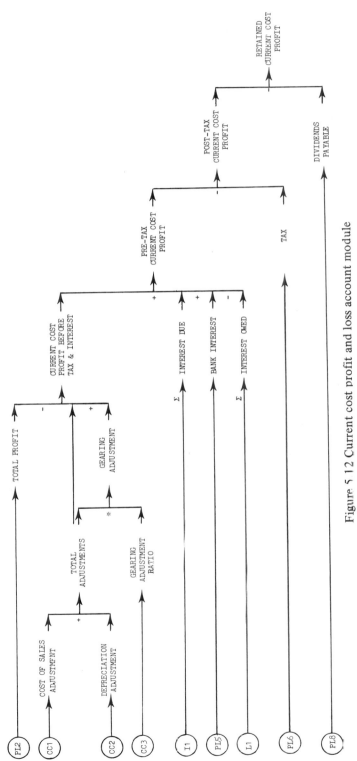

Figure 5 12 Current cost profit and loss account module

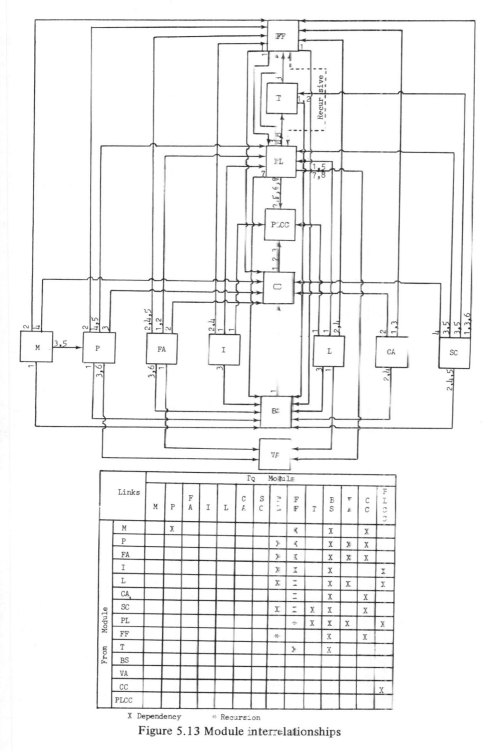

Figure 5.13 Module interrelationships

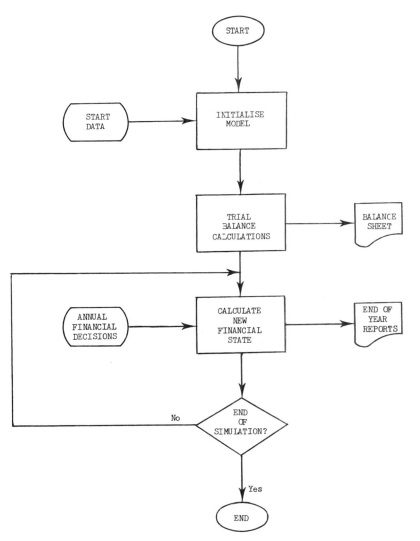

Figure 5.14 Generalized model flow diagram

capital sectors during the first year would be fed in by the user. The most convenient arrangement could well be to allow a default option whereby values remain
unchanged unless a request to change them is made by the user: this saves repeated
inputting of a large volume of similar data. From this input the program can then
perform the calculations in a number of stages: first module M would be evaluated;
then modules P, FA, I, L, CA and SC; next, after one iteration between them,
modules PL, FF and T would be evaluated producing the first two output reports;
finally the remaining reports from modules BS, VA, CC and PLCC would be

generated. The program would then return control to the user as the next simulated time period is entered, and request input data for the following year's operations. This procedure would be repeated until the simulated time has advanced as far as the planning horizon required.

Once the general program structure has been mapped out, it remains to write the program itself, using whatever modelling system has been selected. The size of this task will depend upon the level of detail required as well as upon the flexibility of the system and the availability of personnel trained in its use. At one extreme of simplicity, this actual model has been implemented in the Basic language on a Commodore 'Pet' microcomputer in a form which might be suitable for a small or medium-sized business, while it is also obviously capable of elaboration into something more appropriate to a large multidivisional corporation possibly incorporating direct links to existing corporate databases and information systems. The completed program would need to be tested on a suitable set of data to eliminate any programming or logical errors before it could be used for planning purposes. It might then be employed in a 'what if' mode by management to investigate the financial implications of alternative decisions.

PART 2 OPERATIONAL PLANNING MODELS

The distinction made earlier between revenue and capital financial cycles serves as a useful if not completely rigid division between the material in this Part of the book and that in Part 3. In the main the models that are described here have been developed to provide guidance for short-term financial control, even though the time horizon used in some cases extends over a number of years. They therefore place most emphasis on revenue flows. The scale of application discussed varies from that of a small firm to that of a large industrial corporation, but in each case the methods used could easily be adapted to use in business units of any size from small independent enterprises or cost centres within larger companies to more substantial organizations with highly developed divisional structures.

Marketing is the only part of corporate activity which actually generates revenue and so it is appropriate that this Part begins with a description in Chapter 6 of a methodology which has been used to assess the product range being offered for sale. This study is of particular interest for the use made of interactive computer programs and of the direct incorporation of financial reports. There is a considerable literature dealing with market planning models, but less has been published concerning practical production planning work (as opposed to theoretical academic studies of idealized production processes). Accordingly Chapter 7, which describes some simple models which have been used to assist planning in a large nationalized industry, is of importance, not only for the outline of the models used but also for its discussion of the wider context in which they were developed. Chapter 8 returns to the marketing scene, this time at the 'sharp end', and includes three abbreviated case studies of models used in pricing products. This is an account of the conceptually straightforward but practically valuable work that may be done using financial models. Bankruptcy statistics attest to the problems faced by many small companies in managing their cash balances. Chapter 9 describes an approach, tailored to the small firm but adaptable for a larger unit, which could be used by management to avert these dangers. In Chapter 10 a rather different approach to cash management, based on mathematical-programming techniques is outlined;

this is included, although it is a theoretical account, because of the growing awareness of such techniques and of their potential in this field. The following account
in Chapter 11 describes a typical example of one of the most familiar applications
of financial modelling to company budgeting. Such applications are often an ideal
starting point for modelling in a company, since as well as dealing with a recurring
problem facing many organizations, that of rapidly consolidating budgetary projections across a company, they offer management the opportunity of examining
alternatives and of refining a budget through a number of iterations. This Part of
the book concludes with an examination of the use of discounted cash-flow methods
in an important and frequently encountered investment decision relating to the
leasing or purchase of equipment.

Financial Modelling in Corporate Management
Edited by J. W. Bryant
© 1982 John Wiley & Sons Ltd.

6

A Computer Model for Aiding
Product-line Decisions*

BARBARA JACKSON AND BENSON SHAPIRO

6.1 Introduction

Product-line decisions form the basis of marketing strategy. Too often, however, product managers make such decisions without givng proper consideration to their broad strategic implications. They do not systematically consider the conflicting goals of marketing managers, who tend to prefer broad product lines, and of manufacturing managers, who like narrow cost-efficient product lines. Managers too frequently make these decisions on a tactical basis. Determining the most appropriate product-line lengths and characteristics can be accomplished in a more systematic way with a computer model. The actual process of constructing the model can begin to clarify the product-line decisions, and once the model is completed and working, the sales and profit implications of different product-line decisions become readily apparent. In this chapter the basic approach product managers can take to put together an industrial product-line computer model is outlined. A paper company product line is used to illustrate how one model was assembled, but this example represents an approach that can be tailored to different businesses.

6.2 Product-line Policy in the Paper Industry

Among the products made by a large paper manufacturer is a line of index paper, which is a stiff stock used to make menus, index cards, and promotional flyers.

*Reprinted by permission of the *Harvard Business Review*. 'New way to make product line decisions' by Barbara B. Jackson and Benson P. Shapiro (May–June 1979), Copyright © 1979 by the President and Fellows of Harvard College; all rights reserved.

Each day the company's product manager faces questions about adding and deleting items in the line.

Should we add a new pale green colour to our offerings of index paper? Or should we instead extend the weight range of index offerings and begin to market a heavier grade? Should we do both and evolve into a full-line supplier? Or should we cut back some of the existing items in the company's index line and concentrate resources on a more limited range of offerings?

Such mundane questions form the practical day-to-day basis of product policy. (Product policy can be defined as the management of a company's product and service offerings.) The decisions made on such questions can be viewed as basic building blocks of marketing strategy. Too often, however, these basic decisions are made without any real consideration of their strategic implications. Thus strategies simply evolve to support initial tactical decisions.

One problem with these decisions is that marketing and manufacturing managers frequently disagree about the appropriate number of items to include in a particular product line. Marketers want a broad product line. Manufacturing managers stress a short product line with long production runs and reduced set-up costs and machine changeovers. The decision on line length is important in both financial and organizational terms.

A line longer than needed, on the one hand, faces high costs from increased inventory, production changeovers, and additional order processing and transportation. An overly long line also creates confusion in marketing to distributors, sales people, and customers.

An overly short line, on the other hand, results in different cost problems. Potential losses include sales, competitive position, and economies of scale. Distributors and sales people may reduce their marketing effort.

The financial impacts of either type of mistake are clear. The organizational impacts arise because the costs of the two types of mistake are felt most heavily by separate parts of the organization. A mistake in either direction can create costly problems in different company areas. The costs of the overly short line fall most directly on the marketing area. Conversely, costs associated with a line that is too long hit hardest in the manufacturing area.

Determining the appropriate product-line length is only part of the problem. The other part is determining a sensible set of characteristics for each item in the line. Each must be positioned appropriately with regard to other items in the line, customers' needs, competitive offerings, and the company's own manufacturing process and marketing strategy.

6.3 Computerized Alternative for Product-line Management

A more systematic approach to managing product lines is possible. It involves using a computer model that can be put together through a joint effort between the product manager and a computer programmer. The reader should note here that what we are really suggesting is an approach rather than a single, general model. Thus product managers can tailor models to their own product lines.

The actual process of beginning to assemble a computer model forces managers to think more deeply than is customary about their product offerings and those of their competitors. Managers can be led to ask important questions about their product-line items, including such hard or unpleasant questions as those concerning competition and cannibalization, which involves a company's new items stealing sales from its existing items.

Also, if they are to explore fully the implications of product-line changes, managers must extensively manipulate numbers involving such issues as competition, cannibalization, and manufacturing. In searching for the best positioning of a product line's items, managers should manipulate the numbers for a variety of possible configurations. Most managers simply do not have the time to perform lengthy calculations for each of many possible decisions about items. A computerized aid can mechanize the numerical analysis so that the manager can spend time on judgmental matters rather than on computation.

Thus the two primary aims of a computerized model for product-line planning are to help the manager through a carefully constructed process for considering product-line changes and to handle the many calculations needed to evaluate the profit impact of such changes. To overcome the shortcomings of existing approaches, the model should have the following characteristics:

(1) It should consider the costs involved in manufacturing and distributing operations along with the impact of changes on the sales of other product-line items.
(2) It should enable marketing managers to vary their sales estimates easily and to gain a feel for the sensitivity of how variations will affect forecasted profits.
(3) It should help managers visualize their company's product offerings in terms of customers' needs and competitive offerings.
(4) It should be relatively easy to use even though the data requirements will necessarily be considerable. (In fact, as we shall discuss later, data collection is by far the most difficult part of the process. Data requirements should thus be made as reasonable as possible. The outputs of the model should be given in terms that the managers understand and consider important—in, for instance, gross margins and net profit.)
(5) It should be simple enough to make the issues clear, yet complex enough to capture the essence of the real-world problem.

6.4 Making a Product Map

As a first step in constructing a computer model, a product manager should make use of the product-space, or product-map, concept A product map identifies a small set of relevant dimensions for defining and comparing one company's product line

Table 6.1 A product map (product space)

	White	Buff	Canary	Red
90 weight			■○	
110 weight	△	■△		
140 weight	■○	■○△	○	○
155 weight		■△	■	■

■ The user company makes this product.
○ Competitor A makes this product.
△ Competitor B makes this product.

with those of competitors. (The basic concept of placing products in a product space has existed since the late 1950s. It was developed by Wroe Alderson, Hans Brem, Lee Preston, Volney Stefflre, Norman Barnett, Richard Johnson and others.)

Table 6.1 is a heavily disguised diagram of the index paper offerings of a large paper company from which we first developed the ideas for this chapter. For our index example, the relevant criteria have been identified as weight and colour. By convention, items are offered in 90, 110, 140, and 155 basis weights. (Basis weights are measures of thickness.) Colours for our disguised version of the actual market are white, buff, canary, and red. On the map, we use different symbols for each competitor to show what combinations of weight and colour each competitor offers. Thus, as indicated in Table 6.1, our company has seven items in its product line. Competitor A offers five items, while Competitor B offers four.

Diagrams like this enable managers to visualize their own and competing companies' positions in the market place. For example, a diagram may help to emphasize that one competitor specializes in one part of the space, that another sticks to a different segment, and that yet another aims for overall coverage.

Product spaces are useful in describing other industrial lines as well. In small electrical motors, one might find that the most important product dimensions are torque and horsepower. In a space for electric drill bits, cutting power and life of the bit might be characterized as the two most relevant dimensions.

Such product maps can be incorporated into computerized models as a powerful way of describing product-line markets. Users can then experiment with changes in the individual items within the space. Selecting two dimensions seems to make the best use of the manager's ability to assimilate data because few people can think in more than two dimensions.

Many managers feel initially that *their* products and markets are far too complex to be summarized in only two dimensions. Ultimately they discover that two basic dimensions will usually suffice if the criteria are carefully chosen. It may be, for example, that while an electric motor can be specified in up to 20 or more dimensions, some of the criteria, such as base plate size, are defined by others, such as horsepower and torque. Often industry tradition or standards specify these relationships. To simplify the situation further, products are typically offered at only certain specified points in the range of the relevant dimensions. Thus attention can often be limited to relatively few points along a dimension that at first appears to be continuous.

6.5 Designing the Model

How can the product map be used to construct a workable computer model; Primarily it can be done by assembling the most relevant data and relationships among them for the model. Not surprisingly, that is easier said than done. Data collection especially is a tedious and time-consuming task.

The kinds of data required can be illustrated by reference to the product map in Table 6.1, which shows the offerings of the user company and its two competitors. Existing sales for each item and each competitor are built into the model. In practice, of course, many such figures are only estimates. The paper products are assumed to be commodities for which one price per product prevails industrywide. The prices for the items currently being offered are built into the model, as is information on manufacturing capacity, materials and labour costs, batch sizes, and output rates. The model also starts with a rough estimate of the total manufacturing capacity for each competitor.

In a process industry of the type being considered, changing from one item to another in the production sequence involves both time and materials costs. The time cost is obvious. The materials cost is incurred because scrap material is produced as the machine is changed from one item to another. In changing from pink to green paper, the machine goes through a phase during which a mixed colour of little value is produced. Consequently, the index paper model must consider the order in which items are made and the time required to make changes in such features as paper weight and colour. The model also needs the value of each unit of scrap produced during changeover, which is approximately equal to the value of the pulp in the scrap.

Finally, cost estimates per dollar of sales of the raw materials, the work in process, and the finished goods inventories are required. When the user varies the number of items offered during the computer model's operation, the model assumes that finished goods inventories per dollar of sales vary but that the work in process and raw materials inventories per dollar of sales do not change.

The initial set of data is entered into the computer by a computer programmer. Once that task is completed, a manager communicates with the computer through a TV-like terminal. The user types requests for analyses and responds to questions posed by the computer.

6.6 Using the Model

For the index paper model, which we call PROFIT (for Product Offering Interactive Technique), the program begins by providing an income statement for the product

```
.RUN PROFIT

REVENUE:                    40Cl.
COST OF GOODS:              2144.
----------------------------------
GROSS MARGIN:               1857.
SCRAP CREDIT:                153.
SCRAP COST:                  420.
FIXED COST:                  200.
CARRYING COST:                72.
----------------------------------
EARNINGS BEFORE TAX:        1319.

OUR UTILIZATION (HOURS):   76.81%
COMPETITORS' UTILIZATIONS (UNITS):
                    82.50%  87.50%
```

Figure 6.1 Initial model outputs

line, as illustrated in Figure 6.1. In all the computer illustration exhibits, the parts of the dialogue that the user has typed have been underlined to distinguish them from the parts that the computer has typed, and explanatory comments have been identified by smaller type. In Figure 6.2 the model asks the manager what to do next. It offers the options of adding and dropping items, of inflating and deflating either unit sales or price levels across the industry, of changing individual item sales and changing price values, and of simply requesting assorted information about the product space.

Expansion or contraction of industry sales and prices is an important tool for such a cyclical industry as the paper industry because such expansion or contraction enables the product manager to understand the impact of industry changes on the existing product line; also, the changes enable the product manager to test the impact of industry-wide swings on possible changed versions of the paper company's product line.

It is often useful in models such as this one for the computer to ask brief, almost cryptic questions. A user who does not understand the questions responds with a question mark to request more information. Once users become accustomed to the program, they respond to the short questions rather than wait for the extended explanations. In Figure 6.2, the model offers the user a collection of options, and the user requests a description of the product space. The model then asks which information the user wants and provides a list of what is available. In this list, the term *estimates* appears repeatedly. The model uses smoothing techniques to estimate the prices, direct costs, or other quantities for items on which it does not have complete information. (It provides smoothed estimates only when it has data on nearby actual items in the space.)

The user is always asked for approval before a smoothed figure is used. The model does not impose these values. The values do, however, prompt the user. Figure 6.2 continues with examples of the user's requests for other descriptions of the product space—competitive offerings and sales as well as market shares.

Next, as Figure 6.3 shows, the user asks to increase unit sales for all products

```
OPTION? ?
AVAILABLE OPTIONS:
  A    ADD AN ITEM
  D    DROP AN ITEM
  F    RUN FINANCIAL PROJECTIONS
  PS   DESCRIBE PRODUCT SPACE
  IU   INFLATE OR DEFLATE INDUSTRY UNIT SALES
  IP   INFLATE OR DEFLATE ALL PRICES
  S    CHANGE INDIVIDUAL SALES FIGURES
  PR   CHANGE INDIVIDUAL PRICES
  PC   PROGRAM-SUGGESTED CHANGES
  $    STOP
```

                                                        Request for description of the product space

```
OPTION? PS  ◄
WHICH INFORMATION? ?
AVAILABLE INFORMATION:
  PS   PRODUCT SPACE
  S    SALES
  D    INDUSTRY UNIT DEMAND
  P    PRICES
  P*   PRICES AND ESTIMATES
  O    OUTPUTS/HOUR
  O*   OUTPUTS/HOUR AND ESTIMATES
  C    DIRECT COSTS
  C*   DIRECT COSTS AND ESTIMATES
  B    BATCH SIZES
  MS   OUR MARKET SHARES
  GM   GROSS MARGINS
  G*   GROSS MARGINS AND ESTIMATES
  $    NO FURTHER DESCRIPTION
```
                                          Request for information about which competitors offer which items
```
WHICH INFORMATION? PS  ◄
WHICH COMPETITOR (0=US)? 0
  ROWS GIVE     WEIGHT:      90  110 140 155
  COLS GIVE        COLOUR:WHT BUF YEL RED
  .   .   *   .  ◄
  .   *   .   .  ◄                                          Our company
  *   *   .   .  ◄
  .   *   *   *  ◄
```

```
WHICH INFORMATION? PS
WHICH COMPETITOR (0=US)? 1
  ROWS GIVE     WEIGHT:      90  110 140 155
  COLS GIVE        COLOUR:WHT BUF YEL RED
  .   .   *   .  ◄
  .   .   .   .  ◄                                          Competitor A
  *   *   *   *  ◄
  .   .   .   .  ◄
```

```
WHICH INFORMATION? S
WHICH COMPETITOR (0=US)? 1
  ROWS GIVE     WEIGHT:      90  110 140 155
  COLS GIVE        COLOUR:WHT BUF YEL RED
 ****** ******  100. ******                   Competitor A's sales
    0.     0. ****** ******        (****** means no company offers the item;
  400.   550.   350.   250.  ◄        0. means other companies sell the item,
 ******   0.     0.     0.                       but Competitor A does not)
```

```
WHICH INFORMATION? MS
  ROWS GIVE     WEIGHT:      90  110 140 155
  COLS GIVE        COLOUR:WHT BUF YEL RED
 *****  ***** 60.00 *****  ◄
 0.00  57.14 ***** *****  ◄                               Our market shares
42.86  34.48  0.00  0.00  ◄
 *****  60.00 ***** *****
```

```
WHICH INFORMATION? $
```

Figure 6.2 Descriptions of the product space

by 8%. Such industry-wide expansions are particularly important in the paper
industry. Then the user requests a financial summary. Within seconds, the model
provides the original case, the new results, and dollar and percentage variances.

```
OPTION? IU
FACTOR? ?
GIVE FACTOR BY WHICH TO INFLATE OR DEFLATE INDUSTRY  UNIT SALES -
AS A DECIMAL (FOR EXAMPLE, 1.05)
FACTOR? 1.08  ◄──────────────────────────────────         Unit sales will be raised 8%
OPTION? F  ◄
                                                          Request for financial results
                  THIS CASE     BASE CASE     VARIANCE     VAR %
REVENUE:            4321.         4001.         320.        8.0
COST OF GOODS:      2315.         2144.         171.        8.0
-----------------------------------------------------------
GROSS MARGIN:       2006.         1857.         149.        8.0
SCRAP CREDIT:        164.          153.          11.        7.4
SCRAP COST:          451.          420.          31.        7.4
FIXED COST:          200.          200.           0.        0.0
CARRYING COST:        78.           72.           6.        8.0


-----------------------------------------------------------
EARNINGS BEFORE TAX:  1442.        1319.         123.        9.3

OUR UTILIZATION (HOURS):     82.87%
COMPETITORS' UTILIZATIONS (UNITS):    89.10%   94.50%
```

Figure 6.3 Inflating unit sales industry-wide

In Figure 6.4, the user asks to restore the original case and then to add a new product. The user approves the smoothed values for price and other quantities. The user must also specify where the new item will be placed in the production sequence (so that changeover costs can be calculated). The dialogue thus encourages its marketing users to consider the manufacturing implications of their decisions. Then, making sure that the user considers primary demand, sales taken from competitors, cannibalization from existing items in the line, and any other changes, the model leads the user through a series of questions about sales of the new item.

The model thus imposes a discipline on the manager's judgment about the item addition. Throughout the process, the computer tabulates how much the user has identified in new item sales and checks to see that all such sales come from an identified source. It also alerts the user to errors, such as transferring sales from an item that is not produced. The exhibit ends with the user's request for a financial report summarizing the results of the product addition. The user can see that revenues have risen 7%, that inventory costs have gone up 9.9%, and that scrap costs have increased 7.9%. The net pretax earnings gain is 7.5%.

Figure 6.5 shows a similar sequence in which the user drops an item from the line and is led through a careful series of questions for allocating the previous sales of that item. The figure ends with a financial summary.

Such computerized aids allow the user to experiment with product line changes in a matter of minutes. An hour or two at the terminal with carefully throught-out analyses should result in a substantial increase in a product manager's understanding of the likely results of product-line changes and also of the effect of such changes on revenues, changeover costs, and earnings.

6.7 Implementing the Model

Notice in the foregoing examples what the model does and does not do. It *does* impose a discipline on the planning process. But the model *does not* exercise judgment itself. The judgments come from the user, who is presumably a knowledgeable product manager. The model organizes those judgments and, in seconds, explores their profit implications, which it then presents to the user in output reports.

The model just described is specific to a particular product line. Some of the assumptions made in the previously described model would be highly inappropriate for other types of businesses, particularly those not involving continuous production processes. Even the sequence of questions asked by the model should be tailored to an individual product manager's needs and views.

For example, the index paper product manager mentioned earlier was a firm believer in the importance of being a full-line supplier. Accordingly, the first version of the model included a question asking about overall changes in sales levels when individual items were added or dropped. The manager was required to give a specific factor to quantify the sales effects (something he did not find very easy to do).

A product manager for a second company was equally adamant about saying that there was no such thing as the 'full-line house effect'. Consequently, the question was omitted from the second version of the model.

More generally, if managers are required to make difficult quantitative judgments, the least the model can do is to leave the managers free to formulate their judgments in whatever ways they find most natural.

We chose our design approach because we believe that the relationships among items in an industrial product space are simply not yet understood well enough to allow a formal statistical (or other) model of the demand relationships.

We made our choice of a simulation model without any attempt to have the model optimize the product offerings on its own for similar reasons. We think that computerized aids such as the one described here impose considerably more structure and careful analysis on product-line decisions than is usually the rule in industrial product-planning situations.

We do not think it possible at this time to build more formal statistically based models that choose decisions or forecast sales.

6.8 Conclusions

It would be inappropriate to conclude this discussion without at least some consideration of specific steps that can be taken to implement such a model. Three basic steps are required:

(1) A model must be designed. The basic design must be done by the manager, not by the computer programmer. This task involves identifying the appropriate dimensions for the product space and deciding which aspects of the manufacturing process are critical enough to be included in evaluating possible product-line changes. Even more difficult is the task of deciding which aspects of the manufacturing process and market place are less crucial and can be

simplified or ignored with relative safety. (Most managers seem to begin the process believing that *all* the details are critical.) The design step also involves decisions about how the model can request information from managers in ways most likely to elicit sound judgments.

The product manager should then work with a good programmer to complete the details of the model design. Together they must flesh out the specification of just how the program should calculate sales, costs, and other measurements. The manager and programmer must also decide what the program's output reports will be and design the dialogue through which the user and the program will communicate. These input and output design decisions are extremely important; in practice they often receive little attention, and computer programs

```
OPTION? ?
AVAILABLE OPTIONS:
  A    ADD AN ITEM
  D    DROP AN ITEM
  F    RUN FINANCIAL PROJECTIONS
  PS   DESCRIBE PRODUCT SPACE
  IU   INFLATE OR DEFLATE INDUSTRY UNIT SALES
  IP   INFLATE OR DEFLATE ALL PRICES
  S    CHANGE INDIVIDUAL SALES FIGURES
  PR   CHANGE INDIVIDUAL PRICES
  PC   PROGRAM-SUGGESTED CHANGES
  B    SAVE CURRENT POSITION AS BASE CASE
  R    RESTORE LATEST BASE CASE
  $    STOP
```

The user restores the original base case

```
OPTION? R ◄
PREVIOUS BASE CASE MADE CURRENT
```

Original financial results

```
OPTION? F ◄

REVENUE:                4001.
COST OF GOODS:          2144.
------------------------------
GROSS MARGIN:           1857.
SCRAP CREDIT:            153.
SCRAP COST:              420.
FIXED COST:              200.
CARRYING COST:            72.
------------------------------
EARNINGS BEFORE TAX:    1319.

OUR UTILIZATION (HOURS):  76.81%
COMPETITORS' UTILIZATIONS (UNITS):    82.50%   87.50%
```

```
OPTION? A
     WEIGHT INDEX,        COLOUR INDEX: 3,3 ◄
PRICE=  2.14     OUTPUT/HR= 18.00     DIRECT COST=   0.91
```
A 140-weight canary paper will be added

Model's estimates are accepted by the user

```
OK? Y ◄
BATCH SIZE? 20
WHAT IS PRECEDING ITEM IN PRODUCTION SEQUENCE? 4,3
COMPETITOR,   UNIT SALES ◄
     1          350. ◄
   TOTAL        350. ◄
OUR SALES OF NEW ITEM? 200
OPTION FOR OTHER SALES CHANGES? ?
AVAILABLE OPTIONS:
  I    INDIVIDUALLY ENTERED SALES CHANGES
  P    PROMPTED SALES CHANGES
  D    DESCRIBE CURRENT SALES FURTHER BEFORE PROCEEDING
  E    END CHANGES
```
Summary of the current situation for the new item

```
                                                      Model will lead the user with a series of questions
OPTION FOR OTHER SALES CHANGES? P ◄
OF OUR     200. IN SALES, HOW MUCH (TOTAL)  COMES FROM COMPETITORS? 50
OF THE     150. REMAINING, HOW MUCH IS NEW PRIMARY DEMAND? 75
    75. IS CANNIBALIZATION.
LIST TRANSFERS FROM OTHERS OF THE SAME    WEIGHT:
TRANSFER: ?
GIVE     COLOUR INDEX AND UNIT SALES TRANSFERRED
OR TYPE $ TO INDICATE NO MORE TRANSFERS TO SAME    WEIGHT
TRANSFER: 1,20 ◄
TRANSFER: 2,35                          20 units come from weight 3, colour 1 (140-weight white)
TRANSFER: $
LIST TRANSFERS FROM OTHERS OF SAME     COLOUR:
TRANSFER: 2,15
CHANGE UNACCEPTABLE - WE DO NOT MAKE ITEM  2, 3     ◄        Model catches an error
GIVE    WEIGHT INDEX AND UNIT SALES TRANSFERRED           ◄
OR TYPE $ TO INDICATE NO MORE TRANSFERS TO SAME    COLOUR ◄
TRANSFER: 4,15
TRANSFER: $                  The user has not yet accounted for all sales of the new item
    5. REMAINS: ◄
TRANSFER: ?
SPECIFY TRANSFER BY GIVING    WEIGHT INDEX,    COLOUR INDEX AND CHANGE
OR TYPE $ TO  REQUEST DESCRIPTION FIRST
TRANSFER: 4,2,5
ANY OVERALL CHANGE IN OUR BUSINESS? N
ANY FURTHER INDIVIDUAL CHANGES? N

                                            The user requests the financial results
OPTION? F ◄

                THIS CASE    BASE CASE    VARIANCE    VAR %
REVENUE:        4280.        4001.        279.        7 0
COST OF GOODS:  2284.        2144.        140.        6 5
-----------------------------------------------------------
GROSS MARGIN:   1996.        1857.        139.        7.5
SCRAP CREDIT:   165.         153.         12.         7.8
SCRAP COST:     453.         420.         33.         7.9
FIXED COST:     200.         200.         0.          0.0
CARRYING COST:  79.          72.          7.          9.9
-----------------------------------------------------------
EARNINGS BEFORE TAX:  1429.  1319.        110.        8.3

OUR UTILIZATION (HOURS):  82.96%
COMPETITORS' UTILIZATIONS (UNITS):  80.00%  87.50%
```

Figure 6.4 Adding a product

are consequently unwieldy and difficult to use. Thus the programs may wind up not being used as often as they should be.

(2) A strongly user-oriented computer program for accepting inputs from the user and for performing the relevant calculations must be written. Managers seem to be most concerned about this step, but in practice we find it the easiest of the three. Once the program has been designed properly, the actual coding (or writing the program) is relatively straightforward.

(3) A data collection step, which involves gathering all of the sales, production, and financial data needed is necessary. As has been noted, the process is painfully tedious. Some of the numbers are known only roughly. In such cases, estimates must be used.

Even more of a problem is the fact that many companies do not routinely collect and maintain data in forms that are useful for evaluating product-line changes. One can argue that the collection process is most useful for such companies because it can help identify issues and inconsistencies that might

```
OPTION? D
     WEIGHT INDEX,       COLOUR INDEX: 3,2 ◄──────────────  The 140-weight buff will be dropped
COMPETITOR,  UNIT SALES
      0           465.
      1           550. ◄──────────────────────────────────  The current situation for 140-weight buff
      2           400.
   TOTAL         1415.
OPTION FOR SALES CHANGES? P                                  ◄
OF OUR    465. IN SALES, HOW MUCH GOES TO COMPETITORS (TOTAL)? 300
GIVE RATIOS FOR DIVIDING THE SALES AMONG  COMPETITORS:
COMP 1: 2
COMP 2: 1
OF THE     165. REMAINING, HOW MUCH IS LOST TO  THE INDUSTRY? 75
      90. TRANSFERS TO OTHERS OF OUR OWN ITEMS:
LIST TRANSFERS TO OTHERS OF SAME    WEIGHT:                  The user accounts for all of
TRANSFER: 1,25                                               our sales of the item
TRANSFER: 5
LIST TRANSFERS TO OTHERS OF THE SAME      COLOUR:
TRANSFER: 2,35
TRANSFER: 4,30
ANY OVERALL CHANGE IN OUR BUSINESS? N
ANY FURTHER INDIVIDUAL CHANGES? N
OPTION? F ◄─────────────────────────────────────────────
                                                            The financial implications
                  THIS CASE   BASE CASE    VARIANCE    VAR %
REVENUE:            3530.       4001.        -471.      -11.8
COST OF GOODS:      1859.       2144.        -284.      -13.3
-----------------------------------------------------------
GROSS MARGIN:       1671.       1857.        -187.      -10.0
SCRAP CREDIT:        132.        153.         -21.      -13.5
SCRAP COST:          361.        420.         -58.      -13.9
FIXED COST:          200.        200.           0.        0.0
CARRYING COST:        64.         72.          -8.      -11.8


-----------------------------------------------------------
EARNINGS BEFORE TAX: 1178.       1319.        -140.      -10.6

OUR UTILIZATION (HOURS):  67.56%
COMPETITORS' UTILIZATIONS (UNITS):   90.00%  95.83%
```

Figure 6.5 Dropping a product

not otherwise be addressed. It also facilitates communication between marketing and manufacturing areas.

Making the best product-line decisions involves developing a deep understanding of the strategic impact of tactical decisions about product-line items. Computerized aids of the sort described in this article provide the necessary rigorous structure along with a fast calculating aid that removes much tiresome 'dogwork'.

Such an approach appears to be most useful in two types of situations.

The one involves companies that make frequent item changes, such as producers of nuts and bolts, grinding wheels, and paper. For such companies, a computerized aid helps make a frequent tedious task less onerous and more careful.

In the other type of situation, such models can have substantial impact on product lines with very few items and infrequent changes, such as lines of manufacturers of heavy equipment or jet aircraft engines. Each decision has great impact and must be carefully analysed from many points of view.

Thus a computerized aid provides a means of quickly testing many possible options, of identifying the most feasible options, and of then devoting additional resources only to those options that meet the initial criteria.

Financial Modelling in Corporate Management
Edited by J. W. Bryant
© 1982 John Wiley & Sons Ltd.

7

Plant Planning Models in the Coal Industry*

Brian Harrison and Anthony Baker

7.1 Introduction

This chapter describes a set of plant planning models which have been developed jointly by accountants and operational researchers. It is based on a paper written in 1973. One significant change since then is that the oil and gas exploration activities (mentioned below as part of the organization) have now been taken over by the British National Oil Corporation, but this change does not affect the main financial modelling activities described.

The models are simple from the viewpoint of applied mathematics but they are designed to be practically useful in the process side of the Coal Industry. Firstly, to give the background, the chapter describes the practical situation of Coal Products Division (CPD), the process division of the National Coal Board (NCB). Further sections describe the approach to the construction of several models and then discuss their use and value in practice. The chapter ends with several lessons of the collaboration being drawn together.

7.2 Coal Products Division

CPD is the process division of the National Coal Board, concerned with the commercial exploitation of the derivatives of coal and with some linked ventures such as offshore exploration for natural gas. As such, CPD is a wholly owned subsidiary, with its own Board of Directors, the Chairman and Deputy Chairman of which are members of the Board of the NCB.

CPD operates in effect three main businesses as shown in Figure 7.1. The whole activity is quite large—an annual turnover (1973) of £100 million on a capital

---

*Reproduced by permission of the Operational Research Society from F.B. Harrison and A. Baker, 'The Accountant takes to Models', *Operational Research Quarterly*, 25(1), 3–18.

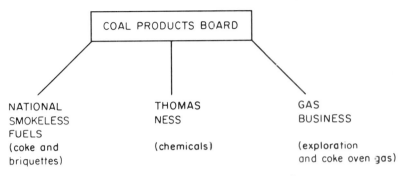

Figure 7.1 Coal products organization

investment of some £60 million—and is growing fast, especially on the associated companies and offshore exploration fronts. In Coking Group, for example, 13 plants process some 6 million tons of coal a year to produce over 4 million tons of Coke, some 25% for the iron foundry market, 12% for blast furnaces and the remainder for the domestic and industrial heating market. Briquetting Group, producing special smokeless fuels for the domestic customer, has 4 plants, 2 of which are still under development. The sales here are currently some 1.25 million tons a year but they could rise to 2 million tons in the future.

The Thomas Ness Group handles the tar by-products of the coking process. It makes various pitches and solvents and some well-known building trade materials such as 'Synthaprufe' and 'Hyload'. Also, the chemicals interest of CPD extends to various joint-owned companies processing further by-products of coke making.

One significant by-product, coke-oven gas, is sold on contract to Gas Boards and to private industries. And allied to coke-oven gas, there is the CPD stake in offshore exploration for natural gas, which now involves 10 partnerships with 23 companies. So CPD is not only a large business; it is considerably diverse with many separate chemical-engineering processes and it involves, for the most part, a chain of dependence between the various products that are made from the original coal.

7.3 Why Think of Using Models?

Granted the wide product range, why did CPD consider using models; that is to say, mathematical techniques aimed at evaluating situations and influencing decisions? It is perhaps facile to work out the reasons after the event. Inevitably the first stages were experimental—the idea caught on in small ways through people talking and working together. Only later was a more formal programme worked out and agreed as a fully argued process. However, it is possible to look back and identify issues that were live in the minds of managers, planners and accountants, when the operational research and computer-minded men were around to suggest what they could do.

The first of these issues was forecasting and budgeting for individual process plants in the short term. In the past this process was done by consultation between accountants at CPD Headquarters and the plant managers and accountants. Forecasts and budgets for the plants covered a year, but they took six months to do by hand. The result was that any individual plant forecast could almost be relied upon to be out of date—as market or coal supply changed or the inevitable cost increase happened. This was specially irritating because the planning process for a given plant is in principle simple enough—such a plant operates a 'chemical' process with known yield ratios of products. But with the various chains of products, the 'cascade' effect of one change (for example, of coal to be carborized) made for a long job in preparation of one forecast or budget, and it made revision of a forecast pretty well impossible in any sensible time.

The second issue which caused CPD to search for some help was the medium-long-term planning of the business, the solid fuel and chemicals part in particular. Here it was not so much that existing processes were too slow to react to the real situation—there just was not any formal process to project the markets and production situations together in a numerical way. Now the issue is very live—many of the CPD plants are falling due for rebuilding and the questions are 'should a plant be rebuilt and, if so, how?' We need to try and take a look perhaps 20 years ahead on:

(1) The coal supply position—where do we get our raw materials?
(2) The market position—to whom do we sell which product, and at what price?

To look that far ahead is no doubt speculative and CPD realize that judgment and risk are all important. To say the least, though, it is desirable to have a facility that can readily look at many different alternative plans involving numbers, and answer the question 'what would happen if. . .?'. There are so many 'ifs' in this situation that pen and paper in the accountant's hand are likely to be insufficient. A controlled computer exercise always seemed desirable, not to supplant the planning process, but to undertake the calculations that people would not have time to do themselves.

A further set of issues of considerable importance to CPD is the negotiation of various contracts and bids. These cover contracts perhaps for export for coke of different types, perhaps for gas supplies to different clients. Negotiating price clauses, price-review periods and discount rates, tends to be a complicated business where we need to be able to react quickly to a counter proposal to clinch a deal. Obviously many calculations are made before the parties come together, but further quick calculations are vital when large sums of money are at stake. So here, too, we look for some computer-modelling procedure to give us help in particular instances.

These are just three situations which we saw requiring calculations which could be done quickly and accurately. Our manual planning and accounting methods were not wrong, but we could not adjust them quickly, and if we were not careful, events might pass us by. That is why we gave a cautious welcome to any process—modelling, computing or otherwise—that offered help.

7.4 The Range of Models Developed

One of the themes in the discussion above is the interdependence of many of the quantities to be calculated in any plant or budget. It was tempting to try to construct one large model reflecting all the links between the products and their raw materials. Such an all embracing model would be slow to set up and get working, and would be unwieldy in the face of changes. While this is not the place to argue for or against such large models, we have consciously moved away from the 'one large model' approach.

Rather, the approach has been to provide managers and accountants with individual models tailored to particular situations. This involves an acceptance that the results from one model may be filtered through management judgment and policy before being directly used or being fed into another model. One grants that this approach provides a ready means for an 'all by hunch' manager to ignore the results of the model. On the other hand, such a manager is unlikely to have commissioned a model in the first place. In short the policy has been to go for several small and relatively simple models each geared to answering a manager's 'What would happen if. . .?' question.

The relationship between the various models developed (as they relate to the planning and control process of CPD as a whole and to individual plants) is best described by dealing in turn with models for short-term planning and budgeting and those for longer-term planning.

Within a timespace of a year, coking-plant management may need to take several decisions about the quantity of coal to be bought for carbonization at a particular plant. Also depending on market trends and the engineering condition of the plant, production levels may be set and revised at times throughout the year. Two kinds of models have been constructed to help this situation and the way they influence each other is shown in Figure 7.2.

The 'coal supplies model' is run for each coking plant where there can be a choice of coal input. It presents plant technical management with a list of preferred coals which achieve a blended feed coal of desired quality at least cost to CPD. The model is formulated in the standard mathematical form known as linear program (L.P.), which suggests a 'best' choice of plan (in this case, a least-cost plan) subject to constraints on the choice. Here the constraints are provided by the main measures of quality: content in the coal of ash, sulphur, volatile matter, moisture and also a swelling index measuring a volume change as coal is carbonized. There is considerable point in using the model to explore the effect of more stringent quality requirements and also to allow for judgments about coal properties that cannot readily be quantified.

The 'plant budget model' is available in slightly different forms for 12 plants

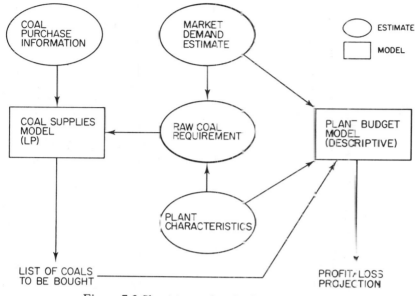

Figure 7.2 Short-term planning/control models

where it is used by managers and group accountants. Its function is to relate a planned production policy at the plant and an estimated market demand for each type of coke to the revenues and costs to be generated at the plant. It then produces a profit and loss account. The model thus integrates the plans of production management with the accountant's figures—not just for one set of conditions at one time as does one budget, but for as many different estimates and revisions as necessary as the year proceeds. The form of this financial model is discussed later in Section 7.5.

In the longer term, say 2–15 years, decisions and plans have inevitably to be broad-brush. The main decisions on this timescale concern the nature and timing of coke-oven rebuilding and rationalization to meet various possible levels of demand. This in turn interacts with the necessary supply of coking coal to the plants.

Figure 7.3 shows the relation between the three kinds of model that are used to help CPD, as a corporate body, decide what to do. The 'demand model' partly relies on a market-research analysis for all solid fuel and partly on statistical projections of past trends. The 'coal supplies model' is a larger version of the method used for individual plants mentioned above. It transforms a total demand across the country for colliery blends of various qualities into a suggested list of individual coals. While likely prices and transport costs are included, it would be fairer to view the model as making suggestions about a sensible pattern of supply rather than about a supply at absolutely minimum cost.

The 'corporate model' evaluates a suggested national CPD production policy (which includes rebuilding plants and converting individual plants to produce other

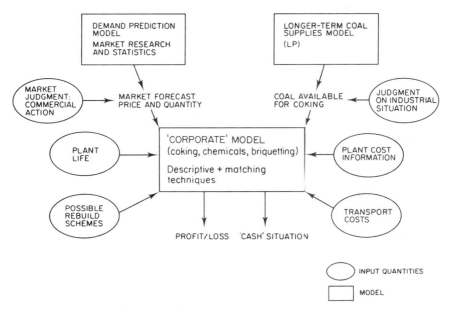

Figure 7.3 Longer-term planning models

types of coke) against demand estimates for products. The model can cover up to 25 years and includes physical summaries of production and pattern of supply to individual geographical markets. The results from the corporate model show the financial consequences of possible policies both in terms of profit and loss and of cash requirements. As with the plant budget model, the corporate model is central to the theme of this paper and will be discussed in more detail in Section 7.6.

7.5 Financial Model for Coking-plant Budgets

The financial model for a coking plant is widely used and is a good example of the simple accountancy-based model. As a reminder, the model produces an answer in physical and financial terms to the question: 'What would happen if this plant were operated in this way while market demand is at this level?'

The stages of the model are outlined in Figure 7.4 and are:

(1) Analysis of planned operating policies to produce the yield of products (six grades of coke, gas benzole, tar, ammonia). This also relates the yield of ammonia to the amount of sulphuric acid needed to make ammonium sulphate.
(2) Matching of production/marketing levels to give sales and stock levels.
(3) Build up of operating costs relative to operating policy.
(4) Stock value adjustments (accounting 'provisions') to guard against loss of realizable value owing to deterioration of product, etc.
(5) Presentation of results in stock change tables and profit and loss account.

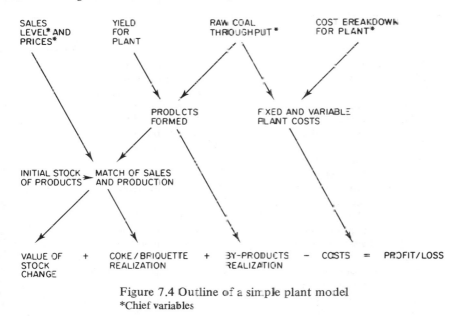

Figure 7.4 Outline of a simple plant model
*Chief variables

Viewed as mathematics, this means constructing equations to derive the 93 headings in Figure 7.5 from each other, from chemical engineering quantities (such as the yield ratio of a grade of coke from a given plant operated in a given way), from production levels and from market levels and prices.

Some equations in the model are trivial, of course. Thus:

total fuel carbonized = total coal charge − total oil charge.

Others embody time-honoured formulae to vary costs with level of operation. Thus several equations have the effect:

Power, heat and light charge
= 0.8 (unit charge for steam raising + unit charge for plant electricity)

$$+ 0.2 \left(\frac{\text{actual fuel carbonized}}{\text{norm fuel carbonized}} \right) - \text{norm fuel carbonized}$$

−value for steam sold + cost for oven gas and methane underfiring.

Such a formula is based partly on a graph of how individual costs vary with throughput. When maintenance on batteries of ovens is being carried out, plant throughput is substantially reduced and the graph is not difficult to establish by linking up four or five known points in a range. In other cases formulae are part of the engineering design of the plant. The product yields, the steam produced and the gas requirement for underfiring the ovens can be so deduced. Other equations summarize accounting analyses, particularly for the valuation of coke held in stock.

Contents of array d

1. Total fuel carbonized
2. Total coal charge
3. Value of coal charge
4. Total oil charge
5. Value of oil charge
6. P & L total foundry sales
7. Foundry net stock movement
8. Total P & L foundry production
9. P & L foundry provision
10. Effective cobbles production
11. Effective trebles prodction
12. Effective doubles production
13. Effective singles production
14. Cobbles net stock movement
15. Trebles net stock movement
16. Doubles net stock movement
17. Singles net stock movement
18. P & L cobbles production
19. P & L trebles production
20. P & L doubles production
21. P & L singles production
22. P & L cobbles provision
23. P & L trebles provision
24. P & L doubles provision
25. P & L singles provision
26. D & I sales
27. D & I stock change
28. D & I total productions
29. D & I provisions
30. P & L breeze productions
31. Breeze net stock movement
32. P & L breeze provision
33. Breeze production ex-screening
34. Value of foundry disposals
35. Value of D & I sales
36. Value of breeze disposals
37. Value of coke sales
38. Value of foundry stock-change
39. Value of D & I stock change
40. Value of breeze stock change
41. Value of coke stock change
42. Value of breeze ex-screening
43. Value of breeze ex-ovens
44. Value of foundry production
45. Value of D & I production
46. Value of breeze production
47. Value of total coke production
48. Coke sales
49. Coke stock change
50. Total coke production
51. Coke provisions
52. Production of tar
53. Production of benzole
54. Production of ammonia
55. Amount used of $H_2 SO_4$
56. Value of tar
57. Value of benzole
58. Value of ammonia
59. Value of $H_2 SO_4$
60. Coke-oven gas produced
61. Gas for underfiring
62. Calculated coke-oven gas sales
63. Gas available to Gas Board
64. Gas sales
65. Transfers to CWM power station
66. Value of gas sales
67. Value of gas transfers
68. Other own use gas
69. Value of other own use gas
70. Price of P & L GFU
71. Value of P & L GFU
72. Oven gas disposals
73. Value of oven gas disposals
74. Total gas production
75. Value of total gas production
76. Value of disposals
77. Total value of production
78. Stock increase or decrease
79. Value of production
80. Market rebates
81. Value of production less M.R.'s
82. Provisions
83. Income
84. Value of raw materials
85. Income less raw materials
86. Total power, heat and light
87. Process materials
88. Plant hire
89. 'Other expenses'
90. Total operating costs
91. Income less raw materials operating costs
92. m
93. ind

Figure 7.5 Variables in a plant model

In summary there are some 50 estimates and other inputs to the model and the model consists of over 200 equations which derive the profit and loss from the parameters.

In this form of model no account is taken of cash flow. The net cash flow for a plant differs from the profit and loss figure. One reason is that coke in stock (e.g. in the summer months) is given a value in a profit and loss statement but not as a cash flow. Moreover, many transactions entered in the accounts in a month will not really be paid then from the bank account. The payment of rates and telephone bills are but two examples of different credit periods. This lack of cash-flow projection is no worry for individual plants which do not have separate bank accounts anyway. It is allowed for in the corporate model, where capital expenditure items can also be incorporated.

When you have over 200 equations to calculate the profit and loss for a plant, the obvious thing to do is to store it as a computer program—and our practice is no exception. The plant models are all operated through a teletype 'conversational' terminal to the IBM 360/65 computer at NCB Computer Services at Cannock. Use of such a terminal ensures local access to a model by local management and accountants, and they can obtain a profit and loss statement as in Figure 7.6 in 20 seconds, little time more than the time taken to print it out. The procedure is speeded up by a control program which enables revision of the input estimates on an exception basis.

The teletype terminal is set up in the NCB to have access to only a part of the computer's memory. The corporate model for longer-term planning is therefore accessed in London through a larger terminal connected to the full facilities of the computer. The limited storage space available to the conversational terminals has also ruled out the plant budget models being written in one of the specialized financial modelling languages now widely offered. This has not really been a great disadvantage since such languages usually make their impact on the program writing and testing stage: our experience is that these stages are less time consuming.

Agreeing the scope of the model and transforming the accountant's logic initially to algebra dominates the time to construct models. Our experience of plant budget and profit and loss models has now reduced the effort in the construction to that of one man working for a month.

7.6 Corporate Model for Production Policy Planning

So far it may seem that all the models are like the plant budget models—a well-established procedure for providing information for planning or control. But other models go further in their methods. Figure 7.7 shows an outline of the logic of the Corporate Model which evluates Coking and By-Products Group operating policy against market demand over several years. A first look reveals that the logic is essentially similar to a plant budget model for a year. Breakdown of overall production level into products and comparison with demand estimates appears much the same. There are, however, two additional features worthy of mention.

PROVISION RATES AND STOCK MOVEMENTS

	Loss provision	Degrade provision	L & M provision	To stock	From stock
Foundry	−1020.4	622.9	66.1	1590.2	1830.5
Cobbles	−296.7	−133.0	−111.1	635.7	231.7
Trebles	−523.1	−193.7	−196.6	930.0	215.0
Doubles	−160.2	−113.8	−63.6	284.9	53.4
Singles	0.0	0.0	0.0	0.0	0.0
Breeze	−41.1	0.0	−57.1	1350.4	0.0
Total coke and breeze	−2041.5	182.4	−363.0	4791.2	2330.7

PROFIT AND LOSS ACCOUNT SUMMARY: MONTH 1

	Unit	% Yield/(ton fuel carbonized)
Fuel carbonized (tons)	42 898	
Coke production	32 657	76.127
Breeze produced (tons)	1 510	3.520
Total coke and breeze	34 167	79.647
	Amount	£/tfc
Income		
Disposals	421 298	11.453
Stock increase (+)/decrease (−)	10 625	0.248
Value of production	501 923	11.700
Less market rebates	372	0.009
Value of production after MRs	502 295	11.709
Stocking provisions	−2 222	−0.052
Total income	500 073	11.657
Raw materials	323 353	7.538
Total income less raw materials	176 720	4.120
Expenditure		
Power, heat and light	39 775	0.927
Plant hire	1 782	1.042
Process materials	699	0.016
Other expenses	74 876	1.745
	117 876	2.730
Profit/loss after rebate	59 588	1.389

Figure 7.6 Plant profit/loss statement

Firstly, a cash statement is produced in addition to profit and loss. This is of considerable interest, to say the least, at corporate level, because provision for working capital has to be agreed with the NCB along with any capital funding. The

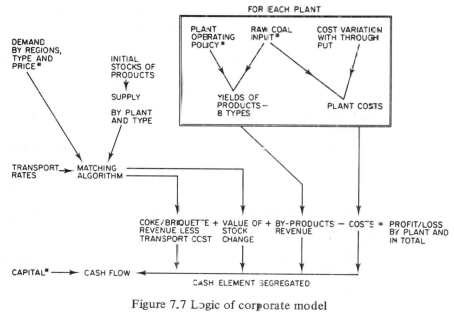

Figure 7.7 Logic of corporate model
*Chief quantities to be varied

cash statement also gives a measure of the money tied up in stock of coke from year to year and the debtors/creditors position. This latter is measured yet again according to accountant's experience, because the model does not monitor day to day financial transactions as such. As an aside, a separate month-by-month cash-flow projection model is currently envisaged.

A second complication is in the matching process between generated product levels and market demand. In the corporate model production and market demands are matched for half a dozen areas of the country at once. The matching of individual markets to the supply coking plant is done in such a way that the financial contribution (price less production and transport cost) is exploited. A similar method has been used, also within the corporate model, where breeze (finely ground coke needed in the process) has to be supplied to each coking plant from one of a few coking plants with breeze grinding equipment.

A simplification in almost all of the models is in their disregard of random fluctuation of performance figures. The logic usually answers the question 'What if. . .?' using only average figures. This is adequate for most of the models. Uncertainty about performance is provided for when you have a means of rapidly revising a calculation on a new assumption. But in one instance—the model for gas contracting mentioned briefly earlier—it was necessary to get the feel of being at risk over several years, and a probability distribution was introduced to provide typical histograms of revenue, return on investment and other financial measures. The point, however, about this and the other refinements was that they were carried out by the accountants and operational research model builders in partnership and they were built onto models in which confidence was already established.

7.7 Provision of Data for the Models

The formulae which make up the models and computer programs which store them are useless by themselves. They require accurate and up-to-date information to work on, data on likely sales and on production costs and yields. Providing good data and in particular designing a method to collect and revise them may sometimes be more difficult than writing the model in the first place. Our experience has not been that extreme, but it has differed in the cases of the two main types of model.

The plant budget models pose no real difficulty in data requirement. Much is essentially fixed, either by the nature of the process (e.g. the yield of various products) or by a declared policy for the year (e.g. the unit value at which products are to be accounted while they are held in stock). These data are held in an 'annual' file, whereas other information, notably on prices and sales, is held in a 'monthly' file which allows regular variation of the figures. Collecting these data takes up a couple of days for the local administrative staff and this would have to be done even without a model. Recording the data on a computer file takes a couple of hours' typing at a terminal keyboard. With this done, the files need major revision only once a quarter, though changes to individual items can be made at any time. And of course, it is the essence of the procedure that if one figure in the data is changed, the new profit and loss projection can be made without having to change or remember any other figure.

By contrast the longer-term corporate model does pose some difficulty in its data handling. Some of the data are speculative, e.g. sales levels some years ahead. Moreover, information has to be extracted from several sources; from production management on possible plant-operating policies, from accountants on likely cost and inflation rates, from marketing men on likely demand for products and on transport arrangements. Inevitably assumptions from each source may not be consistent with each other, e.g. a special product made at one plant may be jeopardized by a plant-rebuilding proposal. Such cases are not really alarming, because the model results can pinpoint a clash of view that might otherwise be left half-stated. More worrying are the trivial data errors that can arise in putting the information from every plant onto a computer file. Such exercises tend to be 'one-off' and regular maintenance of up-to-date data is much more of a problem than in the case of the short-term budget models. We are attacking the problem of data errors by simplifying the design of data collection forms and by establishing checking procedures on the data even before the model is run.

7.8 The Use of the Models and their Value

Now that these models are working, the obvious question to ask is: 'Are they useful, even valuable to practical management?' The short answer is: most are useful and some are very valuable. This section indicates why this is so.

On the planning side, the short-term budget models for the solid-fuel plants are regularly used by the local managers and accountants. It would be naive to imply that the budgeting/planning process has been cut from months to minutes, but the budget now can be done in the time it takes to argue and agree the assumptions, and the resulting plan can be kept up to date. The managers find they need to 'play tunes' on the plants, particularly around the time when plant budgets need to be revised, and we now have the facility to do this from CPD Headquarters too. One tune to play locally, for example, is in getting a good blend of raw materials from week to week. Small quantities of South Wales coke breeze may cost a lot to transport around into various blends—what can we get away with, in the light of other materials that are available? What effect does this have on the yield of coke from coal—and on the costs and revenue?

The longer-term corporate model is operated as an adjunct to the planning discussions in various committees and is useful because it shows all the plants in their interrelations and the way they affect our financial situation. We simply must have this information to support decisions to rebuild particular plants which cannot justly be viewed in isolation from each other.

The value of these planning models is very clear to the user, but how is one to justify them to the outsider? The main point is that CPD can now do something that could not be done before without a model—examine a range of plans based on a permutation of assumptions and strategies. Though it takes time to build up a model, when it is built up and checked it is guaranteed to be accurate in its logic. This is not a point to be despised, particularly when the alternative is a back-of-the-envelope rough exercise done with your boss wanting the results yesterday!

The models were not originally designed to reduce staff and save money that way, though they have done so. We found that in some instances a few posts at plants no longer needed to be refilled once the plant budget model existed. This is always an area for careful consideration and it is impossible to guarantee in advance that a model will save staff.

The great value of these models though, once established, has been through the speed of reaction. Outstanding here is the application of models to contract negotiation, where they have been invaluable. It is impossible, for commercial reasons, to illustrate by example. But a procedure which quickly evaluates CPD's commercial opponent's proposals and enables us to suggest a more profitable counter-proposal puts us in a much stronger position. There is no doubt that models, in fulfilling this role, have been worth a good deal to CPD in making more advantageous contracts in several instances. Again this could not have been done by the usual quick hand calculations—the proposals and counter-proposals were complex and speed and accuracy were of the essence.

Our reliance on the basic accounting logic might be challenged as canonizing an age-old procedure which ought to be questioned instead. This is an arguable view; but we believe the more constructive approach is to focus attention on the basic logic as it is translated into the model and in due course seek improvement in the logic using the model as a test bed.

Already attention has been focused on the matching of production and demand and the breeze-grinding operation in the corporate model, and the model is beginning to influence existing practice. Moreover, the print-out of the corporate model is used to show the alternative effects of allocating stocking charges back to plants or keeping the whole stocking activity controlled on a corporate basis. Our contention is that an accepted model can preserve the right logic and it can readily be used to try out a simplified or otherwise improved idea for a change.

Something which is not easy to predict in advance is the 'spin-off' from a model-building programme. In CPD's case this provided an intensification of some earlier work the operational research men had been doing on choosing blends of coal for individual plants. This work is well established now with substantial savings in transport cost being achieved, and individual local technical officers are aware how their coal-buying programme should relate qualities of a blend to cost of purchase. Another 'spin-off' has been the concurrent introduction of the small computer terminals. This is something of a chicken-and-egg situation in relation to the models since each made possible the existence of the other. Local staff have learnt how to use these terminals and with operational research help use a variety of small programs perhaps too simple to be called 'models'. There are currently over 300 small programs in use. These are helping to improve quality control and to direct attention where safety aspects need improving at individual plants. At CPD Headquarters the staff can readily calculate the effect of a CPD wage-increase proposal, and can do a great variety of cash-flow appraisals for capital-investment projects. All are in no doubt relatively small in themselves but are all well worth having.

Almost nothing has been said about the effort of developing the range of models. The total operational research commitment to CPD over this period is about 3 men for 18 months, but some of that effort deals with topics not brought out in this chapter. What must be included though is the managerial and accountant's efforts in commissioning models and discussing their logic. This has had its rewards in the benefits the plant budget models in particular have brought. This is not to deny that investment of sponsors' resources in time and patience is significant and is a prerequisite for useful procedures to be developed.

7.9 Conclusions

A snapshot of work in CPD on financial modelling has been described. New models are always being developed and old ones are being refined or revised; and for models to remain of use, this is how it should be. However, it is appropriate to reflect briefly here on our experiences.

The practice of going for relatively small models for one sponsoring manager seems to be right. Moreover, a procedure which answers a manager's 'What if. . .?' question quickly allows a place for judgment, risk and intuition: it also avoids what often appears a fundamental weakness of large optimizing models, the exclusion of managerial style.

What seems entirely healthy is the way that accountants and operational research people meet and pool their ideas on CPD topics. It may lead to a model—it may not. But if it does lead to a model, the model will clearly be commissioned, the method will be agreed jointly and the results respected. This seems quite an achievement, but we know there is plenty more to be done.

Financial Modelling in Corporate Managemen
Edited by J. W. Bryant
© 1982 John Wiley & Sons Ltd.

8

Pricing Models in the Imperial Group

STEPHEN LYUS AND GEOFFREY WELLS

8.1 Introduction

The operational research section of the Imperial Group have built models to help companies determine their pricing policy from a *market* point of view. These have involved customers' perception of quality *vis à vis* competitors, and estimates of the influence of price on sales volume. These models are complex statistically and the interpretation of the answers is always a cautious activity. In contrast, the models described in this chapter are not complex and are of an accounting rather than an operational research nature. They are mechanical in the sense of doing no more than simple arithmetical operations, but their benefit often lies in this simplicity. They have normally been very easy to develop, they save substantial clerical effort and they give much more rapid results than can be achieved through manual systems. They have been very useful within our Group in producing good-will between Management Services and Accounting departments, and so provide a sound base from which to develop further systems.

In the remainder of this chapter, examples of some costing-type models are given. These fall into three distinct areas both as regards the field of application and the pay-off of the modelling activity. Firstly, models which have been developed in the imported cigar and the cardboard box markets are described. These show the value of models that react to changing exchange rates. Secondly, a model is outlined which has been used for beer costing. This demonstrates the value of a system that will undertake a lot of detailed calculations accurately and will react quickly to duty changes. Finally, a costing model is discussed which has been used in grocery pricing by Smedley–HP and which illustrates the value of a model that reacts to commodity price changes and which links in with budgeting and four-year planning.

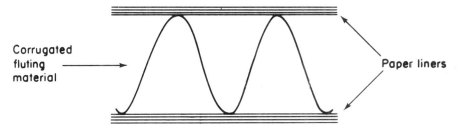

Figure 8.1 Corrugated board construction

8.2 Imported Cigar and Cardboard Box Models

Introduction

The performance of Sterling in the international money markets has recently been an important factor in determining the prices charged by U.K. companies. This section describes two examples from within the Imperial Group where the exchange rates of Sterling are major determinants of a product's profitability. The two companies concerned are Imperial Tobacco (Imports) Ltd, and Ashton Containers Ltd, and their trading activities are now briefly described. (The Imperial Group has since disposed of its interest in Ashton Containers.)

Imperial Tobacco (Imports) Ltd, imports foreign cigars and cigarettes and operates a sales force to market them throughout the U.K. The best known brand name is probably Henri Wintermans, but they have a wide range of products and this involves three currencies; the Dutch guilder, the Swiss franc and the Danish kroner. Apart from duty, the most important cost factor is the purchase price in the foreign currency, and a model has been developed to carry out the costing calculations.

Ashton Containers Ltd, manufacture corrugated packing cases from corrugated board which consists of paper liners and corrugated fluting material that are bound together with adhesive. Usually the corrugated end product consists of one fluting, as shown in Figure 8.1.

The materials used in the process come from various countries including U.S.A., Norway, Sweden, Finland, Portugal and the U.K. There are nineteen different types of paper liners and two main fluting materials and the possibility of having different liners for the top and bottom of the board means that there are a very large number of final board grades. The calculations are in fact done for 225 grades. Thus there are many calculations dependent on a few exchange rates.

The Model Structures

The Imperial Imports model performs the detailed costs and gross profit calculations, by month, for each of the 26 major brands of cigar. The company total gross profit and turnover is also produced, as well as sub-totals by cigar manufacturer.

Examples of the type of reports that are generated by the model are shown in Figures 8.2–8.4. Figure 8.2 shows the build-up of costs for two brands of cigars, the unit being 100 cigars. As an extra security procedure the actual print-out used refers to brands as numbers and only the accountants involved have access to the code. A subtotal is formed over all brands for each manufacturer as shown in Figure 8.3, followed by a further aggregation over manufacturers as in Figure 8.4. A further tabulation is produced in which a suggested new retail selling price is shown, and the cash margins and the percentage margins earned by the retailer are also calculated under the different quantity discounts operating. The whole process is covered in the model from, say a change in the Dutch guilder rate to a change in the retail price at a U.K. outlet. The model contains a feature whereby historical monthly sales volumes can be held within the model and can then be used as a basis for automatically calculating seasonal factors. A change need only be made to the annual sales and the model will break this total down into monthly sales volumes.

In the Ashton Containers application there are two models. The first calculates the supplier price in Sterling per hundred square metres of board, given carriage and other costs. The logic diagram for the supplier price model is shown in Figure 8.5.

The next model takes as input these supplier prices and calculates the following:

(1) The average price for a material, taking into account the various tonnages from different suppliers.
(2) A return on capital figure to be added to the material price.

The logic diagram for (1) and (2) is shown in Figure 8.6.

(3) The cost of the liners and fluting per hundred square metres.
(4) The final board grade cost, being the addition of the various elements required for that particular board.

The logic diagram for (3) and (4) are shown in Figure 8.7.

Figure 8.8 illustrates the output from the first model, whilst Figure 8.9 shows the results of calculations described in (1)–(3) above, and Figure 8.10 is an example of the final board grade cost report ((4) above).

The Models in Use

The Imperial Imports model was originally designed for helping in the preparation of the annual budgets, and has been in use since 1974. However, it has also been extensively used within the year whenever changes in the U.K. selling price are being considered. There has, of course, to be more stability in the U.K. Sterling price charged to the public than that reflected by the exchange rates which vary on

ICL-DATASKIL PROSPER MK3BON:- 25/8/77 AT 22/25/35
OPERATION SHEET

BRAND:	NOV	DEC	JAN	FEB	MAR	APR	MAY	JUN	JUL	AUG	SEP	OCT
	11											
PURCHASE COST	3.6145	3.6145	3.6145	3.6145	3.6145	3.6145	3.6145	3.6145	3.6145	3.6145	3.6145	3.6145
LANDING	0.0300	0.0300	0.0300	0.0300	0.0300	0.0300	0.0300	0.0300	0.0300	0.0300	0.0300	0.0300
BOND	0.0000	0.0000	0.0000	0.0000	0.0000	0.0000	0.0000	0.0000	0.0000	0.0000	0.0000	0.0000
TOTAL IN BOND COST	3.6445	3.6445	3.6445	3.6445	3.6445	3.6445	3.6445	3.6445	3.6445	3.6445	3.6445	3.6445
DUTY	5.8938	5.8938	5.7000	5.7000	5.7000	5.7000	5.7000	5.7000	5.7000	5.7000	5.7000	5.7000
CARR. IN CLEAR	0.0050	0.0050	0.0050	0.0050	0.0050	0.0050	0.0050	0.0050	0.0050	0.0050	0.0050	0.0050
TOTAL DUTY PAID COST	9.5433	9.5433	9.3495	9.3495	9.3495	9.3495	9.3495	9.3495	9.3495	9.3495	9.3495	9.3495
DESPATCH MATERIALS	0.0240	0.0240	0.0240	0.0240	0.0240	0.0240	0.0240	0.0240	0.0240	0.0240	0.0240	0.0240
LABOUR	0.0390	0.0390	0.0390	0.0390	0.0390	0.0390	0.0390	0.0390	0.0390	0.0390	0.0390	0.0390
CARR. OUT	0.0960	0.0960	0.0960	0.0960	0.0960	0.0960	0.0960	0.0960	0.0960	0.0960	0.0960	0.0960
COST OF SALES	9.7023	9.7023	9.5085	9.5085	9.5085	9.5085	9.5085	9.5085	9.5085	9.5085	9.5085	9.5085
GROSS PROFIT PRE-TAX	2.2977	2.2977	2.4915	2.4915	2.4915	2.4915	2.4915	2.4915	2.4915	2.4915	2.4915	2.4915
POST-TAX	2.2977	2.2977	2.4915	2.4915	2.4915	2.4915	2.4915	2.4915	2.4915	2.4915	2.4915	2.4915
SELLING PRICE	12.0000	12.0000	12.0000	12.0000	12.0000	12.0000	12.0000	12.0000	12.0000	12.0000	12.0000	12.0000
% GP ON NET SP	19.1	19.1	20.8	20.8	20.8	20.8	20.8	20.8	20.8	20.8	20.8	20.8
WEIGHT (LB/100)	0.6000	0.6000	0.6000	0.6000	0.6000	0.6000	0.6000	0.6000	0.6000	0.6000	0.6000	0.6000

****

BRAND: 12

PURCHASE COST	5.3012	5.3012	5.3012	5.3012	5.3012	5.3012	5.3012	5.3012	5.3012	5.3012
LANDING	0.0300	0.0300	0.0300	0.0300	0.0300	0.0300	0.0300	0.0300	0.0300	0.0300
BOND	0.0000	0.0000	0.0000	0.0000	0.0000	0.0000	0.0000	0.0000	0.0000	0.0000
TOTAL IN BOND COST	5.3312	5.3312	5.3312	5.3312	5.3312	5.3312	5.3312	5.3312	5.3312	5.3312
DUTY	11.7876	11.7876	11.7876	11.7876	11.7876	11.7876	11.7876	11.7876	11.7876	11.7876
CARR. IN CLEAR	0.0150	0.0150	0.0150	0.0150	0.0150	0.0150	0.0150	0.0150	0.0150	0.0150
TOTAL DUTY PAID COST	17.1338	17.1338	16.7462	16.7462	16.7462	16.742	16.7642	16.7642	16.7642	16.7642
DESPATCH MATERIALS	0.0480	0.0480	0.0480	0.0480	0.0480	0.0480	0.0480	0.0480	0.0480	0.0480
LABOUR	0.0780	0.0780	0.0780	0.0780	0.0780	0.0780	0.0780	0.0780	0.0780	0.0780
CARR. OUT	0.1920	0.1920	0.1920	0.1920	0.1920	0.1920	0.1920	0.1920	0.1920	0.1920
COST OF SALES	17.4518	17.4518	17.0642	17.0642	17.0642	17.0642	17.0642	17.0642	17.0642	17.0642
GROSS PROFIT PRE-TAX	0.5482	0.5482	0.9358	0.9358	0.9358	0.9358	0.9358	0.9358	0.9358	0.9358
POST-TAX	0.5482	0.5402	0.9358	0.9358	0.9358	0.9358	0.9358	0.9358	0.9358	0.9358
SELLING PRICE	18.0000	18.0000	18.0000	18.0000	18.0000	18.0000	18.0000	18.0000	18.0000	18.0000
% GP ON NET SP	3.0	3.0	5.2	5.2	5.2	5.2	5.2	5.2	5.2	5.2
WEIGHT (LB/100)	1.2000	1.2000	1.2000	1.2000	1.2000	1.2000	1.2000	1.2000	1.2000	1.2000

****

Figure 8.2 Imperial Imports: brand reports (From G. E. Wells, *The Effect of International Exchange Rates on UK Inflation*, reproduced by permission of Prosper User Group)

1977/78 BUDGET SUMMARY (£000s)
BURGER SOHNE

	NOV	DEC	JAN	FEB	MAR	APR	MAY	JUN	JULY	AUG	SEP	OCT	TOTAL
BURGER LONG													
SALES VOLUME	1356	565	753	697	1036	697	810	829	904	866	848	1639	11000
GROSS PROFIT	31.2	13.0	18.8	17.4	25.8	17.4	20.2	20.6	22.5	21.6	21.1	40.8	270.3
TURNOVER	163	68	90	84	124	84	97	99	108	104	102	197	1320
BURGER SWISS													
SALES VOLUME	1468	624	810	759	1131	759	878	911	979	945	928	1806	12000
GROSS PROFIT	8.0	3.4	7.6	7.1	10.6	7.1	8.2	8.5	9.2	8.8	8.7	16.9	104.2
TURNOVER	264	112	146	137	204	137	158	164	176	170	167	325	2160
BURGER PANATELLA													
SALES VOLUME	3065	1313	1705	1567	2350	1567	1820	1912	2051	1982	1912	3756	25000
GROSS PROFIT	97.3	41.7	56.5	52.3	78.4	52.3	60.7	63.8	68.4	66.1	63.8	125.3	826.8
TURNOVER	460	197	256	235	353	235	273	287	308	297	287	563	3750
TOTAL													
GROSS PROFIT	136.5	58.1	83.2	76.7	114.8	76.7	89.1	93.0	100.1	96.5	93.6	183.0	1201.3
TURNOVER	887	377	492	455	680 NOBEL	455	528	550	592	571	556	1085	7230
PETIT CIGARILLOS													
SALES VOLUME	1647	693	867	780	1213	780	953	953	1040	1040	1040	1993	13000
GROSS PROFIT	16.1	6.8	9.9	8.9	13.8	8.9	10.9	10.9	11.9	11.9	11.9	22.7	144.5
TURNOVER	132	55	69	62	97 LA PAZ	62	76	76	83	83	83	159	1040
WILDE CIGARILLOS													
SALES VOLUME	1530	765	998	931	1363	931	1064	1097	1197	1131	1131	1862	14000
GROSS PROFIT	6.2	3.1	4.7	4.4	6.4	4.4	5.0	5.1	5.6	5.3	5.3	8.7	64.2
TURNOVER	92	46	60	56	82	56	64	66	72	68	68	112	840
WILDE CIGARROS													
SALES VOLUME	1943	760	989	919	1378	919	1078	1131	1201	1166	1131	2385	15000
GROSS PROFIT	-74.5	-29.1	-35.0	-32.5	-48.8	-32.5	-38.2	-40.0	-42.5	-41.3	-40.0	-84.4	-538.9
TURNOVER	194	76	99	92	138	92	108	113	120	117	113	239	1500
TOTAL													
GROSS PROFIT	-68.3	-26.0	-30.3	-28.2	-42.4	-28.2	-33.2	-34.9	-36.9	-36.0	-34.7	-75.7	-474.7
TURNOVER	286	122	159	148	220	148	172	179	192	184	181	350	2340

Figure 8.3 Imperial Imports: manufacturer reports (From G. E. Wells, *The Effect of International Exchange Rates on UK Inflation*, reproduced by permission of Prosper User Group)

ICL-DATASKIL PROSPER MK3BON :- 25/08/77 AT 22/26/34

1976/77 BUDGET SUMMARY (£000s)

	NOV	DEC	JAN	FEB	MAR	APR	MAY	JUN	JULY	AUG	SEP	OCT	TOTAL
HENRI WINTERMANS													
GROSS PROFIT	396.3	98.0	145.8	135.1	201.4	135.1	160.2	166.7	177.2	171.4	182.8	531.6	2501.6
TURNOVER	3181	786	1044	970	1441	970	1151	1197	1270	1230	1294	3812	18346
BURGER SOHNE													
GROSS PROFIT	136.5	58.1	83.2	76.7	114.8	76.7	89.1	03.0	100.1	96.5	93.6	183.0	1201.3
TURNOVER	886.7	377.2	492.0	455.4	680.4	455.4	528.2	550.4	592.3	571.3	555.7	108b.1	7230.0
NOBEL													
GROSS PROFIT	16.1	6.8	9.9	8.9	13.8	8.9	10.9	10.9	11.9	11.9	11.9	22.7	144.5
TURNOVER	131.7	55.5	69.3	82.4	97.1	62.4	76.3	76.3	83.2	83.2	83.2	159.5	1040.0
LA PAZ													
GROSS PROFIT	−60.3	−26.0	−30.3	−28.2	−42.4	−28.2	−33.2	−34.9	−36.9	−36.0	−34.7	−75.7	−474.7
TURNOVER	286.1	121.9	158.8	147.7	219.6	147.7	171.0	170.0	192.0	184.4	180.9	350.2	2340.0
PANTER													
GROSS PROFIT	53.8	22.9	32.4	31.2	47.4	31.2	35.8	37.0	41.6	38.2	37.0	74.0	482.6
TURNOVER	516.7	220.9	269.7	258.3	393.2	258.3	295.7	307.1	344.5	318.4	307.1	614.1	4103.9
GRAND TOTAL													
GROSS PROFIT	534.4	159.8	241.0	223.8	335.0	223.8	262.8	272.6	293.8	282.1	290.5	735.6	3855.3
TURNOVER	5002	1562	2034	1893	2832	1893	2223	2310	2482	2387	2420	6021	33060

Figure 8.4 Imperial Imports: overall budget summary (From G. E. Wells, *The Effect of International Exchange Rates on UK Inflation*, reproduced by permission of Prosper User Group)

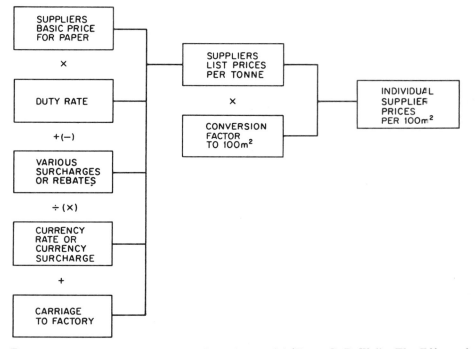

Figure 8.5 Ashton Containers: supplier price model (From G. E. Wells, *The Effect of International Exchange Rates on UK Inflation,* reproduced by permission of Prosper User Group)

a daily basis. It is usual to produce several sets of output based on different assumptions about future exchange rates. The model produces 22 pages of output and only takes 2 minutes to run on the computer. It was written by Imperial Group Management Services for the Chief Accountant of Imperial Imports.

The two programs for the Ashton Containers model were written by an accountant, who had attended an in-house training course in the ICL financial planning language, Prosper. It is run on an *ad hoc* basis several times a year by the Accountants Department and has been an important link in the costing process at Ashtons. The programs have also been kept up to date by them, with only very occasional support from computer specialists. The clerical effort involved in the old manual system was about 2 man-weeks whilst the run time of the models is about 5 minutes in total.

8.3 Beer Costing Model

Introduction

This application is concerned with producing the product standard costs by packaging type and size for all the different beer recipes brewed by Courage Ltd.

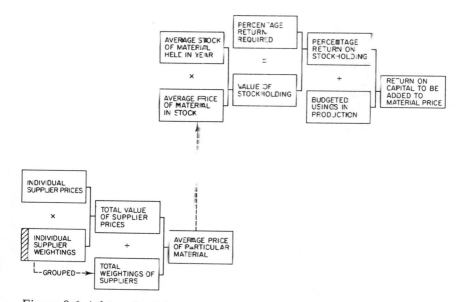

Figure 8.6 Ashton Containers: material average price and return on capital models (From G. E. Wells, *The Effect of International Exchange Rates on UK Inflation*, reproduced by permission of Prosper User Group)

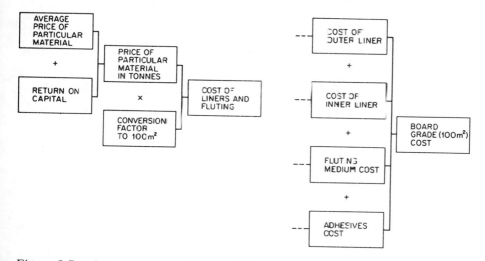

Figure 8.7 Ashton Containers: liner and fluting cost and board grade cost models (from G. E. Wells, *The Effect of International Exchange Rates on UK Inflation*, reproduced by permission of Prosper User Group)

The term 'product standard cost' means the material and duty cost of each beer in its final packaged form. The model mirrors the brewing process, which is shown schematically in Figure 8.11 and which is now briefly outlined.

ICL-DATASKIL PROSPER MK3B ON :- 27/10/77 AT 17/02/39

ASHTON CONTAINERS LTD PT003

TEST JUTE LINER PRICES

	S/C %	125G/M2		150G/M2		200G/M2		300G/M2		400G/M2	
		TONNE £	100M2 £	TONNE £	100M2 £	TONNE £	100M2 £	TONNE £	100M2 £	TONNE £	100M2 £
J. BLOGGS (KENT) 1/9/76		238.91	2.99	230.93	3.35	221.61	4.43	216.95	6.31	216.95	8.68
J. SMITH (YORK) 1/9/76		243.16	3.04	235.17	3.41	225.86	4.52	221.20	6.44	221.20	8.85
W. BAILEY 5/7/76		242.56	3.03	234.17	3.51	224.87	4.50	225.21	6.76		
R. BROWN & SON 1/7/77		232.33	2.90	224.67	3.37	217.02	4.34				
T. LOONEY INC 17/7/76				241.38	3.62	223.74	4.47	219.15	6.57	219.15	8.77
ST JOHNS MILL 17/7/76				242.43	3.64	224.79	4.50	220.20	6.61	220.20	8.81
BISHOP 17/7/76				245.10	3.68	227.46	4.55	222.87	6.69	222.87	8.91
ALBION 2/8/76						216.27	4.33				

EXCHANGE RATE USED	$	1.7559
DO	SWKR	8.4425
DO	NRKR	9.6125
DO	FNMK	0.0000

Figure 8.8 Ashton Containers: suppliers' prices report (From G. E. Wells, *The Effect of International Exchange Rates on UK Inflation*, reproduced by permission of Prosper User Group)

MATERIAL	SUBSTANCE GM2	PRICE PER TONNE	RETURN ON CAPITAL	DELIVERED PRICE PER TONNE	COST PER (100M2)
KRAFT	100	337.154	9.385	346.539	2.079
KRAFT	101	228.726	9.385	238.111	2.976
KRAFT	102	221.309	9.385	230.694	3.460
KRAFT	103	214.521	9.385	223.906	4.478
KRAFT	104	214.521	9.385	223.906	5.038
KRAFT	105	214.521	9.385	223.906	6.717
KRAFT	106	214.521	9.385	223.906	8.956
B I INER	100	181.211	6.279	187.491	2.344
BLEACHED KR	100	368.302	17.799	386.181	4.634
BLEACHED KR	101	365.164	17.799	382.963	5.744
OYSTER KRAFT	100	263.470	17.799	281.269	3.516
OYSTER KRAFT	101	254.971	17.799	272.770	4.092
OYSTER KRAFT	102	254.971	17.799	272.770	4.773
PIG WHITE K	100	644.186	17.268	661.453	5.292
POLY BROWN K	100	460.949	17.268	478.217	3.587
TJL	100	219.760	2.010	222.109	2.776
TJL	101	212.541	2.349	214.890	3.223
TJL	102	204.385	2.349	206.734	4.135
TJL	103	199.528	2.349	201.877	6.056
TJL	104	199.528	2.349	201.877	8.075
CHIP	100	146.052	2.674	148.726	1.859
CHIP	101	146.052	2.074	148.726	2.603
MIDDLES	100	141.691	3.352	145.043	5.599
MIDDLES	101	141.691	3.352	145.043	6.991
MIDDLES WATER	100	170.791	0.976	171.767	6.270
MIDDLES WATER	101	170.791	0.976	171.767	7.987
SEMI CHEM	100	169.538	2.317	171.855	1.925
SEMICHEM	101	169.538	2.317	171.855	2.183
SEMI CHEM	100 COARSE - FLUTE				2.791
SEMI CHEM	101 COARSE - FLUTE				3.165
SEMI CHEM	100 FINE - FLUTE				2.566
SEMI CHEM	101 FINE - FLUTE				2.909

→ The weighted average price of a paper liner from various suppliers

Figure 8.9 Ashton Containers: liner and fluting cost report (From G. E. Wells, *The Effect of International Exchange Rates on UK Inflation*, reproduced by permission of Prosper User Group)

ICL-DATASKIL PROSPER MK 3B ON :- 25/10/77 AT 01/06/15   ASHTON CONTAINERS LTD

PT001 MATERIAL BASIS
STANDARD BOARD GRADES
COARSE FLUTE

CODE NO	BOARD	GRADE	MAKE-UP	CALIPER MM	WEIGHT (100M2) T	COST (100M2) £
E002	105K	103T	100SC		.06	15.76
E003	103K	103T	100SC		.061	13.52
E006	101K	101K	100SC		.062	8.94
E008	100B	100C	100SC		.063	7.19
E009	100B	100B	100SC		.064	7.67
E015	100C	100C	100SC		.065	6.70
E016	101K	100C	100SC		.066	7.82
E017	101C	100C	100SC		.067	8.19
E042	102T	102T	100SC		.068	11.26
E047	101T	100C	100SC		.069	7.62
E048	103K	103K	100SC		.07	11.94
E049	100W	101K	100SC		.071	10.60
E050	100OY	101K	100SC		.072	9.48
E056	103K	102T	100SC		.073	11.60
E079	101K	101T	100SC		.074	8.74
E116	102K	101K	100SC		.075	9.42
E117	102K	102K	100SC		.076	9.67
E118	102K	100T	100SC		.077	9.91
E119	101OY	101T	100SC		.078	9.85
E131	101W	100K	100SC		.079	11.71
E132	101W	101T	100SC		.08	11.95
E147	106K	104T	100SC		.081	20.02
E157	102K	102T	100SC		.082	12.16

The cost of E047 corrugated board manufactured by Ashtons, consisting of:

→ 101T
→ 100SC
→ 100C

Figure 8.10 Ashton Containers' board grade cost report (From G. E. Wells, *The Effect of International Exchange Rates on UK Inflation*, reproduced by permission of Prosper User Group)

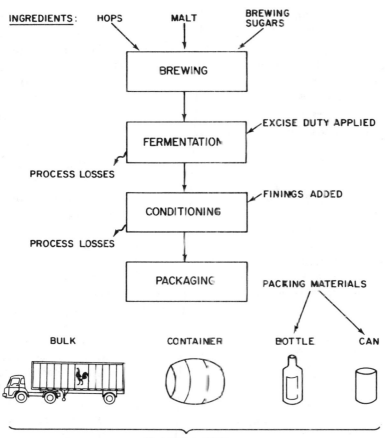

Figure 8.11 Courage: the brewing process

(1) Brewing   Raw materials are used in accordance with traditional recipes to produce a brown sweet liquid. These raw materials include various types of malt, hops and sugars, depending on the particular beer.

(2) Fermenting The brown sweet liquid is fermented, becoming eventually what we know as beer. However, it is not fit for consumption until it has passed through the third stage.

(3) Conditioning Here, with the aid of finings, various haze-forming substances (yeast and certain proteins) are precipitated leaving the beer clear and ready for packaging.

(4) Packaging   Courage beers are packaged in various types of containers ranging from 36 gallon casks to one-third pint bottles and 10 ounce cans.

The cost of the beer must cover both the basic raw materials and also the various substances added. Since these additions are usually in liquid form, volume adjustments to the costs must be made. To this must then be added the cost of the various packaging materials, which include crown tops, labels, cans, non-returnable bottles and cartons. Losses arise *(of a duty-paid product!)* at each of the first three stages of the process, mainly due to transfers between the various plants but also as a result of the processes themselves. Further losses occur at the packaging stage and again must be taken account of in costing.

The Model Structure

The model has been designed such that there are four separate programs corresponding to the four regional operating companies, plus a consolidation program to provide a national picture.

Each operating company model has its own input of budgeted prices of raw materials and budgeted usage of those materials within defined brew sizes. The production departments provide the budgeted process losses, the types and sizes of packaging, and the gravities. The final important common input to all the models is the beer duty rate, provided by H.M. Customs and Excise. Each of the company programs then produces a detailed stage-by-stage report of the way that each standard cost is built-up. An example of the report produced for one fictitious beer is given in Figures 8.12–8.14. The report is laid out in terms of the cost per barrel (36 gallons) at each stage of the process. Figure 8.12 gives the details of the price times quantity calculations for each raw material that is used in this particular beer. Figures 8.13 and 8.14 describe the brewing process followed by the beer. At most stages there are liquid additions of various ingredients, the amount of these additions being taken care of by volume adjustments to bring the costs back to a cost per barrel basis. After the filling stage is shown the cost on a pro-rata basis for each size in which the beer is packaged: these final lines, one for each package size, are the product standard costs. It will be noted that they do not include any elements for labour, distribution or overheads.

The standard costs are picked up by the consolidation program, and a useful summary is produced. However, the main reason for generating this program is that some of the beers are produced at several locations to the same recipe, and the Courage accounting system requires the national average cost of these over all locations weighted by budgeted throughput. The program provides these averages, as well as the consequent national averaging variances attributable to each operating company.

The Use Made of the Model

The model was produced to help in the production of the 1977/78 budget and has been used since then for this purpose. It has also been used for providing the costs which are used to value the finished goods and work-in-progress stocks at the financial year-end. Finally, it is occasionally used when major external suppliers significantly increase their prices.

The computer model replaced a manual system, which involved one man–week of calculations at each operating company, by one that requires one man–day at each operating company to complete the input forms and a suite of programs that takes two hours to produce the standard costs for about 220 products.

The consolidation program mentioned above requires no further input apart from the supply of volume data for each operating company. An additional benefit is that now the standard costs are stored on computer files, other programs can access the files to produce, say, a flex-budget comparing budget and actuals. It will also be extremely easy, if and when the beer duty rate is increased, to produce new standard costs, as only one line of input needs to be changed.

8.4 Smedley–HP Foods Pricing Model

Introduction

Smedley–HP Foods Ltd, produces a wide range of canned, bottled and frozen foods. The products are classified into the following groups: bottled sauces under HP, Daddies and Lea & Perrin labels; pickles under the Epicure label; baked beans under HP and Smedley labels; fruit, vegetables and other recipe products such as soups and spaghetti under the Smedley label; and frozen meats and vegetables under the Ross label. There is also a wide range of products under customer-own labels with a number of them prepared to special recipes In total, there are 72 different types of product with up to six different sizes for each.

Government price control legislation provided the impetus necessary to start using computer models to help decision making. The problem posed was, given a total amount of price increases allowable under price-control legislation, how should this be allocated over products? This might not at first appear a very complicated process, but when trying to increase prices to the maximum amount allowed, whilst taking into account retailers' margins, competitors' prices and sales volumes, the number of combinations involved makes the process very laborious. Once this problem had been successfully resolved, other parts of the laborious Price Commission work were tackled. These were the allocation of overhead costs to products and the basic raw material cost calculations.

The Model

The first, very simple, program took as input current and proposed future retail selling prices, and calculated the standard 1000-case rate based on a specified retailer's margin and the number of items in each case. Figure 8.15 gives an example of the output. The model calculated the amount of the increases based on the

ICL-DATASKIL PROSPER MK3B ON:- 10/10/77 AT 16/47/04
CONFIDENTIAL
COURAGE BREWING LIMITED

PRODUCT STANDARD COSTS

SCHEDULE 1
BUDGET YEAR 1977/78

COURAGE LIMITED
PLANT: LONDON

SOUTHWARK ALE

ORIGINAL GRAVITY 1031
PRIMED GRAVITY 1031

MATERIALS		STD. PRICE	STD. VALUE	STD. COST PER BRL.
		£	£	£
A. DUTY				
RATE PER BARREL PER DEGREE (FROM 01/01/77)		0.5808		16.9245
B. BASIC MATERIALS				
MALT PLAIN	2000.00 KG. @	1.3000	2600.0000	10.8333
SUGARS NO. 3 INVERT	5000.00 KG. @	1.4000	7000.0000	29.1667
HOPS COPPER HOPS	100.00 KG @	25.0000	2500.0000	10.4167
STANDARD VALUE PER BREW OF 240 BRLS.			12100.0000	
STANDARD COST PER BARREL - BASIC MATERIALS				50.4167

C. OTHER MATERIALS

SUNDRIES   10.0000

STANDARD VALUE PER BREW OF   240 BRLS.

STANDARD COST PER BARREL - OTHER MATERIALS   0.0417

D. BY-PRODUCTS

GRAIN   500.00   KG. @   0.01000   5.0000
YEAST   200.00   KG. @   0.00900   1.8000

STANDARD VALUE PER BREW OF   240 BRLS.   6.8000

STANDARD SALES VALUE PER BRL. - BY-PRODUCTS   0.0283

E. ADDITIONS	STAGE ADDED	PINTS/ BARREL	O.G.	COST/ PINT	MATERIALS	VALUE £ DUTY	TOTAL
FININGS	FERM	5.0000		0.0300	0.1500		0.1500
FININGS	C. TANK	6.0000		0.0300	0.1800		0.1800

Figure 8.12 Courage: material costs report

ICL - DATASKIL PROSPER MK 38B ON:- 10/10/77 AT 16/47/13
CONFIDENTIAL
COURAGE BREWING LIMITED　　　　PRODUCT STANDARD COSTS　　　　SCHEDULE 3
BUDGET YEAR 1977/78

COURAGE LIMITED　　　　SOUTHWARK ALE　　　　ORIGINAL GRAVITY 1031
PLANT: LONDON　　　　　　　　　　　　　　　　PRIMED GRAVITY 1031

CHILLED FILTERED AND CONDITIONED BEER

1. STANDARD PRODUCTION LOSSES

	LOSS	YIELD
(A) FERMENTATION	5.00 %	95.00 %
(B) TRANSFER	%	%
(C) WARM CONDITIONING	%	%
(D) COLD PROCESSING	4.00 %	96.00 %
(E) FILLING (1) BOTTLES	3.00 %	97.00 %
(11) CANS	%	%
(111) CONTAINERS	3.00 %	97.00 %
(1V) TANKS	%	%

2. COST PER BARREL BREWED

	MATERIALS	£ DUTY	£ TOTAL
BASIC MATERIALS (PER SCH. 1)	50.4167		50.4167
OTHER MATERIALS (PER SCH. 1)	0.0417		0.0417
EXCISE DUTY (PER SCH. 1)		16.9245	16.9245
COST PER BARREL BREWED	50.4583	16.9245	67.3828

ADDITIONS IN FERMENTATION:

		MATERIALS	£ DUTY	£ TOTAL
FININGS	5.0000 PINTS	0.1500		0.1500
COST PER	293.0000 PINTS	50.6083	16.9245	67.5328
COST PER BARREL BREWED		49.7447	16.6357	66.3804

3. COST PER BARREL TRANSFERRED

	MATERIALS	£ DUTY	£ TOTAL
COST PER BARREL BREWED, AFTER LOSS 1 (A)	52.3629	17.5113	69.8741
COST PER BARREL TO COLD TANK	52.3629	17.5113	69.8741

Figure 8.13 Courage: product standard cost report (first part)

COURAGE BREWING LIMITED

SCHEDULE 3 CONTINUED
BUDGET YEAR 1977/78

COURAGE LIMITED
PLANT: LONDON

PRODUCT STANDARD COSTS

ORIGINAL GRAVITY 1031
PRIMED GRAVITY 1031

SOUTHWARK ALE

	MATERIALS	£ DUTY	£ TOTAL
4. COST OF COLD TANK STOCK			
COST PER BRL. EX SECTION 3	52.3629	17.5113	69.8741
ADDITIONS IN CONDITIONING TANK:			
FININGS 6.0000 PINTS	0.1800		0.1800
COST PER 294.000 PINTS	52.5469	17.5113	70.0541
COST PER BARREL IN COLD TANK	51.4705	17.1539	68.6244
5. TRANSFER TO BRIGHT BEER TANK			
COST PER BARREL EX COLD TANK (SECTION 4)	51.4705	17.1539	68.6244
COST PER BARREL IN BRIGHT TANK, AFTER LOSS 1(D)	52.6152	17.8686	71.4838
6. CONTAINER FILLING			
COST PER BARREL BEFORE FILLING (EX SECTION 5)	53.6152	17.8686	71.4838
COST PER BARREL PACKAGED, AFTER LOSS 1 E(111)	55.2734	18.4213	73.6946
7. COST PER CONTAINER SIZE			
22 GALLON CONTAINER	33.7782	11.2574	45.0356
11 GALLON CONTAINER	16.8891	5.6287	22.5178

Figure 8.14 Courage: product standard cost report (second part)

Product	Current		Proposed		Volume	Rev.	GP %	
	RSP	1000 rate	RSP	1000 rate	Cases	Incr.	Old	New
Carrots UT	12p	2.10	13p	2.27	200 000	£34 000	47	45
Celery A1	10p	1.75	11p	1.93	20 000	£3 600	52	50
Celery A2								
Beetroot A1								

Figure 8.15 Smedley–H.P.: selling price increase report (Reproduced with permission from R. Botwright, *The Adoption of Prosper into Budgeting, Planning and Price Commission Application Systems*)

sales volumes for the following twelve months and also gave the gross profit percentages. In addition it produced four other tabulations showing the effect of 0.5p and 1p variations in either direction in the future retail selling prices. Thus there were five print-outs for each group of products. If in the base case there had been an over-recovery, then the subsidiary print-outs were used to juggle the prices manually.

The overhead allocation program calculates overhead rates per case on a moving annual average basis. This basis was agreed with the Price Commission as a result of the high seasonality inherent in most of the lines. These rates are then increased to take into account recent price levels. For example, in the case of manufacturing overheads, for which the calculations are shown in Figure 8.16, the cost for each location is summarized into thirty expense classifications and the volumes are listed. The program accumulates these amounts with those of the previous eleven periods for that factory and then allocates the cost of each expense category between product groups on bases previously determined. Overheads for the same product grouping from other factories are added and the resulting total is then divided by the volumes to produce rates per case. As well as the annual figure, this process is also carried out on the data for the last three months.

The construction of a raw material cost program was an ideal application for modelling as these costs were continually being re-calculated, incorporating price, usage and recipe variations for latest estimate and standard costing. The program was built up in stages, according to the different product groups. It took, as input the ingredients, their costs and the raw material usages, and then calculated the raw material price costs, as illustrated in Figure 8.17.

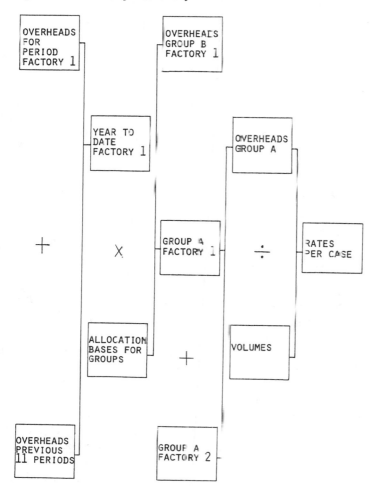

Figure 8.16 Smedley–H.P.: manufacturing overheads model (Reproduced with permission from R. Botwright, *The Adoption of Prosper into Budgeting, Planning and Price Commission Application Systems*)

The Models in Use

Over a period of about a year (1975) computerized financial planning became totally acceptable within Smedley-HP. From small beginnings when all input data used to be put on punched cards, the system has been extended to accept data on magnetic tape and to make use of existing information on current computer files.

In the case of the two Price Commission models much data had previously to be

Ingred.	Usage 1000 cases	Price Oct. 1975	Price 1975/76	£/case base	£/case 1975/76
1	0.219	65.15	63.00	14.27	13.80
2	0.007	227.00	173.70	1.59	1.31
3	0.002	750.00	770.00	1.50	1.54
4	0.233	400.00	325.00	93.20	75.72
5					
6					
7					
8					
9					
10					

Figure 8.17 Smedley–H.P.: raw material costs/usages report (Reproduced with permission from R. Botwright, *The Adoption of Prosper into Budgeting, Planning and Price Commission Application Systems*)

manually input. Now, for the 'price increases' model, it is only necessary to input the proposed Recommended Selling Prices (R.S.P.) and the new cost prices. The previous R.S.P.'s, old cost prices, sales forecasts, selling prices and other figures are all extracted from existing computer files.

For the 'manufacturing overheads' model, all relevant information is taken directly from the company computerized nominal ledger system. When carried out manually, this operation took many days and mistakes were possible. Further, because of the time factor, it was only undertaken when a price increase notification was under way. Now each product group's overheads are calculated in this manner every month, thus making overhead increases become more apparent.

The 'raw material cost' model is also used to derive some of the input for the budget model that was written once the three models which have been described were working. Continual developments have been made since that time, one of which has been the extension of the budget model into four-year planning using the information that is already on file as base data.

Overall, financial planning has been very successful in Smedley–HP as it has meant that greater control has been achieved because more detailed information is produced more regularly. Another important aspect is that when the plans are being revised in this detail a greater degree of reliance can be placed on them. With more regular updates, Smedley–HP are able to react much more quickly to counteract the effect of adverse changes to the current plans, particularly in the critical area of cash flow. Alternatives to plans can be considered by means of 'what if' questions so that contingency plans can be drawn up in advance, whereas previously these could only be considered in terms of generalities. Finally, as managers have been relieved of the burden of carrying out calculations they have been able to spend more time in thinking and in planning.

Acknowledgments

We would like to acknowledge the invaluable help of Messrs. T.A. Daniel, J.E. Lancaster, P.W. Moss and D.L. Willett in the preparation of this chapter.

Financial Modelling in Corporate Management
Edited by J. W. Bryant
© 1982 John Wiley & Sons Ltd.

9

The Use of Computers in Cash Management for the Small Company*

TONY RANDS AND BOB VAUSE

9.1 Introduction

Monitoring the movement of cash and controlling the cash flow is currently one of the key problems facing management in the smaller company, and the increased numbers of company liquidations over the last few years seem to indicate a failure to achieve this minimum requirement for business survival by many firms. However profitable a company may appear in its profit and loss account, if it fails to concentrate sufficient attention on cash flow management it can put its continued growth, and indeed survival, at considerable risk. The only certain means of ensuring survival in today's business climate is to maintain sufficient cash flow and liquid balances to cover payments to creditors. A company must always be able to pay its bills when they fall due. It is a lack of liquid cash funds that causes bankruptcy, not a low or negative profitability. For this reason the profit shown in the company's profit and loss account has long been seen as only one indicator of corporate success and management performance. The cash-flow statement is now seen by most managers as equally important as the profit and loss account, and the key indicator of the company's potential for growth or survival.

Unfortunately many small company managers concentrate their efforts solely in the generation of sales revenues and associated costs, and use profit as the main indicator of their business's success or failure. They pay little attention to cash-flow forecasting and control as, mistakenly, they believe this is a complex and difficult task. Indeed, for most small companies the only time when any real effort is put into cash-flow forecasting is when the bank manager requests a cash budget to

---

*Revised with permission of the publisher from C. A. Rands, R. Vause, and K. G. Pemberton, 'Using Computers in Small Company Cash Management', *Accounting and Business Research* (16) Autumn 1974.

back up a request for loan or overdraft facilities being made by the company. Typically, once this exercise has been completed, the cash budget is relegated to the bottom drawer of the manager's desk and forgotten whilst he concentrates once more on generating sales.

The first sign of cash difficulties for a company is often that there is insufficient cash in the bank to pay a supplier. Management's response to this situation is often arbitrary and unplanned, consisting of an attempt to speed up the collection of cash from customers or applying to the bank for a short-term facility using the debtors expected to pay in the coming period as security. This solution is only, at best, a short-term palliative, and does little to get to the root causes of the company's difficulties. For a more exhaustive approach to the problem a series of questions must be considered:

(1) How was the cash crisis discovered?
(2) Did one particular decision precipitate the situation?
(3) What steps should be taken to remedy the situation?
(4) Could the crisis have been discovered earlier?
(5) How can similar situations be avoided in the future?

In recent years considerable advances have taken place in analytical techniques applicable to cash-flow control which can assist management to answer these questions. In parallel with these techniques there has been an even more rapid development in computer hardware and software, so that today for a few hundred pounds management can acquire for their company the computational power to analyse large and complex problems in a manner which a few years ago was, due to high capital costs, only open to the very large organizations.

It is the purpose of this chapter to consider how computer models of cash flow can provide ready and effective assistance to the management of the small company, to control cash flow, to predict potential cash-flow problems, and to provide assistance in determining what steps to take to remedy the situation.

9.2 Cash-flow Problems and Models

The cash flow of a company, and the residual cash balances at the end of each period, are the result of quite complicated movements in turning money into materials and services which are sold. The cash eventually received can once more be used to circulate within the company to generate further cash flows and profit, and to cover payments of taxation or dividends as well as to re-invest in capital assets necessary for the growth of the company.

At the simplest level, companies can develop a cash budget providing details of the cash movements expected within the coming period. This is achieved by translating the sales, production and other budgets into real cash-flow terms: when is the company going to have to pay cash out? This can be shown as:

	Month 1	*Month 2. . .*	*Total*
Opening cash balance	100	100	100
Cash inflow (sales)	300	400	700
	———	———	———
Total cash available	400	600	800
Cash outflow (expenses)	200	400	600
(capital)	–	100	100
	———	———	———
Closing cash balance	200	100	100
	———	———	———

This is an example of a cash budget that many small companies will have supplied to their bank managers to assist in their loan or overdraft requests. It provides details of the manner in which the operations of the company, producing and selling goods, as well as investing in capital items (new machines or vans, for example) are going to be shown in the cash flow and balances for the coming period. The cash budget can show when money will be required to finance operations and when this, together with any interest, can be repaid.

This form of cash-flow forecasting or budgeting is quite simple. The difficulties management face in real life are normally due to a number of complementary factors, such as time delays between the purchase of goods or raw materials and their sale and the eventual receipt of cash from the customers, seasonalities in trading which may cause large overdraft requirements at particular times each year, and the payment of lump sums (Corporation Tax and VAT, for example) during the year. Many of these factors impinge on each other in a complex manner, making it difficult for the small company manager to predict effectively cash movements and balances even a short time ahead. It is this that explains why many small company managers rely heavily on just knowing what their current cash position is, and making a series of day-to-day decisions relating to cash control under the mistaken assumption that in this way they are really in control of the company's cash flow. This approach, as many managers have learnt, can be a quick path to disaster.

The main difficulty facing managers trying to forecast cash flow is to allow for the interaction between the various factors which dictate cash movements within the firm, and it is towards assisting this process that most of the analytical techniques developed in recent years have been directed. The application of cash-flow modelling techniques allows the manager to build a model that represents the main structural elements in the company and the way in which they interact (for example, sales order patterns, sales deliveries, cash receipts from customers, etc.); by completing a series of calculations within the model, and receiving predictions from it in terms of cash flows for areas of specific concern, the manager is effectively simulating the operations of the company without having to await the actual events taking place. This provides the advantage of allowing a manager

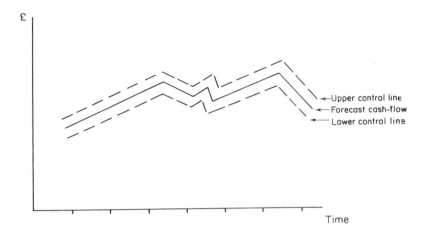

Figure 9.1 Cash-flow control chart

to feed into the model a series of possible alternative choices of action open to the company, together with likely outcomes to see, well ahead of the event, the expected impact upon the company's cash flow. The model anticipates the likely future impact of management action or policies and allows time for them to be assessed in order that the best alternative may be discovered.

Often a particular area of difficulty arises because many of the variables involved in the company's cash flow are subject to random fluctuations, and act to disguise the true cash-flow pattern developing. This means that in order to develop a truly useful cash-flow model, it must be possible to incorporate a facility to enable the manager to identify quickly whether adverse trends are developing. This can be achieved by isolating the trends from the random movements in cash that inevitably occur within any company. The adoption of a system of control charts, similar to those used in quality control, can assist in this process. Control lines can be drawn within which the cash flow is expected to fall. Should the actual cash flow move outside the range of the control lines, then this may act as a stimulus to the manager to question whether there is an adverse trend developing (see Figure 9.1).

Inherent in many methods involving forecasting cash flows is the problem that the manager can only develop a single best estimate of the firm's likely cash flow, and is not offered the facility to develop effective control lines for any possible variations from this resulting from random fluctuations in cash movements. Thus these models may inform the manager what the overall cash flow is likely to be, but make it difficult for him to decide when corrective action should be initiated, or when no action should be taken. These models tend to have more application in cash-flow forecasting and planning rather than in day-to-day cash-flow control.

Often the reason why cash-flow models only allow the prediction of expected or most likely cash-flow outcomes, and do not indicate possible variations in cash flow, is that calculating such variations is often complex and time consuming when related to the small company. For just this reason it is a distinct advantage if cash-flow modelling can be accomplished with the use of computers, as these can be used to perform the rather tedious calculations necessary to determine likely cash-flow variations. Until quite recently the cost involved in using computer facilities, and the complexity and cost of cash-flow modelling designed for computer operation, has outweighed, for the small firm, any possible advantages which might occur.

Within the last few years this situation has changed quite dramatically. Firstly, computers have been reduced in both size and cost, so that today a machine will easily fit in the desk space previously occupied by a typewriter, and at minimal cost can offer the same computational capacity as machines of ten or so years ago requiring a special building to house them, with a cost of several million pounds. In addition, developments in modelling techniques allow models to be built that only require basic readily available company data, and which may be programmed simply by a manager with little experience in computer technology or programming.

This chapter continues with a description of the manner in which such a simple computer-modelling exercise can be effected to meet the needs of the small company.

9.3 A Computer Modelling Method for Managing Cash flows in Small Companies

The computer model described here has been developed at the Oxford Management Centre. It is suited to the needs of small companies because it is relatively easy to build the model and program the computer, whilst the information required is only basic data that any properly managed small company should have available.

Standard Program Blocks

A major difficulty in the development of a computer model of cash flow is to ensure that the model can represent the actual flows of cash, materials and services in the company. As each company is to a large extent unique in the kinds of services it offers and the relationships between the different cash-flow elements, this means no single standard cash-flow model may be used for all small companies. Instead, each company requires an individual model to be constructed for it alone, building the basic elements of cash-flows in the same way as they interact within the real company.

Building different elements together has always been one of the major difficulties with traditional computer programming, but developments in software now allow the various elements to be brought together simply and easily. A key feature of the model developed at Oxford, therefore, is that it contains blocks of computer programs which represent standard cash-flow operations. All a manager has to do is to bring together these blocks following the same structural relationship as

Table 9.1 Some examples of cash-flow operations and program block identifiers

Cash-flow operation	Identifying code of program block	Symbols in cash-flow diagrams
Running balance	B	
Delay	D	B
Net VAT owed	V	D
Forecast	F	V
VAT rate	R	F
		R

exists in his company. In the Oxford model, he may do this directly from his cash-flow statements, in the way that is described below.

Each standard block of computer program that corresponds to a cash-flow operation is recognized by an identifying code. In modelling the system, it is only necessary to refer to the identifier, and the computer will place the cash-flow program corresponding to it in any position relative to other program blocks that is dictated by the manager. The modelling system contains a number of different program blocks that correspond to different elements of cash flows. Examples of these are shown, together with their identifying codes, in Table 9.1.

Constructing a Simple Cash-flow Model

To illustrate how a model may be constructed using this method, a simple example of a company shipping goods ex-stock and receiving cash at some time later from its debtors will be used. The first stage is to develop a flow diagram of the cash movements using appropriate symbols. This is given in Figure 9.2, where it can be seen that a forecast of the goods shipped is used, with a delay between this and the receipt of cash. The balance between the goods shipped and the receipt of cash gives the outstanding debtors; this is achieved by keeping a running balance between goods delivered and cash received later for those goods.

If the problem were slightly different, and the manager concerned could forecast sales orders received but not deliveries because of internal delays within the stock-handling system, then Figure 9.2 could be modified easily to give Figure 9.3.

In order that a flow diagram may be programmed into the computer each separate block must be identified by a number, and these have been added to Figure 9.3. The flow diagram is converted into a computer program by using a table that specifies the block number from which each cash-flow element receives its inputs. In this table, each line refers to a different cash flow block, and the layout of each line follows a format which tells the computer where inputs come from. The format for each line is:

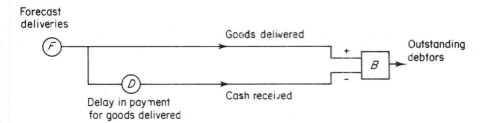

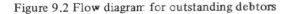

Figure 9.2 Flow diagram for outstanding debtors

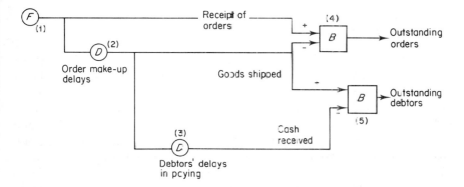

Figure 9.3 Modified flow diagram for debtors model

Block Number Title	Block Type	Source of Input 1	Source of Input 2	Source of Input 3

Following this format means, for instance, that the line for the delay in making up orders for shipment in Figure 9.3 would appear in the computer program as:

Block Number Title	Block Type	Source of Input 1	Source of Input 2	Source of Input 3
2	D	1	0	0

The zeros under Inputs 2 and 3 indicate that the delay has only one input.

Using this table format means that a computer program corresponding to the flow diagram of Figure 9.3 may be written quickly and simply by a manager once the method of writing the table format has been learned. Moreover, it is easy to change the model structure by merely changing the flow diagram, and making appropriate corrections to the table. The complete program for Figure 9.3 is shown in Table 9.2, with negative signs indicating that the balancing elements are deducting rather than adding.

Table 9.2 Computer program for Figure 9.3 showing inputs to each cash flow element

Block number	Block title	Block type	Input 1	Input 2	Input 3
1	Order forecast	F	0	0	0
2	Order delay	D	1	0	0
3	Debtor payment delay	D	2	0	0
4	Order balance	B	1	−2	0
5	Debtors balance	B	2	−3	0

Operating the Model

Once the model structure has been defined by the manager, he is in a position to operate the model and predict the behaviour of areas of special interest to him. In order that the model may be operated, it is necessary for the computer to be fed with certain basic data, such as values for expected orders received, the nature of the delay patterns, opening values for running balances such as outstanding debtors and others. Once the model is developed, the manager may specify what outputs he requires and these may be printed either numerically or graphically.

The manner in which a typical cash model would assist a manager is shown in Figure 9.4. There are a number of inputs to the model, namely the manager's forecasts of the external environment, e.g. the receipts of sales orders, and decisions the manager expect to make. These decisions could be one area where the manager may want the model to help him determine strategies, such as the most viable manufacturing policy given seasonalities in demand. Built into the model are the relationships between cash-flow elements that have already been described, as well as the values of these elements, such as opening cash balances and the length of delays. Outputs from the model may be predictions of net cash balances, or other factors that will help the manager to investigate the cash-flow impact of his policies.

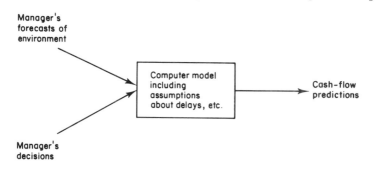

Figure 9.4 Operation of the model

One special feature of the model is the manner in which delays are computed and used during the operation of the system. These may be calculated from the data readily available in most small companies, and do not require a special additional study to determine the average delay length or the nature of the statistical variations about it. A typical input into the computer that allows it to calculate delays is shown in Table 9.3, which contains twelve months' past data for sales deliveries and outstanding debotrs corresponding to the flow diagram of Figure 9.2. The contents of this table may be input to the computer and the average delay in cash receipts represented by the debtors, as well as the statistical variation contained, will be calculated within it. These values may then be used for predicting the appropriate delay during the subsequent simulation. When applied to the data in Table 9.3 this method shows the average credit taken by customers to be 2.62 months, and the statistical variation about this (assumed to be Normally distributed) has a standard deviation of 0.234 months.

9.4 An Example of the Application of the Method

The Company

In order to show how the computer modelling method may be used, its application to a small electronics company will be described. This company manufactured electronic equipment which was marketed through a chain of distributors into the retail network. The company's operations were essentially the assembly of equipment from purchased-in components, and the supply ex-stock of equipment against orders received from distributors.

The basic data from which a cash flow model was developed is shown in Table 9.4. This shows the movements of cash into materials, labour, and other variables, for the year previous to the cash exercise. It can be seen that the data contained in Table 9.4 is no more than the fundamental necessary to monitor the cash flow of the company. It can also be seen that the company uses some of its own conventions of accounting, e.g. that materials and overheads creditors are kept together.

Flow Diagram

The first stage in building a model for the firm was to develop a flow diagram that represented the cash movements within the company. Clearly there is a flow of materials into the company based on orders placed at suppliers, and there is a flow of products leaving the company based on orders received from customers. These materials generate a cash outflow and a cash inflow that has to be balanced against the outflows of cash into labour and overheads. An initial flow diagram related to this application is shown in Figure 9.5. It can be seen that this has been built using the structure of Figure 9.3 to represent both the outflow of materials as products

Table 9.3 Records of past sales and debtors

	Jan	Feb	March	April	May	June	July	August	Sept	October	Nov	Dec
Sales delivered	19 344	21 943	19 425	23 002	27 625	25 030	12 015	29 553	24 246	17 180	29 233	41 164
Opening debtors	71 000	70 818	60 609	62 328	73 727	73 862	69 709	68 934	74 412	59 596	57 928	77 473

Table 9.4 Basic data for cash-flow model

	Jan	Feb	Mar	Apr	May	June	July	Aug	Sept	Oct	Nov	Dec
Orders received	18 000	31 000	32 000	35 645	36 000	22 610	16 735	55 875	11 200	7 200	33 260	42 050
A Sales delivered	19 344	21 943	19 415	23 002	27 625	25 030	18 015	29 553	24 246	17 180	29 233	41 164
C Mats. bought	5 450	10 101	8 653	17 919	6 903	7 963	5 402	10 057	9 456	5 464	7 619	12 219
Labour:												
Weekly	6 088	6 744	8 096	7 009	7 652	9 810	6 822	10 236	7 241	4 970	9 726	9 720
Monthly	2 500	2 465	2 465	2 700	2 710	2 830	2 446	2 560	2 856	2 693	2 444	2 363
C O/H incurred	4 500	2 800	7 100	4 344	4 281	4 122	6 076	6 011	7 531	2 620	2 865	4 955
B Debtors	71 000	70 818	60 609	62 328	73 727	73 862	69 709	68 934	73 312	59 596	57 928	77 473
D Creditors (Mats + O/H)	30 294	25 990	23 726	40 280	37 487	39 747	37 463	40 858	46 049	36 901	23 031	35 479
Bank (OD)	13 980	110 000	110 533	113 821	122 748	115 508	122 573	112 379	120 390	114 095	112 748	107 359
WIP	38 000	48 000	62 500	75 620	84 240	82 595	81 315	107 860	95 030	85 220	89 470	90 530
Creditors + O/H payments	10 674	7 224	12 635	15 160	16 509	8 952	15 781	13 340	10 707	17 065	7 474	31 481

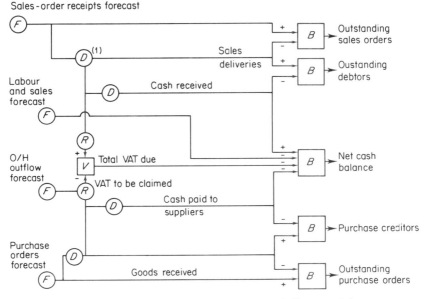

Figure 9.5 Initial flow diagram for cash-flow model

and inflows as components for assembly. Additionally other factors have been added, such as outflows of cash for wages and salaries, overheads, VAT and Corporation Tax.

However, in developing the flow diagram to represent cash flows in the company, a problem occurred because unfortunately the data contained in Table 9.4 does not allow the calculation of parameters relating to certain variables in the model. For instance, in the sales element of Figure 9.5, it can be seen that following receipts of orders from customers, goods are shipped out at a later time, the balance between the two representing outstanding sales orders. In order for the value of delay (1) to be calculated, both the past order receipts *and* levels of outstanding orders are required, so that the equivalent of Table 9.3 may be input to the computer. However, examination of Table 9.4 shows that the company has kept records for orders received from customers, but no record of outstanding sales orders. The managers in the company therefore have no way of knowing what deliveries could be made against receipts of orders, and what the delay time is in satisfying these orders. However, sales-delivery values for the year are available, so that given an opening (or closing) value for outstanding orders on the company, remaining values of outstanding orders for the individual months of the year may be deduced.

At this point the manager developing the model had to make a choice, because he found the model he wanted to construct did not match the data he had available. The choice to be made was either to collect more data so that he might construct the model he wanted, or to modify the model he wanted in line with the data

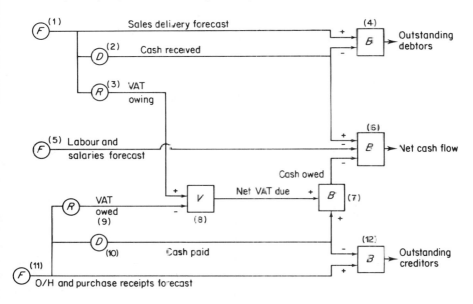

Figure 9.6 Amended flow diagram for cash-flow model

available. In this case the company did not keep a running balance of outstanding customer's orders, and moreover did not at that time have any means of finding the closing balance for the year. It was therefore forced to adopt the second choice above, namely modifying the flow diagram of Figure 9.5 to suit the data available. This meant that instead of feeding in forecasts of order receipts from customers, a forecast of deliveries had to be made (in other words the sales achieved). With other modifications made, the initial flow diagram of the company developed into the model shown in Figure 9.6 It can be seen that purchase receipts and overheads have been combined.

The amending of models to match available data is one of the crucial areas in cash planning, and in the modelling of any type of problem. Figure 9.6. shows a model that matches the data available in the company, but does not necessarily accurately represent important areas relevant to the cash-flow problem. For instance, it is possible that delays between receiving sales orders and shipping goods are important to the cash flow of the company. However, the computer model does not contain this aspect of cash flow, and therefore the managers will be unable to analyse it. To be effective managerially, therefore, cash modelling must quickly enable managers to think about the type of information they are recording, and its relevance to cash planning. In this case it may have been to the advantage of the company to record outstanding sales orders, and thereby be able to assess the effects of delays in satisfying these orders, by incorporating them in the computer model.

Table 9.5 Computer program for cash-flow model

Block number	Block title	Block type	Input 1	Input 2	Input 3
1	Sales delivery forecast	F	0	0	0
2	Debtors payment delay	D	1	0	0
3	VAT on receipts	R	1	0	0
4	Debtors balance	B	1	−2	0
5	Labour forecast	F	0	0	0
6	Net cash balance	B	2	−5	−7
7	Cash owed	B	8	10	0
8	Net VAT owing	V	3	−9	0
9	Purchase VAT rate	R	11	0	0
10	Payment delay	D	11	0	0
11	O/H forecast	F	0	0	0
12	Creditors balance	B	11	−10	0

Programming and Operation of the Model

The computer program related to the flow diagram of Figure 9.6 can now be written in the tabular form that has been previously described. The program itself is shown in Table 9.5.

The first stage in model evaluation is for the computer to calculate the values of delays in the cash-flow system corresponding to Blocks 2 and 10. As explained earlier, the delay represented by Table 9.3 (rows A and B of Table 9.4) is 2.62 months with a variation having a standard deviation of 0.234 months. This is the debtors' delay, which corresponds to Block 2. The amount of credit taken by the company (Block 10) is calculated from rows C and D of Table 9.4, which give a mean delay of 2.88 months with a variation having a standard deviation of 0.186 months.

To operate the model, these values for delays were used for the period to be investigated, as it was assumed that payment patterns would not be changing quickly. Forecasts, and decisions likely to be taken in the company, were then fed into the model a typical set being given in Table 9.6. This shows the sales deliveries the manager expects to be made, given the orders already on hand and the priorities quoted to customers. At the same time the manager has included the materials he expects to receive, given the orders placed on suppliers and the additional orders placed to satisfy orders on hand. Table 9.6 also contains the manager's estimate of the labour costs required to meet these planned delivery patterns.

Some of the outputs from the model for these inputs are shown in Figures 9.7–9.11. Figure 9.7 shows the expected cumulative receipts of cash predicted by the model and includes the cumulative deliveries planned by the company. In Figure 9.7, therefore, the vertical distance between the lines represents the debtors of the

Table 9.6 Forecasts used by cash-flow model

	January	February	March	April
Sales deliveries anticipated	28 600	33 000	38 500	38 500
Mats. received	9 900	11 000	11 000	12 100
Labour: Weekly	9 300	9 600	10 000	10 500
Monthly	2 600	2 600	2 400	2 900
O/H	7 000	7 000	7 000	7 000

company, the initial distance corresponding to the opening debtors at the end of December (i.e. £77 473). It can be seen in Figure 9.7 that the computer has predicted the region in which the actual cumulative cash received is likely to fall, and has therefore given an indication of the possible variations in cash received over the months January to April. Figure 9.8 meanwhile shows the cash inflow expected in any single month, and also contains control lines which indicated the maximum and minimum likely cash inflow in a single month It can be seen that the general level of uncertainty on cash inflows in individual months (shown in Figure 9.8) is proportionately greater than the uncertainty on the cumulative inflows over several months (shown in Figure 9.7). The use of cumulative values is explained in a number of statistical textbooks and will not be explained here.

The computer will print outputs from any of the blocks specified in the program shown in Table 9.5. In this instance the management were interested in the cash outflows to pay creditors as well as the overall net cash flow. Figures 9.9 and 9.10 show the cumulative cash outflows likely to be incurred to creditors, as well as the individual expected cash outflow for each month. These two charts correspond to Figures 9.7 and 9.8 for cash received, whilst Figure 9.11 shows the expected net cash flows in the company over the period of time covered by the forecast of Table 9.6.

9.5 The Value of a Model

Models used as part of management decision-making can help managers in a number of ways, and this is particularly true in the case of cash-flow models. The most obvious use for a model is to predict likely outcomes, given events that managers believe will take place. In the example just described, the computer model has been used primarily to do that, and Figures 9.7-9.11 represent predicted cash inflows and outflows, together with expected net cash movements.

However, models may effectively be used to help managers identify where specific constraints in their businesses lie, and where major sensitive areas are likely to be. These two aspects of modelling are most important where cash planning is concerned, as the identification of constraints and sensitivities are essential to obtain control over cash flows. Here the ability to use computers to operate the

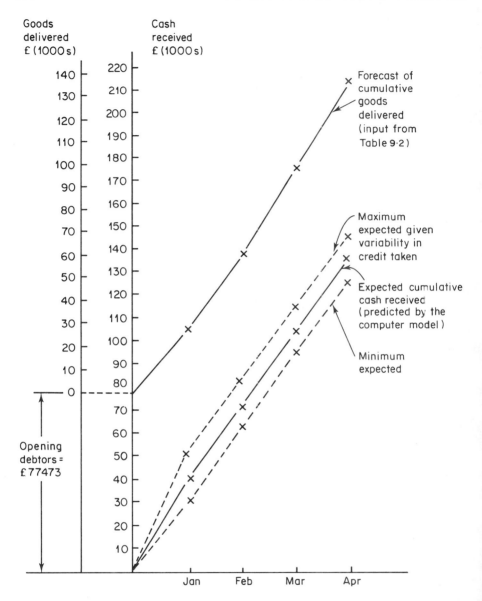

Figure 9.7 Cumulative forecast of cash received

models is an advantage, as these can quickly do the necessary calculations to determine where constraints operate and which areas are sensitive.

For instance, the graph line for cash received in Figure 9.7 is partly conditional on the manager's estimate of what deliveries of sales goods will be made from January to April. If in any month the company does not quite meet the delivery plan, the cash inflows at a later date will be affected. The manager may easily judge

£ (1000s)

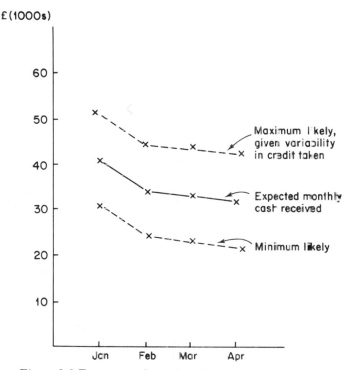

Figure 9.8 Forecast cash received for individual months

the effects of not achieving the delivery plan by re-running the computer model and feeding in alternative delivery patterns that could occur. From the results of this return, the manager may judge when and to what extent cash inflows will be affected by changes in delivery patterns. It can be seen that, for instance, if the company does not fulfil the January sales delivery target, this will make no difference to cash inflows until March, because cash receipts for January and February will come from goods already delivered in October, November and December. The computer model will indicate to what extent cash receipts beyond March are likely to be influenced by a failure to meet January's deliveries target, and the manager can judge how important maintaining deliveries is in the control of the total net cash flow.

The ability of computer models to allow managers to calculate quickly the effects of alternative decisions or events on future outcomes means they may prove useful in helping managers formulate policies. This is particularly valuable whenever seasonal variations in business occur. For instance, the cash model described has been used by the managers of a company manufacturing goods with a marked seasonal trade to determine an acceptable manufacturing policy, given that during sales troughs continued production to meet the next peak generally caused large overdrafts to occur, with high interest charges. The managers could have performed the calculations manually, but this would have been very time con-

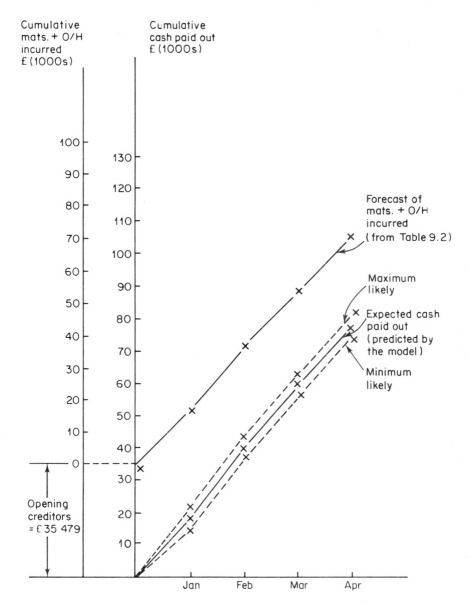

Figure 9.9 Forecast of cumulative cash paid out and cumulative materials + overheads incurred

suming and tedious, which in fact meant the calculations were never done. However, with a computer model, the effects of alternative manufacturing could be calculated quickly so the managers could judge which policies were likely to be the most successful.

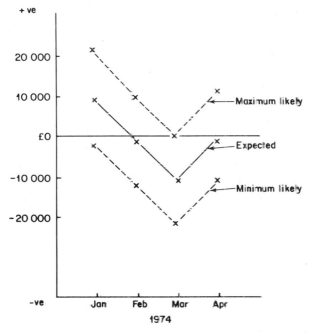

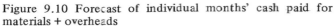

Figure 9.10 Forecast of individual months' cash paid for materials + overheads

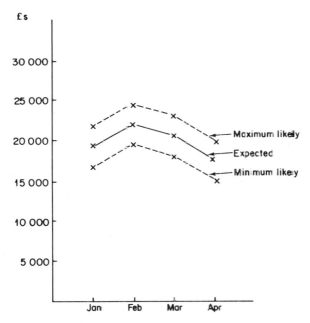

Figure 9.11 Net cash flow in the company

9.6 Conclusions

This chapter has covered the broad application of modelling techniques using computer or microcomputer hardware and software to problems of monitoring and control in the cash flow of the smaller firm and discusses one type of model. Given the current state of the art in these areas and further likely developments in computers, the small firm should be encouraged to assess seriously the introduction of some form of mechanized assistance within this area of planning. There are additional advantages too, in that although the hardware may immediately assist in cash-flow forecasting and control, it may also offer the potential of a wider range of future applications within the overall operation and control of the business. By undertaking the initial efforts of understanding and applying computer modelling to cash planning, management may be able to create a ready-made tool for further applications within their companies.

Financial Modelling in Corporate Management
Edited by J. W. Bryant
© 1982 John Wiley & Sons Ltd.

10

Linear Programming in Cash Management: A Technical Note

ROBERT HILL

10.1 Introduction

The management of cash is the one facet of management of business enterprises that is most often unplanned. The cash position often follows a feast or famine pattern and cash management commonly can be described as crisis management. That is, the amount of cash available is not given management attention unless it is insufficient to meet the cash needs for the enterprise. Cash is a scarce and expensive resource. Because the availability of cash in the operation of a business is critical, a workable cash management programme should be developed and used. Such a programme should be easily understood by management and provide a realistic approach to the problem of managing cash resources of the firm. The firm's cash management policy reflects a firm's need for liquidity, its ability to meet its maturing obligations, and its ability to realize the value of its assets in cash.

The risks of inadequate liquidity are apparent. A firm can be destroyed, never to recover, by not maintaining sufficient cash to avoid the crisis of cash shortages. The costs of too little cash varies from trade discounts foregone, bills unpaid, bad credit, services unable to be provided, to bankruptcy. Cash decreases the risk of insolvency and avoids costs connected with missed payments and frequent short-term borrowings of small amounts. However, cash is not a productive asset—cash balances earn no returns. The opportunity cost of an idle cash balance is the amount of revenue that could be earned by the cash if it were invested by the firm in productive assets. This opportunity cost should be understood to be revenues lost to the firm. The amount of cash to be held involving a trade-off between the risk of cash insolvency and the benefits of higher productivity, is the crux of cash management. The greater the amount of cash held by the firm, the less the risk of being confronted with an insolvent situation, but with larger cash balances profitability will be reduced because of the absence of earnings on the cash being held. Because of the risk inherent in a very low liquidity position, managers should exercise some degree of risk avoidance, but over-compensating with cash holdings that are too large results in a reduction in return on investment. The optimum cash level maximizes returns with acceptable risk.

Three motives for holding cash can be identified. First, cash may be held as a precaution to provide for sudden expenditures that arise due to unexpected contingencies. Secondly, the speculative motive holds cash ready for profit-making opportunities that may arise and is a function of the expectations of the managers of the firm. Finally, cash needs to be held to enable a firm to meet payments arising in the ordinary course of operations. This last motive is known as the transaction motive. For a more extensive discussion of the reasons for holding cash the reader is referenced to Baumol (1952), Johnson (1975) and Miller and Orr (1966).

10.2 Common Approaches to Solving the Cash-management Problem

In the financial literature, textbook cash-management problems begin with a forecast of revenues and expenditures from which a *pro forma* cash budget is developed. In that statement, the financial planner may observe seasonal cash deficits and surpluses. The planner's response to anticipated operating cash deficits in the classic cash-management case is to hold a safety stock of liquid assets accumulated from cash surpluses or to arrange for additional bank credit sufficient to cover cash needs. While this decision may result in meeting the cash requirements of the organization, it contains no cost minimization or optimization methodology.

Baumol (1952) and Miller and Orr (1966) describe inventory approaches to cash management that are directed toward minimizing the cost of cash management. Baumol's economic order quantity model treats cash expenditures as a steady flow through time. The identification of a fixed brokerage fee for selling marketable securities to obtain cash, and an opportunity cost of holding cash, allows the financial manager to determine the optimal average cash balance. Since cash expenditures are less constant than assumed in the Baumol model, the solutions it provides are less applicable to real cash-management problems. In contrast to Baumol's approach, the Miller–Orr model assumes uncertainty with regard to cash expenditures. Upper and lower control limits and a target cash balance, determined by the model, theoretically allow a financial manager to maintain a cash balance within acceptable upper and lower bounds.

While both of the approaches to cash management described above were important advances in the theory of finance, neither approach provides an operational plan for managing cash surpluses and deficits where expenditures do not occur evenly over time or, at the other extreme, are not a random series of events. With data in the form of a *pro forma* cash budget and with borrowing and lending rates stated, a linear programming model may be developed to provide an optimal solution to bank loans required, receivables to be pledged, and investments to be made during a specified time period. The optimal solution to a cash-management problem should minimize the net interest cost (interest paid less interest earned) of providing sufficient cash balances to meet anticipated expenditures.

The linear programming approach to cash management described below assumes that while the revenues and the expenditures for the firm are known in advance, these expenditures and revenues may vary from period to period. In a practical situation where the revenues and expenditures over the planning horizon are not known with certainty, the randomness inherent in any problem can be accommodated by holding a minimum cash balance.

10.3 An Example of the Linear-programming Approach to Cash Management

A simple working-capital problem has been developed to illustrate how linear programming can be used to minimize the costs of maintaining a desired level of cash over a six-month planning horizon. This problem is, in essence, a cash budget giving monthly cash receipts and monthly cash disbursements along with a minimum cash balance. The accumulation of these figures gives the cash that the financial manager must obtain from short-term sources. These data are given in Table 10.1.

In order to have a simple example, the short-term sources of cash are limited to the pledging of receivables, the postponement of payments to suppliers or a six-month loan taken out at the start of January. Other sources could be included but would not change the basic complexion of the problem. For this example the interest charges are assumed to be 3% per month for pledged receivables, the loss of a 5% cash discount if payments to suppliers are postponed for one month, and 1% per month, payable monthly in advance, for the six-month term loan. Any surplus cash can be invested in short-term government securities and earn ¼% per month, payable at the end of the month.

The obvious solution is to obtain a six-month term loan of a sufficient size to insure adequate funds will be available over the planning horizon; in any month invest any surplus cash in short-term government securities. This solution utilizes the least monthly cost source of cash and its simplicity is appealing. In order to meet the requirements of the problem the loan needs to be $22 905.34. The net interest cost after the interest earned on government securities is accounted is $1337.72. The calculations underlying these figures are given in Table 10.2.

This intuitive solution to the cash-budgeting problem may or may not be a good solution. While it utilizes the least expensive source of funds, it must do so for the entire six-month period. The other, more expensive, sources are available on a month-by-month basis and perhaps should be used to some extent. One way to determine the optimal mix of short-term financing is to formulate the problem as a linear program and then solve it. This has been done and the formulation is given in Table 10.3, while the optimal solution is given in Table 10.4.

Table 10.1 Six-month cash budget

	January	February	March	April	May	June
Accounts receivable at start of month	$110 000	$106 000	$100 000	$ 90 000	$96 000	$100 000
Monthly cash collections	95 000	100 000	108 000	95 000	93 000	98 000
Cash outflows for operations	105 000	110 000	105 000	100 000	90 000	85 000
Cash from operations	(10 000)	(10 000)	3 000	(5 000)	3 000	13 000
Initial cash	2 000	(8 000)	(18 000)	(15 000)	(20 000)	(17 000)
Cumulative cash from operations	(8 000)	(18 000)	(15 000)	(20 000)	(17 000)	(4 000)
Minimal cash balance	3 000	3 000	3 000	3 000	3 000	3 000
Cash surplus of deficit	(11 000)	(21 000)	(18 000)	(23 000)	(20 000)	(7 000)
Payments to suppliers (net after taking 5% discount)	5 000	15 000	10 000	10 000	20 000	15 000

Table 10.2 Intuitive solution

The rationale behind the calculations determining the amount of the term loan, if no other sources of short-term fund are used, is to determine the loan amount that insures in at least one month the surplus cash is zero while in all other months it is positive. To accomplish this an iterative expression is developed for the amount of surplus cash available in each month as a function of the amount of the term loan. This function is set equal to zero for a month and a required loan size for each month is calculated. In order to insure that the minimal cash balance is maintained the loan is set equal the largest of the required monthly loan sizes.

Calculation of Required Loan Size and Interest
Earned from Short-term Government Securities

$(K = \text{loan size})$

Month	Interest payment	Money loaned	Interest earned
January	0.01K	$0.99K - 11\,000$	$0.002\,475K - 27.5$
February	0.01K	$0.982\,475K - 21\,027.50$	$0.002\,456K - 52.57$
March	0.01K	$0.974\,931K - 18\,080.07$	$0.002\,437K - 45.20$
April	0.01K	$0.967\,369K - 23\,125.27$	0
May	0.01K	$0.957\,369K - 20\,125.27$	$0.002\,393K - 50.31$
June	0.01K	$0.949\,762K - 7175.58$	$0.002\,374K - 17.94$

Largest K is found when April's money loaned is set equal zero.
$$0\,967\,369K - 23\,125.27 = 0$$
or
$$K = \$23\,905.34$$

The optimal solution is to obtain a six-month term loan of $22 492.19 and to pledge $1367.03 in receivables in April. The net interest cost of this solution is $1313.73. This is a 1.8% decrease from the intuitive solution. While this is a very modest improvement, other problems with more variation in monthly cash requirements or with more competitive sources of short-term funds would show substantial improvement.

Both of these solutions have been very precisely stated. This precision may be misleading. It assumes that the cash budget given in Table 10.1 is completely accurate and that the sources of cash can be conveniently used in any amount. In practice, the cash budget is based on estimates of revenues and expenses and may be substantially different from actual cash flows that occur, and the sources of cash may be 'lumpy'. Consequently, the intuitive solution of obtaining a term loan of $23 905.34 might be adjusted to a term loan of $24 000 while the linear-programming solution might be adjusted to obtaining a term loan of $22 500 and pledging April receivables of $1400.

In conclusion, the linear programming model provides a methodology for minimizing the net interest cost of borrowing to meet cash needs. Provision is made for planned expenditures without overinvestment in liquidity.

Table 10.3 Formulation of problems as a linear program

Let X_1 = the dollar amount of the six month term loan
　　X_2 = the dollar amount of receivables pledged in January
　　X_3 = the dollar amount of receivables pledged in February
　　X_4 = the dollar amount of receivables pledged in March
　　X_5 = the dollar amount of receivables pledged in April
　　X_6 = the dollar amount of receivables pledged in May
　　X_7 = the dollar amonnt of receivables pledged in June
　　X_8 = the dollar amount of payments deferred for 30 days in January
　　X_9 = the dollar amount of payments deferred for 30 days in Febraary
　　X_{10} = the dollar amount of payments deferred for 30 days in March
　　X_{11} = the dollar amount of payments deferred for 30 days in April
　　X_{12} = the dollar amount of payments deferred for 30 days in May
　　X_{13} = the dollar amount of payments deferred for 30 days in June

Constraint Set

(1) $X_2 \leqslant$ 110 000	(4) $X_5 \leqslant$ 90 000	} Receivables 3%
(2) $X_3 \leqslant$ 106 000	(5) $X_6 \leqslant$ 96 000	
(3) $X_4 \leqslant$ 100 000	(6) $X_7 \leqslant$ 100 000	
(7) $X_8 \leqslant$ 5 000	(10) $X_{11} \leqslant$ 10 000	} Postponement of payment to suppliers (5%)
(8) $X_9 \leqslant$ 15 000	(11) $X_{12} \leqslant$ 20 000	
(9) $X_{10} \leqslant$ 10 000	(12) $X_{13} \leqslant$ 15 000	

January flow constraint:
　　(13)　$0.99X_1 + X_2 + X_8 \geqslant 11\ 000$
February flow constraint:
　　(14)　$0.982\ 475X_1 - 1.027\ 5X_2 + X_3 - 1.050\ 1X_8 + X_9 \geqslant 21\ 027.50$
March flow constraint:
　　(15)　$0.974\ 931\ 19X_1 - 0.000\ 068\ 75X_2 - 1.027\ 5X_3 + X_4$
　　　　　$- 0.000\ 125\ 25X_8 - 1.050\ 1X_9 + X_{10} \geqslant 18\ 080.06$
April flow constraint:
　　(16)　$0.967\ 368\ 52X_1 - 0.000\ 068\ 92X_2 - 0.000\ 068\ 75X_3 - 1.027\ 5X_4$
　　　　　$+ X_5 - 0.000\ 125\ 56X_8 - 0.000\ 125\ 25X_9 - 1.050\ 1X_{10}$
　　　　　$+ X_{11} \geqslant 23\ 125.269$
May flow constraint
　　(17)　$0.959\ 786\ 94X_1 - 0.000\ 069\ 09X_2 - 0.000\ 068\ 92X_3$
　　　　　$- 0.000\ 068\ 75X_4 - 1.027\ 5X_5 + X_6 - 0.000\ 125\ 88X_8$
　　　　　$- 0.000\ 125\ 56X_9 - 0.000\ 125\ 25X_{10} - 1.050\ 1X_{11} + X_{12} \geqslant$
　　　　　$\geqslant 20\ 183.082$
June flow constraint:
　　(18)　$0.952\ 186\ 4X_1 - 0.000\ 069\ 27X_2 - 0.000\ 069\ 09X_3$
　　　　　$- 0.000\ 068\ 92X_4 - 0.000\ 068\ 75X_5 - 1.027\ 5X_6 + X_7$
　　　　　$- 0.000\ 126\ 19X_8 - 0.000\ 125\ 88X_9 - 0.000\ 125\ 56X_{10}$
　　　　　$- 0.000\ 125\ 25X_{11} - 1.050\ 1X_{12} + X_{13} \geqslant 7\ 233.5398$

Objective function: minimize
　　　　$251.623\ 65 + 0.045\ 393\ 7X_1 + 0.030\ 069\ 44X_2 + 0.030\ 069\ 27X_3$
　　　　$+ 0.030\ 069\ 09X_4 + 0.030\ 068\ 92X_5 + 0.030\ 068\ 75X_6$
　　　　$+ 0.027\ 5X_7 + 0.052\ 726\ 51X_8 + 0.052\ 726\ 19X_9 + 0.052\ 758\ 8X_{10}$
　　　　$+ 0.052\ 725\ 56X_{11} + 0.052\ 725\ 25X_{12} + 0.0501X_{13}$

Table 10.4 Optimal solution to the linear program

The term loan should be equal $22 492.19. The only other source of funds should be the pledging of $1 367.03 of receivables in April. The amounts put into short-term government securities are:	
January	$11 267.27
February	1 070.51
March	3 848.27
April	0
May	0
June	14 183.12

10.4 Shortcomings of These Cash-management Tools

All cash-management methods have advantages and disadvantages. For example, the manager is always faced with deciding whether a complex, difficult to under-stand method that works very well is better than a simple, easy to understand method that works reasonably well. The trade-off between complexity and simplicity, between realism and ease of use in perhaps the most critical decision a manager faces when he is choosing a managerial decision-making method.

In particular, the linear programming method of determining cash-management tactics is optimal if the required assumptions are met. In the example given a number of assumptions are made. Some of the assumptions are particular to this application of linear programming, while some are required due to the linear programming methodology itself.

A critical assumption is that of certainty in cash flows during the planning period. This assumption is due to the linear programming methodology. Modifying the linear programming cash-planning method to account for uncertainty in the cash flows cannot be satisfactorily accomplished easily. The example illustrates one method for allowing for uncertainty maintaining a minimum cash balance. This 'safety stock' is intended to allow for small variations in cash flow to occur without major disruptions to the financial system. Other *ad hoc* methods such as applying sensitivity analysis and parametric programming to the problem are often utilized (Wagner, 1975) in determining the effects of changes in the problem being analysed.

Additionally, the linear programming approach does not easily account for such transactions costs as initiation fees for loans. In this example they were ignored. Incorporating these types of costs in linear programs is very difficult and in practice is rarely accomplished. The linear program also assumes all of the variables are continuous. For example, the optimal solution requires a term loan of $22 492.19. In practice this amount may be inconvenient or impossible. As suggested above, a term loan of $22 500 might be more appropriate and could be selected without incurring a substantial increase in cost. When such a rounding approach is followed, it is important to check that all of the constraints are still satisfied.

References

Baumol, W. J. (1952). 'The Transactions Demand for Cash: An Inventory Theoretic Approach', *Quarterly Journal of Economics,* **66**, November 1952, 545–556.

Johnson, R. (1975). 'Managing Your Working Capital: Cash Management', *Hospital Financial Management,* **29**, January 1975, 20–22.

Miller, M. H., and Orr, D. (1966). 'A Model of the Demand for Money by Firms', *Quarterly Journal of Economics,* **80**, August 1966, 413–435.

Wagner, H. M. (1975). *Principles of Management Science,* Prentice-Hall, Englewood Cliffs, New Jersey.

Financial Modelling in Corporate Management
Edited by J. W. Bryant
© 1982 John Wiley & Sons Ltd.

11

Budget Modelling in the Construction Materials Industry

IAN CRAWFORD

11.1 Introduction

Before describing the make-up of the budgeting model used within TAC, some details of the company and its management accounting systems will be given.

The Company

TAC Construction Materials Ltd is one of the largest companies in the Turner & Newall Group and one of the principal manufacturers of asbestos cement products in the U.K. The main products include asbestos cement roofing and cladding material, pipes and flat sheets. The company also produces certain electrical and mechanical products and has recently diversified into the manufacture of building blocks. TAC has been in existence since about 1930, though the beginnings can be traced back to about 1870, and it now operates six factories throughout England. In 1976 the company was split into five divisions:

Building & Insulation (B & I) Division
Pipes Division
Engineering Materials (EM) Division   } Four trading divisions
Block Division
Service Division (includes Finance and Personnel Departments)

Management Accounting System

A standard costing system has been in operation for a number of years. However, the budgetary control system commenced in 1969 and has evolved into a comprehensive system over the period since then. The process of preparing the annual budget follows a standard approach. This involves collecting data from a number of sources covering:

sales volumes (home and export);
selling prices;
selling-price increases;
standard costs or standard gross margins;
cost of all departmental budgets (about 60 in total).

We also include certain variances in the budget since the standard costs are based on realistic standards at an authorized capacity level. However, because of a number of factors likely to affect production we include an amount to cover the fact that:

(1) the authorized hours will not be worked, and/or
(2) the standards will not be achieved e.g. higher breakages and rejects, lower output rates, etc.

11.2 Model Development

Until 1976 the company produced quarterly accounts and the budget was manually prepared. However, when Turner & Newall introduced monthly accounts throughout the Group it was decided to look at the possibility of computerizing the budget routine with hopefully the following advantages:

(1) reducing the manual calculations, especially with monthly accounts;
(2) reducing compting;
(3) reducing typing load;
(4) providing facilities for sensitivity runs.

In computerizing we had to decide at what level to input data. Should we start:

(1) at product level (about 10 000), at which level standard costs are produced,
(2) at product family level (about 200), where a family is a group containing a number of different sizes, thicknesses etc. of products, or
(3) at product group level (about 20), which contain a group of product families.

The product family level was chosen since all reports issued are at this level and it also kept the input data and model to a more manageable size.

The first model was based on the PROSPER package and run on our own in-house ICL computer. The system was mainly developed by the Management Systems Department and because of changes in personnel and organizational structure proved difficult to run. Management systems personnel had to carry out any changes and run the model.

In 1977 a Group computer was introduced and TAC removed their own ICL computer in the July before the budget had been prepared. It was therefore necessary to change to a different modelling system and the FCS package marketed by EPS Consultants was chosen because:

(1) it is specially written for budgeting and financial applications;
(2) it is easy to understand and write the logic;
(3) it can be operated by non-computer personnel;
(4) modifications can be carried out by accountants;
(5) data can be input by accountants;
(6) a hierarchy section had just been introduced which made it easier to define the relationship between various input levels;
(7) it was expected to be possible later to use FCS on the Group computer, although initial implementation was through Comshare bureau services.

In fact point (7) above was well founded and when in 1979 the Group Computer Centre offered a timesharing service which included FCS, the model was transferred to the Group computer.

11.3 The Budget Model

The financial model that is now to be explained is the current FCS budgeting model. After describing the model, its use for control purposes, its benefits and its future developments will be discussed.

A basic premise of the model was that it should be simple enough to be operated by non-computer personnel both in terms of changing the logic and inputting data. However, certain advantages arose through using the Computer Department:

(1) simplification of certain parts of the model;
(2) introduction of easy-to-understand instructions for display when starting to run the model through a question-and-answer section.

The model will be considered in four parts: structure, input, operation and output.

Model Structure

In order to describe the model structure it is necessary briefly to outline the main features of the FCS modelling system. The key entities handled are called files and there are three types. All basic calculations performed by a model are defined in *logic files* in which the relationships between financial variables are stated. These contain the logic for all computations in the form of equations relating variables to one another. In many applications of financial modelling essentially similar calculations may have to be carried out for a range of activities and the results consolidated for reporting purposes: for example, a single model may apply to the costing of a number of products. This is where the second kind of file, the *hierarchy file,* is used. This describes the structure of the consolidation to be carried out, and permits repetitive model logic to be incorporated without having to be expressed in full every time it is required. The third and last file type is the *data file* which, as might be expected, simply contains the input values for calculation variables.

The TAC model was required to produce the following eight reports:

(1) quarterly report showing turnover and gross profits by product family for each division, called the Gross Family Trading Account (GFTA);
(2) monthly report showing sales volume, turnover and gross profits by product family for each division;
(3) summary of quarterly turnover and gross profits by division;
(4) monthly divisional profit statements;
(5) quarterly divisional profit statements;
(6) monthly company profit statement;
(7) quarterly company profit statement;
(8) summary trading account detailing on a quarterly basis the carriage, distribution, selling, research and administration budgets by department (these are the Non-manufacturing Expenses (NME)), and giving the company net trading profit.

The system that was developed consists of a number of interlinked files through which calculation and output are ordered in particular manner. This structure makes it possible to ask 'what if' questions at various levels of consolidation and, through the use of files containing the results of intermediate computations, avoids the need for a complete re-evaluation of the entire system each time. Taking the above sequence of reports as a guide, the modelling system first calculates the GFTA for each division in turn (Reports (1) and (2) above), and then these results are con- solidated into the company-wide picture given by Report (3). Next, divisional NME are calculated for each division by combining specific expenses for the division with a proportion of central company expenses allocated on a turnover less carriage basis. Reports (4) and (5) can then be generated and consolidation then produces Reports (6) and (7). Finally Report (8) is output, bringing together the NME and GFTA results into a summary trading account.

The file basis that is used contains five principal files for each division: both logic and data files for GFTA and NME calculation and a hierarchy file defining the divisional structure. Additional logic and data files relate to central company expenses. The files are identified by a two-digit code. Thus the first digit denotes the division (B & I = 1, Pipes = 2, E & M = 3, Blocks = 4) and the second digit the model (GFTA = 1, NME/Profit Statements = 2). For example, DATA 21 is the data file for the Pipes Division GFTA calculation, while RESULTS 42 holds the results of the NME calculations for Block Division. These codes are used in the diagrams describing the modelling system below.

Though the logic for the GFTA is basically the same for all four divisions, it was decided to have a separate logic file for each division as each division could then be operated independently and there was less chance of incorrectly changing data for the wrong division. The only section of the model requiring data from all four divisions relates to the allocated costs of Central Services. In summary, the principal files are:

4 hierarchy files defining the divisional structures
4 logic/data files/for GFTA
5 logic/data files/for NME

in addition to files for producing the various reports.

Before setting up the logic files the hierarchy structure had to be defined for each division. The hierarchy structure is defined by section numbers, these numbers being consolidated at various stages eventually to produce the overall divisional/company consolidation. Figure 11.1 shows how the hierarchy is defined for Electrical Products and each division has its own independent hierarchy file. It can be seen by looking at one set of product families how the hierarchy builds up into a total company picture, the product families' section numbers being used for both home and export information. Therefore in looking at each division we have:

B & I	49 product families	6 product groups
Pipes	24 product families	6 product groups
EM	26 product families	4 product groups
Block	5 product families	3 product groups

and by applying the hierarchical structure the consolidations can be calculated. Once the hierarchies had been defined, the next stage was the build-up of the logic for the GFTA.

The principal calculations of the GFTA can be broken down into product family calculations and product group calculations The product family calculations are carried out for each section number and are as follows:

(1) Annual sales volume (tonnes) $\times$ Seasonality factors (breaks volume down into months.

(2) Once the monthly tonnage is available, the monthly turnover and gross margin can be calculated and hence quarterly and annual totals. The calculations are based on the following relationships:

turnover = volume $\times$ selling price
gross margin = *either* volume $\times$ (selling price $-$ standard cost)
        or turnover $\times$ gross margin %

requiring as data input the selling price, monthly selling price increases, and either the standard cost or gross margin percentage.

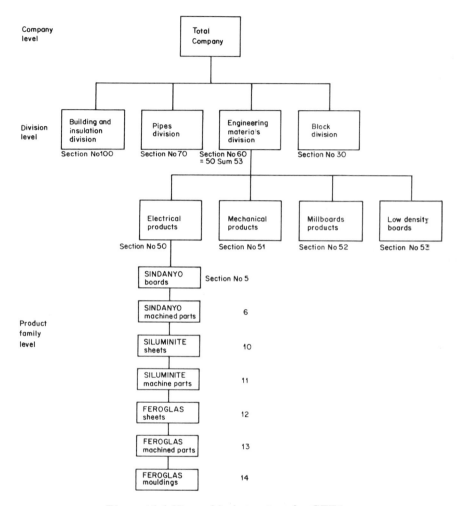

Figure 11.1 Hierarchical structure for GFTA

The model calculates the turnover and gross margins for each section number (home and export). After aggregation at product group level, certain variances are input and the model apportions these between home and export sales. The hierarchical commands are then applied and Reports (1)–(3) produced. Though part of the non-manufacturing costs, carriage rates (which may be related to either volume or turnover) and cash discounts as a percentage of turnover are calculated in this part of the model. These calculations are carried out at a product group level.

The NME model is not built up in the same hierarchical fashion as the GFTA and does not use section numbers. The logic is basically similar for each division except that each obviously includes different departments. There are five logic

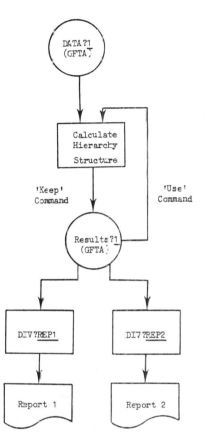

Figure 11.2 Gross family trading
account for each division (Reports
1 and 2)

files comprising four divisional files and one total company file, the latter handling
expenses to be allocated. These produce not only details of non-manufacturing
costs but also give the profit statements.

The first stage of evaluation involves the transfer of the results of the GFTA
model and data from the company NME file to divisional files. This transfers the
following information previously produced by the GFTA Logic

(1) carriage and cash discounts;
(2) turnover, both divisional and company (to enable the allocation of central
    costs to be carried out);
(3) turnover and gross profit figures (to enable the profit statement to be produced),

as well as details of the central costs to be allocated from the NME file. Additionally

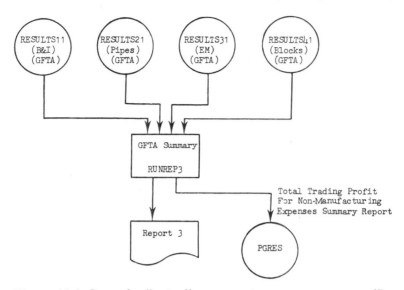

Figure 11.3 Gross family trading account company summary (Report 3)

for each division data are input covering departmental selling, research and distribution budgets. The data can be input either monthly or quarterly (in which case they are broken down into months on 5/4/4 basis). Once the proportion of central costs to be allocated to each division has been calculated these can be added to specific divisional NMEs.

The logic for calculating the non-manufacturing costs for each division is simple and consists of adding a number of row numbers in the relevant file. Thus for example, for B & I Division distribution costs, the four defined costs, Stockroom (row 20), Forwarding (row 21), Scottish Depot (row 22), Erith depot (row 23), are added to give the distribution costs (= row 20 + 21 + 22 + 23).

The results from the GFTA file and NME file are then brought together and the profit statement of Reports (4) and (5) produced. Again the logic for the profit statement is a simple addition or subtraction of rows.

The total company profit statement is finally produced by bringing together the results from the four divisional NME files and adding the results of each line. This file is also used to produce the detailed report of non-manufacturing expenses.

Model Input

Data forms were designed for the input to and creation of GFTA and NME files. Since the input forms were to be completed and input by non-computer personnel it was decided to keep them simple. The GFTA input uses two forms, one for product family data (Figure 11.7) and one for product group data (Figure 11.8).

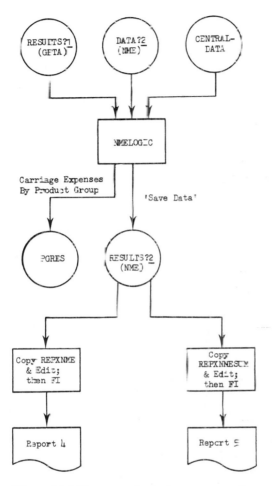

Figure 11.4 Non-manufacturing expenses for each division (Reports 5 and 6)

The NME data consist of departmental budgets for division and central services which are entered via two further forms (Figures 11.9 and 11.10). Data can be either punched onto tape by punch operators or input directly by VDU.

Before any data can be input the information has to be collected from a number of sources throughout the company. Sales information is built up from the recommendations of the sales managers who use the knowledge of their representatives and economic forecasts supplied by Turner & Newall. Computerized forecasting techniques are not therefore used, the budgets being based on individuals' assessments. A number of different departments are involved in establishing factory costs covering factory, research, quality control, buying and accounts departments.

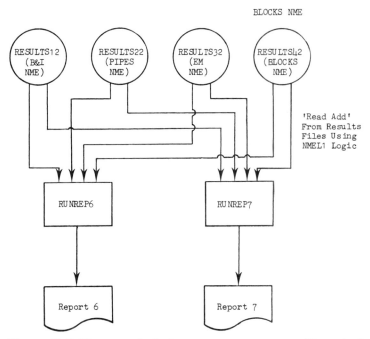

Figure 11.5 Non-manufacturing company summary (Reports 6 and 7)

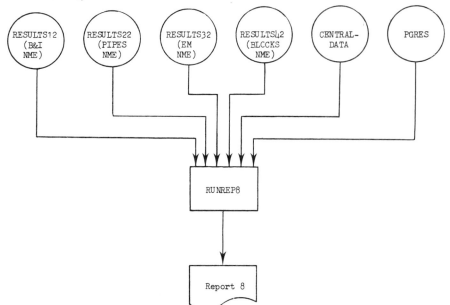

Figure 11.6 Summary trading budget

Period 1-13   1 = Year
2-13 = Months

1	2	3	4	5	6	7
8	9	10	11	12	13	

*SE

Seasonability factor	10, U,							
Selling-price increase	11, U,							
Old selling price	12, U,	*						
Tonnes	13, U,							
Old turnover	´4, U,							
Old gross margin (%)	15, U,	*						
Old standard cost	l6, U,	*						
Cost price factor	17, U,	*						

FAMILY DATA—EXPORT

Seasonability factor	20, U,
Selling price increase	21, U,
Old selling price	22, U,
Tonnes	23, U,
Old turnover	24, U,
Old gross margin (%)	25, U,
Old standard cost	26, U,
Cost-price factor	27, U,

END

Figure 11.7 Form for product family data

1	2	3	4	5	6	7
8	9	10	11	12	13	

*SE

Capacity variance	30, U,	
Price variance	31, U,	
Manufacturing variance	32, U,	
Stock revaluation	33, U,	
Carriage—home	34, U,	
(% or rate)		
Carriage—export	35, U,	
(% or rate)		
Cash discount (%)	36, U,	

END

N.B. Carriage Rates—B&I ⎫
            Pipes ⎬ £/tonne (m²)
            Blocks ⎭
            EM   % of turnover

Figure 11.8 Form for product group data

Again the build-up is from personal forecasts based on relevant information. Departmental budgets are built up by individual managers. For both factory and departmental budgets, we try to get the managers to build up the budgets from an estimate of the resources that they require rather than to use previous year figures with a percentage added. Once data have been received and agreed by the managers they are approved by the appropriate director.

Model Operation

As mentioned previously an advantage of using computer personnel is that they are able to simplify certain aspects of the model. It is in the area of running the model that their expertise was most useful.

To operate the model a set of questions and answers has been set up through which the user interacts with the financial planning system. A typical sequence might be as follows, where the user response is underlined:

Which Division B & I (1) Pipes (2) EM (3) Blocks (4)?   <u>1</u>
Do you want to work with GFTA (1) or NME (2)?   <u>1</u>
Do you want to calculate (1) or print results (2)?   <u>1</u>
Do you want:
     the quarterly GFTA report for this division   (1)

1	2	3	4	5	6	7
8	9	10	11	12	13	

Monthly or Quarterly
Stockroom, packing & despatch 20, U,
Forwarding 21, U,

Quarterly only
Marketing and admin. 30, U,
Regional sales—N 31, U,
Regional sales—S 32, U,
Export sales 33, U,
Export commissions 34, U,

Commercial exps. 36, U,
Publicity 38, U,
Gen. selling pensions 39, U,

Development 46, U,

Interest 54, U,

Monthly
Non-trading items, divisional 55, U,
Extraordinary items 56, U,

END

Figure 11.9 Form for non-manufacturing expenses

the monthly GFTA report for this division	(2)	
the summary of All Divisions GFTA	(3)	
to go on to NME	(N)	
to stop	(S)	
or to do another division?	(A)	1

It can be seen from the above instructions that individual sections of the model can be run independently. Following any changes to individual section number data, subsequent calculations can be limited to that section number if desired. Results are saved, in case any sensitivity runs are required, and the reports printed.

Model Output

The reports that are produced are shown in Figures 11.11 to 11.14. These reports have been so constructed that they are in the same format as the financial accounts issued on a monthly and quarterly basis.

	1	2	3	4
Buying	1, U,			
Fin. accounts	2, U,			
Man. accounts	3, U,			
Man. services	4, U,			
Comp. ops.	5, U,			
H.O. services	6, U,			
General services	7, U,			
Pensions funding	8, U,			
Mfg. cost of sales	11, U,			
Personnel	12, U,			
Central services	13, U,			
Traffic	16, U,			

1	2	3	4	5	6	7
8	9	10	11	12	13	

| Non-trading items | 19, U, | | | | | | |

END

Figure 11.10 Form for centrally allocated expenses

Figure 11.11 Gross family trading account (Report 1)

TAC CONSTRUCTION MATERIALS LIMITED

GROSS FAMILY TRADING ACCOUNT (HOME)

		FIRST QUARTER			SECOND QUARTER		
	TURN £	GROSS £	PROF %		TURN £	GROSS £	PROF %
MILLBOARD - MB600	98141	9716	9.9		95025	9407	9.9
MILLBOARD - MB626	8755	2084	23.8		8477	2018	23.8
MILLBOARD - MB121	12963	3798	29.3		12551	3678	29.3
MILLBOARD - MB800	97929	36723	37.5		94820	35558	37.5
MILLBOARD - BFB9	69091	9673	14.0		66898	9366	14.0
MILLBOARD - OTHER							
FELTS PFR	388209	62502	16.1		445603	89545	20.1
GROSS MARGIN	675088	124496	18.4		723375	149570	20.7
CAP VAR H							
PRI VAR H		14000	2.1		4000	.6	
MAN VAR H		-12654	-1.9		-12252	-1.7	
STK REV H		16000	2.4		14000	1.9	
MILLBOARD & FELTS	675088	141842	21.0	72337	155318	21.5	

11.4 Use of Model in Planning Process

Planning in TAC takes place in two distinct stages. In April/May a long-term planning document is prepared. This is a strategic rather than a control document. Once the long-term plans have been approved, then work can commence on the short-term plan. Then during August/November short-term planning is carried out. This includes the preparation of the trading budget which forms the basic control document for the financial year beginning in January.

Once the budget has been agreed by the company directors it is summarized and submitted to Turner & Newall, where it is consolidated with the budgets of all other Group companies. If the consolidated plan does not meet Group requirements, unit companies will be told to review their budgets. The acceptability of the budgets is discussed at a planning meeting between the directors of each company and Turner & Newall Group personnel. When the budget has been accepted by Turner & Newall it not only becomes the basic control document for the year but indicates what decisions may have to be taken during the year, e.g.

(1) capacity planning for machines with a link to stock control policy;
(2) anticipated price increases and dates;
(3) wage and salary awards that can be afforded;
(4) when looking at cash-flow aspects, what action needs to be taken on debtors or creditors to achieve cash requirements;
(5) cost savings required if required profit is not being achieved.

17:20:1

	THIRD QUARTER			FOURTH QUARTER			ANNUAL TOTAL	
TURN	GROSS	PROF	TURN	GROSS	PROF	TURN	GROSS	PROF
£	£	%	£	£	%	£	£	%
99698	9870	9.9	96583	9562	9.9	389447	38555	9.9
8894	2117	23.8	8616	2051	23.8	34741	8268	23.8
13169	3858	29.3	12757	3738	29.3	51439	15072	29.3
99484	37306	37.5	96375	36141	37.5	388608	145728	37.5
70188	9826	14.0	67995	9519	14.0	274171	38384	14.0
369949	74342	20.1	346406	69611	20.1	1550166	295997	19.1
661382	137320	20.8	628731	130621	20.8	2688571	542006	20.2
							18000	.7
	-9641	-1.5		-12653	-2.0		-47000	-1.7
	15000	2.3					45000	1.7
661382	142679	21.6	628731	118168	18.8	2688571	558006	20.8

```
                    TAC CONSTRUCTION MATERIALS LIMITED
                    --- ------------- --------- -------
                          GFTA - HOME TRADE
                          ---- - ---- -----
                          JAN     FEB     MAR    APRIL     MAY

        MILLBOARD - MB600
        --------- - -----
        TONNES      (H)        96      83      83      96      75
        NEW PRICE(H)       373.75  373.75  373.75  373.75  373.75
        NEW TURN    (H)     35829   31156   31156   35329   28040
        NEW GM      (H)      3547    3084    3084    3547    2776
        NEW GM%     (H)        10      10      10      10      10

        MILLBOARD - MB626
        --------- - -----
        TONNES      (H)         3       2       2       3       2
        NEW PRICE(H)      1158.05 1158.05 1158.05 1158.05 1158.05
        NEW TURN    (H)      3196    2779    2779    3196    2501
        NEW GM      (H)       761     661     661     761     595
        NEW GM%     (H)        24      24      24      24      24

        MILLBOARD - MB121
        --------- - -----
        TONNES      (H)         8       7       7       8       6
        NEW PRICE(H)       571.55  571.55  571.55  571.55  571.55
        NEW TURN    (H)      4732    4115    4115    4732    3704
        NEW GM      (H)      1387    1206    1206    1387    1085
        NEW GM%     (H)        29      29      29      29      29

        MILLBOARD - MB800
        --------- - -----
        TONNES      (H)        49      42      42      49      38
        NEW PRICE(H)       736.00  736.00  736.00  736.00  736.00
        NEW TURN    (H)     35752   31089   31089   35752   27980
        NEW GM      (H)     13407   11658   11658   13407   10492
        NEW GM%     (H)        37      37      37      37      37

        MILLBOARD - BFB9
        --------- - ----
        TONNES      (H)        19      16      16      19      15
        NEW PRICE(H)      1343.98 1343.98 1343.98 1343.98 1343.98
        NEW TURN    (H)     25224   21934   21934   25224   19740
        NEW GM      (H)      3531    3071    3071    3531    2764
        NEW GM%     (H)        14      14      14      14      14

        MILLBOARD - OTHER
        --------- - -----
        TONNES      (H)         -       -       -       -       -
        NEW PRICE(H)            -       -       -       -       -
        NEW TURN    (H)         -       -       -       -       -
        NEW GM      (H)         -       -       -       -       -
        NEW GM%     (H)         -       -       -       -       -

        FELTS PFR
        ----- ---
        TONNES      (H)       413     251     247     391     305
        NEW PRICE(H)       425.88  425.88  425.88  447.17  447.17
        NEW TURN    (H)    176092  107030  105087  174694  136553
        NEW GM      (H)     28351   17232   16919   35105   27441
        NEW GM%     (H)        16      16      16      20      20
        ---------------------------------------------------------
        MILLBOARD & FELTS
        --------- - -----
        TONNES      (H)       588     403     398     565     442
        NEW PRICE(H)            -       -       -       -       -
        NEW TURN    (H)    280825  198103  196160  279428  218519
        NEW GM      (H)     50983   36912   36600   57738   45153
        NEW GM%     (H)        18      19      19      21      21
```

Figure 11.12 Gross family

JUN	JULY	AUG	SEPT	OCT	NOV	DEC	TOTAL
83	104	79	83	104	83	71	1042
373.75	373.75	373.75	373.75	373.75	373.75	373.75	373.75
31156	38945	29598	31156	38945	31156	26482	389447
3084	3856	2930	3084	3856	3084	2622	38555
10	10	10	10	10	10	10	10
2	3	2	2	3	2	2	30
1158.05	1158.05	1158.05	1158.05	1158.05	1158.05	1158.05	1158.05
2779	3474	2640	2779	3474	2779	2362	34741
661	827	628	661	827	661	562	8268
24	24	24	24	24	24	24	24
7	9	7	7	9	7	6	90
571.55	571.55	571.55	571.55	571.55	571.55	571.55	571.55
4115	5144	3909	4115	5144	4115	3498	51439
1206	1507	1145	1206	1507	1206	1025	15072
29	29	29	29	29	29	23	29
42	53	40	42	53	42	36	528
736.00	736.00	736.00	736.00	736.00	736.00	736.00	736.00
31089	38861	29534	31089	38861	31089	26425	388608
11658	14573	11075	11658	14573	11658	9909	145728
37	37	37	37	37	37	37	37
16	20	16	16	20	16	14	204
1343.98	1343.98	1343.98	1343.98	1343.98	1343.98	1343.98	1343.98
21934	27417	20837	21934	27417	21934	18644	274171
3071	3838	2917	3071	3838	3071	2610	38384
14	14	14	14	14	14	14	14
-	-	-	-	-	-	-	-
-	-	-	-	-	-	-	-
-	-	-	-	-	-	-	-
-	-	-	-	-	-	-	-
-	-	-	-	-	-	-	-
300	367	225	235	299	324	152	3510
447.17	447.17	447.17	447.17	447.17	447.17	447.17	425.88
134356	164178	100767	105005	133571	144715	68120	1550166
26999	32992	20249	21101	26841	29081	15689	295997
20	20	20	20	20	20	20	19
452	557	359	386	488	475	281	5404
-	-	-	-	-	-	-	-
225428	278019	187286	196077	247412	235788	145531	2688571
46680	57593	38946	40781	51442	48761	30417	542006
21	21	21	21	21	21	21	20

trading account (Report 2)

```
         TAC CONSTRUCTION MATERIALS LIMITED
         --- -------------- ---------- -------
            SUMMARY TRADING ACCOUNT
            -------- -------- -------
               QUARTERLY SUMMARY
               ----------- -------
                                FIRST QUARTER      SECOND QUARTER
                                ----- -------       ------ -------

  TURNOVER  H                      995743             1323187
  TURNOVER  EXP                       -                   -
  -------- ---
  TURNOVER  TOTAL                  995743             1323187

  GROSS  MARGIN  H                 271565              438449
  GROSS  MARGIN  EXP                  -                   -
  ----- ------ ---
  GROSS  MARGIN  TOTA              271565              438449

  CAP  VAR  TOTAL                     -                   -
  PRI  VAR  TOTAL                   3000                6000
  OTH  VAR  TOTAL                  -5300               -17700
  STOCK  REV  TOTAL                35200               35200
  ----- --- -----                 -----               -----
  GPAV  T                         256765              461949

  CARRIAGE                       -166465             -214291
  DISTRIBN                        -27319              -26489
  SELLING                         -46388              -39359
  SELLING  -  COMM/GE             -41684              -52030
  SELLING  -  PUBLICI             -11000              -11000
  DIV  SERV  -  DEV                -5825               -5825
  DIV  SERV  -  TECH                  -                   -
  ADMIN  CENTRAL                  -65745              -65093
  PENSION  FUNDING                -14566              -14566
  ------- -------                 ------              ------
  TOTAL  NON-MANUF  C            -378932             -428653
  ----- --------- -
  NET  MARGIN                    -122227               33296

  PROFIT/LOSS  ITEMS              -12136               -4282
  INTEREST  CHARGES               -19000              -19000
  -------- -------
  NET  PROFIT/LOSS               -153362               10014
  EXTRAORDINARY  ITE                  -                   -
  NET  PROFIT  BEFORE            -153362               10014
  --- ------- ------             -------               -----
```

Figure 11.13 Divisional trading account (Report 5)

A complete set of budget reports is issued to the directors whilst divisional managers receive a set of their division's reports. Therefore each manager is in a position to see what he is expected to achieve in relation to the budget.

As already mentioned, the trading budget is the basic control document, and all accounts have a comparison of actual and budget. During the year monthly reports are produced explaining differences between actual and budget. Depending on the reasons for the differences and the trends in variances, decisions are taken as to what further action, if any, is necessary if the plan is to be achieved. However, no firm rules can be laid down as to the action to be taken, since it will necessarily depend on the circumstances.

23:15:

THIRD QUARTER	FOURTH QUARTER	ANNUAL TOTAL
----- -------	----- -------	------ -----
1825493	1719876	5864294
-	-	-
1825493	1719876	5864295
677755	710664	2098431
-	-	-
677755	710664	2098432
-	-	-
2000	-2000	9000
-11200	-13100	-95000
35600	-	106000
-----		------
704155	695564	2118431
-316878	-283830	-981464
-27741	-26905	-108455
-39361	-39358	-164466
-64587	-61947	-220247
-11000	-11000	-44000
-5825	-5825	-23300
-	-	-
-65585	-65223	-251646
-14566	-14566	-58265
------	------	------
-545543	-508654	-1861840
-------	-------	--------
158612	186910	256591
-11217	-11177	-38812
-21000	-27000	-86000
------	------	------
126394	148733	131779
-	-	-
126394	148733	131779
------	------	------

During the planning cycle, once the initial data have been input they can quickly and easily be amended for any number of sensitivity runs. What sensitivity runs are usually undertaken? The key figures affecting the forecast are sales volume, selling prices and costs, and these are the items that are most frequently amended in sensitivity runs. Changes may be made because:

(1) figures are considered too optimistic or pessimistic by the directors;
(2) reassessments are made of the relationship between volume and selling prices.

Even before the forecasts are submitted to the directors, the divisions would probably carry out two or three sensitivity runs on sales volume and price.

TAC CONSTRUCTION MATERIALS LIMITED

SUMMARY TRADING ACCOUNT

	FIRST QUARTER	SECOND QUARTER
SELLING EXPENSES		
B&I DIVISION		
MARKETING	40640	40640
HOME SALES	171577	170238
EXPORT SALES	18540	18540
CONTRACTS & MATLS	41851	41849
SALES SERVICES	98116	98115
COMMERCIAL EXP	105000	105000
B & I DIVN	47072	474382
PIPES DIVISION		
MARKET/ADMIN	37132	35682
REG SALES - N	25001	25001
REG SALES - S	21291	21291
EXPORT SALES	10563	10613
EXPORT COMMISS	14063	14063
COMMERCIAL EXP	16113	16113
PIPES DIVN	124163	122763
EM DIVISION		
MARKETING	0	0
ENG MATLS - HOME	22787	22788
ENG MATLS - EXPOR	15835	16160
MILL, FELT & PAPE	4725	4725
MARINE PRODS	0	0
SALES SERVICE	16145	16145
COMMERCIAL EXP	26723	28223
EM DIVN	8620	88041
BLOCKS DIVISION		
ALFRETON SALES	25388	25388
HALTON SALES	21000	13971
COMMERCIAL EXP	15950	15950
BLOCKS DIVN	623 8	55309
PUBLICITY	103000	103000
GENERAL SELLING E	302432	317488
TOTAL SELLING EXP	1153922	1160983

SERVICE AND ADMINISTRATION EXPENSES

FINANCE/ADMIN		
BUYING	17190	17190
FIN ACCS	94492	91043
MAN ACCS	17477	17475
MAN SERV	38523	36523
COMPUTER OPERATIC	87133	87085
H.C. SERVICES	202055	201621
GENERAL SERVICES	154960	154960
PENSION FUNDING	153500	153500
SERV & ADMIN SUB-	76530	759397

Figure 11.14 Part of summary

THIRD QUARTER	FOURTH QUARTER	ANNUAL TOTAL	% TURNOVER
40640	40640	162560	.3
171265	172600	685680	1.3
17140	17140	71360	.1
41851	41849	167400	.3
98116	98103	392450	.7
105000	105000	420000	.8
474012	475332	1899450	3.5
32728	32868	138410	.3
24999	26299	101300	.2
21287	22287	86156	.2
10562	10702	42440	.1
14062	14062	56250	.1
16112	16112	64450	.1
119750	122330	489006	.9
0	0	0	.0
22787	22788	91150	.2
16160	16160	64365	.1
4725	4725	18900	.0
0	0	0	.0
16145	16145	64560	.1
26722	28222	109890	.2
86539	88040	348885	.6
25388	25388	101552	.2
13973	13970	62914	.1
15950	15950	63800	.1
55311	55308	228266	.4
103000	103000	412000	.8
357024	337179	1314124	2.4
1195636	1181189	4691731	8.6
17190	17190	68760	.1
91442	90443	367420	.7
17627	17965	70544	.1
39023	39023	153092	.3
85459	85460	345137	.6
196104	201990	801770	1.5
163480	154960	628360	1.2
153500	153500	614000	1.1
763825	760531	3049083	5.6

trading account (Report 8)

TAC CONSTRUCTION MATERIALS LIMITED

SUMMARY TRADING ACCOUNT

	FIRST QUARTER	SECOND QUARTER
CENTRAL SERVICES		
PERSONNEL	63662	62842
CENTRAL SERVICES	17340	17215
CENTRAL SERVICES	81002	80057
TECHNICAL SERVICES		
B&I DIVN		
DEVELOPEMENT	79296	79295
GRC DEVELOPEMENT	40625	40625
PRCD ENG	0	0
QUAL CONTROL	0	0
ADMIN	0	0
PIPES DIVN		
DEVELOPEMENT	1600	2550
OTHERS	0	0
EM DIVN		
DEVELOPEMENT	0	0
QUAL CONTROL	0	0
PRCD SERVICES	0	0
PROJECT ENGINEERI	0	0
BLOCKS DIVN		
DEVELOPEMENT	5825	5825
TECH SERVICES SUB	1273	128295
MANUFACTURING SERVICES		
B&I DIVN		
MANFG SERVICES SU	0	0
CARRIAGE		
ROOFING AND CLADD	264780	273541
FLAT SHEETS	31940	28628
INSULATION PRODUC	14572	12950
MOLLDED PRODUCTS	31361	27870
CONTRACTS AND MAT	1547	1375
PIPES PFR	4646	4129
TAC PIPES	126671	112580
ELECTRICAL PRODUC	6514	6896
MECHANICAL PRODUCT	8884	9347
MILLBOARD & FELTS	3692	3979
GAS CONCRETE	129729	145411
LIGHT AGGREGATE	36736	68880
CARRIAGE SUB-TOTA	661073	695685
DISTRIBUTION		
STCCK PACK & DFSP	322540	313681
FORWARDING	15674	15671
SCCT DEPOT	16134	16134
ERITH DEPOT	18159	18159
TRAFFIC	10935	10995
DISTRIBN SUB-TOTA	383442	374640
CARRIAGE & DISTRI	1044515	1070224

Figure 11.14 Continued

THIRD QUARTER	FOURTH QUARTER	ANNUAL TOTAL	% TURNOVER
63727	62634	252865	.5
17090	17665	69310	.1
80817	80299	322175	.6
79295	79294	317180	.6
39050	45250	165550	.3
0	0	0	.0
0	0	0	.0
0	0	0	.0
1250	1450	6850	.0
0	0	0	.0
0	0	0	.0
0	0	0	.0
0	0	0	.0
0	0	0	.0
5825	5825	23300	.0
125420	131819	512880	.9
0	0	0	.0
341261	284997	1164578	2.1
38109	38968	137645	.3
15338	14843	57703	.1
33081	32014	124326	.2
1672	1618	6214	.0
4142	4008	15924	.0
114541	110823	464615	.9
6740	7312	27461	.1
9177	9925	37334	.1
3756	3569	14996	.0
243078	224790	743008	1.4
73800	59040	238455	.4
884696	791906	3033256	5.6
327470	318615	1282306	2.4
15673	15671	62689	.1
16134	16142	64544	.1
18159	18522	72999	.1
10995	10995	43920	.1
388431	379945	1526458	2.8
1273126	1171851	4559714	8.4

As the company is a part of the Turner & Newall Group, it is not necessary to assess the effects of tax changes, since all taxation is dealt with at the Head Office.

The model has certainly made the preparation of the trading budget a more practicable exercise, especially in terms of altering the budget. Also as each division's logic and data are kept separate, changes in individual divisions can be made without affecting any other division's plans.

11.5 Future Developments

The budget system as described above is now running reasonably smoothly and so it remains to discuss possible extensions. Already modelling work has been carried out to generate cash-flow and balance-sheet details. These models are simple to operate and run. Divisional and total company reports both on a monthly and quarterly basis are produced in a format that complies with reporting requirements. These models are not directly linked to the trading-budget model but information on sales, profit and cost of sales is used. The data required to operate the model consist of:

> fixed assets covering opening balances, depreciation, disposals, capital expenditure, investments;
> stock level as volume or percentage of sales;
> debtor days for home and export;
> days for trade creditors;
> sundry debtors, creditors, provisions;
> inter-company balances.

There is not a larger number of calculations, the principal ones being calculations of stock, debtors, and creditors, with the other items being input directly. Once the balance sheet has been produced the next stage is the cash-flow calculation, where further information is input concerning profit levels. Information from the balance-sheet file is transferred to the cash-flow file and by sorting the appropriate data a cash-flow statement can be produced. This model is run on the Group computer using the FCS package, and though the logic files are the same for each division, separate logic and data files are again maintained. For the total company position the four divisional files are brought together.

Regarding new developments, three possible extensions of the existing models are contemplated:

(1) linking the budget information to the nominal ledger so that the computer will produce a set of financial reports automatically showing actual and budget;
(2) producing other reports showing departmental budgets and factory budgets;
(3) providing budget information to be used by marketing departments for re-forecasting during the year.

11.6 Conclusion

I have not tried in this chapter to explain the detailed operation of the budget model in use at TAC. What I have attempted to show is the importance of the model within TAC, and how it has been structured to meet the company's organization structure. The model is flexible enough to cope with organizational changes and is not too cumbersome to make it unwieldy to operate.

Financial Modelling in Corporate Management
Edited by J. W. Bryant
© 1982 John Wiley & Sons Ltd.

12

Comparison of Alternative Financing Methods

LEWIS CORNER

12.1 Introduction

All firms regularly require finance to support existing activities, replace aging equipment, and undertake new investment projects. Many methods of finance are available, including the issue of share capital, mortgages, debentures, private loans, institutional loans, cash, hire purchase, and leasing. When choosing how to finance a particular requirement it is important that all the relevant factors should be appreciated. At one level the decision may involve general matters of policy, such as the desirability or feasibility of diluting the current share capital, whether a piece of equipment is to be treated as a capital or revenue item, and so on. When these questions have been settled a number of financing options may be equally acceptable in principle, in which case cost is the predominant factor in determining the final choice.

In what follows the main emphasis will concern the cost evaluation of cash purchase, loan or hire purchase, and leasing using Discounted Cash Flow (DCF) methods. It is assumed that the more qualitative aspects of financial planning have already been fully considered, and other forms of finance have been rejected. Quantitative models can only be sensibly applied to roughly similar options, and it would be misleading to claim that DCF techniques have much to offer in helping to resolve the higher-level decisions.

The evaluation methods to be described are restricted to the cost appraisal of the financing options. Before this stage is reached an earlier analysis may be necessary to justify the proposed expenditure of investment for which funds are being sought. This preliminary hurdle may be omitted for some items, such as office equipment or commercial vehicles, which are regarded as essential for the continuing normal activity of the organization.

The general principles of purchase and lease finance are given, followed by simple examples of the appropriate DCF calculations. Finally some robust conclusions are stated which should obviate the need to repeat the evaluation every time a new acquisition is proposed.

12.2 Financing Methods

Cash Purchase

Cash purchase can only be regarded as an option when a firm is not in a net borrowing position. If a purchase is made at the expense of an increased overdraft it is really a loan purchase, since it commits the firm to increased interest payments on the higher borrowings. The possibility of making a cash purchase is a luxury for most firms, but even when cash is available it is not necessarily the cheapest option. If the effective borrowing rate for loan purchase, hire purchase or leasing is less than the opportunity earnings rate for cash, it makes sense to use the cash for the alternative investment.

Loan Purchase

Finance may be available through an increased overdraft or other loan facilities. Many firms prefer to retain the maximum overdraft allowed to use as working capital, rather than use some of their bank credit to purchase specific pieces of equipment for which other forms of finance can be found. Loans may be arranged at fixed interest, or be tied to current lending rates which fluctuate unpredictably in the long term. When calculating the true cost of loan purchase, interest charges must be taken into account as they reduce the corporation-tax liability.

Hire Purchase

Hire purchase differs from loan purchase in that ownership of the item does not transfer to the hirer until the final payment has been made. This is not normally an important factor since a firm undertaking a hire-purchase agreement would do so with every intention of meeting the obligations, and eventually becoming the owner. An important tax feature of hire purchase is that the hirer claims the capital allowances immediately, although title to the equipment will not be acquired until some future date, possibly several years ahead.

Hire-purchase companies may offer a variety of repayment schemes, devised to appeal to firms with different projected cash-flow patterns. For equipment which becomes substantially more expensive to maintain as it ages, decreasing payment schedules may be available so that the total hire purchase and maintenance cost remains almost constant.

Hire-purchase schemes have been devised which allow the hirer to choose when to terminate the agreement, the final payment depending on the time at which it is made. No matter what contract is the most attractive, all interest charges are tax deductible.

Leasing

Equipment leasing has become an increasingly popular method of finance since its introduction in modern form in the U.K. in the early 1960s. The primary distinguishing characteristic of leasing is that the lessee does not have the right to acquire ownership at any time, title remaining with the lessor until the agreement is terminated. As the owner, the lessor claims any investment allowances, and is able to pass this benefit to the lessee by reducing the leasing payments accordingly. The firm leasing a piece of equipment treats it as a revenue rather than capital item, and the full leasing charges can be used to offset corporation tax.

Not surprisingly for a relatively new form of finance, there have been several tax loopholes in the U.K. which have made leasing particularly attractive for some types of organization and equipment. Until recently non-profit-making bodies, such as local authorities and universities, were able to lease and indirectly claim tax allowances which they would not have received had they purchased the same item. Car leasing has been another buoyant sector of the leasing market, but tax law changes have removed some of the earlier advantages, especially for more expensive vehicles.

An equipment-leasing contract normally specifies a primary period, related to a conservative view of the useful operating life, during which the lessor recovers his initial outlay and earns a profit. In most cases this may be followed by an indefinite secondary period involving nominal payments of perhaps 1% of the original value per year. When the item is finally sold or scrapped the lessor is usually allowed to keep a substantial part, say 75-95%, of the proceeds. The lessor's interest in the equipment is strictly financial; the benefits of warranties, the responsibilities for insurance and maintenance, the negotiation of price and supplier, all fall to the lessee.

Most leasing companies will quote a variety of different terms, depending on the length of the primary period, the frequency of payments, whether they are in advance or arrears, and so on. Typically the rates are per £1,000, and the lessor's only real concerns are whether the contract is suitable for the equipment, and the creditworthiness of the lessee.

The major advantage of leasing occurs when the lessee is not in a position to claim immediately the tax allowances available to a purchaser. A possible non-cost advantage is that leased equipment is not capitalized; many companies feel this is an appropriate way to treat items which are essential but not directly productive, such as vehicles and computers.

Contract leasing is a similar arrangement in which the lessor uses the equipment over part of, rather than all, its operating life. For such schemes the payments are higher, but the advantage to the lessee is that the contract can be terminated subject to a preordained period of notice. The evaluation of contract leasing introduces a number of factors which are difficult to quantify, and hence include in DCF appraisals. Under such an agreement the lessee gains protection against obsolescence and the problems of selling an unwanted partly used item. Contract leasing may offer extra benefits, such as 'free' maintenance, and provision of alternative equipment in the event of breakdown.

In the last few years the previously clear-cut distinction between hiring and leasing has become blurred. Using ownership as the distinguishing factor, there are now available hiring contracts which are leases, and leases which are hiring contracts!

12.3 DCF Appraisal of Financing Terms

The true costs of finance cannot be determined by simply adding the after tax cash flows. Most arrangements will endure for several years, so the timing of the cash flows, as well as their magnitudes, must also be considered. DCF methods deal with such problems by translating future cash flows to present values by means of one or more discount rates. In what follows it is assumed that the reader is familiar with DCF principles, and the ideas of Net Present Value (NPV) or Net Present Cost (NPC).

In order to calculate the NPC of a financing option, a detailed table of cash flows should be prepared. This must include the obvious flows, such as hire purchase or leasing charges, and the effects on the tax position. If equipment is purchased, tax allowances can be claimed, leading to reduced future corporation-tax payments. Similarly finance charges, when choosing loan or hire purchase, and leasing charges are tax deductible. An analysis which fails to include tax relief is incorrect, and liable to lead to false conclusions.

Although the DCF calculations are straightforward, the analysis is not entirely free from difficulty. Perhaps the main problem is the selection of the discount rate, because this can critically affect the results. Gillett (1972) compares cash purchase, hire purchase and leasing, and produces tables showing cash purchase to have the lowest NPC at a discount rate of 5%, hire purchase at 7% and leasing at 10%. The least controversial advice is to use the after-tax borrowing or earning rate for the firm, depending on whether it is in a net borrowing position or not.

The firm's tax position is also vital to the analysis since the cash flows resulting from tax relief must be logged at the correct time. If there are no accumulated profits, the benefits of investment allowances and tax relief on interest will be deferred, affecting the NPC.

For the options being considered the disposal value of the equipment is not likely to present a problem, particularly if the lessor allows the lessee to keep the greater part of any sale proceeds.

Care must be taken to account for any difference in operating costs between financing methods, for example some leasing terms may include service and repair, whereas these must be added to the cost of purchasing. Extra costs which are the same for all finance schemes may be excluded from the analysis.

Another source of uncertainty concerns future corporation tax rates, tax rules and interest rates. If the calculations are performed assuming low interest rates, perhaps loan purchase will have the lowest NPC. Should general interest rates subsequently rise, what appeared to be the cheapest finance may turn out to be the most expensive, as hire purchase and leasing payments are usually fixed at the time the contract is made.

12.4 An Illustrative Example

In this section, simplified analyses are given to compare the costs of financing £1000 worth of equipment; the alternatives to be considered are cash purchase, loan purchase and leasing. All auxiliary revenues and expenditures are assumed to be the same for each alternative, and hence are not included in the analysis.

For ease of presentation it has been unrealistically assumed that tax relief on investment allowances and finance charges is received immediately. In practice there will be delays before tax payments are due, but it would be easy to adjust cash-flow tables to account for such lags.

A time unit of one year has been chosen, but in many cases a more natural period may be a half year, quarter or month. Corporation tax is 50%, and equipment owners can claim a 100% first year allowance.

Cash Purchase

The £1000 purchase price is paid immediately. This investment reduces tax liability by £500 (50% of £1000), hence the net cash outflow in the first year is £500. There are no cash flows associated with cash purchase in subsequent years.

Loan Purchase

The equipment is purchased with a 10% loan, requiring repayments of £239.82 for each of five years. Each payment can be broken down into principal and interest components. Since no interest has accrued by the time of the first instalment, the outstanding loan balance reduces by £239.82 to £760.18. At the beginning of the second year interest of £76.02 is due, hence the principal component of the payment is £163.80. Similarly the interest charges can be calculated for each year.

Tax relief derives from the first year allowance and interest paid on the loan. In year 1 corporation tax liability reduces by £500 because of the 100% allowance; in years 2-5 tax relief is 50% of the interest components.

Table 12.1 Cash flows for cash, loan and lease finance

Cash Purchase					
Year	1	2	3	4	5
Cash payment	−1000.00	−	−	−	−
100% allowance	1000.00	−	−	−	−
Tax relief	500.00	−	−	−	−
Net cash flow	−500.00	−	−	−	−
Loan Purchase					
Year	1	2	3	4	5
Loan payment	−239.82	−239.82	−239.82	−239.82	−239.82
principal	239.82	163.80	180.18	198.19	218.01
interest	0.00	76.02	59.64	41.62	21.80
100% allowance	1000.00	−	−	−	−
Tax relief	500.00	38.01	29.82	20.81	10.90
Net cash flow	260.18	−201.81	−210.00	−219.01	−228.92
Lease					
Year	1	2	3	4	5
Lease payment	−250.00	−250.00	−250.00	−250.00	−250.00
Tax relief	125.00	125.00	125.00	125.00	125.00
Net cash flow	−125.00	−125.00	−125.00	−125.00	−125.00

Lease

The leasing terms are £250 per year for five years. Each leasing payment is fully tax deductible, reducing the amount of corporation tax paid by £125. Because ownership of the equipment remains with the lessor the first year allowance cannot be claimed.

Table 12.1 shows the detailed cash flows for the three options over the five year life of the investment.

Table 12.2 shows the net present costs, at several discount rates, for each method of finance.

12.5 Discussion

The figures used in the preceding example are not realistic, but indicate the kind of results that could be expected if the analysis were performed with actual borrowing or leasing terms.

Cash purchase will always appear cheaper if discounting methods are not employed, while the NPC for leasing, loan purchase or hire purchase will decrease as the discount factor is raised, because payments are spread over several years.

In general the true costs for both hire purchase and leasing are likely to be similar no matter what discount factor is selected, since the finance company rates are calculated to yield approximately the same returns. If a decision is merely between hire purchase and leasing, the reasons for choosing one rather than the

Table 12.2 Net present costs

Discount rate (%)	0	4	8	12	16
NPC cash purchase	500.00	500.00	500.00	500.00	500.00
NPC loan purchase	599.55	513.41	448.84	388.79	336.60
NPC lease	625.00	573.74	539.02	504.67	474.77

other are more likely to involve the desirability of ownership, whether the item is regarded as a capital or revenue item and so on, rather than the marginal cost differences.

Finance house interest charges, whether in explicit form or implied by the hire and lease terms, will normally be slightly higher than those for bank overdrafts. For a firm in a borrowing position, finance by means of an increased overdraft is probably the cheapest alternative of all. However most firms, and possibly banks too, do not like overdraft facilities to be used in this way, preferring to keep them for other contingencies.

If DCF methods are used to compare finance options, the most important error to avoid is the comparison of cash purchase with some alternative, whilst failing to recognize that the cash will come from a loan. Several calculation procedures have been proposed so that a single analysis will implicitly compare leasing with loan purchase, but these are often rather difficult to understand. It is less confusing to determine the interest rate for borrowed cash, and make an explicit comparison along the lines described.

These general conclusions assume that a firm is in a tax-paying position, but if the tax allowance available to a purchaser cannot be claimed, then leasing is likely to be the cheapest method fo finance—providing that the leasing company is satisfied that the lack of profit is only temporary, and that the potential lessee is a sound credit risk.

No permanent conclusions can be drawn about the relative merits of different methods of finance. Successive governments, or even the same government in successive years, are liable to change the regulations concerning investment allowances, the rate of corporation tax, the size of deposits for hire purchase, and many other factors that might affect the costs.

It would be foolish to decide once and for all that a particular form of finance should never be used, because future changes in the financial world could reverse the results of previous evaluations. However, when cost comparisons are required, DCF methods must be used, and close attention must be paid to current tax legislation when constructing cash flow tables.

Reference

Gillett, E. R. (1972). 'Leasing—in perspective', *Accountancy*, 83(944), 24–8.

PART 3 STRATEGIC PLANNING MODELS

The case studies in this section are mainly concerned with balance-sheet items as opposed to the emphasis on the profit-and-loss account which was evident in Part 2. The time horizon considered is generally greater than two or three years, and the implications of the decisions involved are often far-reaching, including some which might alter the whole emphasis of an organization's activities and of its arena of interest. Strategic planning is of course a discipline in itself, and the case studies included here cannot explore in any depth the processes by which alternative futures are conceived. They do, however, demonstrate the part that can be played by modelling in assessing these alternatives.

In the first case, given in Chapter 13, the use of a simulation model to carry out sensitivity analyses on proposals for a major industrial development is described. This is coupled with a related study to evaluate the tradeoff between capital and operating costs in alternative designs of facilities to be provided as part of the development. Investment appraisal is also the subject of Chapter 14, which is concerned with the evaluation of proposals for corporate expansion. The models described here place a refreshingly realistic emphasis on fiscal and financial aspects instead of concentrating, as is more usual, on operating details. Chapter 15 contains the first of two discussions on the implications of alternative dividend policies and shows through a simple example how some very fundamental modelling could assist management decision-making in this area. The second discussion of dividend policy given in Chapter 16, shows how simulation models might be used to explore dividend growth scenarios and their consequent benefits for shareholders. It is hoped that these two contributions will draw attention to an important but often neglected area of financial modelling application. Finally, the role of models in the analysis of acquisitions is considered in Chapter 17. Acquisitions and mergers are perhaps the corporate development strategies with the most significant strategic implications, and so a structured approach to financial analysis is particularly important here.

Financial Modelling in Corporate Management
Edited by J. W. Bryant
© 1982 John Wiley & Sons Ltd.

13

Financial Models for Industrial Development Strategy

LEO BRESSMAN, JAMES BROWNE AND JOHN DROBNY

13.1 Introduction

The Port Authority of New York and New Jersey is a self-supporting corporate agency. It was created as the Port of New York Authority in 1921 under the terms of a bi-state treaty, and given responsibility to plan, develop, and operate terminal, transportation and other facilities of commerce, and to improve and protect the commerce of the bi-state Port without burden to the taxpayer. In 1972, the Authority's name was changed to identify more accurately its status as a bi-state agency of New York and New Jersey.

The Port Authority is responsible for operation of six interstate tunnels and bridges, the regional system of three airports and two heliports, seven marine terminals, three bus terminals, a truck terminal, the World Trade Center and a network of six Trade Development offices. In addition, the Port Authority Trans-Hudson Corporation (PATH), a subsidiary of the Port Authority, has responsibility for operation of the PATH rapid transit system, which links Newark, Jersey City and Hoboken with lower and mid-Manhattan. In total, these facilities represent an investment of close to $4 billion.

In 1978, bi-state legislation was passed to enable the Port Authority to move into a new area of endeavour-industrial development. The passage of the legislation capped two years of preliminary planning. This planning included evaluation of the economic feasibility of several inner city industrial parks, each of which was coupled with a resource recovery facility.

The Port Authority's traditional approach to evaluating the economic feasibility of a new project has been to weigh annual net revenues (gross revenues less operating and maintenance expenses) expected to be generated by the project, against debt service (equal annual payments based on capital costs) that would be incurred by the project. This computation is based on single-point or 'most-likely' estimates for each of the key factors—e.g., revenues, capital costs, inflation rate. It is usually carried out for a single year, either a typical year or the first full year of operation. Implicit in this approach is the assumption that the cost and revenue flows will be relatively stable once full operation is achieved.

In a world where cost inflation rates often exceed revenue escalation, the traditional approach does not take into account some of the risks involved. Analysis based on a single 'typical' year assumes an environment in which, after a construction period, revenues and costs are stable and predictable. While this type of analysis might be acceptable for a tunnel or bridge financially supported by toll revenues, it is inappropriate for a project such as an industrial park in which cash flows are expected to vary significantly by year. Moreover, because the general area of industrial development is a new one for the Port Authority, and because there are so many uncertainties and complexities associated with developing and operating inner-city industrial parks, it was decided that the traditional approach to evaluating economic feasibility would not provide decision-makers with adequate information on the project's risks and potential returns. It was felt that what was needed was an approach that would account for the variabilities inherent in the most relevant factors, resulting in an evaluation of risk and identification of conditions yielding each possible level of return.

The objective of such a method is to provide the decision-maker with a clear picture of the relative risk (i.e. the range of possible outcomes and the probable odds of financial success or failure in light of uncertain foreknowledge). Port Authority top management also wanted to know which of the many assumptions about the future were most critical and just how much the expected financial results would be affected by changes in those key assumptions.

It seemed clear that some sort of computer simulation would be necessary. Although the technique of computer simulation had never been used at the Port Authority for financial analysis, simulation had been used regularly in operational analysis (e.g. evaluating PATH rapid transit train schedules (Browne, 1966), planning airport passenger and baggage flow at Kennedy Airport (Browne, Lui, and Nanda, 1972), designing the World Trade Center elevator system (Browne and Kelly, 1968)), and was well accepted by Port Authority management. To meet the need for a more complete financial analysis, therefore, a study team, comprising staff from the Management Services, Planning and Development, and Finance Departments, developed a financial simulation model to obtain the expected return and the dispersion about this expected return for an investment proposal under given assumptions. This model was used specifically for performing risk and sensitivity analyses on one of the proposed industrial park complexes. While similar approaches have been used in the private sector (Hertz, 1964), this model represents, as far as we know, one of the first uses of such an approach to evaluation of the expected financial returns on investment in the public sector. Such analyses are especially important in organizations which, like the Port Authority, are fully self-supporting and do not have access to tax revenues for financial support.

In carrying out the overall project's financial simulation, it became clear that the resource recovery plant was of great importance in the project economics and that critical decisions had to be made on the design of the resource-recovery facilities. These decisions involved trade-offs between capital and operating costs. Because of the emphasis on decisions to be made, i.e. controllable variables, a deterministic model was used to evaluate the resource recovery facility, whereas a probabilistic model was used in the previous overall project evaluation.

The resource recovery facility would require a capital investment in excess of $100 million and site preparation for the total industrial park area might require an investment of approximately $50 million. In addition to these Port Authority expenditures, investments by industrial park tenants would bring the total to more than $500 million.

Because two distinct simulation methodologies were used, the following sections include a discussion of both. The first section addresses the probabilistic approach to the industrial park application (Bressman *et al*, 1978). After a section on the background of resource recovery operations, the deterministic modelling approach to this analysis is presented (Bressman, Browne and Drobny, 1980).

13.2 Industrial Park Model

In general, the methodology used for the probabilistic model was to assign values to each of a set of critical (basic) variables in accordance with assigned probabilities, and then to calculate annual revenue and cost flows over the project's life based on these values. The yearly cash-flow data were then integrated to obtain three measures of overall financial impact. This process was repeated a number of times to provide the basis for risk and sensitivity analyses.

The development process for the model involved four components:

(1) selection of basic dynamic variables;
(2) Monte Carlo simulation;
(3) revenue/cost generator;
(4) measures of financial impact.

The following sections describe these components in some detail and outline how they were applied to the Port Authority's industrial development project.

Selection of Basic Dynamic Variables (BDVs)

The first step in building the model was to select input variables (BDVs) based on two criteria:

(a) they were expected to significantly affect the outcome of the project; and
(b) they were subject to a significant degree of uncertainty.

For the industrial park project, the following eight BDVs were chosen by a multidisciplinary study team:

(1) *Marketability schedule*—the number of years to market the industrial park to full capacity.
(2) *Resource Recovery Construction Duration*—the number of years to construct the resource recovery plant.
(3) *Revenue Inflation Rate*—the annual rate at which the industrial park's revenues escalate.
(4) *Cost Inflation Rate*—the annual rate at which the park's capital and operating costs escalate.
(5) *Resource Recovery Total Construction Cost*—the uninflated capital cost for constructing the resource recovery plant.
(6) *Ground Rent/ft²*—the annual ground rent to be charged to tenants of the industrial park.
(7) *Tipping Fee*—the amount in dollars per ton that the municipality agrees to pay the Port Authority for disposal of its garbage.
(8) *Tenant Power Ratio*—the proportion of power produced by the resource-recovery plant to be sold by the Port Authority to tenants of the industrial park. Any remaining power would be sold to the local utility.

These eight variables were judged by the study team as the most critical out of fifty variables identified in the formulae for calculating annual revenues and costs.

Monte Carlo Simulation

After the BDVs were selected, an uncertainty profile (probability distribution) was developed for each. Because of the subjective nature of this task, the uncertainty profiles were developed jointly by team members possessing expertise in financial, engineering and marketing areas. For the eight BDVs involved in our application, both normal (skewed and unskewed) and discrete distributions were permitted. Figure 13.1 is an example of an uncertainty profile for 'revenue inflation rate', one of the project's BDVs.

Once the probability distributions were assigned, a Monte Carlo simulation was performed. For each run, individual values for each of the BDVs were selected independently, based on their individual probability distributions and random combinations of these BDV values were obtained, simulating possible future situations. For the Port Authority's industrial development project, 200 combinations were simulated to ensure a statistically valid sample. (In order to obtain an error no greater than ±0.05 in the revenue/cost ratio—one of the measures of

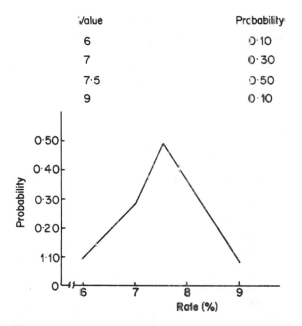

Value	Probability
6	0.10
7	0.30
7.5	0.50
9	0.10

Figure 13.1 Revenue inflation rate—uncertainty profile. *Note*: The distribution shown is hypothetical

financial impact defined in a subsequent section—with a 95% confidence level, it was necessary to simulate 200 combinations.)

Revenue/Cost Generator

Once the desired number of BDV combinations were obtained, they were input, one set at a time, into the revenue/cost generator (R/C generator) program, which calculated the annual cash flows of the project over its 30-year life. Based on the values of the BDVs, formulae contained within the R/C generator calculated yearly revenues and costs associated with the construction and operation of the industrial park complex. Table 13.1 contains a list of the revenues and costs generated.

Each of these revenues and costs were generated by appropriate formulae stored in the R/C generator program. Many were dependent on one or more of the BDV values selected. As an example, land selling costs (in thousands of dollars) were calculated as follows. (Please note that the numerical values stated below are hypothetical.)

For years 1 and 2:
$$\text{cost}_1 = 500$$
$$\text{cost}_2 = 450$$
For years 3 to X:
$$\text{cost}_i = \left(\text{cost}_{i-1} - \frac{450 - 300}{X - 2} \right) Y_i.$$

Table 13.1 Revenue and cost centres

	Land	Buildings	Resource recovery
Capital costs	Stabilization Utilities Paving Landscaping Contingency Engineering Appraisal	Construction	Construction
Operating and maintenance costs	Selling Insurance Security and maintenance Administration Payments in lieu of taxes	None*	Operating and maintenance Supplemental fuel† Payments in lieu of taxes
Revenues	Ground rent Government aid	Building rent	Tipping fees Fuel sales Ferrous metal sales Government aid

*It is assumed that tenants will be responsible for all operating and maintenance costs related to the buildings.
†It is assumed that power will be purchased from the local utility and provided to the tenants at a reduced cost until the resource-recovery plant is operational.

where X is the first year of full occupancy (one of the BDVs) and Y_i is the appropriate cost inflation factor (another of the BDVs) for Year i.
For years $(X + 1)$ to 30:
$$\text{cost}_i = 50Y_i.$$

After formulae such as the above were used to calculate all of the costs and revenues listed in Table 13.1, the R/C generator produced output consisting of many sets of combined annual revenues and costs over the 30 years of the project's life.

Measures of Financial Impact

The next task was to calculate annual financial measures for each set of cash flows (revenues and costs), generated in the previous step, which allowed runs of the model to be compared easily. This task required that some criteria of financial success or failure be defined. Three measures were chosen:

(1) *Present-valued revenue/cost ratio (R/C ratio)*—This measure was obtained by discounting all revenues and costs to present value, using the projected cost of capital as the discount rate. The ratio was then calculated by dividing the

cumulative present value of 30 years of net revenues (revenues minus operating costs) by the cumulative present value of capital costs.

(2) *Internal rate of return (IRR)*—The discount rate at which the cumulative present value of revenues equalled the cumulative present value of total costs (capital and operating).

(3) *Time-valued payback year (TVP year)*—The first year in which the cumulative present value of revenues equals the cumulative present value of total costs (i.e. the time at which the capital funds invested would be recovered through net revenue flows).

13.3 Applications of Industrial Park Model

Risk Analysis

Figure 13.2 contains a flowchart which shows how the simulation was used to perform the risk analysis. After the 200 iterations were completed and the corresponding measures of financial impact calculated, frequency distributions and risk profiles were plotted for each of the measures. The expected (average) return of the project, and the dispersion (variability) about this expected return were then determined. The risk profiles (probability distributions) provided management with the probability that the investment would provide a return greater or less than a certain amount.

Figure 13.3 is a frequency distribution for the range of outcome values of the IRR of the project. (Please note that while the format used is the same, the numerical values presented here are purely hypothetical.) As shown in the illustration, the range of IRR values generated by the model approximates a skewed Normal distribution around a mean of 15.15% with a standard deviation of 3.824%.

The likelihoods of either achieving or bettering specified IRRs were determined from the risk profiles like Figure 13.4. The risk profile shows about a 96% chance of achieving or bettering an IRR of 8.25% (a projected cost of capital), and about a 50% chance of achieving or bettering an IRR of 15.25%. (These values are also hypothetical.)

Sensitivity Analysis

In addition to plotting and analysing the results of the iterations, sensitivity-analyses were performed to determine which BDVs were most critical to the project's financial outcome. The sensitivity analyses were performed by iterating the R/C generator over the range of values for a single BDV, while holding the other BDVs constant at their mean values. The measures of financial impact were then calculated for each iteration and compared to determine the extent to which the individual variable would affect the results.

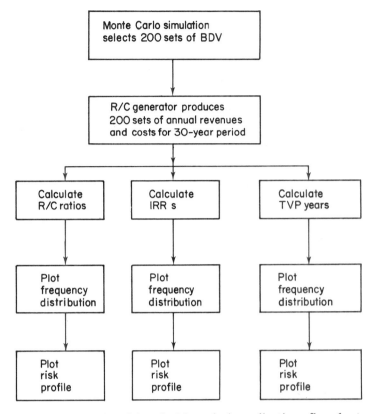

Figure 13.2 Industrial park risk analysis application—flowchart

The statistical range of the resulting set of R/C ratios was used as a measure of the relative impact of the variable on the project's outcome. In addition to the sensitivity analyses based on the BDVs, other assumptions were changed to provide answers to 'what if' questions. These included such changes as eliminating government aid, and not financing certain types of construction in the park.

Through the sensitivity analyses, the relative importance of the different BDVs was determined. More importantly, management attention was directed toward those which could be influenced through contractual agreements, controls or negotiations so that the financial results could be improved. Figure 13.5 flowcharts the mechanics of applying the simulation model to perform sensitivity analyses.

The initial probabilistic model provided top management with information on the risks and possible returns, aiding them in making the GO/NO GO decision on industrial development. In addition, the model highlighted those areas that were critical to the project's financial success. These areas would require further investigation to ensure a financially feasible project. One of these areas was the resource recovery component of the industrial park project.

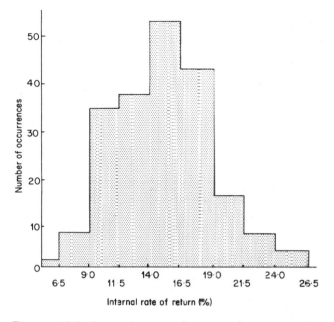

Figure 13.3 Internal rate of return—frequency distribution

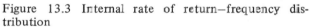

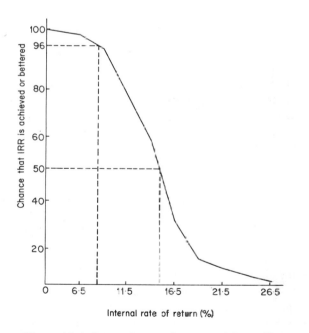

Figure 13.4 Internal rate of return—risk profile

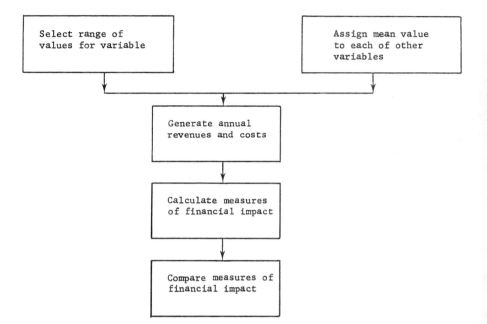

Figure 13.5 Industrial park sensitivity analysis application—flowchart

13.4 Background on Resource Recovery

Basically, resource recovery involves the utilization of solid waste to produce energy in the form of steam or electricity. The concept has gained popularity because of the shortage and escalating cost of fossil fuels, the increasing quantities of solid waste, and the increasing energy requirements of industry. The predominant methods of solid-waste disposal used today (incineration without energy recovery and landfill) squander valuable energy and materials that could be recovered and used effectively in the manufacturing of new products. New York City alone generates approximately 22 000 tons per day of municipal solid waste (MSW). Solid waste must be viewed as a resource rather than a liability because of its high heat content and because of the potentially recoverable materials it contains. Increased utilization of this resource as another source of energy will help us to reduce our demand for conventional sources of energy, such as fossil fuels.

Resource recovery has been proven to be technologically feasible in many European countries. However, depending on the specific technology used and the actual design of the plant, the economics can vary greatly. Today, resource-recovery technologies can turn a waste-disposal problem into an energy resource with minimal environmental consequences. At this time, there are two primary resource recovery technologies that are being evaluated in detail: mass burning and refuse derived fuel (RDF).

The most widely used mass-burning process is direct combustion of unprocessed waste in a waterwall furnace, so called because water-filled tubes are imbedded in the furnace walls to absorb heat and cool the walls. The heat generated by the combustion process is recovered as steam. The quality of the steam is approximately 600 lbf/in^2 and 750°F while the efficiency of the waterwall incinerator varies from 65% to 85%, depending on the type of incinerator used and the quality of solid waste being burned (BTU content). This steam can be converted into electricity. Generally, the only material recovered in the process is low-grade ferrous metal.

Once the steam is produced it is transported short distances for various purposes, or a steam-turbine generator may be used to cogenerate electricity and steam on site. The types and sizes of turbines used, either condensing, non-condensing or automatic extraction, and the overall turbine efficiency, depend on the quantities of steam which can be extracted at various points along the turbine. The system is a closed one with the condensate collected at the end of the turbine and returned to the boiler.

One of the problems involved in the burning of MSW is its variable moisture content. To ensure smooth steam or power production, supplementary fuels (such as oil or gas) must sometimes be burned. The production of refuse derived fuel (RDF) from MSW, by removing non-combustible material and drying the remainder, is one way to overcome this problem. RDF has more uniform physical and energy characteristics and can usually be burned without supplementary fuels. The removal of non-combustibles such as glass, aluminium and ferrous metal before combustion reduces furnace maintenance significantly, and provides a source of revenue from sales of recovered materials. The RDF is then either sold to a local utility that can use the RDF as an efficient fuel replacing coal or oil to generate electricity, or the RDF can be burned on site to produce steam and electricity.

13.5 Resource Recovery Model

The resource recovery deterministic model was designed to simulate three resource recovery technology options: Mass Burning, RDF 'A', which consists of producing refuse derived fuel (RDF) strictly for sale, and RDF 'B' in which some (up to 100%) of the RDF produced is burned at the site. The model was designed to analyse a plant built and operated in either New York or New Jersey.

Input The input parameters required to drive the model fall into two categories: primary and secondary. Primary input must be entered interactively at the terminal every time the model is run. Once the model is loaded and executed, it will begin prompting for the primary input. Figure 13.6 contains a sample run sheet showing this prompting sequence. The first question asks the user to select one of the three technology options. Once this selection is made, the user is prompted for number

```
RRFS13 07/24/80 11:29:21
WELCOME TO THE RESOURCE RECOVERY FINANCIAL SIMULATOR—VERSION 1
ENTER THE PROCESS YOU WISH TO CONSIDER:
1——MASS BURN
2——RDF A
3——RDF B
?
1
ENTER THE NUMBER OF TONS OF MSW PER DAY:
IN THE FORMAT:   MUNICIPALITY, PRIVATE
?
2000, 1500
ENTER THE NUMBER OF MSW COLLECTION DAYS PER YEAR:
?
365
ENTER THE NUMBER OF OPERATING DAYS PER YEAR:
?
302
DO YOU WANT A LISTING OF THE MOST-LIKELY VALUES FOR THE VARIABLES?  Y/N
?
N
HOW MANY VARIABLES DO YOU WISH TO CHANGE? (IF NONE ENTER 0)
?
1
ENTER:   VARIABLE #, NEW VALUE
?
17,.5
WARNING:   YOUR CAPITAL COSTS SHOULD REFLECT A PLANT CAPACITY
OF                       5324.125              TONS/DAY
DO YOU WISH TO ALTER YOUR CAPITAL COSTS —— Y/N
?
N
ENTER THE TURBINE CONFIGURATION YOU WISH TO CONSIDER:
1———AUTOMATIC EXTRACTION
2———CONDENSING AND NON-CONDENSING
?
1
YOUR PEAK KWH DEMAND/HR IS:            59000
ENTER THE # OF AUTO EXTRACT. TURBINES
YOU WANT IN OPERATION AND THE MW RATING
IN THE FORMAT:   # OF TURBINES, MW RATING
?
2,30
```

Figure 13.6 Resource recovery sample run sheet

of tons of solid waste to be processed daily and the number of days per year that the plant will be operational.

After specification of the primary variables, a file consisting of secondary variables relating to the chosen technology is read into the model. There are approximately 200 secondary variables covering all areas including efficiency parameters for boilers and turbines, sale prices for steam and electricity during peak and off-peak hours, sale prices for recovered materials, operations and maintenance costs, inflation factors and capital costs for various components. The

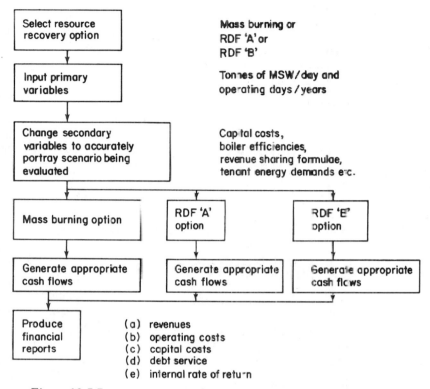

Figure 13.7 Resource recovery financial simulation—logic flowchart

values that are read into the model for each of these variables are the *most-likely* estimates compiled by experts in the engineering, financial and marketing areas. Once these variables are read into the model, the user is given the opportunity to change any combination of variables interactively to reflect the scenario or design alternative that is being analysed.

After changes have been made in the secondary variable file, the user is prompted to select a turbine configuration (automatic extraction, condensing and/or non-condensing) and to select the number and size of turbines desired for the run. Once these decision variables have been entered, the input stage is complete and the simulation begins.

Logic   Figure 13.7 contains a flowchart of the simulation logic performed by the model. The model itself consists of mathematical formulae which generate annual revenues and costs associated with the construction and operation of a resource recovery plant. The formulae generate these annual cash flows over a 30-year period, based on the values that are input for the primary and secondary variables. These cash flows are then reduced to several overall financial measures and ratios and then assembled into a report.

One of the more complex parts of the model involves the mass burning formulae dealing with energy generation and sale. In this section, the model uses heat balance equations and turbine performance factors to calculate the quantities of process steam, heating steam, and electricity produced, given all the input parameters specified. The model then determines the revenue flow resulting from the sale of these types of energy. This module is critical since it deals with the design of the cost-intensive components of the plant.

Output   Once the simulation is performed and the cash flows generated, a financial report is produced containing the following:
(1) the primary variables used for this run;
(2) a record of the changes made to the secondary most-likely file;
(3) annual cash flows;
(4) financial measures including debt service coverage and IRR.

13.6 Applications of Resource Recovery Model

The resource recovery deterministic model had two major applications. First, it served as an aid in the operational planning of the facility by providing a quick economic evaluation of the design strategies and trade-offs. Second, it was used for the negotiating process with municipalities, utilities and tenants, to help establish economic variables, tipping fees, electricity and steam prices, and prices for recovered materials.

While the deterministic model provides the user with a print-out of all two hundred stored values and allows the user to alter any combination of them, the following list will give an idea of some of the specific kinds of evaluations and 'what if' analyses that can be carried out:

(1) Trade-off analysis of higher-efficiency, high-quality boilers and turbines against their greater capital costs.
(2) Evaluation of the effects of delays in construction or in regulatory approvals.
(3) Determination of the effect of different mixes of tenants in terms of their demands for steam and electricity during peak and off-peak periods and by day of the week. This involves the costs of generating or purchasing these utilities.
(4) Once the costs of these utilities have been estimated, the effects of various cost-recovery methods and the economic effects of different prices for peak and off-peak process steam, heating steam and electricity can be explored.
(5) The sensitivity of economic results to varying inflation and interest rates can be gauged for different types of lease agreement and cost-recovery methods.
(6) The effects of payments in lieu of taxes or revenue sharing formulae on overall debt coverage and economic feasibility can be evaluated.
(7) Through a variety of economic evaluations, critical input information can be provided for the basic decision on resource recovery plant technology—mass burning, total RDF or RDF plus on-site process generation.

13.7 Appraisal of the Simulation Approach

When there are a number of variables that can significantly affect the financial results, it is unrealistic and incomplete to analyse results based on a single projection of most likely results. If there are eight important variables, each with three possible values, there are over 6000 (3^8 = 6561) possible outcomes. It does not seem reasonable to base all of one's planning on one possible outcome, any more than one would bet on the assumption that seven will come up on a roll of two dice. The fact that this is the most likely outcome should not be the end of the analysis, but the beginning. How likely is it? What are the other possible outcomes? What are their financial implications and how likely are they? Just as it is necessary to consider all possible outcomes in betting situations to determine if a wager is fair or favourable, the range of possible financial results and their likelihoods should be evaluated to determine whether an investment provides a fair or favourable return. It is important to be aware of the possible outcomes, understand how they can arise, and develop plans to cope with both favourable and unfavourable contingencies. If necessary, one may restructure the project or investment or devise means to identify undesirable conditions and cut possible losses by taking action. In the analysis of projected financial results for the industrial park, it became clear, for example, that low tipping fees led to very poor financial results. Therefore, a minimal level of tipping fee was necessary to ensure a financially viable project.

The use of computer simulation made it possible to evaluate a large number of possible future situations and to analyse their expected results in terms of discounted cash flow and rate of return on investment. By incorporating the known relationships in a computer program, calculations that would be impractical to carry out manually are produced at great speed and with accuracy. It provides a means for easily determining the sensitivity of results to changes in each of the variables. Furthermore, results are automatically summarized and presented in a form designed for the management user.

In the resource recovery application, the use of the computer provided flexibility in selecting assumptions about both management decisions and outside factors. The complete financial analysis was redone automatically and quickly for any combination of decisions and variables specified. Thus, the use of the model facilitates the handling of a complete set of analyses rather than the few limited cases that could be processed manually.

The benefits of modelling and simulation of financial results are by no means limited to the particular objectives, measures and projects that were discussed here. The industrial development project methodology is a straightforward application of a widely used approach. It is essentially the application of Monte Carlo simulation and expected values to discounted cash flow and rate of return analysis. The heart of the model was based on the conventional relationships used to estimate cash flow. The method is potentially applicable to any project or investment involving uncertainties that can significantly affect financial results. In addition to providing information on possible outcomes at the time investments are made, simulation can be used to re-evaluate investments when expectations change.

The resource recovery application was less conventional in its use of a deterministic model. This type of model was more appropriate because the emphasis was on decisions, i.e. choices, rather than uncontrollable variations. Balances and trade-offs involved in key plant design choices were evaluated in a trial-and-error process that also allowed for variations in about two hundred other variables affecting the outcome. Unlike the industrial park application in which many of the basic formulae and relationships were known at the outset from the previous 'most likely' financial projection, the resource recovery model required learning and research on the technologies involved and the development of both engineering and economic models to estimate results. This required a larger study team, incorporating members from the Engineering and Risk Management units. It also required a literature search and a series of visits to operating resource recovery facilities and meetings with equipment manufacturers to obtain the necessary information to develop the model. Similarly, the validation of this model required more reviews to ensure that all aspects of this new endeavour were modelled accurately.

The use of simulation models for complex, but deterministic, operational or financial analyses is often overlooked because the Monte Carlo capability is so well known and easily implemented. It is often desirable, however, to avoid the random variations in results that accompany a Monte Carlo simulation. In an operational simulation of the World Trade Center elevator system, for example, the Monte Carlo demand generation program was run separately from the deterministic model that simulated elevator movements and evaluated system performance (waiting times by floor and direction) (Browne and Kelly, 1968). Thus, any changes in results were attributable directly to differences in the elevator control system logic or in the floor assignments. A deterministic simulation often provides the only practical way to model a complex operation accurately and obtain comparative estimates of service levels based on given assumptions on design and staffing. The deterministic approach shows directly the effects of decisions without the confounding effects of other variables. Of course, any deterministic simulation can be converted to a Monte Carlo one by 'feeding' it input through a random-number generator to provide probabilistic analyses if this is desired.

In general, either type of simulation enables one to analyse a complex situation without making the simplifying assumptions often required in an analytical model. In simulation, the model is specially designed to correspond to the nature of the situation and the specific needs of the decision maker.

Simulation provides much greater flexibility to the model builder, calculation costs are continually decreasing as computers become faster, and the methodology is both easier to understand and better suited to meet any specific information requirements of the manager. For these reasons, analytical models, valuable as they may be for obtaining approximate solutions and as aids in conceptualizing certain problems, will be used less as time goes on. The methods and ways of thinking of pre-computer (the P.C. era) days will gradually be replaced by simulation, a methodology that takes advantage of the new computer capabilities that are now available.

Simulation provides a powerful new way of dealing with the world, analysing quantitative relationships and obtaining information on which to base decisions.

This contrasts with many analytical models which require one to compromise on assumptions to fit the problem to a pre-conceived model for which a solution method is readily available.

13.8 Conclusions

The main benefits of the models consist of an increased capability for more complete analysis and the availability of specific information on the sensitivity of results to key decisions and variables.

These financial simulation models represent the first attempts in the Port Authority to make explicit (i.e. quantify) the risk associated with a major capital investment proposal. The essential difference between the simulation method and the Port Authority's conventional approach to financial analysis is the fact that with the former, many combinations of values of the key variables are evaluated to determine the full range of possible outcomes. For project analyses like the one described, in which no single measure of return is typical or fully indicative of the total project's future prospects, and in which there are many uncertain elements, the simulation approach is superior to the conventional method. In addition to providing the decision-maker with important information on the risks and potential returns of a specific project, it also generates insight that is valuable in determining appropriate courses of action for the implementation phase of the project. This is made possible by the sensitivity analysis and evaluation of alternative scenarios to determine the combinations of conditions most favourable to the project's outcome.

The application of financial simulation methodology was widely accepted by both planners and decision-makers, who continue to use the approach for other proposed projects. It is not practical to estimate the monetary values of benefits derived from the models since they were used as part of the planning process and there is no way to accurately evaluate the alternative decisions and results that might have occurred if they had not been used. It is clear, however, that these studies have fostered a significant change in the way the Port Authority views and evaluates projects. Both the Finance Department and the new Office of Strategic Planning now plan to use risk and sensitivity analysis to evaluate the economics of individual project proposals and the methodology is presently being applied to evaluating a department's long-range (ten-year) forecast.

References and Bibliography

Baumol, W. J. (1972). *Economic Theory and Operations Analysis*, Prentice-Hall, Englewood Cliffs, New Jersey.

Bressman, L. H., Browne, J. J., Nanninga, C. L., and Weintrob, B. (1978). 'Financial Simulation Model: Assessing Project Risk at the Port Authority', *Proceedings of 1978 Winter Simulation Conference*, Miami, December 1978.

Bressman, L. H., Browne, J. J., and Drobny, J. (1980). 'A financial simulation model for a resource recovery plant' paper presented at Joint National Meeting of the Institute of Management Science & Operations Research Society of America, Washington, D.C., May 1980.

Browne, J. J. (1966). 'Simulation of public transportation operations' *Proceedings of First Annual Conference on Simulation in Business and Public Health,* New York, March 1966.

Browne, J. J. and Kelly, J. (1968). 'Simulation of elevator system for the world's tallest buildings', *Transportation Science,* February.

Browne, J. J., Lui, R., and Nanda, R. (1972) 'Simulation of passenger arrivals at airports', *Industrial Engineering,* March.

DeGarmo, E. P., and Canada, J. R. (1973). *Engineering Economy,* Macmillan, New York.

Helfert, E. A. (1972). *Techniques of Financial Analysis,* Richard D. Irwin, Homewood, Illinois.

Hertz, D. B. (1964). 'Risk analysis in capital investment', *Harvard Business Review,* **42**(1), 95–116.

Hertz, D. B. (1968). 'Investment policies that pay off', *Harvard Business Review,* **46**(1), 96–108.

Newendorp, P. D. (1975). *Decision Analysis for Petroleum Exploration,* Petroleum Publishing, Tulsa, Oklahoma.

Van Horne, J. C. (1974). *Financial Management and Policy,* Prentice-Hall, Englewood Cliffs, New Jersey.

Van Horne, J. C. (1977). *Fundamentals of Financial Management,* Prentice-Hall, Englewood Cliffs, New Jersey.

Financial Modelling in Corporate Management
Edited by J. W. Bryant
© 1982 John Wiley & Sons Ltd.

14

Blue Circle's Investment-Planning Models

JOHN DOLBEAR

14.1 Introduction

Blue Circle Industries Ltd is a British company which has developed into one of the largest manufacturers of cement in the world. It is organized into four operating groups together with a small corporate staff providing services to them. The historical genesis of the company is represented by Blue Circle Cement which operates 16 cement works in the U.K. Blue Circle Enterprises represents the group's diversification mainly into the related fields of Building Materials Supply and Merchanting. Blue Circle Overseas (BCO) is a holding company for the group interests in foreign cement works and building material suppliers. Lastly, Blue Circle Technical provides Engineering, Chemical and Geological expertise to the rest of the group and on a consultancy basis to outside companies, besides carrying out basic research and new product developments.

This chapter will attempt to describe only one of the financial modelling activities currently being carried out within the group: one in which the author has been most closely involved.

The Overseas operating group has interests in Asia, Africa, America and Australasia. Typically the investment in these overseas companies is in the range of 30–60% of their ordinary share capital. In addition to this capital, investment is also made in terms of management and technical experience. The group, however, rarely owns 100% of an overseas company, unlike the classic American Multi-national Corporation.

Cement is such a basic material in any developing economy that it is one of the first industries that any Government attempts to establish. Since it is such a low-value, heavy-weight product, the relatively high distribution costs favour production near the potential market. The capital-intensive nature of the processes by which cement is manufactured, however, necessitates careful evaluation of both the raw material and market potential. Whereas there may be many potential sources of capital (e.g. private individuals, government agencies, commercial banks and international development banks), there are few organizations to rival Blue Circle's access to both capital and technical and management expertise. The management of BCO is thus frequently faced with the need to evaluate various investment proposals, both for entirely new cement companies, as well as for expansion proposals from companies in which it already holds a stake.

Faced with this challenge (and problem), what has emerged is a family of long-term financial models, each describing one of the actual or potential manufacturing companies. The family resemblance between the models is great, since they all describe roughly similar manufacturing processes, while at the same time differences in taxation and financing reflect the individuality of each company. The models have helped in the choice between alternative proposals for each project, and whether or not this best proposal should be proceeded with. In those cases where the decision has been made to proceed, the models have been updated with subsequent actual data on costs incurred and the latest estimates of future costs and prices, etc. This is especially critical during the early construction phase of the project, when cost escalation or construction delays might necessitate renegotiation of the financing package.

14.2 Model Development

The question of how the models developed from one another can be tackled in two ways. Firstly, as a straightforward historical account of which model was built first, and second, and so on up to the present time. The alternative approach is, with the benefit of hindsight, to try and link the models together by their logical developmental relationship. We shall begin with the historical approach and then switch to the logical approach in order to avoid repetition and to provide insight into the structural relationship within the family of models.

The first model which was developed for BCO was of an existing company which was proposing to build an additional cement works. Thus although the profitability of the venture had to be judged on the incremental effects alone, the viability of the financial arrangements depended crucially on the cash flow that would be generated by the existing business, so this too had to be modelled. A whole series of runs was performed to assess the effects of alternative plant sizes, phasing of the project, uncertainty regarding the capital costs and uncertainty regarding the sales volume and price.

A rather similar model was then developed for a company proposing to expand one of its existing works. Although this problem was conceptually similar to the previous one, quite a lot of programming modifications were required in order to accommodate the rather different taxation rules and accounting practices.

The next problem tackled was the setting up of an entirely new company, which would build a new cement works on a green-field site. In many ways this represents a rather easier problem to analyse than the previous ones, in that the effects of the 'no go' decision are clearly defined. Closely allied to this problem was that of looking at the acquisition or partial acquisition of an existing cement company, where the investment involved was not only the initial purchase price but also the subsequent pumping in of new capital.

Logically then, we can regard the models as being divided into three levels of complexity. The simplest models represent new companies and acquisitions of existing companies. A second level of complexity involves the expansion of an existing works or the addition of new works. The third level of difficulty (which we have not previously mentioned) concerns the replacement of existing facilities. This last may either represent the replacement of old plant at a works by more modern equipment, a change of process or even the replacement of a whole works by a more favourably situated modern works. The additional difficulty is caused by the treatment of the written-off assets and any scrap value arising, as well as the conceptual problem of determining what were the incremental effects of the project.

Although, so far, we have been talking in terms of financial models of cement works, we also developed the model slightly to cover plants producing other building materials and companies providing technical services.

Another aspect, which did not affect the model as such, but did affect the analysis of the results, was the relationship between the company modelled and the Blue Circle Group. Most of the companies modelled were actual or potential members of the group. In some cases the analysis was carried out on behalf of BCO on a fee-paying basis; in other cases the costs were born by the parent company. We have also had experience of carrying out financial modelling work on a consultancy contract for independent companies not connected with the Blue Circle Group.

14.3 Model Structure

Development Philosophy

The models evolved from one another historically as just described, so it was natural to develop the initial computer program in a similar way by the addition of options to handle the successive enhancements, each controlled by parameters set in the data file. When an old model was required to be rerun, the practice was adopted of updating its data file to conform with the latest version of the program. Then this run was repeated to ensure that no errors had been introduced by the latest programming changes. When this run had been verified, the actual model changes were coded and the new model run. This verification of each model was performed in addition to running each new version of the program with a test pack consisting of three diverse models. The test-pack models were changed with each development, so that at least one of the test models tested out the new facilities. The advantage of revising each model in this way was that only a single version of the program, test models and documentation had to be maintained in terms of computer disc files, tape back-ups, printed listings and typed manuals. This approach minimized the use of file storage space on the computer and eliminated the danger of running the right data with the wrong program.

Computer Language

The model was programmed in FORTRAN IV as this was the most suitable language available at that time on the company's IBM computer. Both time and cost militated against looking for alternative languages. The great advantage of FORTRAN is its universality, thus making the models written in it easily transferred to other machines. It is widely used by Operational Research personnel so it is relatively easy to support and it is very efficient in terms of machine usage once a program has been compiled and loaded.

Its disadvantages are that it is essentially a batch-oriented language and this reduces the rate at which changes can be implemented. However, given the necessity to check quite extensive models when changes had been implemented, the batch processing of them was not too serious a problem. The extensive reports were printed very rapidly on a line printer and these could then be compared with previous runs.

Model Outline

It is customary to set out financial statements with the various accounting items (e.g. cost or revenue) beneath each other down the page (i.e. each accounting item is represented by a row) and each accounting period (e.g. a year or month) is represented by a column representing the values of these items during that period. In calculating this basic matrix of information there are two alternative methods of proceeding: we can either perform all the calculations for a given period first before proceeding to the next period (calculation by column), or we can perform all the calculations for a given accounting item (e.g. capital expenditure) for all of the periods under consideration before proceeding to the next item (e.g. depreciation). Most financial planning packages operate on the latter (row) method by default, but with facilities built in so that, where necessary, one can specify that a subset of the rows is to be calculated period by period. Our model, however, was calculated period by period (the column method) in its entirety.

Referring to the simplified flowchart of the model in Figure 14.1 we see that starting with the opening balance sheet figures, we use forecasts of costs, capital expenditure, sales and other variables to build up the profit and loss account of the company in its first year of modelled operation. A lagging structure is then applied to such items as dividends, taxation, creditors and debtors to arrive at the cash-flow statement of the company for its first year. Then, using the opening

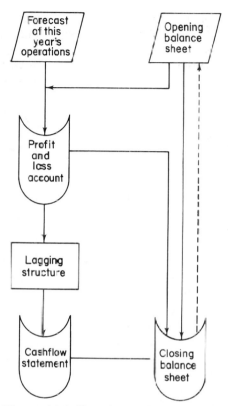

Figure 14.1 Flowchart of calculations performed each period

balance sheet together with the profit and loss account and cash-flow statement, we can calculate the closing balance sheet for the company at the end of its first year. Our closing balance sheet for year 1, of course, becomes our opening balance sheet for the second year. The calculation subroutine can then be called again to obtain all the second-year results. And so the model proceeds from year to year until our specified horizon is reached. Then the various reports which have been requested can be printed out from the results which have been stored each year. Where the horizon specified is sufficiently far ahead for the number of columns not to fit on a sheet of computer printout, the program automatically splits the report so that the later years are shown separately with the appropriate titles, headings and item descriptions repeated.

Both the row and column methods of processing have their advantages. Some calculations are essentially more easily performed by the row method (e.g. straight-line depreciation and write-offs) while others are more easily performed by the column method (e.g. allocating intangible assets to various fixed-asset categories for the purposes of depreciation). The column method, modelling as it does the passage of time, is a more natural method in that it reflects the calculations that would be performed each period if the actual figures turned out to be identical to the estimated figures used in the model. Another advantage of the column method when used with, say, monthly models over 5 years, is that it can be programmed to use much less main computer memory. Each year's data can be read in from backing files, the calculations performed, reports printed and then only the closing balance sheet figures retained before reading in the next year's data and repeating the cycle.

Subroutine Structure

The FORTRAN program consists of a main program which reads in certain control data and then calls the other subroutines as necessary to carry out the particular options specified in this control data. These subroutines are as follows:

INPUT reads in the forecasts for certain items, plus information from which other forecast items can be calculated.
INPRINT prints selected items of the input data.
CALC is the major subroutine which calculates the model for a particular period.

Most of the remaining subrountines define a particular optional report. They all call subroutine HEAD which prints the necessary headings at the top of the page.

CSHFL prints the cash-flow statement which is probably the single most important report.
SHEET prints the balance sheet report.
PROFIT prints the profit and loss account.
NOTES prints some notes to the accounts which elaborate some of the items which have been reported in the balance sheet and profit and loss account.
ALLOW prints details of the tax allowance calculations to enable the modeller to check that these are being performed correctly.
DEPREC prints details of the depreciation calculations for each of the asset categories.
CHARGE prints details of the financial charges incurred on the various debenture and loan stocks.
RATIO calculates and prints the various common financial ratios.
DCF eliminates the financing for the company, calls CALC to recalculate the model, and then calls IRR.
IRR calculates and prints the internal rate of return of the net cash-flow of the company.
BCKDCF iterates backwards to find what percentage change in the contribution is required to achieve a specified target internal rate of return. Each iteration calls DCF in order to calculate the model and the internal rate of return. In

practice somewhere between three and ten iterations were found to be necessary to obtain the desired target internal rate of return to within a tolerance of 0.1%.

Output Reports

The reports produced by the model may be divided into two categories: those whose use was limited to testing the model and data, and those which were used by management to evaluate whether the specified scheme represented a sufficiently profitable and viable investment proposal.

Dealing first with the debugging and validation reports, since a large amount of data had first to be assembled on paper and then typed into the computer, there was obviously scope for straightforward data errors. Some tests were performed on the input data to check for self consistency. Some data were printed out to allow a visual check and some totals printed could be checked against manually calculated totals. Far more important, however, was to ensure that the calculations were being performed correctly and that, as new facilities were added, the original facilities were still working correctly. The most complex calculations concerned:

(1) the financial depreciation for the various fixed asset categories;
(2) the tax allowances (or fiscal depreciation) for the various fixed asset categories;
(3) the draw down, repayment and interest charges of the various categories of loans and debentures.

Each of these topics was therefore the subject of a separate report which enabled the validity of the model logic to be checked by the model builders. These three reports also enabled the validity of the models to be demonstrated to various accountants from external organizations, who came into contact with them from time to time. A fourth report, The Notes to the Balance Sheet, elaborated some of the figures on the balance sheet and demonstrated how items from the profit and loss account had modified the previous year's balance sheet figure to arrive at the present year's balance sheet figure.

Turning now to the reports which were of ultimate use to the financial management of these various projects, the single most important report was probably the cash-flow forecast. This illustrates the build-up of the net cash flow from its various sources and applications and finally arrives at the cash balance of the company at the end of each year. Probably the next most important report is the profit and loss account. This illustrates the contribution that can be expected from the various activities of the company and how this figure is diminished by various fixed costs, taxes and dividends to leave the retained profit in the bottom line. The balance sheet illustrates the position of the company at the end of each year. It is probably of more use to financial managers in the form of the financial ratios. Here, various balance sheet figures are expressed as percentages of each other and various profit and loss items are also expressed as percentages of balance sheet items. The financial

SAMPLE MODEL. NEW KILN STUDY

CASHFLOW STATEMENT

DURING YEAR	1981 (£'000)	1982 (£'000)	1983 (£'000)	1984 (£'000)	1985 (£'000)	1986 (£'000)	1987 (£'000)	1988 (£'000)	1989 (£'000)
TRADING PROFIT	7021	21284	23457	34008	34547	34066	34587	34439	34290
INVESTMENT INCOME	1309	1300	1300	1300	1300	1300	1300	1300	1300
DEPRECIATION	4394	10598	13050	15085	14546	15027	14506	14654	14803
FINANCE CHARGES	0	9954	7496	6098	4908	3766	2587	1535	1154
	------	------	------	------	------	------	------	------	------
	12724	23228	30311	44295	45485	46627	47806	48858	49239
TAXATION	4511	0	0	0	12138	14461	15282	16085	16797
DIVIDEND	1940	2160	2970	2970	2970	2970	2970	2970	2970
	------	------	------	------	------	------	------	------	------
GROSS CASHFLOW	6273	21068	27341	41325	30377	29196	29554	29803	29472
	------	------	------	------	------	------	------	------	------
NEW EQUITY CAPITAL	0	5000	5500	0	0	0	0	0	0
INCREASE IN SHARE PREMIUM	0	0	-5500	0	0	0	0	0	0
NEW PREFERENCE CAPITAL	0	0	-5500	0	0	0	0	0	0
ACQUIRE 1 ST. DEBENTURES	0	10000	0	0	0	0	0	0	0
REDEEM 1 ST. DEBENTURES	0	0	2150	2150	3150	3150	3150	3150	3150
ACQUIRE ACC INT ON 1ST DBNT	1405	1755	600	600	0	0	0	0	0
REDEEM ACC INT ON 1ST DBNT	0	0	491	491	646	646	646	646	646

ACQUIRE DEBENTURE	8000	0	0	0	0	0	0	0	0
REDEEM DEBENTURE	0	0	0	1500	0	0	500	500	500
ACQUIRE VARIOUS BANK LOANS	0	43100	0	0	0	0	0	0	0
REDEEM VARIOUS BANK LOANS	43100	0	0	13420	7420	7420	7420	7420	0
ACQUIRE SUPPLIER CREDIT	6782	0	0	0	0	0	0	0	0
REDEEM SUPPLIER CREDIT	0	0	3183	3183	3183	3183	3183	0	0
ACQUIRE BUYER CREDIT	0	0	0	0	0	0	0	0	0
REDEEM BUYER CREDIT	10000	0	0	2000	2000	2000	2000	2000	0
TOTAL INCREASE OF CAPITAL	16187	69855	-10724	-22144	-16399	-16399	-16899	-13716	-4296
BUILDINGS AT NEW WORKS	1253	6052	3009	303	0	0	0	0	0
PLANT AT EXISTING WORKS	4347	3000	3000	4000	4000	4000	4000	4000	4000
PLANT AT NEW WORKS	48108	23294	12370	7075	3500	3500	3500	3500	3500
PREPROD FIN CHARGES	3768	0	0	-3768	0	0	0	0	0
COMMITMENT FEES	55	55	0	-110	0	0	0	0	0
WORKING CAPITAL NET INCREASE	2646	5000	1455	1772	0	0	2000	0	0
INCREASE IN TRADE INVESTMENT	477	-500	-500	0	0	0	0	0	0
NET CASHFLOW	-38194	54014	-2717	9909	6478	5297	3155	8587	17676
OPENING BALANCE	-13404	-51598	2416	-301	9608	16086	21383	24538	33125
CLOSING BALANCE	-51598	2416	-301	9608	16086	21383	24538	33125	50801

AT END OF YEAR	1980 (£'000)	1981 (£'000)	1982 (£'000)	1983 (£'000)	1984 (£'000)	1985 (£'000)	1986 (£'000)	1987 (£'000)	1988 (£'000)	1989 (£'000)
ORDINARY CAPITAL	25000	25000	30000	35500	35500	35500	35500	35500	35500	35500
RESERVES	19759	25929	35589	44380	58482	71990	85338	99583	114020	128305
PREFERENCE CAPITAL	5500	5500	5500	0	0	0	0	0	0	0
TOTAL SHAREHOLDERS CAPITAL	50259	56429	71089	79880	93982	107490	120838	135083	149520	163805
DEBENTURES & LOANS	32733	48920	107951	85807	70008	53609	36710	22994	18698	9902
	82992	105349	179040	165687	163990	161099	157548	158077	168218	173707

CURRENT ASSETS										
STOCKS	12335	15500	15500	15500	16000	16000	16000	16000	16000	16000
DEBTORS	2969	3500	3500	3500	4000	4000	4000	6000	6000	6000
CASH	1174	0	2416	0	9608	16086	21383	24538	33125	50801
	------	------	------	------	------	------	------	------	------	------
CURRENT LIABILITIES	16478	19000	21416	19000	29608	36086	41383	46538	55125	72801
CREDITORS	10547	11597	6589	5134	4362	4362	4362	4362	4362	4362
BANK OVERDRAFT	14578	51598	0	301	0	0	0	0	0	0
LOAN REPAYMENTS	0	0	5824	22744	16399	16399	16899	13716	4296	8796
TAXATION	4511	0	0	0	12138	14461	15282	16085	16797	17181
DIVIDEND	1940	2160	2970	2970	2970	2970	2970	2970	2970	2970
	------	------	------	------	------	------	------	------	------	------
	31576	65355	15383	31149	35869	38192	39513	37133	28425	33309
WORKING CAPITAL	-15098	-46355	6033	-12149	-6261	-2106	1870	9405	26700	39492
WORK IN PROGRESS	47421	96782	30534	41776	0	0	0	0	0	0
FIXED ASSETS	49546	49499	137493	131582	169651	162605	155078	148072	140918	133615
PREPROD FIN CHARGES	0	3768	3768	3768	0	0	0	0	0	0
COMMITMENT FEES	0	55	110	110	0	0	0	0	0	0
TRADE INVESTMENTS	1123	1600	1100	600	600	600	600	600	600	600
	------	------	------	------	------	------	------	------	------	------
	82992	105349	179040	165687	163990	161099	157548	158077	168218	173707

FOR YEAR	1981 (£'000)	1982 (£'000)	1983 (£'000)	1984 (£'000)	1985 (£'000)	1986 (£'000)	1987 (£'000)	1988 (£'000)	1989 (£'000)
NEW WORKS									
SALES VOLUME ('000 TONNES)	93	575	700	1050	1050	1050	1050	1050	1050
TURNOVER	3820	28750	35000	52500	52500	52500	52500	52500	52500
VARIABLE COSTS	1209	7475	9100	13650	13650	13650	13650	13650	13650
FIXED COSTS EX. DEPRECIATION	817	5151	5151	5400	5400	5400	5400	5400	5400
EXCESS OF INCOME OVER EXPEND	1794	16124	20749	33450	33450	33450	33450	33450	33450
OLD WORKS									
SALES VOLUME ('000 TONNES)	740	750	750	750	750	750	750	750	750
TURNOVER	30592	37500	37500	37500	37500	37500	37500	37500	37500
VARIABLE COSTS	8880	9000	9000	9000	9000	9000	9000	9000	9000
FIXED COSTS EX. DEPRECIATION	10157	10157	10157	10157	10157	10157	10157	10157	10157
EXCESS OF INCOME OVER EXPEND	11555	18343	18343	18343	18343	18343	18343	18343	18343

COMPANY TOTAL

SALES VOLUME ('000 TONNES)	833	1325	1450	1800	1800	1800	1800	1800	1800
TURNOVER	34412	66250	72500	90000	90000	90000	90000	90000	90000
VARIABLE COSTS	10089	16475	18100	22650	22650	22650	22650	22650	22650
FIXED COSTS EX. DEPRECIATION	10974	15308	15308	15557	15557	15557	15557	15557	15557
HEAD OFFICE FIXED COSTS	1934	2585	2585	2700	2700	2700	2700	2700	2700
EXCESS OF INCOME OVER EXPEND	11415	31882	36507	49093	49093	49093	49093	49093	49093
DEPRECIATION	4394	10598	13050	15085	14546	15027	14506	14654	14803
INVESTMENT INCOME	1309	1300	1300	1300	1300	1300	1300	1300	1300
FINANCE CHARGES	0	9954	7496	6098	4908	3766	2587	1535	1154
EARNINGS BEFORE TAX	8330	12630	17261	29210	30939	31600	33300	34204	34436
TAXATION	0	0	0	12138	14461	15282	16085	16797	17181
PROFIT AFTER TAX	8330	12630	17261	17072	16478	16318	17215	17407	17255
PREFERENCE DIVIDEND	660	907	0	0	0	0	0	0	0
ORDINARY DIVIDEND	1500	2063	2970	2970	2970	2970	2970	2970	2970
RETAINED PROFITS	6170	9660	8791	14102	13508	13348	14245	14437	14285

AT END OF YEAR	1981 (£'000)	1982 (£'000)	1983 (£'000)	1984 (£'000)	1985 (£'000)	1986 (£'000)	1987 (£'000)	1988 (£'000)	1989 (£'000)
INVESTMENT INCOME:									
OTHER INVESTMENTS	1309	1300	1300	1300	1300	1300	1300	1300	1300
	------	------	------	------	------	------	------	------	------
	1309	1300	1300	1300	1300	1300	1300	1300	1300
	------	------	------	------	------	------	------	------	------
RESERVES:									
BALANCE BROUGHT FORWARD	19759	25929	35589	44380	58482	71990	85338	99583	114020
RETAINED EARNINGS	6170	9660	8791	14102	13508	13348	14245	14437	14285
INCREASE IN SHARE PREMIUM	0	0	-5500	0	0	0	0	0	0
INCR. IN CAPITAL REDMPT RESV	0	0	5500	0	0	0	0	0	0
	------	------	------	------	------	------	------	------	------
	25929	35589	44380	58482	71990	85338	99583	114020	128305

FIXED ASSETS:

GROSS BOOK VALUE B/F	98399	152107	184453	202832	214210	221710	229210	236710	244210
CAPITAL EXPENDITURE	53708	32346	18379	11378	7500	7500	7500	7500	7500
GROSS BOOK VALUE C/F	152107	184453	202832	214210	221710	229210	236710	244210	251710
CUMULATIVE DEPRECIATION	5826	16424	29474	44559	59105	74132	88638	103292	118095
NET BOOK VALUE	49499	137493	131582	169651	162605	155078	148072	140918	133615
ASSETS FULLY DEPRECIATED	0	0	0	2000	8579	11579	17597	21597	25597

TAXATION:

EARNINGS BEFORE TAX	8330	12630	17261	29210	30939	31600	33300	34204	34436
DEPRECIATION	4394	10598	13050	15085	14546	15027	14506	14654	14803
ALLOWANCES FOR THIS PERIOD	12724	23228	30311	44295	45485	46627	47806	48858	49239
ALLOWANCES B/F	32145	19620	16895	14922	13346	12664	12058	11528	11057
ALLOWANCES C/F	0	19421	15813	2397	0	0	0	0	0
TAXABLE EARNINGS	0	0	0	26976	32139	33963	35748	37330	30102
TAX AT 40.0%	0	0	0	2	2	2	2	2	2
TAX AT 45.0%	0	0	0	12136	14459	15280	16083	16795	17179
	0	0	0	12138	14461	15282	16085	16797	17181

```
ST1B0007              C O R P O R A T E   F I N A N C I A L    M O D E L

14/ 4/80              SAMPLE MODEL. NEW KILN STUDY

                       15.0% + 10.0%   NEW WORKS PLANT

         1981       1982       1983       1984       1985      TOTAL       1981

            0          0          0          0          0          0          0

         1689                                                               534
            0                                                                 0
          169                                                    169         53
       ----------                                                         ---------
         1520                                                               481

                    1520
                       0
                     152                                         152
                  ----------
                    1368

                               1368
                                  0
                                137                              137
                            ----------
                               1231

                                          1231
                                             0
                                           123                  123
                                       ----------
                                          1108

                                                     1108
                                                        0
                                                      111        111
                                                  ----------
                                                     997
```

J.DOLBEAR, OR GROUP, BLUE CIRCLE IND

ALLOWANCE DETAILS

15.0% + 10.0%   NEW WORKS MOBILE

1982	1983	1984	1985	TOTAL	TOTAL
0	0	0	0	0	0
				53	222
481					
0					
48				48	200

433					
	433				
	0				
	43			43	180

	390				
		390			
		0			
		39		39	162

		351			
			351		
			0		
			35	35	146

			316		

YEAR	1981 (£'000)	1982 (£'000)	1983 (£'000)	1984 (£'000)	1985 (£'000)	1986 (£'000)	1987 (£'000)	1988 (£'000)	1989 (£'000)
0.0 % PREPROD FIN CHARGES									
EXPENDITURE	3768	0	0	-3768	0	0	0	0	0
GROSS BOOK VALUE	3768	3768	3768	0	0	0	0	0	0
DEPRECIATION	0	0	0	0	0	0	0	0	0
0.0 % COMMITMENT FEES									
EXPENDITURE	55	55	0	-110	0	0	0	0	0
GROSS BOOK VALUE	55	110	110	0	0	0	0	0	0
DEPRECIATION	0	0	0	0	0	0	0	0	0
TOTAL INTANGIBLE ASSETS									
EXPENDITURE	3823	55	0	-3878	0	0	0	0	0
GROSS BOOK VALUE	3823	3878	3878	0	0	0	0	0	0
DEPRECIATION	0	0	0	0	0	0	0	0	0
3.300 % 3 RD KILN BUILDINGS									
EXPENDITURE	1253	6052	3009	303	0	0	0	0	0
GROSS BOOK VALUE	1253	7305	10314	10617	10617	10617	10617	10617	10617
DEPRECIATION	0	0	0	350	350	350	350	350	350
5.000 % 3 RD KILN PLANT									
EXPENDITURE	3761	18155	9028	1074	200	200	200	200	200
GROSS BOOK VALUE	3761	21916	30944	32018	32218	32418	32618	32818	33018
DEPRECIATION	0	0	1339	1434	1611	1621	1631	1641	1651

	1	2	3	4	5	6	7	8	9
33.300 % EXTRA MOBILE									
EXPENDITURE	226	1089	542	569	500	500	500	500	500
GROSS BOOK VALUE	226	1315	1857	2426	2926	3426	3926	4426	4926
DEPRECIATION	0	0	0	808	974	1141	502	500	500
3.300 % NEW WORKS BUILDINGS									
EXPENDITURE	16642	2750	1500	2533	1500	1500	1500	1500	1500
GROSS BOOK VALUE	31817	34567	36067	38600	40100	41600	43100	44600	46100
DEPRECIATION	0	1141	1190	1274	1323	1373	1422	1472	1521
5.000 % NEW WORKS PLANT									
EXPENDITURE	25607	300	300	1807	300	300	300	300	300
GROSS BOOK VALUE	56146	56446	56746	58553	58853	59153	59453	59753	60053
DEPRECIATION	0	2822	2837	2928	2943	2958	2973	2988	3003
33.300 % NEW WORKS MOBILE									
EXPENDITURE	1872	1000	1000	1092	1000	1000	1000	1000	1000
GROSS BOOK VALUE	3579	4579	5579	6671	7671	8671	9671	10671	11671
DEPRECIATION	0	1525	1858	2221	1034	1031	1000	1000	1000
3.300 % OLD BUILDINGS									
EXPENDITURE	0	0	0	0	0	0	0	0	0
GROSS BOOK VALUE	10771	10771	10771	10771	10771	10771	10771	10771	10771
DEPRECIATION	355	355	355	355	355	355	355	355	355
3.300 % OLD HOUSING									
EXPENDITURE	0	0	0	0	0	0	0	0	0
GROSS BOOK VALUE	4005	4005	4005	4005	4005	4005	4005	4005	4005
DEPRECIATION	132	132	132	132	132	132	132	132	132

YEAR	1981 (£'000)	1982 (£'000)	1983 (£'000)	1984 (£'000)	1985 (£'000)	1986 (£'000)	1987 (£'000)	1988 (£'000)	1989 (£'000)
6.000 % 1 ST. DEBENTURES									
FINANCE CHARGES	1290	1890	1825	1696	1537	1348	1159	970	781
REPAYMENTS MADE	0	0	2150	2150	3150	3150	3150	3150	3150
LOAN OUTSTANDING	21500	31500	29350	27200	24050	20900	17750	14600	11450
0.0 % ACC INT ON 1ST DBNT									
FINANCE CHARGES	0	0	0	0	0	0	0	0	0
REPAYMENTS MADE	0	0	491	491	646	646	646	646	646
LOAN OUTSTANDING	3505	5260	5369	5478	4832	4186	3540	2894	2248
7.500 % DEBENTURE									
FINANCE CHARGES	600	600	600	487	487	487	449	411	373
REPAYMENTS MADE	0	0	0	1500	0	0	500	500	500
LOAN OUTSTANDING	8000	8000	8000	6500	6500	6500	6000	5500	5000

7.250 % VARIOUS BANK LOANS									
FINANCE CHARGES	0	2694	3125	2286	1688	1150	612	74	0
REPAYMENTS MADE	0	0	0	13420	7420	7420	7420	7420	0
LOAN OUTSTANDING	0	43100	43100	29680	22260	14840	7420	0	0
8.000 % SUPPLIER CREDIT									
FINANCE CHARGES	1003	1274	1146	891	636	381	127	0	0
REPAYMENTS MADE	0	0	3183	3183	3183	3183	3183	0	0
LOAN OUTSTANDING	15915	15915	12732	9549	6366	3183	0	0	0
8.000 % BUYER CREDIT									
FINANCE CHARGES	0	400	800	720	560	400	240	80	0
REPAYMENTS MADE	0	0	0	2000	2000	2000	2000	2000	0
LOAN OUTSTANDING	0	10000	10000	8000	6000	4000	2000	0	0
TOTAL									
FINANCE CHARGES	2895	6858	7496	6080	4908	3766	2587	1535	1154
REPAYMENTS MADE	0	0	5824	22744	16399	16399	16899	13716	4296
LOAN OUTSTANDING	48920	113775	108551	86407	70008	53609	36710	22994	18698
OTHER LOAN INTEREST	875	3096	0	10	0	0	0	0	0

ST1B0007 C O R P O R A T E F I N A N C I A L M O D E L J.DOLBEAR, OR GROUP, BLUE CIRCLE IND

14/ 4/80 SAMPLE MODEL. NEW KILN STUDY FINANCIAL INDICES

YEAR	1981 (£'000)	1982 (£'000)	1983 (£'000)	1984 (£'000)	1985 (£'000)	1986 (£'000)	1987 (£'000)	1988 (£'000)	1989 (£'000)
DEBT EQUITY RATIO	87%	152%	107%	74%	50%	30%	17%	13%	6%
CURRENT RATIO	29%	139%	61%	83%	94%	105%	125%	194%	219%
QUICK RATIO	5%	38%	11%	38%	53%	64%	82%	138%	171%
OPERATING PROFIT / TURNOVER	33%	48%	50%	55%	55%	55%	55%	55%	55%
YIELD	2.9%	3.1%	3.7%	3.2%	2.8%	2.5%	2.2%	2.0%	1.8%
RETURN ON SHAREHOLDERS FUNDS	15%	18%	22%	18%	15%	14%	13%	12%	11%
RETURN ON CAPITAL EMPLOYED	6.7%	11.9%	14.2%	20.7%	21.4%	21.6%	21.9%	20.5%	19.7%
DEBT SERVICE RATIO	0.0%	210.3%	125.0%	179.8%	176.6%	176.2%	218.9%	640.1%	346.7%

INTERNAL RATE OF RETURN = 33.80%

INTERNAL RATE OF RETURN OF 20.0 % IS OBTAINED BY MULTIPLYING CONTRIBUTION BY 0.7109

END OF RUN

Figure 14.2 Output reports of Blue Circle model

ratio report also contains the single most important statistic, the internal rate of return of the project. This measures the attractiveness of the project as a whole, independently of how it is financed. (The ordinary shareholders can usually gear up their expected return by replacing some of the equity capital by fixed-interest loans. They pay for this greater expected return, however, by incurring greater risk, as the interest on loans is a fixed cost, whereas the additional equity capital would have shared the risk of having its dividends cut in hard times.)

Model Facilities

In contrast with the majority of models of this type, our emphasis was on fiscal and financial aspects rather than on the operating details. This reflects the areas of greatest uncertainty. While the process and operating details are relatively well defined and consistent from one proposal to another, the fiscal and financial aspects can vary widely from one country to another. Any proposal which had widely different operating details would have probably been ruled out on technical grounds at an earlier stage of the evaluation process. This emphasis on tax and depreciation was reflected in the number of different fixed-asset categories that could be modelled (10) and the number of intangible asset categories (10). Each of these categories could have their own depreciation rate, initial and annual tax allowance rates and method of writing down. In addition, there was provision for various forms of tax holiday, turnover tax and multirate corporation tax. As far as depreciation was concerned, this could be delayed for several years after the capital expenditure had been incurred until the plant actually started production. During this preproduction period, finance charges could be capitalized if required. When production began, preproduction finance charges together with the other intangible assets could begin to be depreciated at the average rate at which the fixed assets were being depreciated or at some specified rate. When production began with the new plant, it was sometimes necessary to scrap old plant, write off some fixed assets, take the final allowance or possibly face a balancing charge. On the other hand, in some cases, facilities were needed to revalue periodically the fixed assets, in order to conform to current cost-accounting practices.

As far as financing the project was concerned, provision was made for ordinary share capital and preference capital which could be drawn down as necessary. Provision was made for a share premium account to accommodate ordinary shares sold at above par and a capital redemption reserve fund, to be set up when preference capital was retired. Up to twelve long-term loans or debentures could be specified, each with their own interest rate and repayment schedule. An annual rate of commitment fees could also be specified to run from any point in time up to the draw-down of the loan. The loans could be acquired or redeemed part way through a year if necessary. Short-term borrowings on overdraft were allowed to cover any cash deficit. Later in the life of the project, when a cash surplus had been achieved, this could be deemed to earn interest at a specified rate. In addition investment income could also be generated from subsidiary companies and trade investments. Provision was made for dividend payments as well as financial charges. Accumulated preference dividends were the first call on after-tax profits and then ordinary dividends. Management and technical fees as well as profit participation by the work force are also catered for in the model.

14.4 Use of the Model

The model has been put to a number of uses over the life of each project. In summary, the initial emphasis during the project appraisal is on profitability, whereas later the emphasis switches to liquidity. Below we describe some of the uses made of the model during the evaluation process. Naturally, no actual project is ever used in all these ways, nor is the sequence of events ever as straightforward. In practice, there are steps backwards to previous stages of the analysis, as new factors come to light, and perhaps, because of lack of time, jumps forward to later stages of analysis.

Profitability

The initial runs of the model are often used to examine the implications of alternative plant sizes, alternative processes or alternative capital expenditure phasing. They have even been used to evaluate alternative locations for a works. At this stage the model is an integral part of the dialogue between the engineers and technical personnel responsible for the technical evaluation and initial plant costings, and the project managers and accountants responsible for the financial evaluation. The single most important figure in choosing between alternative possibilities is the discounted cash flow internal rate of return, but the profit/turnover ratio and return on capital employed are also examined. Other constraints such as the current ratio and quick ratio are relatively easily accommodated by adjusting the debtors, creditors and stocks.

Since relatively few numbers need to be changed to evaluate each alternative, the results can be obtained within a matter of about an hour, and so many more alternatives can now be examined than was possible using manual calculations. The computer model also produces a full evaluation of each alternative, whereas previous manual methods had to concentrate on obtaining only the most critical figures and ratios.

When one or two of the most promising schemes have been identified they may be subjected to sensitivity analysis. This merely means assessing the effects on the schemes of changes in some of the most crucial and uncertain variables—e.g. the volume of sales, the price of fuel, the capital cost of the new plant. In practice, sensitivity analysis is unlikely to differentiate between proposals, but rather give some feeling for the risk inherent in them. Many of the forecast factors are by no means independent, but on the other hand it is very difficult to specify what their relationship is. Therefore, it has not been found possible to perform a comprehensive risk analysis using the model. Rather, the factors are varied independently, although it is known for instance that the sales price of cement is very dependent on its production costs. One method of approach to this problem is to perform a so-called backwards iteration procedure. For any given scenario of, say, pessimistically high capital costs, the model can be set to calculate what the company needs to achieve by way of contribution per unit production volume. Then, assuming a particular production cost, we can calculate the required selling price that would have to be achieved in order to meet the company's target discounted cash flow rate of return. Basically, the program guesses a particular level of contribution and works forward to the internal rate of return that this produces. If this is not within a certain tolerated margin of the required internal rate of return, the program goes backwards and makes another better estimate of the necessary level of contribution. This loop is then repeated until the required internal rate of return has been achieved and the necessary level of contribution has been calculated.

Liquidity

While the engineers and technologists have been refining their plant plans and cost estimates, the accountants and financial managers have been seeking out possible sources of finance. Many diverse institutions and organizations may be involved: banks (both local and international, commercial and intergovernment), governments (national, regional and local, both directly and indirectly via state holding companies and development boards), companies (both local and international) and private individuals (usually local). Additionally, a common source of finance is the manufacturer of the process plant or his government who will usually loan a certain proportion of the capital cost in order to capture the export order. Not only will the sources be diverse, but the legal form of the loan will also be varied—e.g. debenture stocks of various types and seniority, term loans, foreign currency loans, mortgage bonds, etc. Despite these profound differences, the model treats them all identically (although some adjustment in the nominal interest rate may be made outside the model to compensate for currency appreciation of loans denominated in a non-local currency).

When such a financial package is fed into the model, the usual first result is a number of years when there is a surplus of cash and a number of years of deficit. The model is extremely useful at this stage, as very rapidly the acquisition and redemptions of the various loans can be adjusted and the model rerun. After, say, 4 or 5 runs a reasonable package emerges, or at least the shortfall in finance is quantified and banks and other institutions, can be approached with a relatively well-defined requirement. The financial institutions will be interested not only in the timing of the loan repayments and in the net cash flow of the project, but also in such ratios as the debt/equity ratio and the debt/service ratio, as these give them an idea of the level of risk to which their loans are exposed.

Over a period of many months, many financial packages will be modelled as the negotiations with various backers firm up, as the cost estimates are revised, and as interest and currency rates fluctuate. Even when negotiations are concluded and contracts signed, there may still be the need to update and revise the model, as actual capital costs become known and can be substituted for the most likely estimates. Indeed revised estimates of the vital items, such as selling price and production start-up date, may need to be incorporated and the model rerun in order to assess the impact of the latest information.

Many models never reach the stage of being updated as the proposal is rejected and the plant never erected. This in no way means that the modelling effort has been abortive. Indeed it is just as important to highlight projects which are not satisfactory as it is to help in the assessment and planning of ones which are. Of course many other considerations have to be taken into account besides those coped with by the model: considerations of political, economic, and currency instability, considerations of global diversification and competitors' reactions to name but a few. Although they influence variables within the model (such as sales volume), they merit very profound study of themselves.

One of the advantages of using a computerized model is that, when costs are revised and the model needs to be rerun, not only is relatively little effort involved (as few numbers need changing), but also the method of appraisal will be consistent with that previously adopted (possibly many months previously, possibly by a different financial manager). Indeed, not only does the model impose a consistent frame of reference for the same project, but also provides it for different projects, even when the analysis is probably being carried out by different parts of the organization.

Accountancy and Operational Research

The model was initially designed as a co-operative effort between accountants and operational research analysts, the accountants being responsible for the definition of the required output, accounting conventions and methods of calculations, and the operational research analysts being responsible for turning these requirements and rules into a working computer system.

This system was not designed for use by the accountants directly. It was always envisaged that the two professions would work together on any particular project appraisal, with the operational research analyst interpreting the accountant's requirements within the available facilities of the model and, if necessary, extending these to cope with any vital new requirement. This close collaboration had several effects:

(1) It meant that any new model facility could be extremely rapidly incorporated in a working model;

(2) There was little incentive to produce a user-friendly system; rather the data input formats were designed to be used by someone with quite a lot of computer experience (e.g. fixed format fields);

(3) A very efficient system was produced in terms of computer utilization. Little file space was required to store each model. Only a few seconds central processor unit time and a region size of less than 200K bytes was required to run a typical model on an IBM 370/158 at a cost of only a few pounds.

14.5 Conclusions

This family of financial models has reached maturity. Only very minor programming changes have been made over the last couple of years. One possible opportunity for developing the model that has been discussed but not yet implemented lies in extending the model backwards to help in some of the cost estimation that has to be performed to calculate the various capital expenditure amounts. A great deal of effort has to be put into obtaining reasonably accurate estimates and it is felt that automating this could well be cost effective. However, at the moment this possibility is not under active investigation and development resources have been transferred to other financial modelling applications.

This is not to say that the models have stopped being used. Far from it! Besides continuing to update already existing models as cost estimates and situations change, new models of new investment proposals are still being built, but essentially within the existing framework. It has been found that putting together aspects of the already existing models has been sufficient to cover the problems raised by new proposals. No doubt the models are far from perfect, and with extra time, effort and cost they could be improved, but the question that must always be asked is 'Is the extra accuracy worth the extra cost?' Our collective answer has been 'No'. We realize the danger of trying to 'shoehorn' a problem into an already existing model, but equally we realize the danger of suboptimizing by incurring a greater cost in analysis than we can expect to save as a result.

Financial Modelling in Corporate Management
Edited by J. W. Bryant
© 1982 John Wiley & Sons Ltd.

15

Developing Dividend and Financing Policies Using a Computer *

DAVID CHAMBERS

15.1 Introduction

Financial applications in which the computer has so far made the greatest impact have typically been ones where its capacity to store lots of data and its economy in performing routine arithmetic operations have been crucial. This chapter describes work carried out at the London Business School on problems of financial planning, in which the role of the computer was extended from preparation of financial projections to tracing the implications of alternative financing policies and where its crucial advantage lies in the ability to perform not merely arithmetic but also logical operations. Specifically, different financing and dividend policies have been combined in a computer program, together with straightforward routines for making financial projections. The financing policy is expressed in an explicit statement of the conditions under which finance will be raised from different sources; the computer compares values and key ratios generated within the program itself to find which conditions are satisfied. A dividend policy is written similarly as a logical statement of the critical values for particular variables (e.g. earnings, rate of increase in earnings, etc.), critical in the sense that a particular dividend will be paid if the variable falls within a specified range. The computer calculates values of the key variables, identifies the relevant conditions and prints out the stream of projected dividends conforming to the policy.

This approach to strategic planning does not rely on the capacity to store very large quantities of data. It is possible, therefore, to employ a system using a comparatively small and cheap computer, allowing managers to experiment with alternative policies and projections. The advantages of such immediate communication

*Reproduced by permission of the publisher from *Accounting and Business Research*, Autumn 1971, 267–73.

'on-line' with a computer are particularly significant in applications like these to problems of strategic choice, where typically there is no single criterion for ranking outcomes and the reinforcement the manager most needs is some efficient means to explore, alter and compare a wide range of alternatives. With direct access to a computer, it becomes possible to link together the selection of investments, sources of finance and the payment of dividends as one joint problem, and hence to identify interactions between separate elements in the firm's strategic plan which are not apparent when each part is considered in succession.

The approach described below was first developed from inside two small-to-medium sized companies with the cooperation of financial managers. More recently it has been used in reverse, to project company results from the outside under alternative sets of assumptions.

15.2 Policies Identified

Financing Policies

In developing the approach, a number of alternative financing policies were identified with the help of financial managers, and one of these is illustrated in the flow chart of Figure 15.1. This is the policy where managers plan to find any necessary funds in a period first by using any excess cash or short-term investments, then by increasing overdraft, and then if necessary by issuing long-term debt. Calling on the sources of funds in this sequence would be appropriate where, e.g. bank debt is cheaper than long-term debt or where long-term rates are expected to fall.

Within such a policy, there can be many different limits on overdraft. Two limits are used in the examples which follow:

(1) a requirement that current ratio be maintained at not less than a specified value (which places an implied upper limit on the current liability ('bank overdraft');
(2) a simple upper bound, like the 'line of credit' familiar in the U.S.

Long-term debt is allowed to rise only in substantial increments or tranches, and excess funds may be used to reduce long-term debt (again in fixed tranches). Different versions of this policy are stated by specifying values for the required current ratio, the fixed upper limit on overdraft, and the unit size of tranches. The program starts by calculating the net current flow of funds over one period, from all transactions other than financing. The upper limit on permitted bank overdraft is also calculated, from the specified requirement on current ratio. A financial structure for the end of the period is then developed as shown in Figure 15.1. Values of the following parameters are specified by the manager in selecting a particular financing policy:

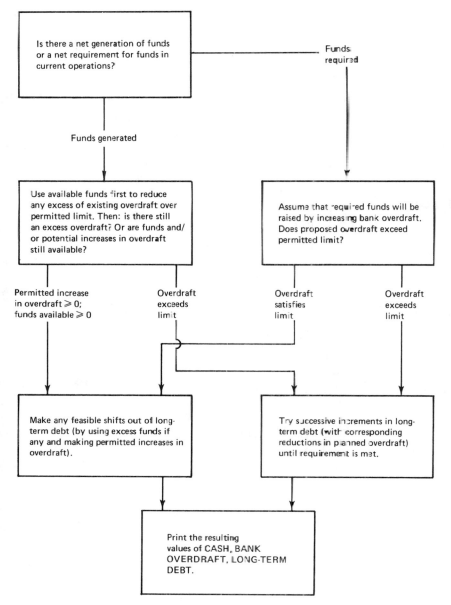

Figure 15.1 Financing policy logic

(1) lower limit on ratio of current assets to current liabilities (as imposed by lending banks);
(2) upper limit on bank overdraft (a separate requirement from (1));
(3) 'policy' limit below which reported cash balances must not fall;

(4) size of the tranche by which (or in multiples of which) long-term debt may be increased;
(5) size of the tranche by which (or in multiples of which) long-term debt may be reduced.

Other financing policies have been analysed in much the same way, but need not be illustrated here: e.g. a policy appropriate to cases where long-term debt is cheaper than money borrowed from the bank, so that funding of debt occurs whenever possible. Further cases have been programmed where successive increments in long-term debt must be separated by a specified interval of time.

Dividend Policies

Two different statements of firms' dividend policy are given below. The form of these statements is fairly typical of those we have encountered, while the numbers used are illustrative.

Dividend policy 1 The target is a cumulative growth of 10% per annum in dividend per share, subject to constraints relating dividend to current earnings, as follows:
—There is a 10% growth in dividend per share if this is consistent with a dividend cover of at least 2. (Dividend cover is here defined as the amount available for distribution to shareholders, divided by the dividend that is actually distributed.) If this dividend cover will not be achieved, dividend is held or cut. It is held at the previous year's value if cover is at least 1. Otherwise dividend is cut by enough to keep cover equal to 1.

Dividend policy 2 The dividend paid in any year is related to the last dividend paid and the earnings in the current year.
—If the last dividend is less than one third of current earnings, then this year's dividend is increased by (say) 10% over the last one.
—If it is more than one third but less than one half of current earnings, then the dividend is maintained.
—If it is more than one half of current earnings, then the latter amount is paid as dividend.

The logic of each of these two policies can be stated (and programmed) very conveniently if three parameters are specified: two critical values for dividend cover, C_H and C_L where the subscripts mean 'high' or 'low', and the target growth rate of dividends, G. The possibilities shown in Figure 15.2. Dividend policy 1 is then expressed by setting C_H, C_L and G at the values (2.0, 1.0, 10%) respectively. For dividend policy 2 the parameters take the values (2.73, 2.0, 10%). Note that policy 2 was expressed in terms of last year's dividend, while the general statement relates earnings to this year's dividend. The condition for dividend increase by 10% under policy 2 can be written as:

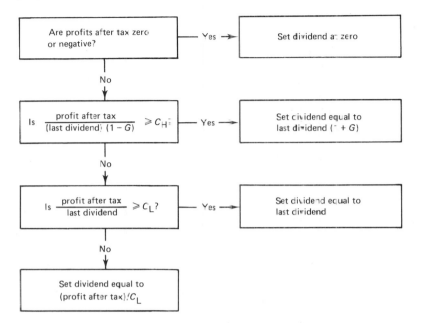

Figure 15.2 Dividend policy logic

$$E_t \geqslant 3D_{t-1}.$$

But if $D_t = 1.1 (D_{t-1})$ this becomes

$$E_t \geqslant 3D_t/1.1 \text{ or } E_t \geqslant 2.73 D_t,$$

where D_t and E_t represent dividend and earnings of year t. The examples therefore illustrate two versions of the same policy, differing only in the values of the three parameters.

Most of the other dividend policies which have been described to us can be represented by increasing the number of critical values for dividend cover beyond the pair used above. Another very simple policy, illustrated in the examples which follow, takes the form: 'Cut dividend to £x and hold it at that rate for y years'.

15.3 Some Numerical Examples

In these examples two dividend policies and two financing policies will be considered, and the financial consequences of adding a significant new project will be projected over three years. The initial balance sheet of Firm X at the end of 1971 is given in Figure 15.3. Financing and dividend policies are as follows:

Financing policy 1: as in Figure 15.1, with current ratio $\geqslant 1.75$.
Financing policy 2: as in Figure 15.1, with current ratio $\geqslant 1.50$.
(In both cases, the fixed upper limit on overdraft is £400 000).

	(£'000)
Assets	
Current assets	
Cash	221
Debtors	878
Stock, work in progress	925
Others	
Total	2024
Less current liabilities	
Creditors	675
Tax payable	70
Bank overdraft	250
Dividend payable	74
Others	
Total	1069
Net current assets	955
Add fixed assets	
Land and buildings	1168
Plant and machinery	188
Others	
Total net assets	2311
Liabilities	
Share capital	937
Reserves	672
Long-term debt	600
Deferred liabilities	102
Total	2311

Figure 15.3 Initial balance sheet of Firm X (31 December 1971)

Dividend policy A: as in Figure 15.2, with $C_H = 3$, $C_L = 2$, $G = 20\%$.
Dividend policy B: 'cut dividend to £50 000 and hold for 3 years'.

Varying Dividend Policy and Financing Policy

Consider first the effects of varying the financing policy while dividend policy (and the use of funds) remains constant. Cases (A) and (B) of Table 15.1 differ in the lower limits imposed on current ratio, and as this limit is raised the firm's freedom to employ increases in bank overdraft as a source of funds is correspondingly curtailed. In case (A) the critical restriction on overdraft consists of the fixed upper bound of £400 000. Case (B) requires a higher current ratio than does (A), and current ratio proves to be the critical restriction on bank overdraft in this case.

Table 15.1 Financial projections under alternative dividend and financing policies

Dividend and financing policies*	(A) Div. policy (1); CR ⩾ 1.50			(B) Div. policy (1); CR ⩾ 1.75			(C) Div. policy (2); CR ⩾ 1.75		
	1972	1973	1974	1972	1973	1974	1972	1973	1974
Financial Projections									
Overdraft limit (£'000)	400	400	400	339	338	338	363	362	362
Actual overdraf (£'000)	377	395	398	327	295	298	327	271	348
Long-term debt (£'000)	700	700	800	700	800	900	700	800	800
Gearing ratio	0.28	0.27	0.28	0.28	0.29	0.31	0.28	0.29	0.28
Current ratio	1.77	1.67	1.67	1.77	1.81	1.81	1.80	1.89	1.77
Dividend payable (£'000)	74	74	74	74	74	74	50	50	50

*Dividend policy (1): as in Figure 15.2 with $G = 0.2$, $C_H = 3$, $C_L = 2$.
Dividend policy (2): 'cut dividend to £50 000 and hold ut at that value'.
CR: Current ratio.

The tighter restriction on overdraft in (B) forces the firm to raise £100 000 in long-term debt in 1973, and gearing rises to 0.31 in 1974 as against the 0.28 of (A).

Next consider an illustration of the effects of varying dividend policy with an unchanged financing policy. The dividend policy of (B) leads in fact in this case to a dividend held at £74 000, since the conditions for an increase at the target rate are not satisfied. In contrast, case (C) requires 1972's dividend to be cut from the previous year's value, to £50 000; and this value is to be maintained for the two years following. This reduction in planned dividend affects the financial projections in two ways. Firstly, the lower dividend means lower current liabilities (specifically a lower 'dividend payable') and this provides room for a bigger overdraft: the limit rises from £338 000 to £362 000. Secondly, the larger retention means that less new debt has to be issued. As a result, 1974's requirements can be met out of over-draft, in case (C), without issuing further long-term debt. The gearing ratio is correspondingly reduced.

The Timing of a Major Investment

Table 15.2 illustrates a routine use of a program of this type. It shows the effect on financial performance of adding one further project whose scale is significant in relation to the firm's existing activities. Assume that accepting this project is consistent with the firm's long-term marketing strategy and that it meets the required standards for estimated DCF return. What will be the impact on reported financial results for 1972–74?

If the investment occurs in 1972, the estimated direct effects on 1973 and 1974 accounts are as follows: this information is entered as a modification to the earlier data.

	1973	1974
Increase in sales	700	700
Increase in fixed costs	150	150
Increase in asset book value	110	

For this illustration, the same figures are moved one year forward if the investment is undertaken in 1973. Alternative data can be accepted with equal ease.

Secondary effects are calculated within the program: e.g. inventories, debtors and creditors are all tied to sales.

In Table 15.2, dividend and financing policies are maintained as in case (B) above, and performance is compared with and without the major investment. It appears that the investment will be effective in reversing the downward trend in profits and in earnings per share over these three years. If it is undertaken at the later date, 1973, profits and return on net assets for that year will both be marginally lower than they would be without the investment. Both values will peak in 1973 if the project is undertaken at the earlier date.

Table 15.2 Effects of a further investment, with alternative starting dates

	(B) No extra investment			(D) Investment in 1972			(F) Investment in 1973		
	1972	1973	1974	1972	1973	1974	1972	1973	1974
Funds required (£'000)	198	68	103	308	−17	−75	198	178	22
Profit after tax (£'000)	252	221	174	244	362	270	252	214	307
Return on net assets	0.10	0.08	0.06	0.09	0.12	0.09	0.10	0.07	0.10
Earnings per share	0.10	0.09	0.07	0.10	0.14	0.11	0.10	0.09	0.12
Dividend payable (£'000)	74	74	74	74	89	89	74	74	89

The investment also makes it possible to satisfy the conditions for an increase in dividend at the target rate of 20%, either in 1973 or 1974.

The financing of this investment is illustrated in Table 15.3. Funds for the initial outlay are obtained in both of the cases illustrated by issuing an extra £100 000 in long-term debt and by an increase of £10 000 in bank overdraft. The behaviour of the gearing ratio matches the time at which this new finance is raised. For an investment in 1972 the ratio starts at a relatively high value and declines over the three years, while for an investment in 1973, gearing will peak in 1973.

15.4 Use of the Program

Results like those in Tables 15.2 and 15.3 can provide managers with useful supplementary information for investment appraisal; alternatively they can be developed by outside analysts to project forward the implications of current policies. An obvious extension is to re-run the cases under alternative dividend and financing policies. The main reason for developing this program for an on-line system, with direct access from a terminal to a central computer, has been to provide the means for experimenting in this way with different combinations of dividend and financing policies and investment opportunities.

The key problem in developing and using approaches like this one is to decide to what extent to aggregate the data on which the program operates. One could develop comprehensive programs to reproduce and manipulate the whole of a firm's system of financial information, which will provide the means for detailed recording and control as well as for strategic planning (Gershefski (1969) and Tyran 1971)). At the other extreme there are many strategic issues which an experienced analyst can resolve with back-of-envelope projections using aggregated data in the broad categories employed in published accounts. The approach described here is perhaps best viewed as an elaboration of back-of-envelope projection, and the case for using a computer in this role is quite separate from the question of whether or not to use one for recording and processing routine accounting information.

It has been our experience that the main investment of time in developing a useful system of this kind comes from managers and financial experts rather than from computer specialists. The primary task is to develop a set of worksheets to form an intermediate link between an existing accounting system and the computer program, using categories which will allow the consequences of different strategies to be isolated. When such a system is being used, much of the work takes place outside the computer, in rearranging or changing the information on a worksheet and hence in providing new summary data on which the program will operate.

Computer programs for projecting forward a set of accounts are now fairly common and this aspect of the system need not be presented in detail. There are, however, two features of its design which are characteristic of any system built for planning rather than for data processing and recording, and which should, there-

Table 15.3 The financing of a further investment, with alternative starting dates

	(B) No extra investment			(D) Investment in 1972			(E) Investment in 1973		
	1972	1973	1974	1972	1973	1974	1972	1973	1974
Financial Projections									
Overdraft limit (£'000)	339	338	338	339	380	285	339	338	375
Actual overdraft (£'000)	327	295	298	337	320	246	327	305	328
Long-term debt (£'000)	700	800	900	800	800	800	700	900	900
Gearing ratio	0.28	0.29	0.31	0.31	0.28	0.26	0.28	0.32	0.30
Current ratio	1.77	1.81	1.81	1.75	1.83	1.80	1.77	1.80	1.81

fore, be emphasized. First, at what stage does the computer accept data from the existing accounting system? This question arises particularly in the treatment of sales and cost data. Second, how much detail should be included in the routines for projecting forward asset values?

In our present system, budgeted sales and the corresponding direct and indirect costs, as developed by the existing accounting procedures (with or without a computer) are taken as inputs.

Assets are grouped in a limited number of categories (ten in the current version), where a single 'category' contains all those assets which are depreciated at (approximately) the same rate, i.e. its depreciation rate is the defining characteristic of a category. The total written-down book value of assets in each category at the starting date is supplied to the computer, together with projected purchases and disposals in each year up to the planning horizon. The most useful projections to be made with this system are those running up to three or four years ahead and over this span there is a strong case for treating all assets as depreciating on the basis of a declining balance. For assets which are in fact on a straight-line basis, the present program makes the approximation of choosing a rate of declining balance to produce the same written-down book value halfway through the asset's remaining life.

The corresponding data for the written-down tax values at the starting date and for planned purchases and disposals are also supplied to the computer, and the program calculates book and tax value in each category for each reporting date up to the horizon. Since tax depreciation rates do not in general coincide with book rates a separate classification into up to ten categories is maintained for calculation of tax.

Projects which are still under consideration are described on individual worksheets, using the same categories as in the basic projections for their effects on sales, costs and assets.

The program is so arranged that the user, at a computer terminal, can try alternative values for direct cost, tax rates, interest rates on debt and ratios of stocks, debtors and creditors to sales for any accounting period.

The most important change of direction which we have made while developing this work has been in the treatment of new equity. In principle this can be handled in much the same way as increments in long-term debt: the flow chart is revised to show the circumstances under which management will issue new shares. Such conditions for expanding the share issue were written into the earlier versions of our financing policies. In practice it is not easy for managers to write an exhaustive statement of policy on new equity taking into account such factors as share price and market expectations. By contrast, with an on-line computing system it is a simple matter to increase the equity and run the program again if, for example, the first results show an unreasonably high gearing ratio. For these reasons we currently favour planning the issue of equity, and weighing up the factors affecting its volume and timing, outside the computer program.

15.5 Relation to Optimization Methods

This chapter has described the current status of one of two connected approaches, developed at the London Business School, to the control problem of treating investment, financing and dividend decisions simultaneously. Other work in formulating this approach has been described by Packer (1971) and by Judge and Melville (1970).

As described in this chapter, the manager himself specifies feasible policy combinations and then decides what disposition of results (as provided by the computer) he prefers. The computer calculates for each combination a merit rating which is stated in more than one dimension: e.g. 'profit in 1972 'return on assets in 1974', 'earnings per share in 1972', etc., and in the process of searching for better combinations the manager has to formulate his preferences between outcomes each of which has many dimensions.

The parallel development has been in extending optimization methods (viz. DCF appraisal, and modelling by linear programming) to deal simultaneously with investment, financing and dividend policy.

This complementary approach starts with limits which must be satisfied by particular indices of financial performance (e.g. 'reported earnings must exceed £1.5 million') and uses the computer to explore all the feasible combinations of investment, financing and dividend policy, using a single merit-rating. Current applications of this work are presented by Chambers (1971, 1972). Together, the two approaches offer reasonable grounds for believing that the computer can now be used operationally for the simultaneous analysis of investment, financing and dividend decisions.

References

Chambers, D. J. (1971). 'The Joint Problem of Investment and Financing' *Opnl. Res. Qtly.*, **22**, 267–95.

Chambers, D. J. (1972). 'Dividend Plans and Balance Sheet Management', *Journal of Business Finance*, **4**(4), 17–25.

Gershefski, G. W. (1969). 'Building a Corporate Financial Model', *Harvard Business Review,* **47**(4), 61–72.

Judge, F. C. and Melville, M. R. (1970) *'Computer-assisted Financial Policy and Planning',* Sloan Programme Paper, London Business School, London.

Packer, J. J. L. (1971). 'The Projection of Financial Results', *Long Range Planning,* **3**(3), 49–53.

Tyran, M. R. (1971). 'A Computerised Decision-Simulator Model' *Management Accounting,* **52**(9), 19–26.

Financial Modelling in Corporate Management
Edited by J. W. Bryant
© 1982 John Wiley & Sons Ltd.

16

Financial Planning Models Including Dividend Growth*

JOHN GRINYER

16.1 Introduction

During recent years the technology of computing has changed dramatically, but our knowledge of the behavioural processes which influence the actions of corporate management and of investors has changed little. Some new theories of finance have been constructed and developed, but the difficulties of testing them have been such that none could claim to be validated adequately by reference to empirical data. There has therefore been little change in the general nature and objectives of the planning process a rational manager would wish to undertake.

The author's perception of the objectives of financial management has moved away from the conventional shareholder wealth maximization view, towards a satisficing approach. Management objectives are discussed fully in this chapter and their implications for financial policy-making are considered. In particular, the appropriateness of dividend growth as a suitable measure for financial evaluation is examined below. Some computer simulation models which have been developed to investigate investment options using such measures are then presented and assessed in the concluding sections.

16.2 Shareholder Wealth and Financial Management

Management Objectives

It seems realistic to suggest that the average top manager of a public company is primarily motivated by a desire to satisfy personal, and possibly organizational,

---

*Reproduced by permission of the publisher from John R. Grinyer, 'Financial Planning Models Incorporating Dividend Growth Elements', *Accounting and Business Research* (10), Spring 1973.

goals rather than to maximize the wealth of that unknown group of people who are the shareholders. Most financial theories are, however, based on the assumption that management would wish to analyse financial aspects of decisions by reference to shareholder wealth, so it seems necessary to consider whether such an assumption seems valid. This would seem to be the case if:

(1) existing and potential shareholders are able to influence the future position of the managers and organization, and
(2) such shareholders are sufficiently sophisticated and in receipt of sufficient information to make a reasonable evaluation of the shareholder wealth generation prospects of the company and the extent to which management is acting to realize those prospects.

Given (1), the existence of (2) would imply that failure of management to act in accord with shareholders' interests would lead to shareholder action with unpleasant consequences for top managers or other members of the organization.

Existing and potential shareholders are able to influence the future position of the organization in a number of ways, including direct intervention by means of appointments to the Board of Directors and indirect intervention such as the sale or purchase of shares, (which affects the share price and so alters both the availability to the company of future funds raised by a share issue and its desirability as candidate for a takeover bid). Since maintenance of an adequate share price and retention of the loyalty of the majority of shareholders may be pre-requisites for maintenance of control by the existing managements of many companies, and therefore for the satisfaction of any of their personal or organizational goals, condition (1) above seems generally to hold.

Does the large scale of institutional activity which dominates the stock markets for equity shares mean that condition (2) is met? Although it is doubtful whether the information available to institutional investors is sufficient for them to forecast company prospects accurately, a fair picture of management's attitudes in decision making and of possible trends in wealth generation should be possible. If management realizes this, it is likely that it will be motivated towards achieving at least a satisfactory performance in terms of shareholder wealth generation which, in the absence of conflicting aims, could best be achieved by maximizing shareholder wealth.

The real world seems too complex and uncertain to allow shareholder wealth maximization to predominate in the management decision process. Recent discussions with a number of senior managers of U.K. public companies has demonstrated a widespread opinion that shareholders are entitled to a fair return for the risks they are taking but that the corporate organization does not exist primarily to serve them. In the U.S.A., also, there is evidence that management does not pursue shareholder wealth oriented models (Gabrowski and Mueller, 1972). It appears that management is interested in the satisfactory achievement of a number of, possibly conflicting objectives.

The weighting given by management to the achievement of different objectives seems likely to vary over time and according to the particular circumstances facing the company when decisions have to be taken. Similarly, weightings may also depend on the forecast outcomes of different possible courses of action being considered. It can therefore be argued that the most useful models for processing financial forecasts concerning major decisions are not optimizing algorithms, but simulation models which project outcomes by reference to several, incommensurate, measures and leave management to decide which of the available sets of outcomes it prefers. If this argument is accepted it becomes necessary to identify the measures which seem most appropriate for the analysis of the financial implications of possible decisions.

Quantifying Shareholder Wealth

The achievement of satisfactory performance in the generation of wealth for shareholders requires a model by reference to which this may be measured. A possible measure is the present value of the wealth derived by an existing shareholder from holding a share:

$$W_0 = \frac{ES_j}{(1+r)^j} + \sum_{t=1}^{j} \frac{ED_t}{(1+r)^t},$$

where ED_t is the expected value of the cash dividend, net of tax, paid at the end of period t.

j is the period of sale of the share.

ES_j is the expected value of the sale proceeds at the end of period j, of the dividend for period j.

r represents the opportunity cost of the return on investment in other securities of an equivalent risk, and includes a premium for risk.

In making its financial evaluations it would seem, from the above, that management might wish to consider both future dividends and future share prices.

Under the uncertainty generally prevailing in the real world the share price, which is set by market transactions and therefore reflects the expectations of the marginal investors, may be a very imperfect reflection of the present value of future dividends. If management wished to use a decision model on the reasoning underlying the above expression it would need to consider the likely changes in the expectations of investors resulting from the information which they would receive during the period under consideration for planning purposes. Knowledge of the findings of empirical studies of share prices could therefore be useful. There seems to be widespread agreement that share price is significantly affected by earnings (Lorrie and Hamilton, 1973), although it is, of course, possible that the evidence is merely indicative of the capital market impact of the cash flow figures underlying the historical cost figures of earnings. We will assume the importance of earnings, which leaves the significance of dividend policy for consideration.

Dividend Policy

There is wide agreement that under assumptions of perfect markets with no transactions costs or taxation, and with homogeneous expectations on the part of all participants, dividend policy is irrelevant. It is generally agreed that the introduction of transactions costs and of taxation create a situation in which dividend policy *is* relevant and in which the relative desirability of dividends or distributions is affected by the tax and other costs associated with each action. Conflicting evidence about the effect of dividend policy on capital market sentiment and perceptions means that dividend policy is still an area in which considerable 'qualitative' judgment is required.

How should a financial manager react to this situation? Empirical work in the U.K. (e.g. Briston and Tomkins, 1970) and in the U.S.A. (e.g. Lintner, 1956; Brittain, 1966; Fama and Babiak, 1968) indicates that it is likely that the majority of companies follow a policy of paying stable dividends; dividends increase with a lag when management thinks that maintainable profits have increased, but are held constant (if at all possible) in the event of a downward revision of managements' profit expectations. Given these findings and the apparent general disinclination of risk-averse managers to provide useful cash and profit forecasts it seems rational behaviour, on the part of investors, to assume that dividends have an information content. If investors do make such an assumption it is reasonable to suggest that they will act upon it with the result that share price changes will be positively correlated with dividend changes. Of course it is possible to find examples in which this has not been so (e.g. the price of the shares of Lesney Products Ltd fell substantially during 1970 despite an increased dividend in that year). Such apparent contradictions are presumably the result of a substantial re-appraisal by the market of a company's prospects, a re-appraisal based on information other than dividends (e.g. in the case of Lesney the market appears to have changed its assessment of the firm's competitive position). Further, countervailing examples of apparent adverse market reactions to news of dividend reductions are available (e.g. Coates Paton in 1974). We will continue on the assumption that share price changes are positively correlated with dividend changes, and also with changes in profit.

Which Shareholders Should be Considered?

The above shareholder wealth measure indicates that the relative significance of dividends received and share price at the time of sale differs depending on the length of time for which a share is held. As the period lengthens, the present value of the future dividends increases and the present value of the proceeds of the share sale declines, because of the operation of the discount factor. As share prices appear to be influenced by dividend and profit flows it seems that different patterns of such flows, having equal present values of future dividend flows over the planning period, could give rise to different variations in share price and therefore to differing shareholder preference for those flows depending on when the shareholder sells his shares. This argument could be extended to claim that the acceptance of the present value criterion frequently used in project appraisal could adversely affect the interest of some shareholders. This has been illustrated by an extended example in an earlier paper (Grinyer, 1973).

In practice the fluctuating cash flows, interest rates and share prices give rise to extremely complex variations between the interests of different shareholders. Management must therefore implicitly decide which group of shareholders is to receive preferred treatment.

As previously noted, the significance of the sale price to the net present value of holding a share declines as the period for which the share is held lengthens, and so it could be claimed that the net present value method of evaluation is likely to give a reasonably correct analysis so far as very long-term shareholders' interests are concerned. It therefore seems desirable that NPV results should form part of the information presented to management in respect of a financial decision. It may be useful, however, to extend the analysis to incorporate some measure of the welfare of short- and medium-term shareholders—that is, those shareholders who will sell their shares well within the time horizon envisaged for decision purposes by management.

If no attempt is made to smooth the dividend pattern it seems likely that share price will fluctuate for most companies. That would mean that the interests of shareholders selling in each year will probably differ from those of all other shareholders. It is possible that the most satisfactory policy furthering the interests of the majority of short- and medium-term shareholders would be one designed to achieve a stable trend of dividends, preferably growing over time at the maximum maintainable rate. This stability should help to steady share prices so that there is less likelihood of some shareholders losing by reason of marked downward fluctuations in price and could also help to increase long-run share price if it resulted in a reduction in the market rate of discount applied to the firm. The growth should mean that, within the constraint of the achievement of stability, the shareholders receive a growing measure of wealth from their share ownership—both by way of cash received as dividends and by way of increase in share prices. Several reasons can be advanced to show that this management objective of maximization of the compound growth of dividends over the next few years is probably a sensible one (Grinyer, 1973).

Key Variables for Financial Management

At this point it is helpful to review some other variables considered important in financial management. These may be added to those already discussed to provide a set of assessment criteria for investment planning.

It seems likely that management would wish to consider the effect of financial alternatives on reported earnings, since earnings apparently affect share price, and in turn share price affects, and is a reflection of, the attitudes of those within the capital markets to whom management turn for new externally provided funds. Accounting reports have increased relevance if management believes that outsiders are judging its performance by reference to figures of accounting profit. Most people wish to 'win' and it seems reasonable to assume that management will consider the rules of scoring the business game when deciding on their strategy. For this reason, it may be assumed that management would wish to achieve a 'satisfactory' pattern of earnings, i.e. one which they perceive as being likely to persuade outsiders that the resources of the company are being efficiently managed.

One clear lesson of the recent years, at least for U.K. businesses, has been the importance of cash planning. Insufficient cash availability at times of crisis can be embarrassing at best and can be catastrophic at worst. Outsiders also look at firms' reported cash generation as an indication of their viability in the short and in the long term. Few would dispute management's need to forecast the effect of currently considered proposals on the future liquidity of the firm—so it is reasonable to assume that management would wish to include a measure of cash flow in any financial analyses.

If the analyst determines permitted amounts of future expected dividends by reference to cash and to earnings cover constraints, then he can be most sure to avoid creating adverse outsider perceptions of management performance by following a policy of maximizing the growth of dividends over time; for achievement of that objective also attains a pattern of constantly increasing cash flows and accounting earnings. Obviously it is easier to fall short of internally held expectations of growth without creating external perceptions of failure than to fall short of internally held expectations of constant earnings, cash flow and dividends—i.e. the growth element has an in-built security element against the consequences of non-attainment of expectations. On these grounds it seems likely that maximization of the growth of possible dividends is a useful proxy for certain of management's objectives.

On the basis of the above arguments, it seems likely that the significant elements which should be modelled in the financial analysis of each alternative plan considered by management are:

(1) future cash flows generated;
(2) net present values;
(3) the pattern of accounting profit generated;
(4) rates of compound growth of dividends possible;
(5) rankings of alternatives by reference to key variables.

16.3 Dividend Growth Simulation Models

Introduction

During the early 1970s the author constructed several computer simulation models to test the feasibility of providing the information outlined above (Grinyer, 1973).

These models simulated the outcomes of adopting different investment alternatives under two dividend policies, the first of which assumed that maximum dividends would be paid each year (i.e. that there would be no attempt to smooth the dividend stream over time), and the second of which assumed that the dividend stream would be smoothed to achieve the maximum compound rate of dividend growth over a specified period.

For both policies the models calculated:

(1) the net present value per share of after-tax dividend figures, derived after the imposition of constraints for cash availability and profit cover;
(2) the figures of annual profit which would arise, given the dividend policy and assumptions of the rate of return possible on re-invested funds, during the planning period;
(3) the figures of annual cash balances, after payment of dividends, during the planning period.

Maximum rates of compound growth of dividends, possible under each alternative, were calculated in the smoothed dividend run and were used, where appropriate, to provide ranking signals.

Comparison of the net present value figures, mentioned in (1) above, for a single investment alternative provided a measure of the anticipated loss to long-term shareholders from pursuing a policy of compound growth of dividends over the period specified for the model.

Basic Model

The first basic model combined the projected profit and cash flows associated with the existing business of a firm with the estimated flows from alternative investments and with the estimated cash flows associated with alternative financing plans. All of the information outlined above was calculated and printed for each alternative investment and financing combination, including the *status quo*. The model did not take explicit account of the financial risk implicit in gearing, but it did calculate the present values of dividends under a range of rates—thus making possible both a measure of sensitivity analysis concerning interest rates and the exogeneous addition of risk premiums by the analyst if he wished to adjust discount rates for gearing.

Three alternative, mutually exclusive projects were considered. Project 1 was a dummy project, indicating a situation of rejection of other alternatives; project 2 represented diversification into a new area by purchasing a factory and building the new business 'from scratch'; and project 3 represented entry into the desired area by purchase of a subsidiary. Because of problems of quality of staff acquired on the prospective takeover, and the location of the premises (coupled with competitive and technical factors) management believed that the long-term prospects for the subsidiary if it were acquired were much poorer than for the alternative of immediately commencing with its own factory (i.e. project 2) which accounted for the rather unexpected revenue flows for project 3. The model was run in 1970 and incorporated the U.K. tax regime of that year. Table 16.1 shows test input to the model.

The results for one combination of project and finance are shown in Figure 16.1 and Figure 16.2 shows the summary of present values and growth rates for all combinations considered. Detailed assumptions of the model are not discussed in this paper as each user firm would in any event wish to model its own environment and therefore to incorporate its own taxation, financial and accounting assumptions in its decision models. It is interesting to observe from the summary (Figure 16.2) that project 2 combined with finance alternative 3, which is the option with the highest present value per dividend (at 10% it is £2.27) has a growth rate of only 3%. The option with the highest growth potential is project 3 with finance alternative 2, which has a potential dividend growth rate of 8%, but at 10% a present value per share of only £1.96. Obviously management would wish to consider the detailed figures for these options before making its decision—but the test data clearly indicate that dividend growth and NPV can give different signals.

Capital Rationing Model

A second simulation model dealt with the possibility of capital rationing. It would have been suitable for use when considering projects that materially alter the cash and accounting profit flows of a firm which considered that it was in a capital rationing situation. It combined the cash and profit flows of each of a limited number of investment projects to obtain such flows for each possible combination of the considered projects. Flows for each combination were then aggregated with the projected cash and profit figures arising from the existing business (and with cash receipts from sources external to the company in cases in which management considered that such receipts would arise) and the output listed earlier and illustrated in Figure 16.1 was printed for each possible combination of projects.

An example of the use of the model is provided by a run that considered five independent projects which, with the inclusion of project 1 (a 'dummy' project inserted to evaluate the alternative of rejection of all projects), made a total of six projects for evaluation. There were, of course, 63 combinations of such projects. With the test data of Table 16.2, the results of Figure 16.3 were produced, the computer printing lists of present values of dividends and scatter diagrams of such present values and of maximum rates of compound dividend growth possible with each project combination. It can be seen that the output assumes that management would wish to maintain the same rate of dividend growth throughout the total number of years used in the model. However, it would be easy to adjust the model to accommodate measurement over shorter periods.

Clearly, detailed examination, by management, of the computer output relating to each of the possible combinations would have made decisions difficult, if not

Table 16.1

Project alternatives: 1 Dummy (= rejection of other alternatives)
2 Factory purchase
3 Subsidiary purchase

Finance alternatives: 1 No further finance raised
2 All equity capital raised
3 All debt finance raised (repayable in last year of evaluation)

Number of years in evaluation: 15

Project Forecasts:

	Project Alternative		
Project flow (£'000)	1	2	3
Capital Expenditure			
Year 1	Nil	300	1000
Year 2	Nil	200	Nil
Thereafter	Nil	Nil	Nil
Revenue			
Year 1	Nil	Nil	400
Year 2	Nil	Nil	300
Year 3	Nil	50	300
Year 4	Nil	100	300
Year 5	Nil	200	200
Year 6	Nil	300	200
Year 7	Nil	400	200
Years 8–15	Nil	500	200
Depreciation			
Year 1	Nil	Nil	30
Year 2	Nil	Nil	30
Years 3–15	Nil	40	30
Terminal value			
Year 15 (end)	Nil	1000	500

Existing Business Forecast Flows (£'000):
Revenue Years 1–15 : 1000
Depreciation Years 1–15 : 200
Terminal value Year 15 (end): 3000

Other Cash Flows (not connected with existing business, projects or related finance) (£'000):
Year 1 : 100
Years 2–4 : Nil
Year 5 : 500
Thereafter : Nil

Existing capital : £2 000 000
Existing shares issued: 2 000 000
Last dividend declared (gross):£400 000
Corporation tax payable (Year 1) : £320 000
Corporation tax rate 45%
Rate of interest for short-term lending : 20%
Minimum dividend cover required : 1.0

Details of finance alternatives:

Alternative 2 : Finance capital cash flow £1000 per £1000 required, all receivable in Year 1
500 additional ordinary shares issued per £1000 of capital raised
£1000 additional capital not-taxable on distribution per £1000 of capital raised

Alternative 3 : Finance capital cash flow £1000 per £1000 required, all receivable in Year 1
Cash outflow of £1000 per £1000 of capital raised, in Year 15
Debt interest of £100 per annum per £1000 of capital raised

Project 3 and Finance 3

Year	Profit	Unsmoothed dividends		Profit	Smoothed dividends	
		Dividends	Cash balance		Dividends	Cash balance
1	483500	284056	314682	483500	251450	370182
2	518115	304393	573003	510860	269051	379322
3	574030	337243	848752	566395	287885	501717
4	631863	371219	1126070	630977	308037	639743
5	662368	389141	1881028	678260	329600	1264118
6	745413	437930	2178974	771691	352672	1108858
7	778187	457185	2435790	826286	377359	1237394
8	806437	473782	2688903	889706	403774	1434686
9	834279	490139	2941683	958661	432038	1646655
10	862085	506475	3194433	1033082	462281	1875453
11	889888	522809	3447181	1078265	494640	1963902
12	917690	539143	3699928	1141461	529265	2153908
13	945492	555477	3952675	1209200	566314	2345606
14	973294	571810	4205423	1276526	605956	2527302

Present value of dividends at 0.10 rate   Unsmoothed 2.1534   Smoothed 2.1847
Present value of dividends at 0.11 rate   Unsmoothed 1.9823   Smoothed 1.9958
Present value of dividends at 0.12 rate   Unsmoothed 1.8298   Smoothed 1.8284
Present value of dividends at 0.13 rate   Unsmoothed 1.6936   Smoothed 1.6799
Present value of dividends at 0.14 rate   Unsmoothed 1.5717   Smoothed 1.5477
Present value of dividends at 0.15 rate   Unsmoothed 1.4622   Smoothed 1.4298
Maximum rate of compound dividend growth = 0.07

Figure 16.1 Basic model output: results for one project/finance combination

Project No.	Finance No.	Discount rate	P.V. unsmoothed dividends	P.V. smoothed dividends	Max. compound div. growth rate
1	1	0.10	1.9118	1.9223	0.0600
1	1	0.11	1.7578	1.7627	0.0600
1	1	0.12	1.6208	1.6210	0.0600
1	1	0.13	1.4986	1.4948	0.0600
1	1	0.14	1.3893	1.3823	0.0600
1	1	0.15	1.2914	1.2817	0.0600
1	2	0.10	1.9118	1.9223	0.0600
1	2	0.11	1.7578	1.7627	0.0600
1	2	0.12	1.6208	1.6210	0.0600
1	2	0.13	1.4986	1.4948	0.0600
1	2	0.14	1.3893	1.3823	0.0600
1	2	0.15	1.2914	1.2817	0.0600
1	3	0.10	1.9118	1.9223	0.0600
1	3	0.11	1.7578	1.7627	0.0600
1	3	0.12	1.6208	1.6210	0.0600
1	3	0.13	1.4986	1.4948	0.0600
1	3	0.14	1.3893	1.3823	0.0600
1	3	0.15	1.2914	1.2817	0.0600
2	1	0.10	2.2172	2.2217	0.0400
2	1	0.11	2.0320	2.0168	0.0400
2	1	0.12	1.8673	1.8362	0.0400
2	1	0.13	1.7205	1.6768	0.0400
2	1	0.14	1.5893	1.5358	0.0400
2	1	0.15	1.4719	1.4108	0.0400
2	2	0.10	2.1398	2.1470	0.0700
2	2	0.11	1.9602	1.9629	0.0700
2	2	0.12	1.8013	1.7997	0.0700
2	2	0.13	1.6597	1.6547	0.0700
2	2	0.14	1.5331	1.5257	0.0700
2	2	0.15	1.4199	1.4105	0.0700
2	3	0.10	2.2619	2.2705	0.0300
2	3	0.11	2.0736	2.0560	0.0300
2	3	0.12	1.9060	1.8674	0.0300
2	3	0.13	1.7566	1.7011	0.0300
2	3	0.14	1.6231	1.5544	0.0300
2	3	0.15	1.5035	1.4245	0.0300
3	2	0.10	1.9425	1.9617	0.0800
3	2	0.11	1.7864	1.8053	0.0800
3	2	0.12	1.6474	1.6659	0.0800
3	2	0.13	1.5233	1.5413	0.0800
3	2	0.14	1.4124	1.4296	0.0800
3	2	0.15	1.3130	1.3294	0.0800
3	3	0.10	2.1534	2.1847	0.0700
3	3	0.11	1.9823	1.9958	0.0700
3	3	0.12	1.8298	1.8284	0.0700
3	3	0.13	1.6936	1.6799	0.0700
3	3	0.14	1.5717	1.5477	0.0700
3	3	0.15	1.4622	1.4298	0.0700

Figure 16.2 Basic model output: summary statistics

Project 2

Year	Unsmoothed dividends			Smoothed dividends		
	Profit	Dividends	Cash balance	Profit	Dividends	Cash balance
1	96250	56547	203750	96250	33194	243500
2	83809	49238	305571	86747	37509	338827
3	120144	70584	131593	125540	42385	201599
4	129870	76298	186140	140440	47895	277892
5	143627	84380	226667	160979	54122	348025
6	160380	94223	274451	186701	61157	435618
7	165608	97293	279160	200900	69108	465280
8	163654	96146	268005	210246	78092	480654
9	173736	102070	305134	230871	88244	549038
10	182530	107237	327879	250911	99715	603302
11	190011	111631	347046	269779	112678	650201
12	195378	114784	359835	285638	127327	681584
13	201339	118287	376458	301626	143879	712761
14	209355	122996	399879	318780	162583	745456

Present value of dividends at 0.10 rate Unsmoothed 2.2410 Smoothed 2.2475
Present value of dividends at 0.11 rate Unsmoothed 2.0600 Smoothed 2.0359
Present value of dividends at 0.12 rate Unsmoothed 1.8988 Smoothed 1.8492
Present value of dividends at 0.13 rate Unsmoothed 1.7549 Smoothed 1.6840
Present value of dividends at 0.14 rate Unsmoothed 1.6261 Smoothed 1.5377
Present value of dividends at 0.15 rate Unsmoothed 1.5106 Smoothed 1.4078
Maximum rate of compound growth = 0.13

Projects 2, 3 and 6 combined

Year	Profit	Unsmoothed dividends		Profit	Smoothed dividends	
		Dividends	Cash balance		Dividends	Cash balance
1	75900	44591	54100	75900	32019	75500
2	79899	46940	146092	81480	34900	173741
3	120946	30297	0	124571	38041	1924
4	148446	87212	169538	152214	41465	261484
5	160977	94574	191198	171540	45197	319951
6	175108	102876	230748	195187	49265	404200
7	188164	110546	265197	219481	53599	487216
8	196967	115718	285539	242650	58532	563933
9	218071	128117	352711	284188	63799	723935
10	231609	136070	383155	318367	69541	834811
11	244147	140430	383728	354771	75800	928353
12	266453	156541	402317	404510	82622	1062223
13	276588	162495	419782	447009	90058	1201141
14	286510	168324	446456	494105	98163	1365644

Present value of dividends at 0.10 rate Unsmoothed 2.5269 Smoothed 2.5046
Present value of dividends at 0.11 rate Unsmoothed 2.3096 Smoothed 2.2474
Present value of dividends at 0.12 rate Unsmoothed 2.1164 Smoothed 2.0220
Present value of dividends at 0.13 rate Unsmoothed 1.9443 Smoothed 1.8241
Present value of dividends at 0.14 rate Unsmoothed 1.7906 Smoothed 1.6500
Present value of dividends at 0.15 rate Unsmoothed 1.6531 Smoothed 1.4966
Maximum rate of compound dividend growth = 0.09

Figure 16.3 Capital rationing model output: specimen results

Table 16.2

Projects available	:	1	Dummy (= rejection of other alternatives)
Project combinations	:	2–6	Various options
Number of years in evaluation: 15		63	combinations of available projects

Project forecasts

	Project					
Project flow (£'000)	1	2	3	4	5	6
Capital expenditure						
Year 1	Nil	50	100	200	200	70
Year 2	Nil	50	100	100	Nil	100
Year 3	Nil	50	Nil	Nil	Nil	200
Thereafter	Nil	Nil	Nil	Nil	Nil	Nil
Revenue						
Year 1	Nil	100	Nil	50	60	Nil
Year 2	Nil	50	50	70	100	20
Year 3	Nil	Nil	50	70	20	50
Years 4–10	Nil	Nil	50	70	20	100
Years 11–15	Nil	Nil	10	30	Nil	100
Depreciation						
Year 1	Nil	75	Nil	20	20	37
Year 2	Nil	75	20	20	20	37
Years 3–10	Nil	Nil	20	20	20	37
Year 11	Nil	Nil	20	20	Nil	Nil
Years 12–15	Nil	Nil	Nil	20	Nil	Nil
Terminal value						
Year 15 (end)	Nil	Nil	Nil	50	Nil	200

Existing business forecast flows (£'000):

Profit	Years 1–15	:	200
Depreciation	Years 1–15	:	50
Terminal value	Year 15 (end)		

Other Cash Flows (not connected with existing business or projects) (£'000):

Year 1	:	100
Year 2	:	200
Thereafter	:	Nil

Existing capital	:	£400 000
Existing shares issued	:	400 000
Last dividend declared (gross)	:	£50 000
Corporation tax payable (Year 1)	:	£50 000
Corporation tax rate	:	45%
Rate of interest for short term lending	:	10%
Rate of return on internal re-investment of cash surplus to project and dividend requirements	:	20%
Minimum dividend cover required	:	1.0

impossible. Fortunately that was unnecessary, because the summary information printed enabled the majority of combinations to be rejected as being dominated in all respects by other combinations. Only the few combinations that were not dominated by others remained for detailed consideration. For example, out of the 63 possible combinations of projects in a test run utilizing the input of Table 16.2 there were only two (Figure 16.3) for which expectations on all measures were not matched or surpassed by those for other projects.

16.4 Conclusion

It seems unwise of management to make financial decisions on the basis of consideration of only one measure. The outcome of alternative courses of action should, ideally, be estimated and expressed in terms of the several different measures which could provide meaningful information. Management must then decide which set of expected outcomes it prefers, or possibly which set of outcomes it considers that the majority of shareholders would prefer.

The expected future rate of dividend growth possible under alternative decisions seems to be information which could prove useful when choosing between such alternatives, as it can, to some extent, represent a proxy for profit and cash balances and may well indicate the likely direction of movement of share price attributable to the information which investors appear to believe they receive from dividend declarations. In addition, risk-averse, satisficing, managers may prefer alternatives with high potential growth because of the greater opportunities for undisclosed future shortfalls from expectations which they are likely to present.

Construction of some computer models incorporating a dividend growth feature has demonstrated that the inclusion of such a characteristic in financial simulation models is feasible, if believed by management to be desirable.

References

Briston, R. J. and Tomkins, C. R. (1970). 'The Impact of the Introduction of Corporation Tax upon the Dividend Policies of U.K. Companies', *Economic Journal*, **80**, 617–37.

Brittain, J. A. (1966). *Corporate Dividend Policy*, The Brookings Institution, Washington, D.C.

Fama, E. F. and Babiak, H. (1968). 'Dividend Policy: an Empirical Analysis', *Journal of the American Statistical Association*, **63**, 1132–61.

Gabrowski, H. G. and Mueller, D. C. (1972). 'Managerial and Stockholder Welfare Models of Firm Expenditure', *Review of Economics & Statistics*, **54**, 9–24.

Grinyer, J. R. (1973). 'Financial Planning Models Incorporating Dividend Growth Elements', *Accounting and Business Research*, **10**, 145–55.

Lintner, J., (1956). 'Distribution of Incomes of Corporations among Dividends, Retained Earnings and Taxes', *American Economic Review*, **46**, 97–113.

Lorrie, J. H. and Hamilton, M. T. (1973). *The Stock Market, Theories and Evidence*, Richard D. Irwin, Homewood, Illinois.

Financial Modelling in Corporate Management
Edited by J. W. Bryant
© 1982 John Wiley & Sons Ltd.

17

Strategic Analysis for More Profitable Acquisitions*

ALFRED RAPPAPORT

17.1 Introduction

As more and more corporations see acquisitions and mergers as an important part of their growth strategy, the acquisitions market has become intensely competitive, and buyers are paying a substantial premium for target companies. This chapter describes a framework for acquisitions analysis that evaluates both the buying and the selling company and helps the buyer decide, among other things, the maximum price he should pay for a particular company as well as the best way to finance the acquisition.

Less than a decade after the frantic merger activity of the later 1960s, we are again in the midst of a major wave of corporate acquisitions. In contrast to the 1960s, when acquirers were mainly freewheeling conglomerates, the merger movement in the 1970s includes such long-established giants of U.S. industry as General Electric, Gulf Oil, and Kennecott Copper. Because of the decline in the value of the dollar and the greater political stability of the U.S.A., foreign companies also have become increasingly active buyers of U.S. companies during the past few years.

Most acquisitions are accomplished with cash today, rather than with packages of securities as was common in the 1960s. Finally, the current merger movement involves the frequent use of tender offers that often lead to contested bids and to the payment of substantial premiums above the pre-merger market value of the target company. In 1978 and 1979 cash tender offer premiums averaged more than 70% above pre-merger market values.

*Reprinted by permission of the Harvard Business Review. 'Strategic Analysis for More Profitable Acquisitions', by Alfred Rappaport (July–August 1979). Copyright © 1979 by the President and Fellows of Harvard College; all rights reserved.

The popular explanation for the recent merger rage is that the market is 'under-valuing' many solid companies, thus making it substantially cheaper to buy rather than to build. Couple this belief with the fact that many corporations are enjoying relatively strong cash positions and the widely held view that government regulation and increased uncertainty about the economy make internal growth strategies rela-tively unattractive, and we see why mergers and acquisitions have become an in-creasingly important part of corporate growth strategy.

Despite all of the foregoing rationale, more than a few of the recent acquisitions will fail to create value for the acquirer's shareholders. After all, shareholder value depends not on pre-merger market valuation of the target company but on the actual acquisition price the acquiring company pays compared with the selling com-pany's cash-flow contribution to the combined company.

Only a limited supply of acquisition candidates is available at the price that enables the acquirer to earn an acceptable return on investment. A well-conceived financial evaluation program that minimizes the risk of buying an economically unattractive company or paying too much for an attractive one is particularly important in today's seller's market. The dramatic increase in premiums that must be paid by a company bidding successfully calls for more careful analysis by buyers than ever before.

Because of the competitive nature of the acquisition market, companies not only need to respond wisely but often must respond quickly as well. The growing inde-pendence of corporate boards and their demand for better information to support strategic decisions such as acquisitions have raised the general standard for acquisi-tion analysis. Finally, sound analysis convincingly communicated can yield sub-stantial benefits in negotiating with the target company's management or, in the case of tender offers, its stockholders.

Salter and Weinhold (1978) outlined seven principal ways in which companies can create value for their shareholders via acquisition. In this chapter, I will show how management can estimate how much value a prospective acquisition will in fact create. In brief, I will present a comprehensive framework for acquisition analysis based on contemporary financial theory—an approach that has been profitably employed in practice. The analysis provides management and the board of the acquiring company with information both to make a decision on the candi-date and to formulate an effective negotiating strategy for the acquisition.

The approach makes use of an interactive computer model for the evaluations, and while the model structure is not explicitly discussed here, its form and the logical sequence of calculations performed should be apparent from the description below.

17.2 Steps in the Analysis

The process of analysing acquisitions falls broadly into three stages: planning, search and screen, and financial evaluation.

The acquisition planning process begins with a review of corporate objectives and product-market strategies for various strategic business units. The acquiring company should define its potential directions for corporate growth and diversification in terms of corporate strengths and weaknesses and an assessment of the company's social, economic, political, and technological environment. This analysis produces a set of acquisition objectives and criteria.

Specified criteria often include statements about industry parameters such as projected market growth rate, degree of regulation, ease of entry, and capital versus labour intensity. Company criteria for quality of management, share of market, profitability, size and capital structure also commonly appear in acquisition criteria lists.

The search and screen process is a systematic approach to compiling a list of good acquisition prospects. The search focuses on how and where to look for candidates, and the screening process selects a few of the best candidates from literally thousands of possibilities according to objectives and criteria developed in the planning phase.

Finally comes the financial evaluation process, which is the focus of this chapter. A good analysis should enable management to answer such questions as:

(1) What is the maximum price that should be paid for the target company?
(2) What are the principal areas of risk?
(3) What are the earnings, cash flow, and balance sheet implications of the acquisitions?
(4) What is the best way of financing the acquisition?

Corporate Self-evaluation

The financial evaluation process involves both a self-evaluation by the acquiring company and the evaluation of the candidate for acquisition. While it is possible to conduct an evaluation of the target company without an in-depth self-evaluation first, in general this is the most advantageous approach (Rappaport, 1979a). The scope and detail of corporate self-evaluation will necessarily vary according to the needs of each company.

Two fundamental questions posed by a self-evaluation are: (a) How much is my company worth? (b) How would its value be affected by each of several scenarios? The first question involves generating a 'most likely' estimate of the company's value based on management's detailed assessment of its objectives, strategies, and plans. The second question calls for an assessment of value based on the range of plausible scenarios that enable management to test the joint effect of hypothesized combinations of product-market strategies and environmental forces.

Corporate self-evaluation viewed as an economic assessment of the value created for shareholders by various strategic planning options promises potential benefits for all companies. In the context of the acquisition market, self-evaluation takes on special significance.

First, while a company might view itself as an acquirer, few companies are totally exempt from a possible takeover. During 1979 alone, 83 acquisitions exceeding $100 million were announced. The recent roster of acquired companies includes such names as Anaconda, Utah International, Babcock & Wilcox, Seven Up, Pet, Carborundum, and Del Monte. Self-evaluation provides management and the board with a continuing basis for responding to tender offers or acquisition inquiries responsibly and quickly. Second, the self-evaluation process might well call attention to strategic divestment opportunities. Finally, self-evaluation provides acquisition-minded companies a basis for assessing the comparative advantages of a cash versus an exchange-of-shares offer.

Acquiring companies commonly value the purchase price for an acquisition at the market value of the shares exchanged. This practice is not economically sound and could be misleading and costly to the acquiring company. A well-conceived analysis for an exchange-of-shares acquisition requires sound valuations of both buying and selling companies. If the acquirer's management believes the market is undervaluing its shares, then valuing the purchase price at market might well induce the company to overpay for the acquisition or to earn less than the minimum acceptable rate of return.

Conversely, if management believes the market is overvaluing its shares, then valuing the purchase price at market obscures the opportunity of offering the seller's shareholders additional shares while still achieving the minimum acceptable return.

Valuation of Acquisitions

Recently *Business Week* (1978) reported that as many as half of the major acquisition-minded companies are relying extensively on the discounted cash-flow (DCF) technique to analyse acquisitions. While mergers and acquisitions involve a considerably more complex set of managerial problems than the purchase of an ordinary asset such as a machine or a plant, the economic substance of these transactions is the same. In each case, there is a current outlay made in anticipation of a stream of future cash flows.

Thus the DCF criterion applies not only to internal growth investments, such as additions to existing capacity, but equally to external growth investments, such as acquisitions. An essential feature of the DCF technique is that it explicitly takes into account that a dollar of cash received today is worth more than a dollar received a year from now, because today's dollar can be invested to earn a return during the intervening time.

To establish the maximum acceptable acquisition price under the DCF approach, estimates are needed for (a) the incremental cash flows expected to be generated because of the acquisition and (b) the cost of capital—that is, the minimum acceptable rate of return required by the market for new investments by the company.

In projecting the cash-flow stream of a prospective acquisition, what should be taken into account is the cash-flow contribution the candidate is expected to make to the acquiring company. The results of this projection may well differ from a projection of the candidate's cash flow as an independent company. This is so because the acquirer may be able to achieve operating economies not available to the selling company alone. Furthermore, acquisitions generally provide new post-acquisition investment opportunities whose initial outlays and subsequent benefits also need to be incorporated in the cash flow schedule. Cash flow is defined as:

(earnings before interest and taxes [EBIT]) $\times$ (1-income tax rate) + depreciation and other noncash charges — capital expenditures — cash required for increase in net working capital

In developing the cash-flow schedule, two additional issues need to be considered: (a) What is the basis for setting the horizon date—that is, the date beyond which the cash flows associated with the acquisition are not specifically projected? (b) How is the residual value of the acquisition established at the horizon date?

A common practice is to forecast cash flows period by period until the level of uncertainty makes management too 'uncomfortable' to go any farther. While practice varies with industry setting, management policy, and the special circumstances of the acquisition, five or ten years appears to be an arbitrarily set forecasting duration used in many situations. A better approach suggests that the forecast duration for cash flows should continue only as long as the expected rate of return on incremental investment required to support forecasted sales growth exceeds the cost-of-capital rate.

If for subsequent periods one assumes that the company's return on incremental investment equals the cost-of-capital rate, then the market would be indifferent whether management invests earnings in expansion projects or pays cash dividends that shareholders can in turn invest in identically risky opportunities yielding an identical rate of return. In other words, the value of the company is unaffected by growth when the company is investing in projects earning at the cost of capital or at the minimum acceptable risk-adjusted rate of return required by the market.

Thus, for purposes of simplification, we can assume a 100% payout of earnings after the horizon date or, equivalently, a zero growth rate without affecting the valuation of the company. (An implied assumption of this model is that the depreciation tax shield can be invested to maintain the company's productive capacity.) The residual value is then the present value of the resulting cash-flow perpetuity beginning one year after the horizon date. Of course, if after the horizon date the return on investment is expected to decline below the cost-of-capital rate, this factor can be incorporated in the calculation.

When the acquisition candidate's risk is judged to be the same as the acquirer's overall risk, the appropriate rate for discounting the candidate's cashflow stream is

Table 17.1 One company's average cost of capital

	Weight	Cost	Weighted cost
Debt	0.20	0.05	0.01
Equity	0.80	0.15	0.12
Average cost of capital			0.13

the acquirer's cost of capital. The cost of capital or the minimum acceptable rate of return on new investments is based on the rate investors can expect to earn by investing in alternative, identically risky securities.

The cost of capital is calculated as the weighted average of the costs of debt and equity capital. For example, suppose a company's after-tax cost of debt is 5% and it estimates its cost of equity to be 15%. Further, it plans to raise future capital in the following proportions—20% by way of debt and 80% by equity. Table 17.1 shows how to compute the company's average cost.

It is important to emphasize that the acquiring company's use of its own cost of capital to discount the target's projected cash flows is appropriate only when it can be safely assumed that the acquisition will not affect the riskiness of the acquirer. The specific riskiness of each prospective candidate should be taken into account in setting the discount rate, with higher rates used for more risky investments.

If a single discount rate is used for all acquisitions, then those with the highest risk will seem most attractive. Because the weighted average risk of its component segments determines the company's cost of capital, these high-risk acquisitions will increase a company's cost of capital and thereby decrease the value of its stock.

17.3 Case of Alcar Corporation

As an illustration of the recommended approach to acquisition analysis, consider the case of Alcar Corporation's interest in acquiring Rano Products. Alcar is a leading manufacturer and distributor in the industrial packaging and materials handling market. Sales in 1978 totalled $600 million. Alcar's acquisition strategy is geared toward buying companies with either similar marketing and distribution characteristics, similar production technologies, or a similar research and development orientation. Rano Products, a $50 million sales organization with an impressive new-product development record in industrial packaging, fits Alcar's general acquisition criteria particularly well. Pre-merger financial statements for Alcar and Rano are shown in Table 17.2.

Acquisition for Cash

The interactive computer model for corporate planning and acquisition analysis used in the Alcar evaluation to follow generates a comprehensive analysis for

Table 17.2 Premerger financial statements for Alcar and Rano (in millions of dollars

Statement of income (year ended December 31)	Alcar	Rano
Sales	$600.00	$50.00
Operating expenses	522.00	42.50
EBIT	78.00	7.50
Interest on debt	4.50	.40
Earnings before taxes	73.50	7.10
Income taxes	36.00	3.55
Net income	$ 37.50	$ 3.55
Number of common shares outstanding (in millions)	10.00	1.11
Earnings per share	$ 3.75	$ 3.20
Dividends per share	1.30	.64
Statement of financial position (at year-end)		
Net working capital	$180.00	$ 7.50
Temporary investments	25.00	1.00
Other assets	2.00	1.60
Fixed assets	216.00	20.00
Less accumulated depreciation	(95.00)	(8.00)
	$328.00	$22.10
Interest-bearing debt	$ 56.00	$ 5.10
Shareholders' equity	272.00	17.00
	$328.00	$22.10

acquisitions financed by cash, stock, or any combination of cash, debt, preferred stock, and common stock. In this chapter, the analysis will concern only the cash and exchange-of-shares cases. In the cash-acquisition case, the analysis follows six essential steps:

(1) Develop estimates needed to project Rano's cash flow contribution for various growth and profitability scenarios.
(2) Estimate the minimum acceptable rate of return for acquisition of Rano.
(3) Compute the maximum acceptable cash price to be paid for Rano under various scenarios and minimum acceptable rates of return.
(4) Compute the rate of return that Alcar will earn for a range of price offers and for various growth and profitability scenarios.

Table 17.3 Most likely estimates for Rano's operations under Alcar control

	Years		
	1–5	6–7	8–10
Sales growth rate (g)	.15	.12	.12
EBUT as a percentage of sales (p)	.18	.15	.12
Income tax rate (T)	.46	.46	.46
Capital investment per dollar of sales increase (f)	.20	.20	.20
Working capital per dollar of sales increase (w)	.15	.15	.15

Employing the cash flow formula for year 1:
$$CF_1 = 50(1 + 0.15)(0.18)(1 - 0.46) - (57.5 - 50)(0.20 + 0.15) = 2.96$$

(5) Analyse the feasibility of a cash purchase in light of Alcar's current liquidity and target debt-to-equity ratio.

(6) Evaluate the impact of the acquisition on the earnings per share and capital structure of Alcar.

(a) Cash-flow Projections

The cash-flow formula presented earlier may be restated in equivalent form as

$$CF_t = S_{t-1}(1 + g_t)(p_t)(1 - T_t)(S_t - S_{t-1})(f_t + w_t)$$

where

CF = cash flow,
S = sales,
g = annual growth rate in sales,
p = EBIT as a percentage of sales,
T = income tax rate,
f = capital investment required (i.e., total capital investment net of replacement of existing capacity estimated by depreciation) per dollar of sales increase,
w = cash required for net working capital per dollar of sales increase.

Once estimates are provided for five variables, g, p, T, f, and w, it is possible to project cash flow.

Table 17.3 shows Alcar management's 'most likely' estimates for Rano's operations, assuming Alcar control; Table 17.4 shows a complete projected ten-year cash-flow statement for Rano.

Before developing additional scenarios for Rano, I should make some brief comments on how to estimate some of the cash-flow variables. The income tax rate is the effective cash rate rather than a rate based on the accountant's income tax expense, which often includes a portion that is deferred. For some companies, a direct projection of capital investment requirements per dollar of sales increase will prove a difficult task.

Table 17.4 Projected ten-year cash flow statement for Rano (in millions of dollars)

					Years					
	1	2	3	4	5	6	7	8	9	10
Sales	$57.50	$66.12	$76.04	$87.45	$100.57	$112.64	$126.15	$141.29	$158.25	$177.23
Operating expenses	47.15	54.22	62.36	71.71	82.47	95.74	107.23	124.34	139.26	155.97
EBIT	$10.35	$11.90	$13.69	$15.74	$18.10	$16.90	$18.92	$16.95	$18.99	$21.27
Income taxes on EBIT	4.76	5.48	6.30	7.24	8.33	7.77	8.70	7.80	8.74	9.78
Operating earnings after taxes	$5.59	$6.43	$7.39	$8.50	$9.78	$9.12	$10.22	$9.16	$10.25	$11.48
Depreciation	1.60	1.85	2.13	2.46	2.84	3.28	3.74	4.25	4.83	5.49
Less capital expenditures	(3.10)	(3.57)	(4.12)	(4.74)	(5.47)	(5.69)	(6.44)	(7.28)	(8.22)	(9.29)
Less increase in working capital	(1.13)	(1.29)	(1.49)	(1.71)	(1.97)	(1.81)	(2.03)	(2.27)	(2.54)	(2.85)
Cash flow	$2.96	$3.41	$3.92	$4.51	$5.18	$4.90	$5.49	$3.86	$4.32	$4.84

Table 17.5 Additional scenarios for sales growth and EBIT/sales

	Sales growth			EBIT/sales		
		Years			Years	
Scenario	1–5	6–7	8–10	1–5	6–7	8–10
1. Conservative	0.14	0.12	0.10	0.17	0.14	0.11
2. Most likely	0.15	0.12	0.12	0.18	0.15	0.12
3. Optimistic	0.18	0.15	0.12	0.20	0.16	0.12

To gain an estimate of the recent value of this coefficient, simply take the sum of all capital investments less depreciation over the past five or ten years and divide this total by the sales increase from the beginning to the end of the period . With this approach, the resulting coefficient not only represents the capital investment historically required per dollar of sales increase but also impounds any cost increases for replacement of existing capacity.

One should estimate changes in net working capital requirements with care. Actual year-to-year balance sheet changes in net working capital may not provide a good measure of the rise or decline in funds required. There are two main reasons for this: (a) the year-end balance sheet figures may not reflect the average or normal needs of the business during the year, and (b) the inventory accounts may overstate the magnitude of the funds committed by the company.

To estimate the additional cash requirements, the increased inventory investment should be measured by variable costs for any additional units of inventory required rather than the absolute dollar amount of increase in the inventory account (Rappaport, 1979b).

In addition to its most likely estimate for Rano, Alcar's management developed two additional (conservative and optimistic) scenarios for sales growth and EBIT-sales ratio. Table 17.5 gives a summary of all three scenarios. Alcar's management may also wish to examine additional cases to test the effect of alternative assumptions about the income tax rate and capital investment and working capital requirements per dollar of sales increase.

Recall that cash flows should be forecast only for the period when the expected rate of return on incremental investment exceeds the minimum acceptable rate of return for the acquisition. It is possible to determine this in a simple, yet analytical, non-arbitrary, fashion. To do so, we compute the minimum pretax return on sales (P_{min}) needed to earn the minimum acceptable rate of return on the acquisition (k) given the investment requirements for working capital (w) and fixed assets (f) for each additional dollar of sales and given a projected tax rate (T). The formula for P_{min} is:

$$P_{min} = \frac{(f + w)k}{(1 - T)(1 + k)}.$$

Alcar's management believes that when Rano's growth begins to slow down, its working capital requirements per dollar of additional sales will increase from 0.15 to about 0.20 and its effective tax rate will increase from 0.46 to 0.50. As will be shown in the next section, the minimum acceptable rate of return on the Rano acquisition is 13%. Thus-

$$P_{min} = \frac{(0.20 + 0.20)\,(0.13)}{(1 - 0.50)\,(1 + 0.13)} = 0.092.$$

Alcar's management has enough confidence to forecast pretax sales returns above 9.2% for only the next ten years, and thus the forecast duration for the Rano acquisition is limited to that period.

(b) Estimate Minimum Acceptable Rate of Return for Acquisition

In developing a company's average cost of capital, measuring the after-tax cost of debt is relatively straightforward. The cost of equity capital, however, is more difficult to estimate.

Rational, risk-averse investors expect to earn a rate of return that will compensate them for accepting greater investment risk. Thus, in assessing the company's cost of equity capital or the minimum expected return that will induce investors to buy the company's shares, it is reasonable to assume that they will demand the risk-free rate as reflected in the current yields available in government bonds, plus a premium for accepting equity risk.

Recently, the risk-free rate on government bonds has been in the neighbourhood of 8.8%. By investing in a portfolio broadly representative of the overall equity market, it is possible to diversify away substantially all of the unsystematic risk—that is, risk specific to individual companies. Therefore, securities are likely to be priced at levels that reward investors only for the non-diversifiable market risk—that is, the systematic risk in movements in the overall market.

The risk premium for the overall market is the excess of the expected return on a representative market index such as the Standard & Poor's 500 stock index over the risk-free return. Empirical studies (Ibbotson and Sinquefield, 1977) have estimated this market risk premium (representative market index minus risk-free rate) to average historically about 5–5.5%. I will use a 5.2% premium in subsequent calculations.

Investing in an individual security generally involves more or less risk than investing in a broad market portfolio, thus one must adjust the market risk premium appropriately in estimating the cost of equity for an individual security. The risk premium for a security is the product of the market risk premium times the individual security's systematic risk, as measured by its beta coefficient.

The rate of return from dividends and capital appreciation on a market portfolio will, by definition, fluctuate identically with the market, and therefore its beta is equal to 1.0. A beta for an individual security is an index of its risk expressed as its volatility of return in relation to that of a market portfolio (Brigham, 1977). Securities with betas greater than 1.0 are more volatile than the market and thus would be expected to have a risk premium greater than the overall market risk premium or the average-risk stock with a beta of 1.0.

For example, if a stock moves 1.5% when the market moves 1%, the stock has a beta of 1.5. Securities with betas less than 1.0 are less volatile than the market and would thus command risk premiums less than the market risk premium. In summary, the cost of equity capital may be calculated by the following equation:

$$k_E = R_F + B_j(R_M - R_F)$$

where

k_E = cost of equity capital
R_F = risk-free rate,
B_j = the beta coefficient,
R_M = representative market index.

The acquiring company, Alcar, with a beta of 1.0, estimated its cost of equity as 14% with the foregoing equation:

$$k_E = 0.088 + 1.0\,(0.052) = 0.140.$$

Since interest on debt is tax deductible, the rate of return that must be earned on the debt portion of the company's capital structure to maintain the earnings available to common shareholders is the after-tax cost of debt. The after-tax cost of borrowed capital is Alcar's current before-tax interest rate (9.5%) times 1 minus its effective tax rate of 46%, which is equal to 5.1%. Alcar's target debt-to-equity ratio is 0.30, or, equivalently, debt is targeted at 23% and equity at 77% of its overall capitalization. As Table 17.6 shows, Alcar's weighted average cost of capital, the appropriate rate for discounting Alcar cash flows to establish its estimated value, is then 12%.

For new capital projects, including acquisitions, that are deemed to have about the same risk as the overall company, Alcar can use its 12% cost-of-capital rate as the appropriate discount rate. Because the company's cost of capital is determined by the weighted average risk of its component segments, the specific risk of each prospective acquisition should be estimated in order to arrive at the discount rate to apply to the candidate's cash flows.

Rano, with a beta coefficient of 1.25, is more risky than Alcar, with a beta of 1.0. Employing the formula for cost of equity capital for Rano:

$$k_E = 0.088 + 1.25\,(0.052) = 0.153.$$

On this basis, the risk-adjusted cost of capital for the Rano acquisition is as shown in Table 17.7.

Table 17.6 Alcar's weighted average cost of capital

	Weight	Cost	Weighted cost
Debt	0.23	0.051	0.012
Equity	0.77	0.140	0.108
Average cost of capital			0.120

Table 17.7 Risk-adjusted cost of capital for Rano acquisition

	Weight	Cost	Weighted cost
Debt	0.23	0.054*	0.012
Equity	0.77	0.153	0.118
Average risk-adusted cost of capital			0.130

*Before-tax debt rate of 10% times 1 minus the estimated tax rate of 46%.

(c) Compute Maximum Acceptable Cash Price

This step involves taking the cash-flow projections developed in Step 1 and discounting them at the rate developed in Step 2. Table 17.8 shows the computation of the maximum acceptable cash price for the most likely scenario. The maximum price of $44.51 million, or $40.10 per share, for Rano compares with a $25 current market price for Rano shares. Thus, for the most likely case, Alcar can pay up to $15 per share, or a 60% premium over current market, and still achieve its minimum acceptable 13% return on the acquisition.

Table 17.9 shows the maximum acceptable cash price for each of the three scenarios for a range of discount rates. To earn a 13% rate of return, Alcar can pay at maximum $38 million ($34.25 per share), assuming the conservative scenario, and up to $53 million ($47.80 per share), assuming the optimistic scenario. Note that as Alcar demands a greater return on its investment, the maximum price it can pay decreases. The reverse is, of course, true as well. For example, for the most likely scenario, the maximum price decreases from $44.51 million to $39.67 million as the return requirement goes from 13% to 14%.

Table 17.8 Maximum acceptable cash price for Rano—most likely scenario, with a discount rate of 0.130 (in millions of dollars)

Year	Cash flow ($)	Present value ($)	Cumulative present value ($)
1	2.96	2.62	2.62
2	3.41	2.67	5.29
3	3.92	2.72	8.01
4	4.51	2.76	10.77
5	5.13	2.81	13.59
6	4.90	2.35	15.94
7	5.49	2.33	18.27
8	3.86	1.45	19.72
9	4.32	1.44	21.16
10	4.84	1.43	22.59
Residual value	11.48	26.02*	48.61
Plus temporary investments not required for current operations			1.00
Less debt assumed			5.10
Maximum acceptable cash price			$44.51
Maximum acceptable cash price per share			$40.10

$$\frac{\text{*Year 10 operating earnings after taxes}}{\text{Discount rate}} \times \text{year 10 discount factor} = \frac{11.48}{0.13} \times 0.2946 = 26.02$$

Table 17.9 Maximum acceptable cash price for three scenarios and a range of discount rates

Scenarios	Discount rates				
	0.11	0.12	0.13	0.14	0.15
1. Conservative					
Total price ($ millions)	$48.84	$42.91	$38.02	$33.93	$30.47
Per share price	44.00	38.66	34.25	30.57	27.45
2. Most likely					
Total price ($ millions)	57.35	50.31	44.51	39.67	35.58
Per share price	51.67	45.33	40.10	35.74	32.05
3. Optimistic					
Total price ($ millions)	68.37	59.97	53.05	47.28	42.41
Per share price	61.59	54.03	47.80	42.59	38.21

Table 17.10 Rate of return for various offering prices and scenarios

		Offering price			
		$35.00	$38.00	$40.00	$45.00
Scenarios	Total ($) millions	$31.53	$34.23	$35.04	$40.54
	Per share				
1. Conservative		0.137	0.130	0.126	0.116
2. Most likely		0.152	0.144	0.139	0.129
3. Optimistic		0.169	0.161	0.156	0.144

(d) Compute Rate of Return for Various Offering Prices and Scenarios

Alcar management believes that the absolute minimum successful bid for Rano would be $35 million, or $31.50 per share. Alcar's investment bankers estimated that it may take a bid of as high as $45 million, or $40.50 per share, to gain control of Rano shares. Table 17.10 presents the rates of return that will be earned for four different offering prices, ranging from $35 million to $45 million for each of the three scenarios.

Under the optimistic scenario, Alcar could expect a return of 14.4% if it were to pay $45 million. For the most likely case, an offer of $45 million would yield a 12.9% return, or just under the minimum acceptable rate of 13%. This is as expected, since the maximum acceptable cash price as calculated in Table 17.8 is $44.51 million, or just under the $45 million offer. If Alcar attaches a relatively high probability to the conservative scenario, the risk associated with offers exceeding $38 million becomes apparent.

(e) Analyse Feasibility of Cash Purchase

While Alcar management views the relevant purchase price range for Rano as somewhere between $35 and $45 million, it must also establish whether an all-cash deal is feasible in light of Alcar's current liquidity and target debt-to-enquiry ratio. The maximum funds available for the purchase of Rano equal the post-merger debt capacity of the combined company less the combined pre-merger debt of the two companies plus the combined pre-merger debt of the two companies plus the combined pre-merger temporary investments of the two companies. (Net working capital not required for everyday operations of the business is classified as 'temporary investment.')

In an all-cash transaction governed by purchase accounting, the acquirer's shareholders' equity is unchanged. The post-merger debt capacity is then Alcar's shareholders' equity of $272 million times the targeted debt-to-equity ratio of 0.30, or $81.6 million. Alcar and Rano have premerger debt balances of $56 million and $5.1 million, respectively, for a total of $61.1 million.

Table 17.11 Alcar's projected EPS, debt-to-equity ratio, and unused debt capacity—
without and with Rano acquisition

Year	EPS		Debt/equity		Unused debt capacity (in millions of dollars)	
	Without	With	Without	With	Without	With
0	$3.75	$4.10	0.21	0.26	$25.60	$20.50
1	4.53	4.89	0.19	0.27	34.44	9.42
2	5.09	5.51	0.17	0.28	44.22	7.00
3	5.71	6.20	0.19	0.29	40.26	4.20
4	6.38	6.99	0.21	0.30	35.45	0.98
5	7.14	7.87	0.24	0.31	29.67	−2.71
6	7.62	8.29	0.26	0.31	22.69	−7.77
7	8.49	9.27	0.27	0.32	14.49	−13.64
8	9.46	10.14	0.29	0.33	4.91	−22.34
9	10.55	11.33	0.31	0.34	−6.23	−32.36
10	11.76	12.66	0.32	0.35	−19.16	−43.88

Note: Assumed cash purchase price for Rano is $35 million.

The unused debt capacity is thus $81.6 million minus $61.1 million, or $20.5 million. Add to this the combined temporary investments of Alcar and Rano of $26 million, and the maximum funds available for the cash purchase of Rano will be $46.5 million. A cash purchase is therefore feasible within the tentative price range of $35 to $45 million.

(f) Evaluate Impact of Acquisition on Alcar's EPS and Capital Structure

Because reported earnings per share (EPS) continue to be of great interest to the financial community, a complete acquisition analysis should include a comparison of projected EPS both with and without the acquisition. Table 17.11 contains this comparative projection. The EPS stream with the acquisition of Rano is systematically greater than the stream without acquisition. The EPS standard, is not, however, a reliable basis for assessing whether the acquisition will in fact create value for shareholders. (Alberts and McTaggart, 1974; Stern, 1974).

Several problems arise when EPS is used as a standard for evaluating acquisitions. First, because of accounting measurement problems, the EPS figure can be determined by alternative, equally acceptable methods—for example, LIFO versus FIFO. Second, the EPS standard ignores the time value of money. Third, it does not take into account the risk of the EPS stream. Risk is conditioned not only by the nature of the investment projects a company undertakes but also by the relative proportions of debt and equity used to finance those investments.

A company can increase EPS by increasing leverage as long as the marginal return on investment is greater than the interest rate on the new debt. However, if the marginal return on investment is less than the risk-adjusted cost of capital or if the increased leverage leads to an increased cost of capital, then the value of the company could decline despite rising EPS.

Primarily because the acquisition of Rano requires that Alcar partially finance the purchase price with bank borrowing, the debt-to-equity ratios with the acquisition are greater than those without the acquisition (see Table 17.11). Note that even without the Rano acquisition, Alcar is in danger of violating its target debt-to-equity ratio of 0.30 by the ninth year. The acquisition of Rano accelerates the problem to the fifth year. Whether Alcar purchases Rano or not, management must now be alert to the financing problem, which may force it to issue additional shares or re-evaluate its present capital-structure policy.

Acquisition for Stock

The first two steps in the acquisition-for-stock analysis, projecting Rano cash flows and setting the discount rate, have already been completed in connection with the acquisition-for-cash analysis developed in the previous section. The remaining steps of the acquisition-for-stock analysis are:

(a) Estimate the value of Alcar shares.
(b) Compute the maximum number of shares that Alcar can exchange to acquire Rano under various scenarios and minimum acceptable rates of return.
(c) Evaluate the impact of the acquisition on the earnings per share and capital structure of Alcar.

(a) Estimate Value of Alcar Shares

Alcar conducted a comprehensive corporate self-evaluation that included an assessment of its estimated present value based on a range of scenarios. In the interest of brevity, I will consider here only its most likely scenario.

Management made most likely projections for its operations, as shown in Table 17.12. Again using the equation for the cost of equity capital, the minimum EBIT as a percentage of sales needed to earn at Alcar's 12% cost of capital is 10.9%. Since management can confidently forecast pre-tax return on sales returns above 10.9% for only the next ten years, the cash-flow projections will be limited to that period.

Table 17.13 presents the computation of the value of Alcar's equity. Its estimated value of $36.80 per share contrasts with its currently depressed market value of $22 per share. Because Alcar management believes its shares to be substantially undervalued by the market, in the absence of other compelling factors it will be reluctant to acquire Rano by means of an exchange of shares.

To illustrate, suppose that Alcar were to offer $35 million in cash for Rano. Assume the most likely case, that the maximum acceptable cash price is $44.51

Table 17.12 Most likely estimates for Alcar operations without acquisition

	Years		
	1–5	6–7	8–10
Sales growth rate	0.125	0.120	0.120
EBIT as a percentage of sales	0.130	0.125	0.125
Income tax rate	0.460	0.460	0.460
Capital investment per dollar of sales increase	0.250	0.250	0.250
Working capital per dollar of sales increase	0.300	0.300	0.300

Table 17.13 Estimated present value of Alcar equity—most likely scenario, with a discount rate of 0.120 (in millions of dollars)

Year	Cash flow ($)	Present value ($)	Cumulative present value ($)
1	6.13	5.48	5.48
2	6.90	5.50	10.98
3	7.76	5.53	16.51
4	8.74	5.55	22.06
5	9.83	5.58	27.63
6	10.38	5.26	32.89
7	11.63	5.26	38.15
8	13.02	5.26	43.41
9	14.58	5.26	48.67
10	16.33	5.26	53.93
Residual value	128.62	345.10*	399.03
Plus temporary investments not required for current operations			25.00
Less debt outstanding			56.00
Present value of Alcar equity			$368.03
Present value per share of Alcar equity			$36.80

$$*\frac{\text{Year 10 operating earnings after taxes}}{\text{Discount rate}} \times \text{Year 10 discount factor} = \frac{128.62}{0.12} \times 0.32197 = 345.10$$

million (see Table 17.8); thus the acquisition would create about $9.5 million in value for Alcar shareholders. Now assume that instead Alcar agrees to exchange $35 million in market value of its shares in order to acquire Rano. In contrast with the cash case, in the exchange-of-shares case Alcar shareholders can expect to be worse off by $12.1 million.

With Alcar shares selling at $22, the company must exchange 1.59 million shares to meet the $35 million offer for Rano. There are currently 10 million Alcar

Table 17.14 Calculation of loss by Alcar shareholders (in millions of dollars)

Alcar receives 86.27% of Rano's present value of $44.51 million (see Table 17.8)	$38.4
Alcar gives up 13.73% of its present value of $368.03 million (see Table 17.13)	(50.5)
Dilution of Alcar shareholders' value	$12.1

Table 17.15 Maximum acceptable shares to exchange for three scenarios and a range of discount rates (in millions)

	Discount rates				
Scenarios	0.11	0.12	0.13	0.14	0.15
1. Conservative	1.327	1.166	1.033	0.922	0.828
2. Most likely	1.558	1.367	1.210	1.078	0.967
3. Optimistic	1.858	1.630	1.442	1.235	1.152

shares outstanding. After the merger, the combined company will be owned 86.27%—i.e., (10.00)/(10.00 + 1.59)—by current Alcar shareholders and 13.73% by Rano shareholders. The $12.1 million loss by Alcar shareholders can then be calculated as shown in Table 17.14.

(b) Compute Maximum Number of Shares Alcar can Exchange

The maximum acceptable number of shares to exchange for each of the three scenarios and for a range of discount rates appears in Table 17.15. To earn a 13% rate of return, Alcar can exchange no more than 1.033, 1.210, and 1.442 million shares, assuming the conservative, most likely, and optimistic scenarios, respectively. Consider, for a moment, the most likely case. At a market value per share of $22, the 1.21 million Alcar shares exchanged would have a total value of $26.62 million, which is less than Rano's current market value of $27.75 million—that is, 1.11 million shares at $25 per share. Because of the market's apparent undervaluation of Alcar's shares, an exchange ratio likely to be acceptable to Rano will clearly be unattractive to Alcar.

(c) Evaluate Impact of Acquisition on Alcar's EPS and Capital Structure

The $35 million purchase price is just under ten times Rano's most recent year's earnings of $3.55 million. At its current market price per share of $22, Alcar is selling at about six times its most recent earnings. The acquiring company will

Table 17.16 Alcar's projected EPS, debt-to-equity ratio, and unused debt capacity—
cash vs. exchange of shares

	EPS		Debt/equity		Unused debt capacity (in millions of dollars)	
Year	Cash	Stock	Cash	Stock	Cash	Stock
0	$ 4.10	$ 3.54	0.26	0.21	$20.50	$25.60
1	4.89	4.37	0.27	0.19	9.42	35.46
2	5.51	4.93	0.28	0.17	7.00	46.62
3	6.20	5.55	0.29	0.18	4.20	48.04
4	6.99	6.23	0.30	0.20	0.98	46.37
5	7.87	7.00	0.31	0.21	−2.71	44.29
6	8.29	7.37	0.31	0.23	−7.77	40.90
7	9.27	8.22	0.32	0.24	−13.64	36.78
8	10.14	8.98	0.33	0.26	−22.34	28.90
9	11.33	10.01	0.34	0.27	−32.36	21.79
10	12.66	11.17	0.35	0.29	−43.88	12.29

Note: Assumed purchase price for Rano is $35 million.

always suffer immediate EPS dilution whenever the price–earnings ratio paid for the selling company is greater than its own. Alcar would suffer immediate dilution from $3.75 to $3.54 in the current year. A comparison of EPS for cash versus an exchange-of-shares transaction appears as part of Table 17.16. As expected, the EPS projections for a cash deal are consistently higher than those for an exchange of shares.

However, the acquisition of Rano for shares rather than cash would remove, at least for now, Alcar's projected financing problem. In contrast with a cash acquisition, an exchange of shares enables Alcar to have unused debt capacity at its disposal throughout the ten-year forecast period. Despite the relative attractiveness of this financing flexibility, Alcar management recognized that it could not expect a reasonable rate of return by offering an exchange of shares to Rano.

17.4 Conclusion

The experience of companies that have implemented the approach to acquisition analysis described in this chapter indicates that it is not only an effective way of evaluating a prospective acquisition candidate but also serves as a catalyst for re-evaluating a company's overall strategic plans. The results also enable management to justify acquisition recommendations to the board of directors in an economically sound, convincing fashion.

Various companies have used this approach for evaluation of serious candidates as well as for initial screening of potential candidates. In the latter case, initial input estimates are quickly generated to establish whether the range of maximum acceptable prices is greater than the current market price of the target companies. With the aid of a computer model, this can be accomplished quickly and at relatively low cost.

Whether companies are seeking acquisitons or are acquisition targets, it is increasingly clear that they must provide better information to enable top management and boards to make well-conceived, timely decisions. Use of the approach outlined here should improve the prospects of creating value for shareholders by acquisitions.

References

Alberts, W. W. and McTaggart, J. M. (1974). 'The short-term earnings per share standard for evaluating prospective acquisitions', *Mergers and Acquisitions,* Winter 1974, 4.

Brigham, E. F. (1977). *Financial Management: Theory and Practice,* Dryden Press, Hinsdale, Illinois.

Business Week (1978). 'The cash-flow takeover formula', *Business Week,* 18 December 1978, 86.

Ibbotson, R. G. and Sinquefield, R. A. (1977). *Stock, Bonds, Bills and Inflation: The Past (1926–1976) and the Future (1977–2000),* Financial Analysts Research Foundation, New York.

Rappaport, A. (1979a). 'Do you know the value of your company?' *Mergers and Acquisitions,* Spring 1979.

Rappaport, A. (1979b). 'Measuring company growth capacity during inflation', *Harvard Business Review,* 57(1), 91–100.

Salter, M. S. and Weinhold, W. A. (1978). 'Diversification via acquisition: creating value?' *Harvard Business Review* 56(4), 166–77.

Stern, J. M. (1974). 'Earnings per share don't count', *Financial Analysts Journal,* July–August 1974, 39.

PART 4 MODELS IN CORPORATE PLANNING

Many successful applications of financial modelling have been in corporate planning systems where models form an integral part of the management control process. Such models are used not simply to evaluate specific operating alternatives nor to examine particular opportunities for investment, but to assist in the overall development planning of an organization. Typically, then, the models include both revenue and capital components and they are employed to investigate the interactions between these elements, over time periods of up to about five years, in some detail. Corporate planning in any organization is a widely based activity involving management from all functions, and the corporate planning model may act as a valuable medium of communication between these specialists. This also has implications for the model structure, which must be such that it is accessible to all concerned and may be used to highlight trade-offs which have to be made in pursuit of corporate goals.

The two case studies described in this section are both based on experiences in the public sector, but they could equally well have been taken from any of the larger private corporations. In Chapter 18, a planning system which has been designed to assist particularly in the establishment of a social-service organization is described. A useful feature of this report is the discussion of some of the sensitivity tests carried out using the model. The planning system presented in Chapter 19 is essentially intended for the ongoing control of an established organization, and the relationship of the models to the annual planning cycle is described in a uniquely detailed and valuable account.

Financial Modelling in Corporate Management
Edited by J. W. Bryant
© 1982 John Wiley & Sons Ltd.

18

A Computerized Financial Planning Model for Health Maintenance Organizations

JOHN COLEMAN AND FRANK KAMINSKY

18.1 Introduction

Organization and Scope of the U.S. Health-care System

Health care in the U.S.A. is delivered by a wide spectrum of providers and institutions and, although there is some informal connection, they are not linked together in any systematic way. As shown in Figure 18.1 the health-care system is a complex set of competing groups, providing care at six different levels in a bewildering array of settings. Providers operate independently and autonomously with very little, if any, price competition. Because of the way health care is financed by the government and private health-insurance plans, high priority is assigned to acute care, with a noticeable lack of attention to prevention and continuing primary care. As two observers have noted (Sidel and Sidel, 1977):

> it is so fragmented, the responsibilities so diffuse, the levels of control so manifold, and the communication and coordination between its parts so haphazard that—except for the euphemisms 'pluralistic' and 'pragmatic'—the system almost defies brief description.

The American health-care system is massive. In 1977 it was ranked as the second largest industry in the U.S.A., employing over 6.3 million workers. From 1970 to 1977 the number of employees increased by 50% and, as a result, one out of every seven new jobs created in our economy was for the health industry.

Health-care services are provided in a variety of out-patient and inpatient care settings. Ambulatory care facilities such as the doctor's office, group practice

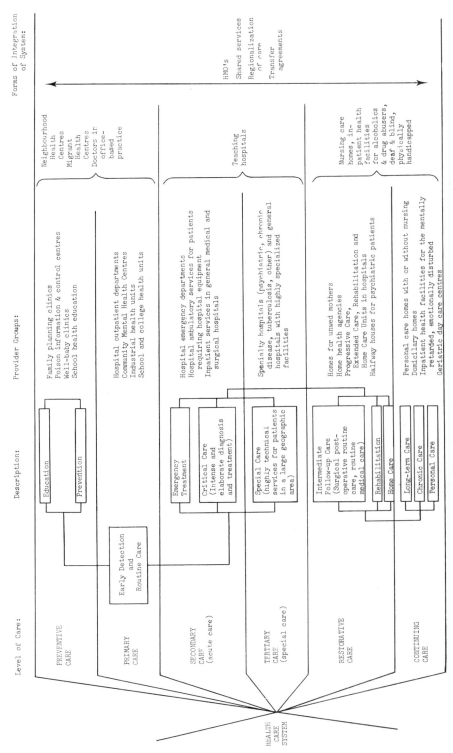

Figure 18.1 U.S. Health Care delivery system

clinics, outpatient clinics in hospitals, neighbourhood health centres, and community health clinics account for approximately 80% of all health-care services.

Inpatient health-care facilities include short- and long-stay hospitals, nursing homes and other facilities, such as those for the mentally retarded and emotionally disturbed. In 1977 hospitals admitted 28 million inpatients and handled 264 million outpatient visits.

About half of all hospitals in the U.S. are owned by non-profit organizations, with another 36% owned by either Federal, State or local governments. Only 14% are owned by profit-making organizations. Nursing homes are operated differently in that 75% are owned and operated by profit-making organizations while 18% are non-profit and the remaining 7% are owned and operated by government.

The U.S. health-care system can be characterized as one with strong community support. Community hospitals represent 83% of the total, handle over 92% of all admissions, account for 77% of all outpatient visits, employ 78% of the industry's labour force and account for 79% of the total cost of hospital care (Rice and Wilson, 1976). By 1976 the number of beds in community hospitals was almost twice that in 1950.

Even though large amounts are provided by public funds, a large part of the U.S. health care system is controlled by the private sector. Prior to the enactment of Medicare and Medicaid in 1965, the public share of health-care expenditures stood at 24.5%. In fiscal year 1977, the public's share reached 42.1%. Between 1970 and 1977, public expenditures for health care increased at an annual rate of 14.5%. Private expenditures for health care also increased rapidly during this period of time but at a slightly lower rate (10.96%).

Cost of Health Care in the U.S.

In addition to being massive, the U.S. health-care system is very expensive. Using percentage of Gross National Product (GNP) as a measure, the U.S.A. ranked among the biggest spenders in the world. The U.S. Department of Health, Education and Welfare (Califano, 1979) estimates the cost of health care to be as much as 206 billion dollars in 1979, a figure translating to 9.1% of the GNP. In 1950 the total cost was 12 billion dollars or 4.6% of the GNP.

Similarly to other industrialized countries, health care costs and expenditures in the U.S. have shown dramatic increases over the last three decades. They have risen faster than the GNP and have increased more rapidly than the Consumer Price Index (CPI) for almost every year since 1950.

Expenditures for hospital care have traditionally acounted for the largest share of the health-care dollar. This share increases each year as hospital costs continue to be the most rapidly growing component of the total cost. By 1978, outlays for hospital care reached 40% of the total, compared with 31% in 1950.

The average cost of a hospital stay rose from $533 in 1969 to $1634 in 1979 and, given present trends, is expected to reach $2660 in 1984.

Recent estimates by the Department of Health, Education and Welfare show that the U.S.A. will soon be spending annually over $1000 per person, and if the cost increases continue unchecked, the total annual bill for the nation's health will exceed $1000 billion at the turn of the century.

Health-maintenance Organizations (HMOs)

During the late 1960s and early 1970s, Federal policymakers became increasingly concerned about ways to curb the chronic inflation of medical expenditures and about methods to guarantee consumers a better return for the increased cost of health care. Numerous controls evolved, many of which were designed to change the financial and organization structure of the delivery system. One initiative to curb spiraling costs and to reduce the inefficiencies in the delivery system was increased federal support to create organized systems of health care that would provide a comprehensive range of health-maintenance and treatment services to voluntarily enrolled populations in exchange for fixed and prepaid periodic payments. Such an organization, called a Health Maintenance Organization (HMO), received national attention in early 1971 as President Nixon sought the support of Congress because, in his words:

> HMOs simultaneously attack many of the problems comprising the health-care crisis. They emphasize prevention and early care: they provide incentives for holding down costs and for increasing the productivity of resources: they offer opportunities for improving the quality of care; they provide a means of improving the geographic distribution of care; and by mobilizing private capital and management talent, they reduce the need for federal funds and direct controls... Because HMO revenues are fixed, their incentives are to keep patients well, for they benefit from patient well-days, not sickness. Their entire cost structure is geared to preventing illness and, failing that, to promoting prompt recovery through the least costly services consistent with maintaining quality. (U.S. Department of Health, Education and Welfare, 1971)

While such organizations can have different sponsors and take on various organization patterns, all of them are designed to integrate, in a balanced structure, the following basic ingredients:

(1) a group of *consumers* who desire pre-paid comprehensive medical care;
(2) a qualified group of *providers* suited to pre-paid medical practice;
(3) *a comprehensive set of medical and health-care services* that meet the needs of its consumers and are within the capacity of the providers to provide;
(4) a *medical facility or group of facilities or offices* in which to provide the necessary services;

(5) an *administrative organization* to plan, coordinate, manage and control the plan's resources; and

(6) *financial resources* for initial and continuous operation.

The generic term HMO is new but the concept has existed for more than 50 years in the form of pre-paid group practice.

In 1971 there were 33 HMO prototypes in the U.S.A. serving an estimated population of 3.6 million. Motivated by Congressional and administration support HMOs have emerged rapidly since that time. The Health Maintenance Organization Act of 1973, PL 93-222, committed the federal government to encourage and foster the development of HMOs and to support their operation for a trial period. Passage of this Act helped increase the number to 125 by 1973, and to 183 by the end of 1974. In late 1979 the number of operating HMOs reached 223 of which 97 were federally qualified. Enrolment in 1979 stood at 8.2 million, more than twice the number being served in 1971. More than 100 new HMOs are now in various stages of development.

One of the principal arguments for advocating the HMO as an alternative to traditional fee-for-service medicine is that it is less expensive because of low hospital utilization rates. The reasons for lower hospital utilization are still being debated, but several are usually suggested:

(1) an emphasis on ambulatory service and good preventive care;
(2) the removal of financial incentives for performing unnecessary procedures.
(3) peer review:
(4) group controls; and
(5) the lower ratio of beds to population (Donabedean, 1969, Roemer and Shonick, 1973 and Greenlick, 1972).

When compared to the traditional fee-for-service health-care system, HMOs have fared well with respect to utilization, total costs and quality of care. Some recent evidence shows that, for HMO enrollees, hospitalization rates and surgical procedures are far lower than in the traditional system; that HMOs provide more ambulatory care; and that health-care costs for HMO members can be as much as 10–40% less than those with traditional forms of health-insurance coverage.

In addition to maintaining somewhat lower costs HMOs have also been able to maintain effectively their members' health and to maintain quality. Although comparative evaluations are difficult, the quality of medical care provided by most HMOs is equal to or better than that provided in comparable fee-for-service delivery systems. While different studies have shown variations in patient attitudes to HMO care, patient satisfaction is generally high and negative responses to a 'clinic atmosphere' are similar to responses from patients receiving care in a private office setting (Romer, 1974).

While the concept of the HMO is still being debated, the evidence continues to mount in support of the HMO as a viable economic alternative to fee-for-service medicine. A recent assessment of various hospital cost-containment strategies singled out the HMO as being a consistent and effective means of reducing hospital costs and of keeping health costs at reasonable levels (Chassin, 1978).

Problems and Prospects in HMOs

The U.S. government expected to have 500 HMOs in operation by 1980, but was beset by many problems. Contined opposition to the HMO from hospitals and the medical profession hindered the program from the start but, more importantly, problems were caused by lack of planning technology and management skills. The lack of expertise in the skills required to develop and manage an HMO resulted in many failures. For example, between October 1974 and May 1975 more than twelve HMOs went out of business due to financial reverses. In December of 1975 there were 23 fewer HMOs in operation compared to May of 1975 (U.S. Department of Health, Education and Welfare, 1975a, 1975b). Several more went out of business between 1976 and 1978. The two most recent failures in 1979 were federally qualified under the HMO Act of 1973. Approximately twenty of the over 200 HMOs now operating are experiencing fiscal problems and could fail in the near future.

Although the number of HMOs that have either failed or are now in trouble is not high compared to those still in operation, the financial losses have been high, especially for those that received from the federal government the maximum loan support of $4.5 million.

Post mortems on failures and fiscal examinations of those now in danger indicate that the primary cause of failure is due to substandard planning and faulty management practices. Most of the problems stem from a lack of experienced planners and a lack of planning methodologies specifically designed for HMOs.

While the HMO program has suffered some reverses and at time has been criticized by the Congress and the General Accounting Office, the program is now receiving strong support by labour organizations, large industries, chambers of commerce, and many Congressional leaders. Because of success in the area of cost containment and because of the ability of an HMO to correct deficiencies in the existing health-care delivery system, the Department of Health, Education and Welfare is now preparing plans to continue supporting HMOs through the 1980s. By 1988, the Department is expecting an increase of almost 300% in HMO enrollment and plans to have over 400 operating HMOs. Based on studies of their competitive impact on the traditional fee-for-service delivery system, HMOs are serving a major role in virtually every major national health-insurance proposal now being discussed in the Congress.

18.2 Planning in HMOs

Design and Developmental Planning of HMOs

Planning an economically viable HMO is by no means simple and the resources involved are by necessity very costly. The planning process often takes 3–5 years before one comes on line and another 4-5 years to achieve financial viability. The cost of planning an HMO can range from $2 to $5 million depending on its organizational form and construction plans, and another $2 to $4 million in loans is usually needed to offset operating deficits that are incurred before revenues finally exceed costs. While both public and private venture capital are usually combined to meet the planning costs and operating deficits, to those that can qualify, most of the capital is provided by the Department of Health, Education and Welfare.

From a cost point of view, it is extremely important that sound and rational business decisions be made to prevent a chaotic start and to reduce the chance of failure at a later date. Measured by both time and money the business risks are substantial. The task of bringing together the essential ingredients of the existing health-care delivery system to create an HMO is technically complex and therefore should embody a systems-planning approach and an orderly, systematic planning process. The need for these can be seen in the flowchart in Figure 18.2 which depicts the major tasks in starting an HMO.

There are many ways to coordinate and manage the various interested parties, study groups, and tasks. Although it is difficult to define all of the steps and procedures needed to bring an HMO to life, the Department of Health, Education and Welfare have developed a planning framework to place into a time perspective the activities and issues involved (Geiser and Ring, 1975, Gumbiner, 1975, Kress and Singer, 1975, Birnbaum, 1976, and U.S. Department of Health, Education and Welfare, 1974). This framework consists of four major phases:

(1) feasibility;
(2) planning;
(3) initial development; and
(4) implementation/operation.

Figure 18.3 presents a schematic diagram showing the various phases, their time relationships, some of the issues addressed, and activities conducted when going from one planning/development phase to the next.

As shown in Fgure 18.3 the concept of incremental decision-making is used. This implies that a decision is made only to proceed to the next appropriate phase, enabling the planning group to stop at each of several points before major resources are committed.

As the planning group proceeds from one planning phase to the next, the number of design activities, analyses and decisions multiply and become more complex. At each new phase the different ways of doing things are examined in finer detail and plans begin to become more detailed. At the start of the planning process choices are examined from a macro point of view and, in each case, are examined later from a micro point of view.

The design of an HMO requires that the planning group study and evaluate, among other things, the medical and economic consequences of alternative benefit-package designs, marketing strategies, organization formats, service-use patterns and operating policies and procedures. The process, which involves thousands of

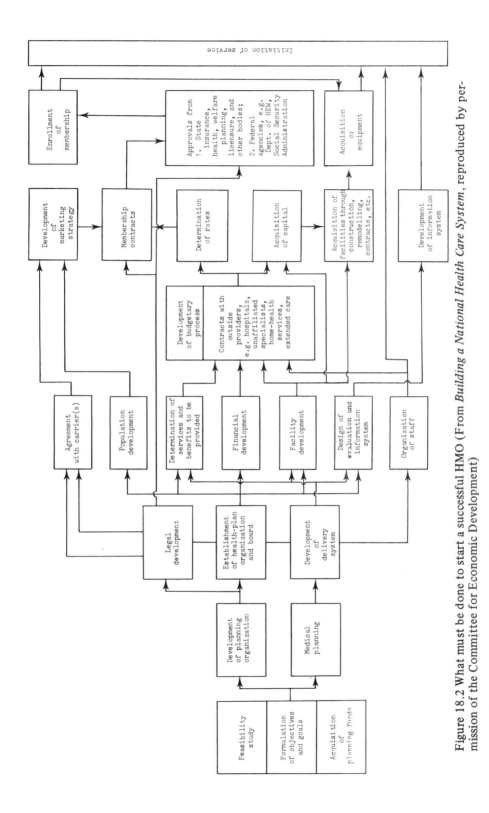

Figure 18.2 What must be done to start a successful HMO (From *Building a National Health Care System*, reproduced by permission of the Committee for Economic Development)

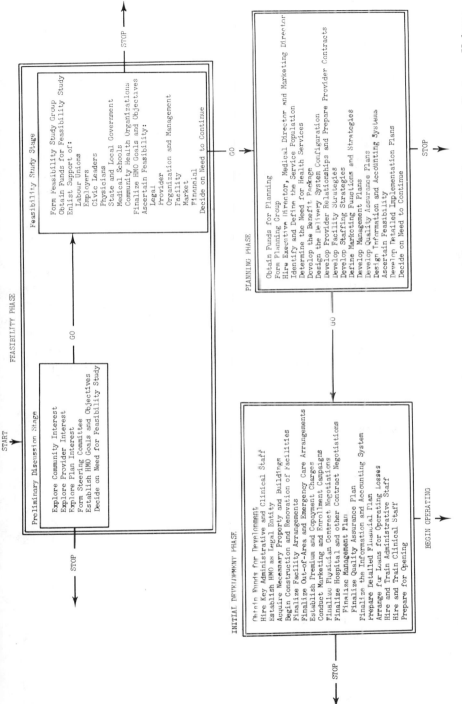

Figure 18.3 The three major phases in HMO development (Reproduced by permission from *Ambulatory Care Systems, Volume IV, Designing Medical Services for Health Maintenance Organizations*, by John R. Coleman and Frank C. Kaminsky: Lexington, Mass.: Lexington Books, D. C. Heath and Company, Copyright 1977, D. C. Heath and Company)

hours of analysis at each step, is an iterative one, with the group proceeding from one design to the next, hoping to find that one 'best' design that is economically feasible while, at the same time, meeting a number of design criteria initially set to guide the planning and decision-making processes.

The HMO Financial Planning Process

The ultimate test of a soundly planned HMO is its ability to achieve quickly an enrollment level producing revenues that exceed costs and to maintain this position for each scucceeding year of operation. Experience has shown that this phenomenon does not happen immediately and that expert financial planning and management skills must be used to keep the HMO financially solvent, particularly during its formative years when it is most vulnerable.

HMO financial planning is concerned with estimating, in advance, the financial requirements and fiscal consequences of the enterprise once it has decided what is to be done. It involves an explicit economic evaluation of alternative courses of action and the selection of the 'best' acceptable alternative for implementation once planners have made policy decisions concerning how the plan is to be managed, what health-care services it will provide and so forth.

An overview of the HMO financial planning process is shown in Figure 18.4. This simplified activity chart shows that the financial needs and requirements of an HMO are outcome measures for a given set of policy decisions and assumptions relating to:

(1) *what* health services are to be covered;
(2) *who* will be eligible to receive them;
(3) *where, when,* and *how* they are to be provided;
(4) *who* will provide them; and
(5) *how* they are to be paid for.

18.3 Financial Planning Models for HMOs

During 1973 and 1974 computer models were suggested and several were later developed for specific HMO planning situations (Moustafa and Sears, 1974, Greene and Grimes, 1974, Hersch and Miller, 1974 and Thompson, 1974). The first models were rather simple in construction and were, consequently, neither adopted for nor adapted to other HMO settings. The model to be described in the sections that follow was the first computerized financial planning model that could be used in any HMO planning situation (Coleman and Kaminsky, 1977a). This particular financial planning model (FPM)—was designed to assist planners in the feasibility and planning phase to determine and evaluate the economic implications of alternative organization designs and operational policies and procedures regarding the services to be included in the benefit package, who will be eligible to receive these services,

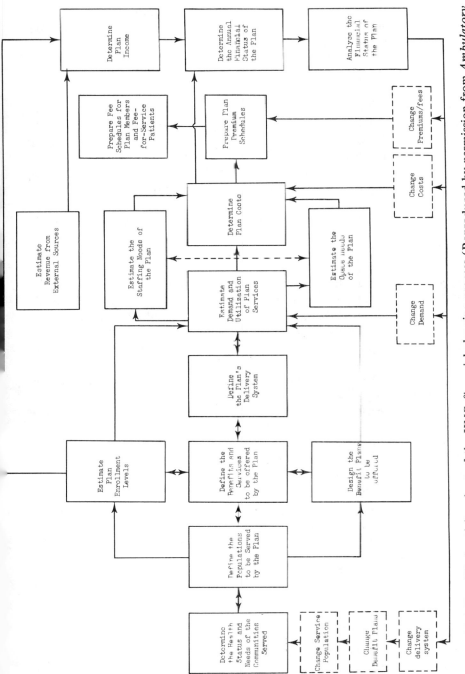

Figure 18.4 Simplified activity chart of the HMO financial planning process (Reproduced by permission from *Ambulatory Care Systems, Designing Medical Services for Health Maintenance Organizations*, by John R. Coleman and Frank C. Kaminsky: Lexington, Mass.: Lexington Books, D. C. Heath and Company, Copyright 1977, D. C. Heath and Company)

how, when, and where these services are to be made available and delivered by health resources in the community, and how much the HMO, its members, and non-members must pay for its services.

An Overview of the FPM

The FPM is a computer-assisted system for determining the economic implications of alternative organizational, financial and operational strategies and policies before the HMO actually begins operation. The model can be used as a simulator and is designed to provide HMO planners with rapid answers to a number of 'what if?' questions that need to be asked before a final HMO configuration is accepted. The FPM provides answers to a number of specific design questions:

(1) What will be the expected annual utilization of the plan's medical and health-care services?

(2) What is the financial impact of various hospitalization rates on the plan and hospital?

(3) What effects will various organizational structures and operational policies for delivering services have on the financial security of the plan and the hospital?

(4) What mix of physicians and allied health and paramedical personnel will be needed to be a direct service provider?

(5) What effect will changes in the mix of medical and health-care services have on yearly costs and revenues?

(6) What external funding should the plan secure during its formative years in order to meet its financial obligations?

(7) What are the effects of the plan's size, and the premium and fee-for-service schedules on annual cash flow and financial security?

(8) What co-payment and capitation fee schedules and membership levels are needed to break even within the first five years of operation?

(9) What physical resources must be made available each year to provide the services on a direct-service basis?

(10 What will be the effect of changes in the socio-economic and demographic characteristics of the subscribing population?

(11) What organizational structure and operational policies will result in low initial operation costs, low indebtedness, early break-even?

(12) What are the annual proforma cost and revenue schedules for each HMO con-figuration to be evaluated?

General Structure of the Model

Figure 18.5 illustrates the general structure of the model. The FPM consists of eight components or 'program modules', an edit/control program, and seven planning models: service population, demand/utilization, staff, space, cost, revenue, and

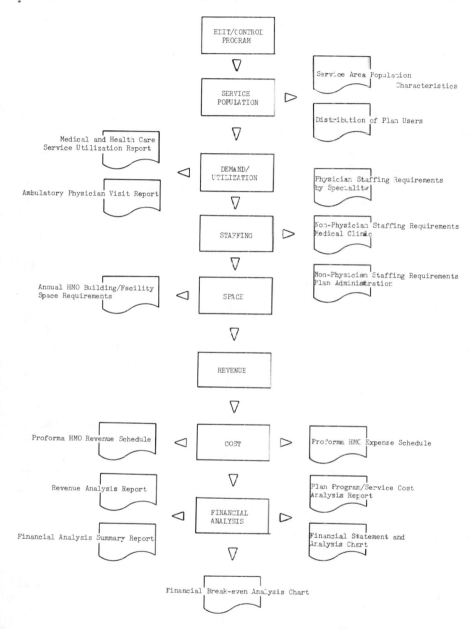

Figure 18.5 Systems diagram of the FPM (Reproduced by permission from *Ambultory Care Systems, Designing Medical Services for Health Maintenance Organizations,* by John R. Coleman and Frank C. Kaminsky: Lexington, Mass.: Lexington Books, D. C. Heath and Company, Copyright 1977, D. C. Heath and Company)

financial analysis. The FPM, the assumptions and the data bases used in its design and all of the modules are completely described in two volumes (Coleman and Kaminsky, 1977b, 1977c).

Input and Output

Input to the FPM consists of two data bases. One is built into the planning model (the HMO DATA FILE) and the other one is provided by the HMO planning group.

The HMO DATA FILE consists of two basic sets of data. The first consists of socio-economic and demographic data for urban and rural areas in various census regions of the country. The second contains service use rates for the different inpatient and outpatient health services a qualifying HMO may provide. Included in this file are inpatient care admission rates, physician and dentist visit rates, and the distribution of hospital admissions and physician visits by medical specialty and visit site. The utilization rates, which are by sex and age group, were obtained from a sample of operating HMOs located throughout the country. Although the HMO DATA FILE is built into the FPM, planners can modify the utilization data if some of these data do not satisfy regional or local conditions.

THE USER DATA FILE, which is also provided by the planning group, is essentially a data base defining the HMO under consideration. This data base contains 21 different sets of design data. Each set is used to indicate the design option to be made by the planners or to specify values of certain design variables and operating variables used to describe the beneficiary population, the benefit packages, monthly premiums, facility and delivery options, hospital and medical-service use rates, compensation schedules, fee schedules, fringe-benefit rates, labour turnover rates, loan and investment data, economic conditions, and organizational and operational strategies and policies. These data are provided for each of the first five years of HMO operation. Table 18.1 lists the contents of the 21 data sets.

These inputs are operated upon by seven FPM modules. The transformation functions for the input data of each module were built with the experience data provided by many first-, second-, and third-generation HMOs.

Output from the FPM consists of 15 planning reports that contain annual and five-year summary information on:

(1) demographics of the beneficiary population;
(2) projected use of health and medical services by programme and physician specialty;
(3) physician staffing requirements by specialty;
(4) non-physician staffing requirements by programme or organization unit;
(5) facility space needs by programme;
(6) proforma revenue schedule by source and programme;
(7) proforma expense schedule by programme;
(8) cash flow and financial needs of the plan.

Table 18.2 lists the different reports and their contents. Tables 18.3–18.5 are illustrative examples of some of the reports for a particular HMO configuration under study.

Sensitivity Analyses

The FPM has been designed with the flexibility of a simulator. For example, financial managers can study the economic behaviour of the HMO when certain operating and design variables remain fixed while others are allowed to vary. Ten such sensitivity analyses have been incorporated into the model.

(1) days of hospital care per 1000 enrolled members;
(2) monthly premiums for individual, family, Medicare, and Medicaid plans;
(3) annual increases in the monthly premiums for plan members;
(4) ratio of family-to-individual premium prices;
(5) annual increases in service fees and charges for fee-for-service patients;
(6) annual salary increases for HMO staff personnel;
(7) annual staff turnover rates for HMO personnel;
(8) annual cost inflation rates for hospital care;
(9) annual cost inflation rates for medical and physician care services;
(10) annual cost inflation rates for dental care services.

Whenever sensitivity analyses are to be conducted, the FPM will use a 'low', 'high', and 'incremental' value provided as input by the user. For example, if the user wants to study the financial impact of different hospital days per year per 1000 members, it can be stipulated that the FPM vary the hospital days per year per 1000 members from say, 400 to 600, in increments of 50 days.

The sensitivity options listed above are but a few of the many that can be computed. Additional analyses can be performed by repeatedly running the FPM under different values for the input variable to be examined. By using the model as a simulator, a large number of designs can be evaluated by the planning group in a short period of time at a reasonable cost.

Examples of the FPM in Typical Planning Situations

A typical HMO Planning situation requires planners to examine a number of feasible designs within a reasonable time and at a reasonable cost. This section illustrates how the FPM can be used to select the 'best' HMO configuration once an initial design has been selected for study. Although a large number of combinations of design and operating variables need to be studied in a real planning situation, only a few have been selected here to illustrate the model's usefulness and versatility. The operating variables for the HMO planning case which follows were chosen from a number of variables studied in an active planning situation. The ones

Table 18.1 Description of the user data file (Reproduced by permission of the publisher, from *Ambulatory Care Systems, Volume V, Designing Medical Services for Health Maintenance Organizations*, by John R. Coleman and Frank C. Kaminsky: Lexington, Mass.: Lexington Books, D. C. Heath and Company, Copyright 1977, D. C. Heath and Company)

User data set	Contents
(1) Geographic, residential and community definition	The census region and types of communities served by the HMO including the fluoridation or nonfluoridation of community water supplies.
(2) Annual prepaid and fee-for-service patient populations	The number of individual, family, Medicare, Medicaid and fee-for-service patents to be served during each of the five years.
(3) Annual enrolment levels for supplemental health services	The number of plan members who have elected supplemental benefits during each of the five years.
(4) HMO organizational form benefit program and service options	The type and scope of service benefits to be provided by the HMO.
(5) Definition of HMO services and program delivery options	The delivery system options chosen to provide for the delivery of service benefits selected by the HMO.
(6) HMO building and medical facility occupancy options	The medical building and facility occupancy options for the medical and administrative components of the HMO.
(7) Service capacity of medical buildings and plan facilities	The service capacity of medical buildings and facilities to be constructed by the HMO during the first five years of plan operation.
(8) Plan member utilization rates for inpatient care services	The birth rate per 1000 women of childbearing age, lengths of stay in inpatient care facilities, and the hospital days of care per 1000 members.
(9) Monthly premiums for 'basic' and 'supplemental' health benefit plans	The initial monthly premiums for individual, family, Medicare, and Medicaid plan members and for all supplemental benefit plans offered by the IIMO.
(10) Annual percentage price increases in plan premiums	The annual increase in premium prices for 'basic' and 'supplemental' benefit plans.

(11) Co-payment fee schedule for HMO plan members

The point-of-service charges for services rendered to plan members.

(12) Other plan member service fees and annual increases in co-payment fees

Other fees for services rendered to members and the annual increases in co-payment fees.

(13)
(14) Service fee schedules for fee-for-service patients

The fees charged nonplan members for services rendered by the HMO.

(15) Monthly SSA cost reimbursement for Medicare

The average monthly cost reimbursement from SSA for Medicare members.

(16) External revenues

External income to the HMO from such sources as grants, gifts, endowments, and so forth.

(17) Service provider compensation options and schedules

The contractual costs to the HMO for contracting with health service groups within the community to provide health services to plan members. These costs are on a capitation and/or unit of service (fee-for-service) basis.

(18) Compensation schedules for HMO staff physician and nonphysicians

The annual base salary for physicians and nonphysicians employed directly by the HMO including those in administration.

(19) Fringe benefit, salary increase, and manpower turn-over rates for HMO staff members

The annual percentage rates of salary increases for HMO employees. Also included are the percentage rates for fringe benefits, and the annual turnover rates for physicians and non-physicians.

(20) Hospital and medical care services cost inflation rates

Annual rates of cost inflation for hospitalization and medical care services including physician, dental, optical, and pharmaceutical services.

(21) HMO loan and plan investment income data

Annual interest rates and payment records for capital borrowed from The Department of Health, Education and Welfare and/or commercial banks to meet operating deficits and for the construction of buildings. Annual interest rates for funds (loans and/or profits) deposited in the bank.

Table 18.2 Description of the HMO planning reports generated by the FPM (Reproduced by permission of the publisher, from *Ambulatory Care Systems, Volume V, Designing Medical Services for Health Maintenance Organizations*, by John R. Coleman and Frank C. Kaminsky:Lexington, Mass.: Lexington Books, D. C. Heath and Company, Copyright 1977, D. C. Heath and Company)

Planning report	Description
(1) Service area population characteristics	Age-sex distribution and socioeconomic data for persons living in the service area of the HMO.
(2) Distribution of plan users report	Age-sex distribution of plan members and fee-for-service patients who will use plan services during the year.
(3) Medical and health care service utilization report	Expected utilization of inpatient and outpatient services for the first five years of plan operation.
(4) Ambulatory physician visit report	Expected number of annual ambulatory visits to physicians by medical speciality.
(5) Physician staffing requirements by speciality	Annual staffing patterns for primary and specialty care physicians for each of the first five years of plan operation.
(6) Non-physician staffing requirements—medical clinic	The yearly staffing patterns for the medical clinic including nurses, laboratory technicians, administrative staff, and dental, pharmacy, home care, and mental health services.
(7) Non-physician staffing requirements—plan administration	The yearly staffing pattern for the administrative component of the HMO.

(8) Annual HMO building facility space requirements

The yearly space needs of fourteen organizational components of the HMO.

(9) Proforma HMO revenue schedule

Estimated yearly income to the HMO from plan operation and external sources including income from borrowed capital and profits if any.

(10) Revenue analysis report

Detailed revenue data by source for the five-year planning period.

(11) Proforma HMO expense schedule

The annual estimated costs of plan operations, including the cost of borrowing capital to meet projected losses during the first five years of plan operation.

(12) Plan program/service cost analysis report

Detailed costs of HMO operations for the year of plan operation. This report is prepared on a yearly basis.

(13) Financial analysis summary report

The financial position of the HMO at the end of each year including when and how much capital must be borrowed and the annual levels of outstanding debt.

(14) Financial statement and analysis chart

The enrolment and financial position of the HMO during each year of plan operation including a graph of revenue vs. cost for the first five years.

(15) Financial break-even analysis chart

A graph indicating the time when the HMO's income balances costs and the number of plan members and fee-for-service atients using the HMO when this occurs.

Table 18.3 Sample FPM utilization report
IIMO group model
Pre-paid medical plan
Medical and health-care service utilization report
Summary

Medical and health-care service	Service unit	Year 1	Year 2	Year 3	Year 4	Year 5
Physician services		16 323	43 394	71 068	94 156	114 818
Home	(visits)	81	216	355	470	574
Inpatient	(visits)	2 203	5 858	9 594	12 711	15 500
Office/clinic	(visits)	14 037	37 318	61 118	80 974	98 743
Hospitalization						
Short-term care						
Non-maternity cases	(number)	370	1 008	1 604	2 039	2 377
Length of stay	(days)	7.2	7.2	7.2	7.2	7.2
Non-maternity-days	(days)	2 663	7 255	11 551	14 683	17 116
Maternity/births	(number)	71	204	338	448	550
Length of stay	(days)	4.2	4.2	4.2	4.2	4.2
Maternity-days	(days)	298	857	1 420	1 882	2 310
Surgical cases	(number)	166	453	721	917	1 069

		Col 1	Col 2	Col 3	Col 4	Col 5
Long-term care						
Admissions	(number)	6	19	32	42	42
Length of stay	(days)	26.0	26.0	26.0	26.0	26.0
Patient days	(days)	156	494	832	1 092	1 352
Psychiatric care						
Admissions	(number)	12	38	61	83	103
Length of stay	(days)	23.0	23.0	23.0	23.0	23.0
Patient days	(days)	276	874	1 403	1 909	2 369
OP mental health	(visits)	861	2 294	3 757	4 978	6 071
Laboratory services						
Outpatient	(tests)	19 537	51 894	84 969	112 571	137 264
Pharmacy services	(prescriptions)	25 266	67 225	110 117	145 901	177 923
Injections	(number)	1 824	4 851	7 945	10 526	12 836
Physical therapy						
Outpatient	(visits)	146	389	637	844	1 029
Radiology services						
Outpatient	(exams)	2 931	7 785	12 745	16 885	20 589
Dental services						
Hygienist	(visits)	1 210	2 975	4 626	5 927	7 116
Dentist	(visits)					
Optical services						
Refractions	(number)	888	2 361	3 866	5 122	6 246
Prescriptions	(number)	532	1 416	2 319	3 073	3 747
VNA home-care visits	(visits)	255	687	1 123	1 487	1 815

Table 18.4 Sample FPM physician staffing requirements report
HMO group model
Pre-paid medical plan
Physician staffing requirements by specialty

Medical specialty	Provide option	Year 1	Year 2	Year 3	Year 4	Year 5
GP/internists	Staff	2.00	5.05	8.26	10.95	13.35
Paediatrics	Staff	1.00	1.93	3.17	4.20	5.12
Obstetrics/gynaecology	Staff	0.50	1.23	2.02	2.68	3.26
General surgery	Staff	0.50	0.97	1.59	2.10	2.57
Opthalmologists	FFS	0.09	0.25	0.42	0.56	0.68
Ear/nose/throat ENT	FFS	0.12	0.33	0.55	0.73	0.89
Orthopaedics	FFS	0.16	0.43	0.70	0.93	1.14
Dermatology	FFS	0.12	0.33	0.55	0.73	0.89
Allergy	FFS	0.06	0.16	0.27	0.36	0.44
Psychiatry	FFS	0.16	0.43	0.70	0.93	1.14
Urology	FFS	0.09	0.25	0.41	0.55	0.67
Radiology	FFS	0.17	0.46	0.75	1.00	1.22
Anaesthesiology	FFS	0.13	0.34	0.56	0.75	0.91
Pathology	FFS	0.07	0.19	0.31	0.42	0.51
Other	FFS	0.06	0.16	0.26	0.35	0.42
Total—psych excluded		5.07	12.08	19.82	26.31	33.07
Staff—psych excluded		4.00	9.18	15.04	19.93	24.30

chosen are those having the greatest impact on the financial security of an HMO and therefore would be likely candidates for sensitivity studies in other planning situations.

(a) Sensitivity of Hospitalization Rates

The deteriorating effects of hospital rates on the annual financial position of the HMO is illustrated by the family of cash-flow curves given Figure 18.6. For this particular design, the monthly premiums for the first year were established at $48 for the individual plan and $120 for the family plan. As shown, the HMO did not have a favourable annual cash flow until the hospital days per 1000 members was started at 625 days per 1000 members and could be reduced each year by 25. If the HMO experiences 625–525 days per 1000 members, it finally reaches break-even in the 38th month of operation, and would have to borrow almost $2.3 million to off-set previous losses. When the hospital days per 1000 members starts out at 725 and is reduced annually by 25 to reach 625 in the fifth year, the HMO could not reach break-even until the 49th month of operation and would need to borrow $3.5 million.

The change in the HMO's financial position after five years of operations is from a cumulative loss of $1.7 million when it is at 725, to a gain of $2.2 million at 625. The impact of excessive hospital days on the cash flow of the HMO is quite obvious.

(b) Sensitivity of Annual Premium Increases

Figure 18.7 illustrates the financial impact on the HMO when the monthly premiums are increased annually at a rate of 8, 9, 10 and 12%, and hospital costs and medical inflation are at 12 and 10% respectively. For three of the cases (8, 9, 10), the HMO finds itself in a position with cumulative losses ranging from $4 to 7 million by the end of the fifth year. If the premiums are increased at 10% annually, the HMO reaches break-even in the 53rd month with an enrolment slightly less than 31 000 members. The amount of capital to be borrowed is $3.9 million. When the premiums are increased each year by 12%, the HMO reaches break-even in the 41st month with an enrolment of just over 24 000 members. While the HMO still has to borrow $2.8 million to meet operating deficits, at the end of the fifth year it will have a net gain of $248 502.

It is obvious from the graph that there are definite financial trade-offs for pricing decisions—namely, the stretch out of the break-even and pay-back periods in return for lower annual rates of premium increases.

(c) Sensitivity of Hospital and Medical Cost Inflation

The annual rate of inflation assumed in the original design was 12% for hospital care and 10% for medical care. Figure 18.8 shows the cash-flow curves for various

Table 18.5 Sample FPM financial analysis summary report
HMO group model
Prepaid medical plan
Financial analysis summary report

Plan revenue–expenses–balance ($)	Year 1	Year 2	Year 3	Year 4	Year 5
Total plan revenue					
Plan operations:	$2 022 402	$6 273 311	$11 614 434	$17 276 586	$23 647 675
Borrowed capital:	$1 137 230	$1 162 542	$573 381	$00	$00
Interest income:	$43,131	$44,091	$21 746	$19 092	$122 361
Total:	$3 202 763	$7 479 944	$12 209 561	$17 295 678	$23 770 036
Total plan expenses					
Plan operations:	$3 159 632	$7 435 853	$12 187 815	$16 668 228	$21 134 378
New loan principal:	$127 456	$130 293	$64 262	$00	$00
New loan interest:	$90 978	$93 003	$45 870	$00	$00
Total:	$3 378 066	$7 659 149	$12 297 947	$16 668 228	$21 134 378
Annual plan balance	($175 303)	($179 205)	($88 386)	$627 450	$2 635 658

Loan interest and principal					
Interest paid—new loans:	$00	$00	$00	$ 00	$00
Interest paid—other loans:	$90 978	$264 763	$462 983	$632 912	$772 285
Principal paid—new loans:	$00	$00	$00	$00	$00
Principal paid—other loans:	$127 456	$395 402	$749 047	$1 130 982	$1 543 473
Total:	$218 434	$660 166	$1 212 030	$1 763 895	$2 315 759
Capital borrowed to date					
New loans:	$00	$00	$00	$00	$00
Bank and other loans:	$1 137 230	$2 299 772	$2 873 153	$2 873 153	$2 873 153
Total:	$1 137 230	$2 299 772	$2 873 153	$2 873 153	$2 873 153

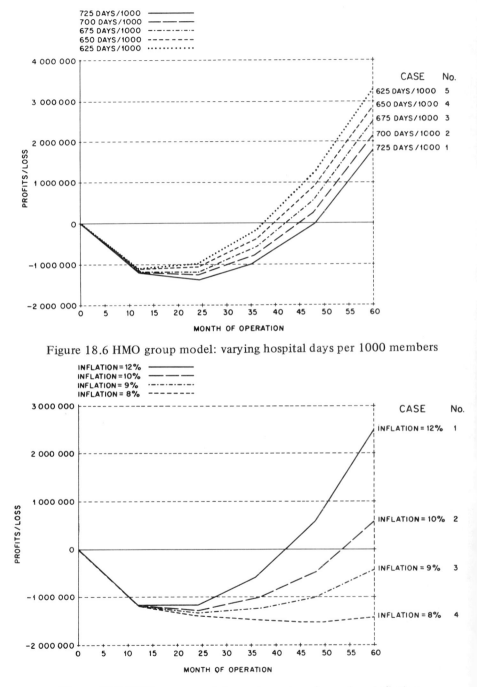

Figure 18.6 HMO group model: varying hospital days per 1000 members

Figure 18.7 HMO group model: varying rates of premium inflation

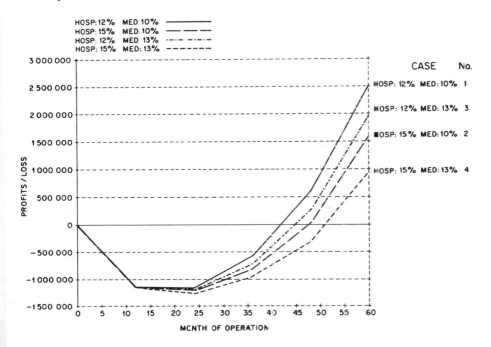

Figure 18.8 HMO group model: varying rates of hospital and medical services inflation

rates of inflation. For case 1, the HMO reaches break-even in the 41st month with an enrolment of 24 180. The amount of capital borrowed is $2.8 million. If medical-care costs increase by 3% over the assumed rate of 10%, the break-even enrolment becomes 25 893 and the time of break-even is pushed back to the 45th month. Cumulative losses for the five-year period total 0.8 million and an additional $175 194 needs to be borrowed.

Cases 3 and 4 have even more negative effects than case 2. For case 3 the break-even enrolment becomes 27 607 and the time is extended to the 43th month. Total cumulative losses are 1.5 million for the period with increased capital borrowing of $303 134. Obviously, case 4 is the worst. Cumulative losses become $2.7 million and break-even doesn't occur until the 51st month.

The effect of higher hospital and medical cost inflation rates over the projected rates illustrates the need for strong cost-containment initiatives by the HMO.

18.4 Implementation of the FPM in Different HMO Planning Settings

The FPM has been implemented successfully and used by several HMO planning groups. In some instances it was modified and adapted to their specific planning needs and used by an HMO design team to select the best configuration from among many alternative choices that appeared to be feasible. In other instances it was used as a design reference for developing an in-house financial model for feasibility planning or financial planning and control for an HMO in operation. Three case examples of how the model was used and its impact on the HMO planning process are presented below. All three cases are for HMOs sponsored or operated by Blue Cross/Blue Shield.

Case example 1 One of the first adaptations of the FPM was by a Blue Cross/ Blue Shield (BC/BS) plan that was in the early stages of an HMO feasibility study jointly funded by the plan, industry, and the federal government. An examination of the FPM by systems analysts and the HMO technical and planning staff members indicated that the model could easily be adapted to satisfy their planning needs in the feasibility, and possibly also in the planning and initial development phases of HMO development, assuming it was concluded at the end of the feasibility study that an HMO would be succesful in the community under study. The model, once debugged, was modified to operate on a commercial time-sharing system that used an IBM 370/158 as its host computer. By using a remote terminal and CMS, a systems analyst and programmer increased the range of values for several of the input variables, modified some of the staffing, cost, and revenue functions, and changed the format and frequency at which output reports could be requested. A plotting subroutine was added to plot financial curves and membership levels.

These changes were not technically difficult and were completed by a systems analyst and systems programmer. The newly rebuilt FPM was installed, debugged, and modified to meet their planning needs in less than one month. Technical staff time for evaluation, model adaptation, evaluation, testing and implementation was approximately 6 man-weeks.

Once the model was operating, the planning team was able to examine in detail several different configurations and to conduct a number of sensitivity analyses on those configurations which showed the most promise. The FPM was installed in such a way that the planning team could ask a number of 'what if?' questions and have the financial impact analyses just minutes later. By using six, and in some cases only three, executive commands the planning team could analyze the financial consequences of their choices. As the planning team became more involved with the model, they began to make refinements, so more economic studies could be done with its assistance.

The average cost per configuration under study ranged from $20 to $30. While it is difficult to estimate the amount of personnel time and cost saved by using the model, its real value and contribution to the design effort became evident during the final three weeks of the feasibility study when many final choices were made and several sensitivity studies had to be done to determine their economic impact on the HMO, a task which would have been difficult to do without a computer model.

Now that they have entered a more detailed planning phase, the FPM is being revised again to provide quarterly and monthly planning reports.

Case example 2 A second user or adapter of the FPM was a BC/BS plan that had already conducted six HMO feasibility studies and was the sponsor of five HMOs as a regular line of business. In this particular case, the HMO planning and development department was initiating its seventh HMO feasibility study and wanted to design and construct a planning model now that they had undergone the pains of manually designing the others and now had several planning and operational data bases that could be more appropriately used by a computerized financial planning model.

Placing the FPM up on the plan's Honeywell 6000 computer was the responsibility of the systems people assigned to work with the HMO planning staff by the Systems Department. Initial installation of the FPM was delayed because of system-compatability problems. However, these and other technical problems were overcome by outside consultation with the original designers of the model and by technical assistance provided by other users.

After final debugging and testing, the model was examined closely to determine if it could be used to meet their short- and long-term planning needs. After their evaluation, minor as well as major program changes were undertaken to construct a model that best suited their planning needs, as well as the needs of several plan operated and sponsored HMOs. Major changes dealt with modifying the time frame of the FPM so it could be used to project month-to-month operations in the first couple of years of operation. Minor changes dealt with modifying the range of values for input variables, modifying some of the functions in the submodels, and adding some special subroutines for additional reports.

The FPM in this particular setting was used primarily as a design reference. While many of the original functions and component models were used frequently to verify some of the planning already completed, others were not because of time and cost factors and because some of the analyses were too far down the planning stream.

Although the level of integration of the FPM with their HMO planning process was not high, its impact on the design of new financial planning models was. The logical construction of the FPM greatly influenced the design of a mini-financial planning model just completed for their operating HMOs. Another financial planning model is under construction that will again use many of the original submodels. This new one is being designed for the ID (Initial Developemnt) phase of HMO development, which means that a good number of the reports will be generated for shorter planning periods during the first and second years of HMO operation. Similar to its predecessor, the new model will be capable of performing several sensitivity analyses. The new model is being designed with real-time, on-line capability.

At the present time, this BC/BS plan is assisting other HMC planning groups involved in HMO feasibility planning studies. The FPM plays a significant role in the technical support services that they are providing.

Case example 3 The third primary user of the FPM in an HMO feasibility study was a BC/BS plan that had just completed an initial feasibility study and there were sufficient indicators that an HMO would be accepted by the community. Time for debugging, for initial testing, and for understanding the model's assumptions, construction and input and output features was spread over a two-month period for members of the HMO planning staff and data-processing personnel assigned to the project. Total manpower expended, including the time to modify some of the input routines and to change several of the staffing, cost and revenue and financial functions, was eight man-weeks. The modified FPM was installed on an IBM 370/158 computer. It was operated using batch processing, with the HMO planners specifying the numbers and types of analyses to be made and data-processing personnel preparing the input cards and the FPM for use. The morning after the requests were made, the planning group was able to review the economic consequences of their decisions. Repeated use of the FPM allowed the HMO design team to look at a large number of designs in a relatively short period of time, helped them to identify the types and amounts of data that must be assembled and analysed in the later stages of HMO development, and sensitized them to the many inter-relating factors that come into play and need to be analyzed when creating an HMO. Adaptation, implementation, and repeated use of the FPM helped the HMO design team to adhere to a logical and systematic approach to HMO design and development planning.

With the BC/BS plan now into the more detailed planning phase of HMO development, the FPM is being used to gauge the financial consequences of making different design choices for a staff model HMO.

Case examples summary It is clear from the above case examples that the FPM has contributed to the state-of-the-art of financial modelling of HMOs by not only being adapted and successfully used in different HMO planning settings, but also by influencing the design and construction of another generation of models. While the FPM is the most generalized HMO financial planning model thus far constructed, its use in different planning settings can only be successful when:

(1) the HMO design team clearly understands the assumptions and logical construction of the FPM and its component submodels;
(2) the HMO design team understand the limitations, exclusions, and capabilities of the FPM;
(3) the HMO design team has the technical capability to change the FPM to meet its specific planning needs; and
(4) the HMO design team will only use the FPM after it has been properly tested to determine its validity and utility.

18.5 Summary and Conclusions

Financially viable HMOs don't just happen, they have to be planned, replanned, and replanned again and again. HMO financial planning is a never-ending, complex process that consumes enormous amounts of time and resources. Sound financial planning requires that HMO planners and administrators recognize the financial implications of their decisions in all stages of the HMO, particularly during the design and early operational stages because many of the decisions are irreversible, and incorrect and hasty ones often result in financial catastrophes.

No computerized financial planning model can guarantee the short- or long-term financial success of an HMO. However, such models can help HMO planners to understand the complex inter-relationships that exist in an HMO.

Hopefully, the FPM and the newer ones now under construction can help the more than 100 HMOs now being designed, and the more than 200 that are now operational, to become and remain economically viable alternatives to the traditional fee-for-service medical care system.

References

Birnbaum, R. W. (1976). *Health Maintenance Organizations: A Guide for Planning and Development,* Spectrum Publications, New York.

Califano, J. A. (1979). Testimony of the Secretary of HEW at the Joint Hearing Before the Subcommittee on Health of the Committee on Ways and Means, and the Subcommittee on Health and the Environment of the Committee on Interstate and Foreign Commerce, House Representatives, March 12, 1979.

Chassin, M. R. (1978). 'The Containment of Hospital Costs: A Strategic Assessment,' Supplement to *Med. Care,* 16(10), 14–20, 46.

Coleman, J. R. and Kaminsky, F. C. (1977a). A financial planning model for evaluating the economic viability of health maintenance organizations. *Inquiry,* 14(2), 176–88.

Coleman, J. R. and Kaminsky, F. C. (1977b). *Designing Medical Services for Health Maintenance Organizations,* Vol. IV, Ambulatory Care Systems, Lexington Books, D. C. Heath, Lexington, MA.

Coleman, J. R. and Kaminsky. F. C. (1977c) *Financial Design and Administration of Health Maintenance Organizations,* Vol. V, Ambulatory Care Systems, Lexington Books, D. C. Heath, Lexington, MA.

Donabedean, A. (1969). 'An Evaluation of Prepaid Group Practice,' *Inquiry,* 6(2), 3–27.

Geiser, L. A. and Ring, M. F. (1975). 'Health Maintenance Organization Feasibility Study Procedure,' *Medical Group Management,* September–October 1975, 32–7.

Greene, L. A. and Grimes, R. M. (1974). 'A Simulation of the Financial Requirements of a Pre-paid Health Care Delivery System,' *Examination of Case Studies in Health facilities Planning,* Proceedings of a forum held at Washington, D.C., 3–4 December, 1973. National Cooperative Services Center for Hospital Management Engineering, Richmond, Virginia.

Greenlick, M. R. (1972) 'The Impact of Prepaid Group Practice on American Medical Care: A Critical Evaluation,' *Ann. Am. Acad. Pol. Sci.,* 399, 100–13.

Gumbiner, R. (1975). *HMO–Putting It All Together,* C. V. Mosby, St. Louis, Missouri.

Hersch, G. and Miller, S. (1974). 'Evaluating HMO Policies with a Computer Simulation Model,' *Med. Care,* 12(8), 668–81.

Kress, J. R. and Singer, J. (1975) *HMO Handbook, A Guide for Development of Prepaid Group Practice Health Maintenance Organizations,* Aspen Systems Corporation, Germantown, Maryland.

Moustafa, A. T. and Sears, D. W., (1974). 'Feasibility of simulation of health maintenance organizations.' *Inquiry,* 11(3), 143–50.

Rice, D. P. and Wilson, D. (1976). 'The American Medical Economy—Problems and Perspectives,' *International Health Costs and Expenditures,* U.S. Department of Health. Education and Welfare, DHEW Publication (NIH) 23–53, 76–1067.

Roemer, M. I. (1974). 'Can Prepaid Care Succeed: A Vote of Confidence,' *Prism,* 2(4), 58.

Roemer, M. I. and Shonick, W. (1973). 'HMO Performance: The Recent Evidence,' *Milbonk Mem. Fund Q., Health and Society,* 51, 271–317.

Sidel, C. and Sidel, R. (1977). *A Healthy State: An International Perspective on the Crisis in United States Medical Care,* Pantheon Books, New York, 53.

Thompson, D. A. (1974). 'Financial Planning for an HMO,' *Health Serv. Res.,* Spring 1974, 68–73.

U.S. Department of Health, Education and Welfare, (1971). *Towards a Comprehensive Health Policy for the 1970s: A White Paper,* Washington, D.C., U.S. Government Printing Office, May 1971, 31–32.

U.S. Department of Health, Education and Welfare, (1974). *HMO Feasibility Study Guide,* Public Health Service, Health Services Administration, Bureau of Community Health Services, Rockville, Md., February 1974.

U.S. Department of Health, Education and Welfare, (1975a). *HMO Program Status Report, May 1975,* PHS, HSA, Division of HMO, Rockville, Md., 1975.

U.S. Department of Health, Education ad Welfare, (1975b). *HMO Program Status Report, December 1975,* PHS, HSA, Division of HMO, Rockville, Md., 1975.

Financial Modelling in Corporate Management
Edited by J. W. Bryant
© 1982 John Wiley & Sons Ltd.

19

Corporate Planning in Local Authorities*

BAL WAGLE

19.1 Introduction

Corporate planning became a fashionable term in the private sector in the early 1960s and there is no dearth of literature on the subject as a result of the vast proliferation of articles, books, seminars and conferences dealing with it. A few organizations in the U.K. and elsewhere have developed corporate planning systems which have been implemented and used with a remarkable degree of success. Nevertheless the authoritative surveys on corporate planning seem to indicate that organized corporate planning is neither as well accepted nor as well practiced as one would expect, and that although planning is carried out in the great majority of organizations it is lacking in coordination and is certainly not as sophisticated as the literature would indicate.

The situation in local authorities is not very different. The local government management process in the U.K came under increasing criticism during the 1960s and 1970s and the need for improvement was constantly stressed. Considerable emphasis was placed on the use of a corporate approach by local authorities (see reports by Maud (1967) and Redcliffe-Maud (1969); Bains (1972) included the statement 'we believe that the need for the corporate approach is beyond dispute if local government is to be efficient and effective'). A more recent report by the Central Policy Review Staff (1977) concludes that many local authorities have done quite a lot in setting-up appropriate management organizations and in introducing some of the methods needed for effective corporate planning and corporate management. These include appointment of a chief executive, introduction of chief officers management teams, establishment of central policy and review committees,

---

*Parts of this chapter are reproduced by permission of North-Holland Publishing Company, Amsterdam, from Bal Wagle, 'Corporate Planning in Local Authorities', *European Journal of Operational Research,* 1, 211-24 (1977).

and setting up of small corporate planning units with responsibilities for coordinating resource allocation from several departments, formulation of options and plans. But the progress in terms of achievement has been much slower than might have been expected. The CRS report goes on to say

> Finally, it is undeniable that corporate action is much harder in times of crises *[presumably referring to the mid-1970s]*. The same is true of reasoning processes of any kind. But the right answer is not to abandon the attempt. We can only repeat the opposite proposition, that these are the times at which it is most important to think hard about alternative policies and to get resources out of ineffective programmes and into effective ones. . . .

As a percentage of G.N.P., local government gross current expenditure in the U.K. increased from 11.4% in 1970 to 13.9% in 1975 (Central Statistical Office, 1976). Local governments therefore control substantial resources, and the need for effective planning is particularly important in view of their public responsibility.

In order to set the modelling system described here in its proper perspective, the organizational structure and responsibilities of the reorganized local authorities as of 1 April 1976 in England and Wales are first reviewed. The nature of corporate planning and associated problems are discussed, and an overall framework of a planning cycle is evolved. The structure of the modelling system is described in depth in Sections 19.6 and 19.7. The type of *ad hoc* questions which often arise in the corporate planning context at the request of senior management, and which can be handled by the modelling system, are discussed in Section 19.8. Section 19.9 addresses the potential role of the modelling system in the formal corporate planning cycle of a local authority. The chapter concludes with some brief comments on the feasibility of the system to other local authorities and areas for future technical (operational research) development.

19.2 Local Government Reorganization

The pattern of local government organization which had existed in the U.K. since the Local Government Acts of 1888 and 1894 came to an end on 31 March 1974. The system which came into existence on 1 April 1974 is a two-tier system of counties and districts throughout England and Wales. Scotland had a similar reorganization on 1 May 1975. As a result of this reorganization the number of authorities in England and Wales were cut by about two-thirds from over 1400 to 425. In England six counties are of a special type. These are the metropolitan counties which are more densely populated urban areas with special problems and characteristics.

The health and water services were also reorganized at this time, a two-tier

Table 19.1 Main functions of the new authorities

Service	Metropolitan County	Metropolitan District	Non-metropolitan County	Non-metropolitan District
Education		*	*	
Social services		*	*	
Housing		*		*
Planning				
structure	*		*	
local		*		*
Highways	*		*	
Traffic	*		*	
Public health		*		*
Libraries		*	*	
Parks and recreation	*	*	*	*
Weights and measures, trade				
descriptions, etc.	*		*	
Licensing		*	*	*
Police	*		*	
Fire	*		*	
England and Wales number	6	36	47	333

system of regional and area health authorities and unitary water authorities being established. Personal health and water supply functions were transferred from the old authorities to these new specific function authorities. This continued the trend of diminution of the range of responsibilities of local authorities which has been noticeable for a number of years (but to some extent compensated by an increased involvement in other activities, e.g. planning and leisure pursuits).

The major functions exercised by each class of authority following reorganization are summarized in Table 19.1. The modelling system described in this paper is designed for a non-metropolitan county. But it would be possible to adapt it for the metropolitan districts quite easily.

19.3 The Corporate Planning Process

A local authority, like any other organization that has to respond to change in its environment, must identify the needs and problems it faces, anticipate future needs and decide on how best these can be met given the various constraints (financial, political and social) under which it has to operate. A local authority must also react dynamically to change, continually reorienting to the changing environment and adjusting its plans and programmes accordingly.

A local authority, like any other individual or firm, has only a limited amount of resources available and must therefore optimize the use it makes of them. From Table 19.1 it is clear that a local authority has to manage an extremely wide range of activities, each one of them providing a service to its citizens, and the rate of progress towards one activity should be balanced against that towards the others. Corporate planning in local government therefore requires that separate committee plans e.g. education, social services, highways, etc., are not evaluated in isolation but as components of a balanced programme designed to achieve the overall aims of the public community serviced by the authority.

Financial resources in a local authority are traditionally allocated through a budget which is also used to authorize and control expenditure and fix the rate levy for one year ahead. It has often been supplemented by a capital programme from one to five years. More recently some local authorities have been preparing multi-year budgets which reflect the revenue implications of all development whether in current or capital account. But even these may be no more than an amalgam of the individual committees' shopping lists, lacking the conscious balance which is required of the corporate approach.

The corporate planning process in local authorities may be summarized as the following five-stage process:

Setting of objectives. Committees establish their objectives and sub-objectives, ideally in relation to community needs, taking stock of existing position;
Generation of strategies. This involves creating plans, possibly with different levels of growth, and expenditure plans for individual activities, within each committee;
Evaluation of strategies. This involves costing the alternatives and measuring their contribution to the objectives;
Choice of plan and implementation. Choosing one of the sets of alternatives involves consideration of priorities between committees. This is thus a matter for the policy committee and the council.
Monitoring and feedback. The plan must be monitored against performance using targets and the traditional budgetary control procedures.

One should not however underestimate the problems of implementing the above corporate approach. For example, the setting of objectives which have to be defined in terms of community needs and are therefore dependent on political interpretation and judgment, is no easy task. Trade-offs between different services are difficult to measure. How does one compare the benefits of a lower pupil/class ratio in relation to three extra home helps, or how does one define need? All these are complex questions but they need to be considered and dealt with if true corporate management or planning is to be introduced.

One can accept that quantitative measurement of some of these trade-offs is a well-nigh impossible task because of the political, social and emotional connotations. With the normal type of operational research model for corporate resource allocation, the output is frequently a pontification upon what is the optimal course to adopt (the underlying model being usually based on mathematical-programming concepts). In the case of a deterministic situation, in which the variables, the inter-relationships and the objectives are clearly defined, this approach may work. But in the local government context it is extremely difficult to visualize the members of a council (the ultimate decision-makers) relying on a mathematical algorithm to pass judgment. Rather they would rely on intuition, experience, and the views of the chief officers who advise them. A planning system which fails to take this into account is unlikely to be of much use in real practice. It is for this reason that we have rejected in the first instance some of the evaluation techniques suggested by researchers such as Nijkamp (1975) and Lichfield, Kettle, and Whitbread (1975). For example, Nijkamp's approach based on multicriteria analysis, requires the precise specification of criteria for measurement, the contribution of each project or programme to these criteria and finally the assigning of weights to the criteria. Given this information, Nijkamp builds up a mathematical technique which can be employed in the selection of projects. He demonstrates the applicability through a simple numerical example. Undoubtedly the method has theoretical attractions, but our experience leads us to believe that much of the data required for applying the technique at a practical level in the local authority environment would be difficult to obtain and almost impossible to implement. In fact, in the U.K. a few local authorities such as Hampshire County and Durham County Councils have attempted similar approaches for project planning and resource allocation in a single department, but have given up after some considerable effort, owing to the practical problems of implementation.

Our overall conclusion is that models for use in corporate planning (at least in local authorities at present) should be capable of measuring the implications of alternative policies in terms of physical and financial variables with a simple resource-allocation algorithm. They should be capable of answering a wide range of 'what if' questions, perhaps in considerable detail, quickly and with adequate accuracy, and of presenting the results in a format which can be readily understood. This could lead to a more rational framework for decision-making and provide a basis for discussion and deliberations between officers and members belonging to different services such as education, social services, or finance. If properly implemeted, the system should thus be capable of tackling the problem of multigroup decision-making and resolving conflicts between groups, which is usually the crucial problem in practical planning situations. The framework for one such system is discussed in Section 19.6.

19.4 Planning System Requirements

During the first half of 1974 the IBM (U.K.) Scientific Centre conducted a feasibility study to identify the role of a computer-based modelling system in local government corporate planning. In-depth interviews were held with 19 local authorities. Structured discussions took place with officers involved in corporate planning, resource allocation and budgeting. Areas covered were the background of the local authority and the nature of the authority's planning and resource allocation process. In the latter context, the role of models and computerized systems were discussed.

The main problem areas in the corporate planning process in which the local authorities felt help was most desirable were the following:

(1) coping with environmental change, particularly rates of inflation and uncertainty governing central government policy;
(2) current budgeting procedures, which were less than perfect and needed improvements;
(3) quantifying objectives and the evaluation of alternatives on a rational systematic basis;
(4) monitoring.

The results of the feasibility study are described in Howard (1975).

The broad conclusions from the feasibility study are summarized below, as these formed the basis for the model described in Section 19.6.

(a) Reorganization would promote a strong move towards corporate management.
(b) Evaluation of and selection between key policy options in the face of a constantly changing environment was a key issue.
(c) Cutbacks in public expenditure were anticipated, so allocation of financial resources and better financial management was of key importance.
(d) Models developed to date tended to concentrate on the operational issues rather than strategic problems.
(e) The few decision-making models lacked credibility as there was a major problem of lack of communication between the model-builder and the ultimate user.
(f) The immediate need was for a system to aid short-term corporate decision-making, short-term meaning three to five years.

It is worth emphasizing that although this survey was conducted in 1974, the views expressed and the problems faced are just the same today for local authority management.

19.5 Background to Development of the Modelling System

Following the recommendations in the above feasibility study, a joint project was launched between the IBM (UK) Scientific Centre, Clwyd County Council and Bradford University Management Centre with the following objectives:

(1) determine the feasibility of a computer-based modelling system as an aid in the corporate planning process in local authorities;

(2) make a preliminary assessment of the impact on the corporate planning process of the use of such a system, the evaluation being based on trials of an experimental subset of the complete modelling system;

(3) make specific recommendations on how the system might be used.

A six-man project team was set up to work on the project. It was recognized that in practice considerably in excess of six persons would be involved, but overall it was envisaged that the full-time equivalent would match the indicated resource input. Management was exercised mainly through a project management team including two persons representing IBM, one representing Bradford University Management Centre and three senior officers from Clwyd County Council (one each from treasury, administration, and one from a key service department initially chosen as social services). This ensured the top management involvement and commitment to the project, so sadly lacking in many modelling projects.

The duration of the project was from January 1975 to March 1977.

19.6 Structure of the Modelling System

The basic modelling system is described in this section. Various user-oriented enhancements are covered in the next section.

The overall structure of the modelling system consists of three interlinking modules dealing with the following:

capital programme;
loans and debt charges;
revenue budgets.

Each of the three modules consists of a number of submodules. Thus, for example, the capital programme module has submodules to represent the capital programme for each of the committees. The reason for using this modular approach is twofold. First, it provides efficiency from the computational point of view both in development and in updating or incorporating revisions; secondly, from the conceptual point of view this type of model representation is easy for the local authority personnel to understand. The activities of the following committees are represented in the modelling system:

education;
social services;
highways;
planning;
transportation;
road safety;

police (joint with Gwynedd County Council);
cultural, recreation and amenities:
  records;
  libraries;
  arts centre;
magistrates' courts;
fire services;
consumer protection;
agricultural estates;
policy, finance and resources.

It would be obviously out of place to describe here in detail the activities of all the committees. What is important to recognize is that each committee has a number of activities for which it has responsibility. Thus in the case of the social services committee the activities number 55, and these are grouped in various ways either according to the client group or to a budgeting classification. Typical activities include homes for the elderly, sheltered housing, day care, meals on wheels, and home helps. Each activity can have a number of projects. Some of these activities have both capital and revenue implications; others, such as the home help activity, have just revenue implications. The total number of activities in a typical authority is between 125 and 150.

Before turning to the three modules, it should be said that the overall approach used in the model structure is similar to that which has been used in many private-sector corporate financial simulation models (see Grinyer and Wooller, 1975). The underlying relationships in the model are of an arithmetical nature, extremely simple and deterministic, but there are thousands of these and outputs of one equation can provide input to another.

Let us now examine the three modules in detail:

Capital Module

The primary objective of the capital module is to calculate the multiyear revenue implications for each new scheme and aggregate this information on an activity, committee or authority basis. The base input data which therefore needs to be fed into the system for each project is as follows:

(1) state of project e.g. planned, approved, on-going;
(2) district in which located (six districts within Clwyd);
(3) number of units of provision, e.g. beds, places;
(4) whether it is a joint user facility;
(5) project size, e.g. new home or centre or extension to existing building, or minor adaptation (such as wiring and installing a lift);
(6) area of land involved;

Output report	: Revenue mplication of capital programme
Committee	: Social services
Activity	: Multi-purpose day centres
Project 1	: XYZ day centre
State of project	: Under construction, new building

Revenue cost description	Estimate 1976/77	Estimate 1977/78	Estimate 1978/79	Estimate 1979/80	Estimate 1980/81
Employees	1000	4000	4000	4000	4000
Premises	500	2000	2000	2000	2000
Supplies etc.	250	1000	1000	1000	1000
Other revenue costs	250	1000	1000	1000	1000
Debt charges	8000	14000	13000	12000	11000
Income	250	1000	1000	1000	1000
Net revenue	10350	23000	22000	21000	20000

Project 2	: ABC day centre
State of project	:
Revenue cost Description	etc.

Figure 19.1 Example of output report from capital module (for illustrative purposes only)

(7) completion year;
(8) operational year;
(9) staff totals (full time/part-time in 10 age groups);
(10) unit costs of staff for each group.

For each scheme the model then calculates the revenue implications for a period of five years as illustrated in Figure 19.1 (the numbers are hypothetical). The costs such as cost of premises, supplies and services, and other miscellaneous costs are calculated either as percentages of employee costs or on the basis of predictive relationships estimated from hisotrical data. For example, in Figure 19.1,

$$\text{cost of employees} = \binom{\text{no. of employees}}{\text{in a group}} \times \binom{\text{cost per employee}}{\text{in the group}}$$
maximum number of groups = 10
cost of premises = 0.50 × (cost of employees)
cost of supplies and services = 0.25 × (cost of employees)
other revenue costs = f(cost of employees, cost of supplies and services).

Debt charges are the interest payments attributable to this project and these are

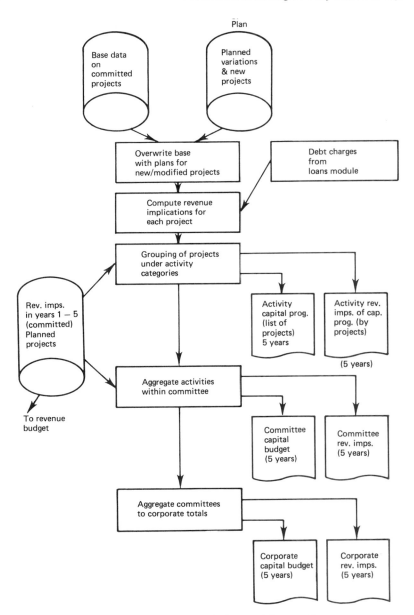

Figure 19.2 Capital module: model operation

obtained from the loans module. The module operation is best shown by the schematic diagram in Figure 19.2.

The capital module can be used to answer a wide range of 'what if' questions concerned with the capital programme, such as shifting starting and completion dates; changing manpower requirements; or investigating the effects of not operating a particular capital project (e.g. a home) for a few months to save revenue costs. The current version of the system contains a representation of the entire capital programme consisting of some 300 projects (70 for social services). A typical application might be to study the financial effect of delaying all capital projects by three months.

Loans Module

This part of the model estimates debt charges for each project, under different assumptions concerning interest rates. Each capital project is allowed a maximum of five project components such as land, buildings, furniture or vehicles. For each of the components the following data need to be input.

(1) start date;
(2) finish date;
(3) source of funds;
(4) capital cost (total);
(5) capital payments:
    (a) to end of previous year;
    (b) in current year (year 0);
    (c) estimates for years 1–5;
    (d) estimates for later years;
(6) repayment period for loan;
(7) percentage of capital cost as government grant.

Given the above data and assumptions about interest rates, this module calculates the debt charges, project by project, for new schemes and can print these out separately without transferring them to the capital module if so required. For each project the calculation is performed on a component basis and these are summed. Thus,

debt charge for project i in year $t = \Sigma$ (debt charges in year t),

where the summation is over the components of the project. The debt charge for each component can be easily calculated using the input data of the type shown in Figure 19.3 and information on interest rates.

The data required for the loans and the capital module is obviously incorporated in one data base. The reason for treating the two modules separately is that some of the debt charge calculations are particularly complex and policy-makers like to treat the financial side of the capital programme independently of the rest.

Revenue Module

This part of the system is designed to produce revenue budgets. The level of detail is therefore considerably greater than that which goes into the new schemes repre-

Project	Source of finance	Start date	Finish date	Estimated total cost	Payments to 31/3/75	Revised payment 1975/76	Estimate 1976/77	Estimate (later years)
XYZ day centre (under construction) (new building)								
—Land	1	03/74		30 000	30 000			
—Building	2	03/75	06/76	138 000	5 000	103 000	30 000	
—Furniture	3		10/76	14 000			14 000	
Total				182 000	35 000	103 000	44 000	
ABC day centre (awaits W.O. approval) (new buildings)								
—Land								
—								
—								
etc.								

Figure 19.3 Input to the loans module

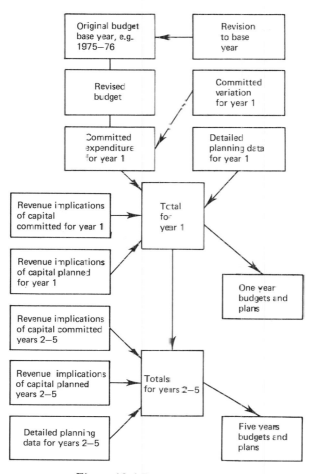

Figure 19.4 Revenue module

sented in the capital module. Detailed data on items such as manpower costs and running costs of a particular activity (such as energy costs for a particular home, costs of laundry, etc) are input to the system. Almost all this data is readily available and is currently used by the local authority accountants in producing the traditional budgets.

The structure of the revenue module is shown in a schematic form in Figure 19.4.

For each of the activities the revenue module thus produces revenue budgets from one to five years. Detailed analysis of the changes with budget variations divided into 'planned' and 'committed' changes are shown under 18 headings. The division on what is committed and what is planned may vary between authorities and by time. It is clear, however, that if so desired, the expenditure which is unavoidable can be called 'committed' and all other expenditure classified under 'planned'. This would enable an authority to estimate what the stand-still budget is and also to

Social services committee—multi-purpose day centres	Activity budget 1976/77			
	Actual expenditure 1974/76	Original budget 1975/76	Revised budget 1975/76	Budget for 1976/77
Expenditure				
Employees	x	x	x	x
Premises	x	x	x	x
Supplies and services	x	x	x	x
Transport	x	x	x	x
Establishment	x	x	x	x
Central establishment charges	x	x	x	x
Agency services	x	x	x	x
Miscellaneous	x	x	x	x
Debt charges	x	x	x	x
Leasing charges	x	x	x	x
Revenue contributions to capital	x	x	x	x
Total expenditure				
Income				
Sales	x	x	x	x
Contributions/charges for service	x	x	x	x
Grants	x	x	x	x
Miscellaneous	x	x	x	x
Total income				
Net expenditure (Clwyd County Council Homes)	x	x	x	x
Clwyd financed places elsewhere	x	x	x	x
Total net expenditure on activity	x	x	x	x

Figure 19.5 Activity formulation (revenue)—example of output report (1)

Social services committee multi-purpose day centres— budget changes 1976/1977	Increase	Decrease
Committed changes		
1. Full year effects of pay and prices increases	x	
2. Full year effects of increase in charges		x
3. Full year effects of changes in service provision	x	
4. Staff salary increments	x	
5. New capital schemes (debt and operating costs)	x	
6. Changes in debt charges and leasing charges	x	
7. Changes in employers contributions (staffing)	x	
8. Unavoidable decreases in income	x	
9. Cost of maintaining improved agency services	x	
10. Increase in central establishment charges	x	
Total committed changes	x	
Planned changes		
11. Non-recurring expenditure (improvements/repairs)	x	
12. Improvements in service (non-capital)	x	
13. Increased provision of agency services	x	
14. Revenue contributions to capital	x	
15. Effect of proposed capital schemes	x	
16. Effect of proposed increase in charges		x
17. Effect of increases in sales; grants etc.		x
18. Planned savings		x
Total planned changes	x	
Analysis of changes		
Less revised budget for 1975/1976	x	
Non-recurring items 1975/1976	x	
Adjusted total for 1975/1976	x	
Plus committed changes 1976/1977	x	
Total committed expenditure (1976/1977 base)	x	
Plus planned changes 1976/1977	x	
Total budgeted expenditure	x	

Figure 19.6 Activity formulation (revenue)—example of output report (2)

estimate where and how any cuts can be made. Although the same type and amount of data needs to be input to the system as in producing traditional budgets, the great advantage of the present module is that it provides a uniform database and that the effects of updates or changes can be very quickly analysed. It provides a rational framework for updating the revenue budget on a regular basis in addition to providing for greater information than the traditional budget. Figure 19.5 and 19.6 illustrate how the information is presented. The total number of these reports for the social services committee is of the order of 150.

Consolidated Model

The modelling system in its present form is capable of producing detailed budgets and plans from one to five years on a project, activity or committee basis. Detailed analysis of changes in the first planning year with budget variations divided into planned and committed changes are shown under 18 headings. In addition, five-year capital programmes are generated on a project, activity, committee and corporate level. On the five-year horizon, alternative planning programs involving new capital- and/or revenue-dependent options can be evaluated within the constraints of forecasts of overall finance availability. The financial effects of such plans are built upon a base of committed expenditure over five years. The effects of inflation are handled at the committee level with six cost categories (such as wages, salaries and fuel) for the first year and just one common factor from years two to five. The forecast of the rate support grant from central government can be estimated either as a percentage of total revenue expenditure or as a percentage of committed expenditure only. The system is then capable of estimating the future rate levy or precept for alternative policies. This is illustrated in Figure 19.7.

The system also provides a wealth of statistical information in the form of 'statistical statements', which provide for each activity data on current service levels, and costs anlaysed over districts and compared with national and local standards; a sort of position audit.

The system can thus provide the local authority officers and members of the council with facilities to model individual activities of the authority separately, but is also capable of producing aggregated reports and analyses automatically from the submodules, and so can provide assessments of alternative policies. It is capable of providing far greater information than the Teesside Model (Fox and Wagle, 1972), albeit over a shorter time horizon.

The total number of reports the modelling system can currently generate for the social services committee alone is about 350 (150 each for revenue and capital and 55 statistical statements). For the whole of the authority this would number about 2000. Not all these reports will, of course, be generated on each occasion. The ability to perform selective reporting is built into the system.

19.7 Enhancements to the Basic Modelling System

The basic modelling system was described in detail in the last section. Three enhancements are now discussed more briefly. Each of these is designed to help the system user.

Programme Planning Subsystem (PPS)

This is a convesational facility designed to aid in the evaluation and selection of options for the various activities. Typical planning options handled for any activity can be summarized as changes in:

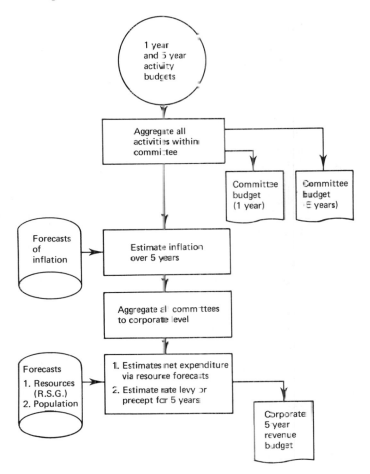

Figure 19.7 Consolidated model

(1) manpower numbers, e.g. home helps, teachers, road-crossing attendants;
(2) service provision, e.g. places in a home or classroom, pupil/teacher ratio;
(3) revenue articles, where the service is of a one-off type, e.g. library items;
(4) project timings, e.g. cancel, defer or advance a particular project;
(5) charges which can be increased or decreased.

   The implications of pursuing options is calculated through a set of simple logical relationships and displayed on a visual display unit in terms of revenue, capital and manpower for five years. Various other analyses can also be performed conversationally: for example, activities can be grouped by client category or type of care provided for a particular activity, and a report generated to examine whether priorities are being satisfied for that committee. Alternatively one can analyse total local authority expenditure in terms of its recipient population as defined by five year age groupings. It is the ability to analyse conversationally the effects of policy changes in various different ways that makes PPS an extremely flexible and versatile tool.

Resource Allocation Subsystem (RAS)

This is a conversational system designed to calculate the allocation of financial resources between committees in such a way as to reflect recommendations and decisions on priorities made by senior management in the authority.

The analysis is performed on the basis of two sets of priorities. The first set consists of development priorities whereby each service committee identifies certain activities as priorities for development. The second set (which helps to compare activities belonging to different committees) is obtained by a ranking of all the council's activities in three priority bands.

This ranking is made according to the degree of importance attached to each activity in relation to the council's key objectives (four in the case of Clwyd County Council—personal development, economic development, safety and protection, and resource utilization). The following categorization is used for each activity:

Band 1   If the activity is regarded as fundamental or crucial to the attainment of a key objective
Band 2   If the activity is regarded as directly contributing to, but not fundamental to, the attainment of a key objective
Band 3   If the activity is regarded as making an indirect contribution to, or supporting other activities in the attainment of, the key objective

This second set of priorities is agreed to by the Policy, Finance and Resources committee (PFR committee) on the basis of recommendations of the chief officers management team.

The basic principle of the resource allocation procedure is firstly to take resources away from each committee on the basis of its relative expenditure in each of the priority bands; then to add or subtract from this any allowable growth or necessary reduction in the council's overall expenditure. In this way a theoretical pool of resource is formed, which is then allocated back to committees on the basis of their relative mix of development priorities. The procedure requires a set of weights which are determined by the elected members and which reflect their view as to the extent to which the three bands contribute towards the achievement of the objectives. The computer system allows the weights to be changed as required.

Detailed Activity Modelling Subsystem (DAMS)

This subsystem complements the PPS. Whereas the latter is concerned with formulation of options at an activity level and the building of these options into committees' and authority programmes, DAMS is concerned with planning and controlling the allocation of resources within an activity.

DAMS is a conversational, generalized system which can be adapted to most activities within a short space of time. The underlying concept is that each activity is characterized by data that link the magnitude of service provided to the client group and to the resources involved.

Typically the authority management will be interested in using these data to monitor cost in relation to service, and service in relation to demand. A range of key management ratios has been incorporated in the system. This enables attention to be directed to schemes or sites which demonstrate marked performance differences.

Besides its function as a tool for regularly monitoring ongoing performance, the system can also be used to introduce possible changes to the plan, and to study their consequent effects on the activity measured.

19.8 Use of the System

Ad hoc questions from senior management often arise in the corporate planning context. These need to be answered quickly and correctly, and presented in a meaningful format to the executives. The modelling system has been specifically designed to answer a whole range of 'what if' questions. These questions could be subdivided into two types; those attributable to an exogenous or external change, and those which are attributable to a particular internal policy. Typical examples of these types of 'what if' questions are:

Exogneous changes
(1) Rate of inflation falling to $X\%$ in 1977 and to $Y\%$ in 1980;
(2) interest rates rising to $A\%$ in 1977, falling to $B\%$ in 1980;
(3) central government increasing its rate support grant contribution to say $X\%$ of local authority expenditure in 1980;
(4) Government directive for no growth in any services over five years—simply meet the roll-over effects of existing commitments.

Internal planning changes
(1) Increase the provision of home helps to meet the Welsh Office planning guideline, over a three-year period;
(2) self-adjustment of service levels to follow population changes in client groups, maintaining constant level of service per head;
(3) service cuts involving a standstill despite increasing demand, non-replacement of staff without redundancy and staff reductions if redundancy is inevitable;
(4) delaying revenue implications of capital projects (keep new homes empty);

(5) moving the 'borderline' between capital and revenue expenditure (e.g. architects salaries and building repairs met from loan, or vehicles financed by leasing rather than capital).

The system can also form an integral part of the local authority's formal corporate planning cycle as discussed in the next section.

19.9 Role of the Modelling System in Clwyd County Council's Corporate Planning

The computer-based modelling system described above has been designed to support the corporate planning process within local authorities. It is therefore appropriate to explain its role in relation to this particular process within Clwyd County Council (the process would appear to be very similar elsewhere (Howard, 1975)).

Clwyd County Council operates a formal corporate palnning system comprising four stages as shown in Figure 19.8:

(1) position statements;
(2) county programme;
(3) programme options followed by preferred programme selection;
(4) budget preparation.

Position Statement Stage

The process starts around February with a review of county services which leads to the production of position statements and the identification of priorities for development. In all, there are six position statements, one for each main committee, and these are divided into activities based on an objective classification of the service. As indicated earlier, social services, for example, has 55 activities. The position statement for each activity describes the particular service, its objective, recommended standard and current level of service within the county. In addition, capital and revenue costs, manpower requirements, and appropriate statistics for the current year, with a projection for a further five years, is shown. Position statements are considered by the relevant committees and are essentially the work of the departments, assisted by the County Treasurer, and the corporate planning unit. The committees identify their priorities for development and any key issues for further study.

Position statement information can be obtained in two forms from the modelling system. The first is the statistical statement discussed earlier, which provides for each activity data on service level and costs, analysed over districts and compared with national and local standards. Other data from the system which are of use in this exercise is provided by the conversational programme planning system. This enables sophisticated analysis of present and projected future service levels

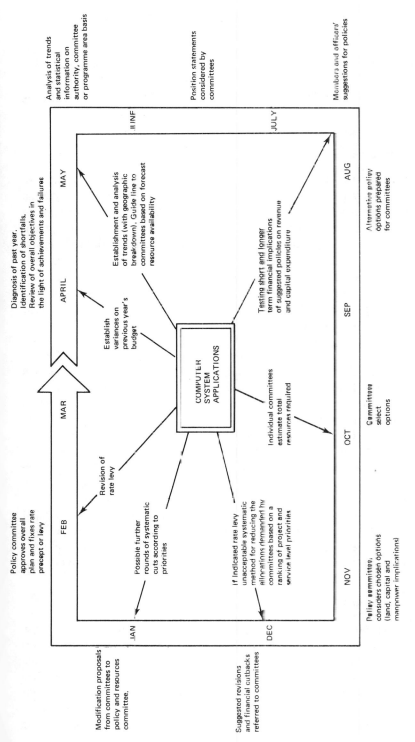

Figure 19.8 Possible applications of the proposed computer system during a local authority planning cycle

and costs, including percentage growth, year-on-year growth, per capita reports and unit cost analyses. These reports and analyses are of use both to service departments and committees in reviewing their own services and establishing priorities, and in more general terms to the corporate planning unit and to the PFR committee.

County Programme Stage

In July the second stage of the corporate planning cycle in Clwyd involves the production of the county programme. The purpose of this document is to provide the PFR committee and the council as a whole with information to assist them in the formulation of guidelines for further expenditure, and its allocation among committee areas. It contains a commentary on the economic situation and central government policy in relation to local government, population forecasts for Clwyd, and comparisons between Clwyd's performance in certain key areas and the performance of other counties of similar size and structure. The document also attempts to set out the projected future resources of the county over a five-year period and to review its future commitments.

The basic modelling system can be used at this stage to produce a set of budgets which reflect a committed, 'roll-over' (or 'service-standstill') situation for the authority over the next five years. By indicating to the system that roll-over estimates are required, all features of the budget which are marked on the data base as being 'planned' are omitted. The processing followed by the model is otherwise exactly the same as for detailed budgeting, and the same formats of reports are available. Clearly at this time of the year some of the detailed individual location and activity level reports are not required, and the printing of these can be suppressed. In its use by service committees and the PFR committee in the setting of guidelines, reports are likely to be most useful at committee and authority level, although individual activity reports can be produced selectively if required.

The reallocation of resources within a static, expanding, or contracting budget may be explored using the resource allocation subsystem, as described earlier. The allocation is provisional, and subject to reconsideration if strong arguments emerge later when the committees have looked in more detail at what they want to do.

Programme Options Stage

Once resources have been allocated to each committee, the third main stage of the corporate planning cycle commences in early autumn. This stage involves the formulation of options for each activity. Programme option statements are produced for each committee, and these indicate the resource consequences of alternative plans. Given the committee priorities and the resource base, the various options available for each activity are considered and from these a preferred programme is selected. The various committee programmes are then brought together for the

PFR committee so that it can assess whether the guidelines and allocations identified at the county programme stage have been adhered to.

The two subsystems which are designed to help with the formulation and evaluation of individual options at the activity or service level are the PPS and the DAMS. The latter is used as a 'what if' tool by the planners in the individual service departments. The basic data established on the data base, either by the stand-still budget or by the stand-still plus existing plans, or by revision of one of these to a new year's price base, are used as the base plan by the PPS.

The function of the PPS is to give general costings for any activity, based on a standard set of rules applied across the authority, and modified by individual parameters for each activity. An alternative additional means of costing options is to use the DAMS, where appropriate, to provide more detailed and more accurate costings for a specific activity.

Once all individual activity/options for a committee have been evaluated and stored, the PPS may be used as outlined earlier to select committee-level programmes. One of these is denoted as the preferred programme for each committee. The preferred programmes for the various committees can be further aggregated to provide the authority's preferred programme.

Annual Budget Stage

The final stage of the cycle is the production of the following year's budget for approval in February or March.

The basic modelling system as described in Section 19.6 is obviously of relevance here. This is the area in which Clwyd County Council have made the most progress since completion of the joint research project in March 1977. For a discussion of specific case studies conducted with the model see Greening, Howard and Wagle (1978) and Duffy and Marlow (1978).

19.10 Conclusion

It is felt that for local authorities committed to a balanced planning cycle (i.e. trying to examine the various activities in a consistent and coordinated manner) the Clwyd type of system, through its integration with the management process, could be of considerable value.

The modular nature of the basic systems and subsystems (PPS, RAS, and DAMS), means that individual local authorities could adopt these systems one at a time. It is not essential that the whole system be implemented before any benefits can be derived. Each of the systems or even a subsystem (e.g. the Capital Program Subsystem, or the Loans Subsystem), could lead to useful benefits in isolation.

The representation of an individual authority structure defining the number of committees, activities, projects and so forth and their relationships (in terms of which location belongs to which activity, which activities belong to which committee, etc.) are all determined by the user of the system and can be readily restructured. The final version of the experimental system in Clwyd, after several such restructurings, contained 13 committees or subcommittees with a total of 130 activities, (of which 55 were in social services) and a total of about 300 locations. Looking at the database, the data files have been designed in such a way as to make their adaptation to use in different organizations a matter of re-defining a small number of reference files, rather than changing computer programs.

Operating requirements are more difficult to specify, since the system is not simply an addition to the workload, but is integrated with other systems and data which are directly or indirectly part of the planning process. It is, however, estimated that these are unlikely to approach even 1% usage of the total computer resources. The total requirements in a year for computer time is likely to be small, although the nature of the planning cycle may produce peaks of work load, which would need careful scheduling.

The statistical statements, the various financial reports, and the conversations on the display screen, have all been designed with the user in mind. The Clwyd County personnel who have used the system with no computing or operational research background, have had very little difficulty with it. The RAS, even in its present simple form, has been of much practical use, though it is generally agreed that this area offers the most potential for further research. Methods need to be developed to handle a wider range of 'what if' questions. For reasons already discussed in Section 19.2, the author tends to favour techniques based on multidimensional scaling or some ranking procedure which would be relatively easy to explain to the user, rather than a formal mathematical-programming approach.

Other techniques for combining judgmental data with quantitive information may also be worth pursuing (Eckenrode, 1965).

A second area for development would be to link the system to a forecasting model. The latter might project population by age, sex, geography and other variables, and so would provide valuable input to the basic modelling system.

In conclusion, it is estimated that a local authority building on the Clwyd experience would be able to develop a comparable system with between seven and ten man-years of effort. Development of individual subsystems would obviously require far less effort. It is envisaged that with as little as 12-24 man-months of appropriate effort, another local authority would be in a position to adapt parts of the system to yield useful results. Any local authority interested in doing so should first study the full project report (Duffy and Marlow, 1978) and the systems documentation (Marlow, 1977). These are available from the IBM (U.K.) Scientific Centre. They are also recommended to discuss the system with the staff in Clwyd County Council, who have offered to demonstrate the interactive components of the system (Local Authorities Management Services and Computer Committee, 1977). On the basis of the general understanding of the system gained in this way, it should be possible to select those parts of it which are of interest and relevance, with a view to adapting them from the Clwyd modelling system.

References

Bains, J. (1972). *The New Authorities—Management and Structure,* H.M.S.O., London.

Central Policy Review Staff (1977). *Relations between Central Government and Local Authorities,* H.M.S.O., London.

Central Statistical Office (1977). *Annual Abstracts of Statistics 1976,* Table 348, H.M.S.O., London.

Duffy, J. A. and Marlow, A. T. (1978). *A Computer-based Modelling System to Aid the Corporate Management Process in Local Authorities,* Report 0095, IBM (U.K.) Scientific Centre, Peterlee, Co. Durham.

Eckenrode, R. T. (1965). 'Weighting multiple criteria', *Management Science,* **12**(3), 180–92.

Fox, R. D. and Wagle, B. (1972). *Long-range Financial Planning Model for Teesside,* Report 0035A, IBM (U.K.) Scientific Centre, Peterlee, Co. Durham.

Greening, R., Howard, K., and Wagle, B. (1978). *Executive Guide for a Computer-based System to Aid the Corporate Management Process in Local Authorities — The Clwyd Project,* Report 0098, IBM (U.K.) Scientific Centre, Peterlee, Co. Durham.

Grinyer, P. H. and Wooller, J. (1975). *Corporate Models Today,* Institute of Chartered Accountants in England and Wales, London.

Howard, K. (1975). *The Scope for Computer-based Systems to Aid Corporate Decision-making in the Short and Medium Term in the Reorganised Local Authorities — A Feasibility Study,* Report 0074, IBM (U.K.) Scientific Centre, Peterlee, Co. Durham.

Lichfield, N., Kettle, P., and Whitbread, M. (1975). *Evaluation in the Planning Process,* Pergamon, London.

Local Authorities Management Services and Computer Committee (1977). *Lamsac Newsletter,* No. 26, 4.

Marlow, A. T. (1977). *The Clwyd Planning Model — Technical Documentation, IBM (U.K.)* Scientific Centre, Peterlee, Co. Durham.

Maud, J. P. R. (1967). *Report of the Committee on Management of Local Government,* H.M.S.O., London.

Nijkamp, P. (1975). 'A multi-criteria analysis for project evaluation: economic-ecological evaluation of a land reclamation project', *Regional Science Association,* **35**, 88–111.

Redcliffe-Maud, J. P. (1969). *Royal Commission on Local Government in England,* H.M.S.O., London.

PART 5
FINANCIAL MODELLING CASE HISTORIES

Financial modelling is emphatically not an academic process, and past experience has shown elegant mathematics and sophisticated programming as more likely to lead to failure rather than forming a pathway to success. The importance of models being developed in close conjunction with (if not by) the user cannot be over-emphasized. Assumptions made in structuring the model must be made explicit and care must be taken in the design of input and output through which the model interacts with the decision-maker or with external databases. More important, but more frequently neglected in the development of financial models, is a consideration of the political context of modelling activity. The balance of power in an organization may be radically modified by the use of financial models which can place evaluation techniques in new hands, while in some cases models may be used with ulterior motives to achieve quite different ends. A modeller must be fully aware of these practical difficulties and the case studies in this section are intended to illustrate the evolutionary process, shaped by the above forces, through which most models emerge.

In Chapter 20 the development of a number of models based on a particular modelling system is described. Of special interest is the account of the computer hardware changes as the project unfolded, with the ultimate application of a mini-computer. The next case history, in Chapter 21, describes the succession of phases through which a programme of financial modelling has progressed in one organization over a comparatively long time period. This is a 'warts and all' account and makes fascinating reading. Chapter 22 also traces the evolution of model building in a company but couples this with a novel structured analysis of the process of model development.

Financial Modelling in Corporate Management
Edited by J. W. Bryant
© 1982 John Wiley & Sons Ltd.

20

Financial Modelling on an In-House Mini-Computer

JOHN MACGREGOR AND PETER WHYTE

20.1 Introduction

Imperial Chemical Industries Limited (ICI) is one of the world's largest multinational chemical companies. Its turnover of £5368 million in 1979 included products as diverse as fertilizers and paints, plastics and explosives, dyestuffs and pharmaceuticals.

This case study concerns the Management Accounting Group of the Treasurer's Department situated at their Head Office in Millbank, London. The Management Accounting Group is mainly involved in collecting, consolidating and analysing financial and management information for presentation to the Main Board, relating to both achieved results, both monthly and quarterly, and forecasts, short and long term.

The collection of actual financial accounting data was already satisfied by a batch-orientated IBM system with some on-line capability. This received a large amount of telexed information from over 150 units world-wide each quarter, which was validated and consolidated to a Group total.

The management information required to aid analysis of these actual results and prepare forecasts was still being collected and processed by hand. It was to speed up the processing and allow more time for thinking that models were developed upon a computer bureau with the help of ICI's Central Management Services.

20.2 Applications and Problems

The first application in 1977 was a straight 'number cruncher'. This was to speed up a comprehensive exchange effect calculation used to analyse the sales and profit

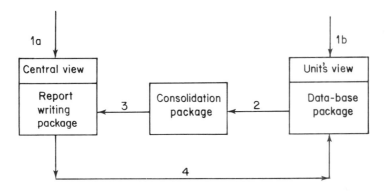

Figure 20.1 The five-year cash-forecasting system

variances shown by the £-sterling financial accounts into 'real' variances and those due to the conversion of results of overseas units at different exchange rates for each period under consideration. In order to achieve the result, data were required to be transferred from the in-house IBM collection system to the bureau via a terminal with floppy discs. This also served as a useful introduction to data management.

The next two applications were concerned with 5-year cash forecasting. These were a unit's view—bottom up, and a central view—top down. The unit's view was essentially a collection of data from UK divisions and overseas units (about 70 in all) of their own cash forecasts which required to be converted into sterling and consolidated to territorial and group totals. This was assigned to a database-type lanaguage—COMPOSIT 77. The central view was a Group-level four-way split which was designed to allow a base case to be calculated and then changes applied to test sensitivities to various strategies. A 'report-writing' package was used for this—DATAFORM. These two systems were successful in achieving their own requirements but incompatible when it was decided that the computer should be able to take the difference between the two views and show the central adjustments required to amend the unit's view to the central view. A third package was employed to consolidate the unit's data to the same level as the central view—PLANMASTER. Finally, the loop was closed so that the central adjustments could be input into the unit's view making it equal to the central view in total but containing all the unit's details. The system therefore evolved over about 18 months (3 planning cycles) as shown in Figure 20.1.

Although operable, the above system had disadvantages:

(1) Three different packages had to be learned.
(2) Time was involved and expense incurred in transferring data between systems.
(3) Effort was needed to maintain the three systems separately but to remain compatible.

(4) The packages produced the numbers, but not in a form which could be directly incorporated in issued reports. Typing was therefore required for final results.

Rationalization was essential and the medium chosen, based on experience in one of the ICI divisions, was FCS-EPS. Both systems were re-written, the central and unit's views still as separate entities, but with the following features:

(1) Sections in the hierarchy of the unit's view were defined both for territorial output reports and to allow the comparison with the central-view analysis.
(2) Although not a true hierarchical model, the central-view data file was defined to compare directly, row for row, with the unit's view.
(3) Input of data into a matrix model allowed extensive on-line validation and correction by cross-checking and check totals rather than a separate batch program run as in a database system.
(4) Currency conversion, carrying forward of closing to opening balances and calculation of related exchange differences coud be made automatic. (This feature saved much time in calculation and recalculation when data were updated.)
(5) Output reports were written in a form suitable for inclusion in published documents.

Development of the systems to this stage had considerable benefits to the department, but there were constraints. These were mainly related to costs. There is always the feeling of a continually ringing cash register at the other end when connected to a computer bureau, and a small data change in a large integrated system can necessitate a very expensiive re-run. The question is also asked 'Is it worth running the system for this extra case? It may cost too much!' Similarly, with the above experience, a whole new vista of possible applications can be seen 'if only it didn't cost so much'.

On the purely logistical side, one or two terminals connected to a bureau via telephone are generally shared with other users and require checking for availability, operating in that room with working papers and coping with bad lines/line noise (especially on final print-outs) when eventually running. It would be much more sensible to have a terminal on the desk which would allow immediate access without charging for every operation performed once the price for the facility had been paid.

20.3 Move to 'In-House'

From the previous bureau experience it had already been decided that FCS–EPS was the modelling system most suitable and when it became known that it was to be offered on a mini, enquiries were immediately commenced. These showed that to replace current bureau usage a configuration including three VDUs and utilizing the current teletype terminal for printing would be available at a price giving a payback period of two years. There was also at the time the possibility of using the software on an ICI Division machine which amounted to the same facilities as the bureau at half the bureau cost. The latter option was resisted as it was felt that greater benefits would accrue from a mini dedicated to the department, but as there was little experience of its hardware reliability or capacity it was agreed to rent the system for a trial period in order to evaluate performance.

The equipment was installed three months later, models readily transferred from the bureau and the cash forecast immediately embarked upon. In order to complete the installation in time for this to take place, a machine intended for EPS was diverted to ICI. This included a 600 lines per minute printer which was not in the original specification but remained 'temporarily'.

During the successful running of the two-month forecast cycle, it became apparent how useful it was to have immediate access to data through a VDU on the desk, especially for checking and referring quickly to data in detail or summary form, whereas a long time had previously been spent maintaining up-to-date manual records. Also, the facility acquired by the accountants in the department prompted more suggestions of routine collecting, consolidating and reporting of data which could be implemented. These could all be considered now as the marginal cost for each application was zero. The main areas covered were monthly sales and profits reporting to the Main Board and tax modelling which is a very complex matrix problem. Through all this time the line printer was becoming more an essential part of the system in order to obtain fast hard-copy reports and those which were too large for the VDU screen.

The developments thus far were certainly cost effective compared to the previous bureau usage but were only using a small amount of the capacity of the machine available. The time was now ripe for the next step.

20.4 In-House Model Developments

A major part of the department's effort was directed to analysis and presentation of the financial data collected quarterly on the IBM system. This consists of end-of-quarter balance sheet and cumulative profit and loss account information. The presentations required are mainly analyses showing the quarterly values derived from cumulatives from the previous and current years together with comment on and detail of the variances between these quarterly figures. Hence, although all the data were collected by computer, much time was expended in deriving and presenting results in the required format. This had not been computerized on the IBM system because the programming effort required to produce satisfactory prints in a lower-level language such as PL1 would be immense and the output difficult to change once completed. In addition to this, the current programming team were completely occupied with maintenance and development of the collection system. Conversely, once the data is entered into the FCS–EPS hierarchical system, extractions, quarterly values, variances and print-outs are relatively easy to produce.

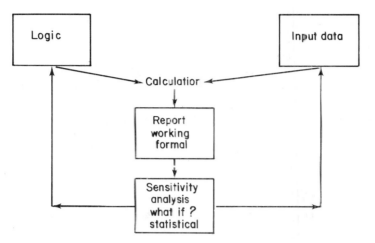

Figure 20.2 Elements of the FCS–EPS system

The first stage of this work was completed in six weeks with consultant programming aid. It included housekeeping routines, conversion of data from the IBM to the mini (a daily tape) and thirty reports suitable for direct inclusion in the published report.

The modelling consultant was used merely as extra resource, given a fairly tight timetable. The vast majority of the ICI Millbank models are written by the management accountants in the Treasurer's Department and a management services programmer-analyst with no previous FCS–EPS experience.

20.5 The FCS–EPS System

FCS–EPS was written by EPS Consultants and first released in 1973. The system has been successfully applied to problems in the area of short-term planning, typically budgetary planning and control; to problems in the longer term, typically the 'five-year plan'; to problems of investment appraisal—new capital, new products, acquisition; and to such problems as manpower planning and even production scheduling. FCS–EPS have over 500 users of the system worldwide.

The system may be divided into four major elements, as shown in Figure 20.2. The LOGIC is the definition of the relationship between variables in the model; for example, revenue equals volume × price. Input data are the forecasts obtained for the variables; for example, volume will be 10 000 per month, price will be £10 until June, then £11.50. These two elements are brought together, and the calculations carried out according to the definitions in logic. Then various reports can be produced; working reports, formal reports and graphical output. Finally, sensitivity analysis may be performed in terms of changes to the data, changes to several input variables, several stepped changes to a single variable, or working to a target; for example, what sales growth is necessary to achieve a minimum target and DCF yield? Changes may also be made to the logic—for example, to evaluate the impact of removing a production constraint. Analysis of a more statistical nature may be employed.

A major factor contributing to the success of FCS–EPS, and indeed of financial modelling systems, is the ease of use. Planners and accountants have been able to develop their own models, ranging from simple to complex. The often fruitless dialogue between planners and the data-processing department, to get even the simplest of models built, has been avoided. The people who know the model they want are able to construct it themselves. An example is given below of the model logic from one of the ICI models.

```
SYSTEM) LOGIC
+ 101 'TRADING PROFIT'
+ 102 'DEPRECIATION'
+ 103 'CAPITAL ALLOWANCES'
+ 104 'STOCK RELIEF'
+ 105 'CASE I '=' TRADING PROFIT' SUM 'STOCK RELIEF'
+ 111 'INTEREST RECEIVED'
+ 112 'OVERSEAS INCOME'
+ 113 'INTEREST PAID'
+ 114 'NON-TRADING ITEMS' = 111 + 112 - 113
+ 121 'TAXABLE PROFIT' = 105 + 114
+ 125 'TAX CHARGED' = 121 AT 52.0
+ END
SYSTEM)
```

FCS–EPS is command driven—the command LOGIC is used to enter the logic or model, CALCULATE calculates the input variables to give calculated variables according to the rules of the logic, LIST prompts for the columns and rows that are to be listed for a 'working paper' report. The commands are self-explanatory, again re-emphasizing the need for ease of use. An example is given below of the data that might be entered for the simple model already described, using, as one might expect, the DATA command.

```
SYSTEM) DATA
* 101,U,100,110,130,135
* 102,U,50,60,65,65
* 103,U,-80,-85,-90
* 104,U,-20,-25,-35,-45
* 111,I,30,5
* 112,I,20,5
* 113,U,*45
* END
SYSTEM)
```

The logic and data are combined using the CALCULATE command, and a LIST of results produced.

```
SYSTEM) CALCULATE
SYSTEM) LIST
COLUMNS? 1-4
ROWS 101-125
```

	1	2	3	4
101 TRADING PROFIT	100.00	110.00	130.00	135.00
102 DEPRECIATION	50.00	60.00	65.00	65.00
103 CAPITAL ALLOWANCE	−80.00	−85.00	−85.00	−90.00
104 STOCK RELIEF	−20.00	−25.00	−35.00	−45.00
105 CASE I	50.00	60.00	75.00	65.00
111 INTEREST RECEIVED	30.00	35.00	40.00	45.00
112 OVERSEAS INCOME	20.00	25.00	30.00	35.00
113 INTEREST PAID	45.00	45.00	45.00	45.00
114 NON-TRADING ITEMS	5.00	15.00	25.00	35.00
121 TAXABLE PROFIT	55.00	75.00	100.00	100.00
125 TAX CHARGED	28.60	39.00	52.00	52.00

```
SYSTEM)
```

A simple REPORT specification can be written, to provide a more formal report, again the report specifications being self-explanatory.

```
SYSTEM) HEADINGS
OPTION: NU
FIRST VALUE,PERIOD STEPS,OMITTING PERIODS? 1980
OPTION: EN
SYSTEM) TITLE
TITLE: TAX CALCULATION
SYSTEM) REPORT
SPECIFICATIONS
  10 SUPROW
  20 BRACKET
  30 ROWS 101-104 UDATA
  40 ROWS 105
  50 SKIP
  60 R111-113 U R114 J S
  70 U'=' R121 U'='
  80 END
```

SYSTEM⟩ DISPLAY
20:41:44 ON 08/07/80

TAX CALCULATION

	1980	1981	1982	1983
TRADING PROFIT	100	110	130	135
DEPRECIATION	50	60	65	65
CAPITAL ALLOWANCE	(80)	(85)	(85)	(90)
STOCK RELIEF	(20)	(25)	(35)	(45)
	-----	-----	-----	-----
CASE I	50	60	75	65
INTEREST RECEIVED	30	35	40	45
OVERSEAS INCOME	20	25	30	35
INTEREST PAID	45	45	45	45
	-----	-----	-----	-----
NON-TRADING ITEMS	5	15	25	35
	-----	-----	-----	-----
	-----	-----	-----	-----
TAXABLE PROFIT	55	75	100	100
	-----	-----	-----	-----

SYSTEM⟩

From this base data various sensitivity analyses can be carried out—single, stepped or targeted.

It is very important to realize that while a modelling system must be fundamentally designed on the basis of the criterion of ease of use, it must also have the ability to model complex problems. Complexity will obviously arise if the logic is itself complex, as will be seen in the description of the tax model. Complexity may also arise if the models are, for example, 'parameterized'—for example, given the parameter of 'current quarter of plan', the respective data files and period, the report headings and contents are accessed. The actual model should not change, given a change to the parameter—current plan period.

A comprehensive modelling system will possess such facilities as logical expression, conditional and unconditional jumps, redefinition of variables, facilities for interpolation and extrapolation, matrix handling and financial functions. Of major importance are: file-handling functions; facilities for directly and indirectly reading or writing data; terminal input/output of both numeric and string characters; issuing of commands in models; means of string comparison and concatenation; features for looping by variable or by period and for nesting loops; and the capability of indirectly as well as directly defining relationships between variables. Many of the models in ICI Treasurer's Department use these facilities; the models are complex, and mainly written not by professional data-processing people, but just by simple planners and accountants! It requires considerable training and experience, but this case study proves what can be done.

A major task facing ICI Treasurer's Department is the consolidation or aggregation of plans. FCS–EPS contains facilities to help the modeller deal with consolidation problems. The facilities are designed to allow complex multilevel consolidations, involving such problems as currency conversion, cost allocation and various inflation scenarios to be simply modelled. Figure 20.3(a) shows the common feature of these applications, the presence of a company tree of hierarchy. Three types of files are required during hierarchical consolidation. One file describes the hierarchy or tree, and contains the description of each section—product, division, company etc., (see Figure 20.3(b)). The logic file is the logic which applies to each section, (see Figure 20.3(c)). Common rows contain data common to all sections, the input rows and calculated rows describe the logic of each section. The logic may vary from section to section, and from level to level in the hierarchy. The data file contains the common data and the data for each section or company. The data are in blocks of rows on the file known as 'sections'. Section zero is reserved for the common data; sections 1 upwards contain data for each company, (see Figure 20.3(d)). The structure of the hierarchy is defined, in terms of the hierarchy file, logic, and data files. The latter is also defined in terms of the zero section, and input rows and consolidated rows for each section. The complete hierarchy may be consolidated by issuing the one command HIERARCHY. Some of the hierarchies used in ICI Treasurer's Department contain several hundred base sections, with over 100 rows of input data for each section and ten or more columns of data. With such a large consolidation, it is important that the modelling system allows not only the rather brutal consolidation of all sections, but control over the various stages of consolidation: control in terms of being able to consolidate a section, using the information immediately below the section, to be able to input and analyse a particular section, and to be able to minimize the cost of recalculating the hierarchy after specified input sections have been changed or updated. These controls and more are specified using keywords with the command HIERARCHY, for example, HIER-ARCHY UPDATED 55.

The normal reporting facilities of the system can be used to look at the results of a consolidation. Any section may be displayed and, of great value, cross-section reports may be produced. A particular row or variable for a group of sections may be displayed in one report, and a particular column or period for a group of sections may be displayed in one report, see Figure 20.4.

The model logic facility, hierarchy and report facility are extensively used in the four applications now described.

20.6 Application A: Long-term Cash Forecast Models

The Central View

This system consists of a main cash-flow model which produces cash-flow statements, profit and loss account, balance sheet and statistics prints. Changes to the

(a) Hierarchical consolidation

(b) The hierarchy file

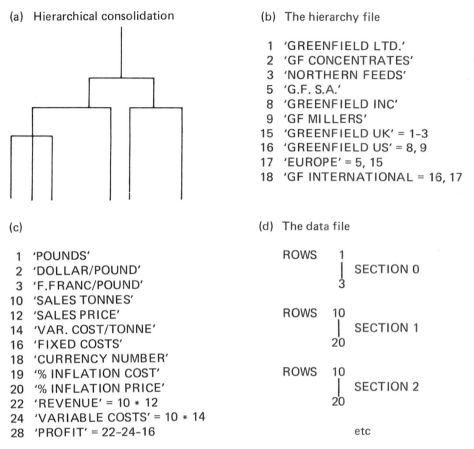

1 'GREENFIELD LTD.'
2 'GF CONCENTRATES'
3 'NORTHERN FEEDS'
5 'G.F. S.A.'
8 'GREENFIELD INC'
9 'GF MILLERS'
15 'GREENFIELD UK' = 1–3
16 'GREENFIELD US' = 8, 9
17 'EUROPE' = 5, 15
18 'GF INTERNATIONAL = 16, 17

(c)

(d) The data file

1 'POUNDS'
2 'DOLLAR/POUND'
3 'F.FRANC/POUND'
10 'SALES TONNES'
12 'SALES PRICE'
14 'VAR. COST/TONNE'
16 'FIXED COSTS'
18 'CURRENCY NUMBER'
19 '% INFLATION COST'
20 '% INFLATION PRICE'
22 'REVENUE' = 10 * 12
24 'VARIABLE COSTS' = 10 * 14
28 'PROFIT' = 22–24–16

ROWS 1
        | SECTION 0
        3

ROWS 10
        | SECTION 1
        20

ROWS 10
        | SECTION 2
        20

        etc

Figure 20.3 The hierarchy structure

basic information may be applied to enable assessments of sensitivity to be made and arrive at a final agreed central forecast. Subsidiary models supply data concerning loan interest, dividends, tax, profit sharing and CCA information. See Figure 20.5.

The base-data file contains four sections of cash-flow data equivalent to the levels at which the forecast is being made. Rows are also provided for opening balances and journal entries which allow the cash-flow movements to be converted into profit and loss and balance sheet forecasts. Statistics such as capital gearing, interest cover and internal generation are then calculated. The model requests the base-file name and calculates and prints all or selected reports. The model also requests the name of a file of changes to be applied to the base. If this is supplied, changes to profit, capital expenditure, working capital, loans and dividends generate subsequent additional interest savings or payments together with tax implications. These may be displayed if required and added to the data input from the base file before printing.

```
SYSTEM) DISPLAY SECTION
SECTIONS? 1-3, 15
```

GREENFIELD LTD.

	1	2	3
22 REVENUE	170000	207000	250000
28 PROFIT	17000	24650	32500

SIMILAR REPORTS FOLLOW FOR SECTIONS 2, 3, AND 15

```
SYSTEM) DISPLAY SECTION COLUMN 3 TITLE
TITLE: EUROPEAN COMPANIES PLAN 1981
SECTIONS? 1-3, 5, 17
```

EUROPEAN COMPANIES PLAN 1981

	GREENFIELD LTD	GF CONCEN.	GF NORTH	G.F. S.A	EUROPE
SALES TONNES	2500	800	4000	1500	8800
PROFIT	32500	113000	54000	17647	217147
	- - - - -	- - - - -	- - - - -	- - - - -	- - - - - -
PROFIT %					
REVENUE	13.0	35.3	12.9	11.1	18.9

SYSTEM) DISPLAY SECTION BY ROW 28

	1979
GREENFIELD U.K.	199500
GREENFIELD U.S	301667
GF INTERNATIONAL	518814

Figure 20.4 Hierarchical reports

The results of calculation can be passed on to a CCA model which adjusts values according to inflation data held on a separate file to enable full CCA profit and loss, balance sheet and ratio reports to be output.

The Units' View

Forecast cash flow, sales, working capital and other sundry information is collected from units in local currency. This is then converted into sterling and consolidated according to the defined hierarchy. (see Figure 20.6.)

The input/validation model requests the section number (i.e. operating unit) to be updated on the original currency file and accepts input from the terminal. At the end of input validation, checks are carried out (e.g. 'movement in cash' row equals sum of individual rows sales rows add up to total) and any errors are displayed. Corrections are accepted and the data re-checked. When all the data are valid, exchange rates from the control file are used to convert movements, opening and closing balances to sterling and calculate exchange effects. The sterling section is then written to a different file. Once all sections have been validated and con-

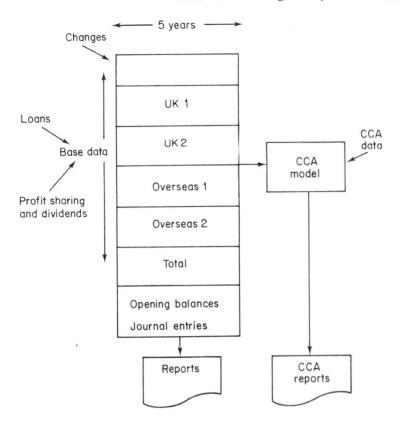

Figure 20.5 The long-term cash-forecast models

verted, the HIERARCHY command is issued to calculate consolidated nodes up to a group total. Two extra hierarchy structures are calculated on the same file to give alternative groupings of sections. All consolidated results are written back to the same sterling data file to enable displays of both input and calculated sections or full BYROW reports. Report models, generally of the BYROW nature, which access the sterling file to print in publishable form analyses of each cash-flow item or territorial cash flows for each year, are also run.

The Central Versus The Units' View

Forecasts submitted by units are statements of their individual profits and expenditure proposals. They must, however, agree in total with Group targets. Therefore it is necessary to compare the units' and central views.

The central view only requires cash-flow details, but at the four consolidated levels. In order to facilitate comparison, the units' view cash-flow rows are numbered identically to the central view and four of the consolidated sections are at the same

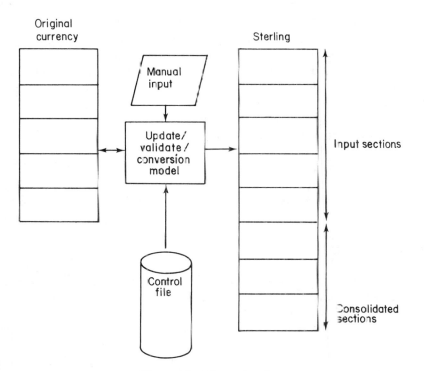

Figure 20.6 The units view

level as the four central view forecasts. The stages required to bring the two fore-casts into line are:

(1) create a central view base-data file from the units' view;
(2) difference the central and units' base files
(3) apply the differences as changes to the units' base file to equal the central view of profit, fixed capital expenditure, working capital increase;
(4) difference the resulting 'centralized' units' view file and the central view to give central adjustments;
(5) input thesse central adjustments into sections reserved for them in the units' view system and reconsolidate.

Reports from the units' view will now show territorial details as given by units but centrally adjusted to come to the central view totals.

20.7 Application B: The Suite of ICI Tax Models

UK Corporation Tax is essentially a set of legal rules for application to the accounts of companies in order to derive the contribution payable to the government. Since in a group situation relatively intricate complications may result from an attempt to optimize the taxation position of the payer, it is an area ideally suited to computerization.

The main model is a five-year forecast and the ICI position is dealt with under four main headings: company, financing, oil and minor subsidiaries. For companies established after 1965, tax is payable in the year after the charge, for those before 1965 it is payable two years after. The optimum situation, which is determined by deterministic simulation, combines the following:

(a) full utilization of tax losses;
(b) full utilization of Group relief;
(c) Group relief taken in the order which leaves residual tax payable in pre-1965 companies.

The model is used for:

(1) Planning purposes—to calculate tax charge, and payments for five year forecast. It enables sensitivities of changes in capital expenditure dividends, loans, etc. to be measured in their effect on tax charges and payments.
(2) Tax planning—illustrating where a future tax problem ought to receive attention, for example, covering overseas charges by overseas income.
(3) Actual results—first-year forecast combined with interim period (e.g. 6 months) figures to produce an interim tax charge which is used in the interim accounts.

Whilst an integrated approach is the aim, which will enable transfers of data between models to take place within the minicomputer, currently there exist auxiliary models, the output from which is used as input in the main model. The models inter-relate as shown in Figure 20.7.

A brief description of each model follows:

Model 1. Capital allowances—takes capital expenditure by each unit split: buildings, plant, motor cars, research, plus written-down value brought forward, and calculates annual capital allowances. This is then used as input in the main model.

Model 2. Overseas income—takes net dividends received from overseas companies and separately grosses them up for underlying tax and witholding tax to give the gross Case V income and WHT which become part of the tax calculation for the company. Double taxation relief (gross) is calculated by the difference between gross Case V and net dividend, and is restricted by reference to 52% of gross Case V income.

Model 3. Other U.K. Subsidiaries—takes main items of tax calculations for 24 companies, including trading profit, depreciation, capital expenditure/allowances, interest received/paid, and calculates taxable profit and notional tax charge. The totals are aggregated into classes of company:

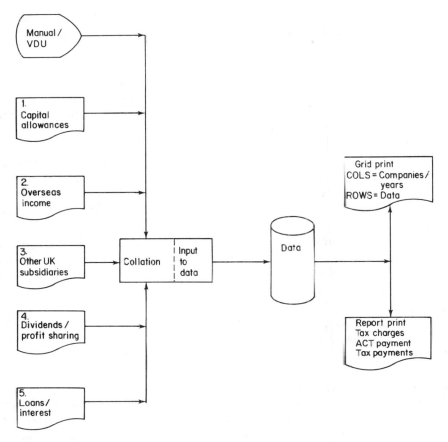

Figure 20.7 The five-year tax model

(a) 50–75% owned
(b) 75% owned
(c) over 75% owned

Categories (b) and (c) are used to provide discrete net totals of taxable profit against which losses for the rest of the group may be offset by 'Group relief'.

The overall totals are part of the input to the main model.

Model 4. Dividend and employees profit sharing—whilst not formally a tax model this provides the dividend charge total for the main model and also the profit-sharing figure which is an allowable deduction for tax purposes.

Model 5. Loans and interest—also not formally a tax model; this provides detail of the loans drawn down and planned for with the relevent interest charges. Different rules are applicable in the main model for different classes of loans, whilst the discrete interest figures are important in determining Case III and charges.

The main model takes detail from the auxiliary models, plus data from the cash-forecast program in order to calculate the U.K. tax charge, ACT utilization and charge, and U.K. tax payments for the current year plus four years forecast. Minor routines also included are the calculation of stock relief, formalization of overseas income and the calculation of trading income for tax purposes.

Specific detail has been built in for the optimizing of group relief, the calculation of tax losses utilized and carried forward, the utilization of ACT by reference to dividends payable in the period and the write-off/credit of ACT by reference to dividends charged, and the payment of mainstream corporation tax after utilization of ACT and including ACT paid in the period, which happens to be by reference to dividends charged in the previous period.

A minor complication is the 'ring-fence' which operates in the oil business. This enables tax losses arising in oil (resulting possibly from excess capital allowances) to be offset against profits in the rest of the group, but losses from the rest of the group may not be offset against oil profits—however they may be offset against 'non-ring-fenced' refining and dealing profits.

The interim accounts model provides the U.K. tax charge for the ICI results for interim (3 months, 6 months and 9 months) accounts. It takes the relevant proportion of certain items from the current year of the main model, for example, capital allowances, stock relief, overseas income, ACT charge/credit and applies these to the trading and interest flows of the interim period.

Attention is given to the inter-relationship between the current-year forecast and the interim accounts charge to ensure that they are consistent in treatment of general items. For example, if the forecast is a taxable loss at trading level, then no tax losses brought forward may be utilized in the interim figures even though this may be a profitable result. The ACT charge/credit is a compensating figure.

The following dimensions give an idea of the size of models:

	Variables	Periods
(1) Capital allowances	2760	5
(2) Overseas income	920	10
(3) Subsidiaries	5712	6
(4) Dividends/profit sharing	103	6
(5) Loans	100	46
Main model	300	24
Interim accounts model	300	24

For model 1, there are 40 input rows + 144 calculated rows, for 15 sections, i.e. 2760 variables; for model 3 there are 32 input rows + 136 calculated rows, for 34 sections, i.e. 5712 variables.

The Capital allowance model has the following structure—rows are model variables, periods are time, and sections are ICI divisions. The overseas income model has a transposed structure—rows are time, periods are variables and the sections divisions. The other U.K. subsidiary model has the usual structure—variables, time and divisions, but uses extensively the FCS-EPS allocation facilities to allocate group items down the hierarchy, and the FCS-EPS facility to change model logic for sections, for example, input and consolidated sections. The various model logics use most of the advanced language facilities described earlier, for example, file handling, looping, and indirect addressing.

Whilst the models have been developed by four people over the last three years the main development has been in the last year for the main model, interim model and models 2 and 3. The smaller models 2 and 3 took a week to write in total spread over a 3-month period. The main model has taken 2-3 months spread over a 9-month period, and the interim accounts model perhaps 2 weeks. All models include logic, job tracks and report specifications, any of which may be subject to amendment at short notice.

Future developments are seen in terms of further enhancement of current systems, for example the provision of more supporting detail, tax creditor, reconciliation for full deferral purposes, and the computerization of inter-relationships between interim accounts and current-year tax models; automatic reading from auxiliary files into the main model; more detail of intra-merger flows of interest for information purposes; formalization of inputs for internal discussion of the resulting tax charge and payments; the updating of the tax model as legislation changes. This could also result from changes in group structure or large changes in data which necessitate an amendment to the logic in the model.

20.8 Application C: Quarterly Profit and Sales Reports

Data are fed down to Head Office from the central computer on a tape suitable for FCS-EPS, and loaded on to the minicomputer into a hierarchy model using a conversion table. For a six-week period during each quarter data arrive daily and are checked with the previous day's data to identify changes. The original data have been telexed from all over the world to the Centre and are 'cleaned-up' before transfer to Head Office.

The tape contains current-quarter cumulative data, and so, given previous cumulative data, each quarter may be derived by differencing. A current annual forecast is also supplied. All data are recorded in operating-unit detail, and using the hierarchical facilities of FCS-EPS, territorial and group totals are derived. The actual hierarchy comprises 390 input sections and 130 consolidated sections, giving 520 in total. Sales and profit data are kept on two separate data files. For sales, an input section comprises 140 rows for 5 time periods, while for profits an input section comprises 170 rows for 5 time periods. The previous year has been constructed in the same format. In total, this represents several hundred thousand data elements! Report specifications are used to output quarterly figures and variances for the current year and previous year as shown in the two examples, Figures 20.8 and 20.9.

Inter-company transfers are easily treated by identifying them on separate rows in each section and inputting contra entries to ensure they cancel out at group level. The hierarchy is used to simply add up the data, and via VDU screens check any data item using section and cross-section displays.

The reports are fairly detailed—headings and selected text are dynamically created, depending on year and current quarter; the de-cumulating depends on current quarter; zeros in columns with no data are blanked out, in columns with data they must appear as dashes; column output positions are variable; variances differ by report and there are many other intricate requirements.

The models have been 'parameterized' to ensure that if, for example, in the current year, the input-section sizes or the number of sections change, then they need not be re-written. An important distinction has been made between the concept of applying logic rules to a data matrix to identify and obtain final numbers, and separate report specifications for the final reports. This helps to differentiate between the two processes of checking and producing the base data, and then reporting on it. Writing and maintaining the system is thus easy to understand and implement.

The consolidations themselves take several minutes to perform, but this again only serves to emphasize the different attitude created by modelling on an in-house mini. All marginal costs are zero, or very nearly so; if the consolidation takes a few minutes that is a fairly good excuse for popping out of the office for a cup of tea!

20.9 Application D: Corporate Report to Board

This is a small hierarchical system of 20 sections, each with 20 data rows. There are 73 columns however, to allow for monthly cumulative data for both actual and budget sales and profits.

Once budgets have been set up for the year, only the current month's actual figures need be input to obtain a comprehensive set of reports for performance monitoring;

20.10 Hardware

Having discussed the reasons for using an in-house mini, and presented the current applications, it is now appropriate to describe the actual mini-computer in ICI Treasurer's Department.

ICI Treasurer's FCS–EPS Minicomputer

FCS–EPS is implemented at Millbank on a timesharing minicomputer, replacing a commercial timesharing bureau. The computer hardware is a high-performance 32-

SCHEDULE 1

GROUP PROFIT AND LOSS ACCOUNT

SCHEDULE 1

1979	1980	Varia-tion		1980	1981 F/c	Varia-tion
£m	£m	£m		£m	£m	£m
			SALES TO EXTERNAL CUSTOMERS (Schedule III)			
—	—	—	United Kingdom	—	—	—
—	—	—	Overseas	—	—	—
—	—	—		—	—	—
—	—	—	TRADING PROFIT (Schedule IV)	—	—	—
—	—	—	After charging depreciation	—	—	—
—	—	—	Exchange gain/loss on net current assets of overseas subsidiaries	—	—	—
—	—	—	Profit less losses from trade investments (Schedule VII)	—	—	—
—	—	—	Interest and financing costs less income	—	—	—
—	—	—	PROFIT BEFORE TAXATION AND GRANTS	—	—	—
—	—	—	Taxation less grants (Schedule VIII)	—	—	—
—	—	—	PROFIT AFTER TAXATION AND GRANTS	—	—	—
—	—	—	Applicable to minorities	—	—	—
—	—	—	PROFIT APPLICABLE TO PARENT COMPANY BEFORE EXTRAORDIN-ARY ITEMS	—	—	—
—	—	—	Extraordinary items	—	—	—
—	—	—	PROFIT APPLICABLE TO PARENT COMPANY AFTER EXTRAORDIN-ARY ITEMS	—	—	—
—	—	—	Less: Preference dividend	—	—	—
—	—	—	EARNINGS FOR ORDINARY STOCKHOLDERS	—	—	—
—	—	—	Less: Ordinary dividend	—	—	—
—	—	—	PROFIT RETAINED FOR THE YEAR	—	—	—
—	—	—	By Parent Company	—	—	—
—	—	—	By Subsidiaries	—	—	—
—	—	—	In Principal Associated Companies	—	—	—
—	—	—		—	—	—

Figure 20.8 EPS report output

GROUP EXTERNAL SALES IN THE UNITED KINGDOM

	1979						1980				
	QUARTERS				YEAR		QUARTERS				YEAR
	1st	2nd	3rd	4th			1st	2nd	3rd	4th	
	£m	£m	£m	£m	£m		£m	£m	£m	£m	£m
UNITED KINGDOM											
Business 1	—	—	—	—	—		—				
Business 2	—	—	—	—	—		—				
Business 3	—	—	—	—	—		—				
Business 4	—	—	—	—	—		—				
Business 5	—	—	—	—	—		—				
Business 6	—	—	—	—	—		—				
Business 7	—	—	—	—	—		—				
Business 8	—	—	—	—	—		—				
Business 9	—	—	—	—	—		—				
Business 10	—	—	—	—	—		—				
TOTAL UK	—	—	—	—	—		—				
OVERSEAS SUBSIDIARIES											
Australasia	—	—	—	—	—		—				
Canada	—	—	—	—	—		—				
Europe	—	—	—	—	—		—				
Indian sub-continent	—	—	—	—	—		—				
United States	—	—	—	—	—		—				
Other Territories	—	—	—	—	—		—				
TOTAL OVERSEAS	—	—	—	—	—		—				
GROUP TOTAL	—	—	—	—	—		—				

Figure 20.9 EPS report output

bit system which was initially installed in October 1979. The hardware/software package was 'black boxed' where possible to provide as simple a transition from bureau usage as possible.

The initial configuration was delivered with the capability to support three simultaneous users, one of whom had substantial experience of using FCS on the commercial bureau. Computer hardware operation experience was limited since the user department was primarily staffed by financial analysts/accountants. The machine was installed with the configuration shown in Figure 20.10.

Progressive enhancement of the hardware has seen the addition of a 600 lines per minute lineprinter, two further VDUs and an extra 120 c.p.s. slave printer. In addition an extra one half megabyte of main memory has been added. The provision of HASP remote job entry to 'talk' to the main IBM computer is also planned.

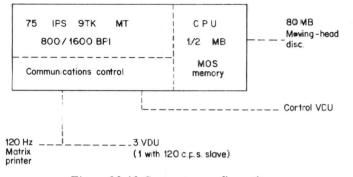

Figure 20.10 Computer configuration

ICI wanted to retain the option to purchase the equipment, so initially the hardware was rented plus hardware/software maintenance. Costs increased with the additional hardware including the planned addition of HASP. The purchase option is now being evaluated—using FCS-EPS no doubt! The provision of the software was part of the overall licensing arrangement. between EPS Consultants and ICI for supply of financial modelling software.

The computer installed uses a memory-mapping technique, whereby programs not requiring CPU time (user is thinking what to do next or drinking his tea again) are rolled out on to disc, thus allowing programs that require processing to gain access to the CPU. The FCS-EPS program, with its integral working area (a specially large version was supplied for certain ICI applications) resides in 400 000 bytes of main memory. Each FCS-EPS user has a separate copy of the program, so as the number of users increases, so the rolling out process swapping increases.

This swapping frequency is more complex than a simple first-in/first-out schedule. A priority system provides for access to the CPU; however, a task automatically migrates to the priority level most suitable for its needs, e.g. a task that is needing to do terminal output/input requires regular small slices of CPU time whiles a calculation-bound task needs to absorb larger slices of CPU time.

A planned enhancement to the FCS-EPS system is the provision of a shared-load module. This means that all users logged will have their own working area but will share the main FCS-EPS program. This simultaneous re-entrant use of the FCS-EPS program considerably increases the number of users on the machine that can achieve satisfactory response.

Timetable of Events

October 1979   Computer installed comprising:
                                Processor and all cabinets
                                ½ Mbyte main MOS memory
                                Disc drive, magnetic tape unit

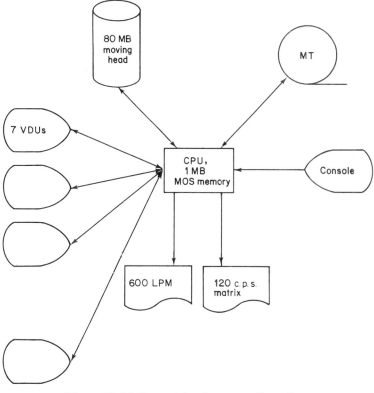

Figure 20.11 Current hardware configuration

4 VDUs and 6 COMMS unit
1 × 120 c.p.s. matrix printer
1 slave printer
600 lines per minute printer
Operating system and associated software

December 1979	2nd slave printer
April 1980	2 extra VDUs
May 1980	½ Mbyte extra memory.

Installation of a computer capable of supporting six or more simultaneous users normally requires some form of operating team. The attitude of ICI was that the availability of the computer had to be maximized, but that the use of an operator was not practical. The fundamental housekeeping requirements on the machine had therefore to be kept to the practical minimum consistent with security.

This was achieved by establishing batch jobs that performed the role of security, and which could easily be run by the last user of the day before system close down. The only operating experience necessary was the ability to select and mount the correct generation magnetic tape. In many respects keeping this housekeeping system as simple as possible and giving the users a very brief description of its operation obviated completely the need for an operator.

Similarly, the simple mode of operation of the magnetic-tape housekeeping software means that files of data may easily be moved from one computer to another, as long as they are kept as symbolic information.

Experience has shown that a computer system capable of running FCS–EPS can be installed in a financial department, and can be successfully used by a relatively non-technical staff. The current hardware configuration is shown in Figure 20.11.

20.11 Graphical Output

The information presented by the systems described has been output in tabular form. A further stage in development will be to present part of this data graphically. Tabular output has little immediate impact and is often hard to comprehend, whereas graphical output is immediate. Figure 20.12 shows several graphs extracted from the ICI 1979 *Annual Report*. It is intended to produce such output, using the FCS–EPS minicomputer graphics facilities currently under development.

Bubble plots may be used to present data. For example, each business division's sales and trading profit may be plotted using data extracted from the five-year plan; the movement in sales and profit and relative size presented; yield curves plotted, breaking down the constituent parts of return on capital to other ratios. For example, return on capital is defined as CCA trading profit divided by gross trading capital employed; this ratio may be re-defined in terms of CCA profit margin, (CCA trading profit divided by sales value) multiplied by the capital ratio (sales value divided by gross trading capital employed). The movement in return on capital can thus be further explored in terms of two other ratios, and simply presented on a VDU screen. Obviously the ratio analysis may be extended. See Figure 20.13 for examples of proposed bubble plot and yield curves.

The graphical presentation of data will be a major development for financial modelling systems.

20.12 Conclusion

The Management Accounting Group of ICI Treasurer's Department have shown how the relatively new concept of financial modelling on a dedicated in-house mini-computer can be successfully implemented. The use of a computer bureau for the initial applications was expensive, correction of small data errors in a large integrated system involved expensive re-runs, sensitivity analysis was restricted by cost, model development not always encouraged—the cash register keeps ringing! The in-house move was easily justified, the benefits were more than expected. A VDU on each accountant's desk gives immediate data checking and presentation, and a feeling of involvement. A major change was a new attitude to modelling, the

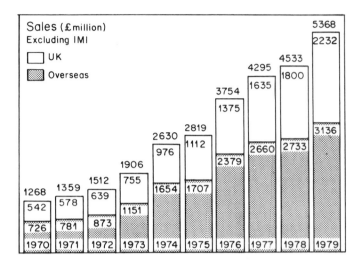

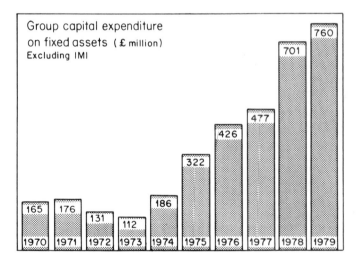

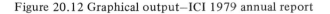

Figure 20.12 Graphical output—ICI 1979 annual report

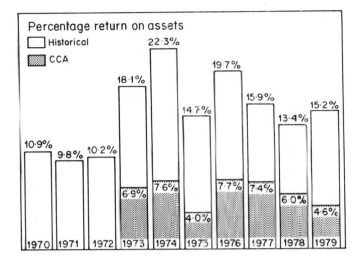

Percentage return on assets

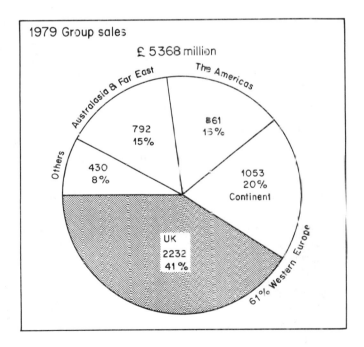

1979 Group sales

£ 5368 million

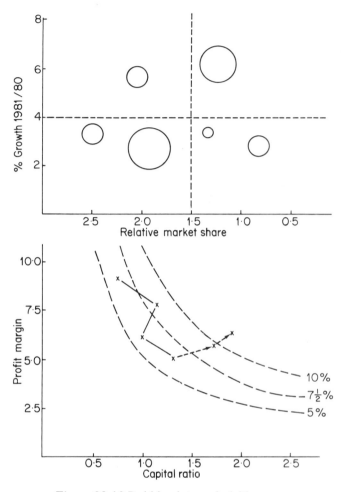

Figure 20.13 Bubble plots and yield curves

marginal cost for each application was zero, the accountants creatively suggested new methods of routine collection, consolidation, analysis and reporting of data. The extent of the current applications has been earlier demonstrated—long-term cash-forecasting models, tax-planning models, quarterly profit and sales reporting, and corporate reports to the Board, direct from the computer print-out to the boardroom.

The above application has shown that non-technical data-processing staff can successfully operate a computer system supporting several users simultaneously; the only operating experience necessary is the ability to select and mount the correct generation magnetic tape.

Financial Modelling in Corporate Management
Edited by J. W. Bryant
© 1982 John Wiley & Sons Ltd.

21

An Experience of Corporate Modelling[*]

JOHN PRECIOUS

21.1 Introduction

This chapter describes the experience gained in the field of corporate computer model-building by one organization over a period of about eight years. Throughout, an emphasis has been placed on the practical aspects of the work: how we approached the technique from first principles; the errors which have been made; and the successes which we feel have accrued. There will be companies which have different or more rapid progress to report, but it is probable that the lessons learned at Tioxide are fundamental and of general relevance to any organization embarking on corporate modelling.

The development process is described below in three parts, the first dealing with the first four years of work, while the other two cover the later phases of modelling carried out during a further succeeding four-year period. These sections were each written at the end of the respective four-year development period which they describe, and so there is added poignancy in the remarks made at the end of Section 21.2 which describe the then anticipated developments, as opposed to the reality described in Section 21.3. It was felt to be instructive to retain this historical dimension rather than to produce a single discussion of the whole modelling programme written with the benefit of hindsight, because it illustrates quite dramatically how perceptions of the growth and value of specific corporate models can change for reasons that are not always easily anticipated.

21.2. When Success can be a Long-term Forecast

This section reviews the first four years of corporate modelling by British Titan Ltd. (later renamed Tioxide Group Ltd). There are three clearly defined phases

---

[*]Parts of this chapter are reproduced by permission of the publisher from J. R. Precious and D. R. Wood, 'Corporate Modelling: When Success Can Be a Long-term Forecast', *Accounting and Business Research*, Autumn 1975, 254–72.

through which we have progressed, and these are described below as seen at the conclusion of this part of the work.

Phase 1

The process of model building by computer began some fours years ago, shortly after finalization of the group's five-year plan. The decision to take our first tentative steps in building an 'in-house' corporate model was made before the experience of compiling this particular plan by hand had receded into the memories of those concerned. That experience (at least to the accounting function) could probably best be summarized as: mass calculation, analysis, compilation and consolidation—repeated several times, to test forecast revisions—which, manually, is a time-consuming process. It was therefore logical to conclude that use of the company's ICL 1900 series computer should, by the very time saved, allow a much closer look at the key variables through the medium of sensitivity analysis. Thus followed our first acquaintance with the ICL PROSPER Programming package.

So the decision was made; but how to begin? And promptly, our first mistakes: we chose to approach the task by straightforward transcription of the recent plan, using the accounting schedules to prepare an outline flow chart. We had unknowingly made two fundamental errors:

(1) We assumed that, by and large, each succeeding reappraisal of medium- and long-term plans would fit the format devised for the most recent manual assessment.
(2) We devoted a relatively small amount of time (approximately two weeks) to the preparation of flow charts.

In other words, reduction of the accounting man-hours became the major objective. It did not, of course, follow that the resultant model would be particularly appealing in a practical sense to anyone other than accountants. Had we been content to merely simplify our own involvement in subsequent reviews, then in some ways the project could have been considered a partial success. But this was not our sole objective. it was not even the most important. We wanted to build a model which could be used by corporate planners to test the broader strategic aspects of possible courses of action open to the group. In this respect, the model was a failure.

Although it it true to say that the PROSPER package has in itself been developed to give better service to the user in terms of operation and output presentation during the last four years, the fact remains that our first corporate model suffered considerably from too much inflexibility. Most of its drawbacks resulted from a combination of this and the two major policy errors mentioned above, all of which were the direct result of our inexperience in this planning technique.

By the time the project was eventually complete, we had assembled a formidable list of items requiring amendment or improvement, which effectively meant a total program overhaul. Some of them are outlined below:

(1) The program was written as one complete model.

It is not difficult to envisage the impact of this decision upon run time and paper: excessive consumption of both. So for example, to observe the effect of a change in sales prices on trading profits, we had to resign ourselves to a twenty minutes wait whilst the model ran from start to finish. Compared with the process of manual adjustments, this is of course an insignificant period. But when a computer is operational for many of the 24 hours in a day, working to closely defined schedules, time assumes a premium rating: one-third of an hour used in this manner equates to a waste of resources.

Thus we learnt the value of time spent in planning a program, and how the use of a number of submodels can help to accelerate the results of sensitivity analysis.

(2) The opportunity to use the results of a series of instructions and forecasts in a different area of model was not used to the full.

Another example may best illustrate this point. The group's manufactured end product demands considerable investment in raw material stocks. To calculate the usage of cost of each raw material, assembly of the relevant stock accounts will obviously be necessary. But when complete, this process will also show the investment in raw material stocks at each period end—which in itself is a major element of working capital, necessary for the compilation of cash flows and balance sheets.

Because we elected to construct trading accounts, cash flows and balance sheets independently of each other, we did not take programming advantage of this obvious financial link. The result was a less efficient model than might otherwise have been the case, and once more the reason was lack of pre-program planning.

(3) There was only one way in which a sales forecast could be calculated.

The chosen method was to assume that finished product stocks would equate to a fixed number of weeks' sales (based on past experience), and with a known production capacity, sales would be the balancing figure. The principle was, of course, perfectly sound. But a planning model which does not offer any alternative means of constructing a key forecast is taking too much for granted: inflexibility again.

(4) The standard of output presentation was poor.

Some figures had been subject to rounding up procedures, but others contained two or three places of decimals. The impact on a casual observer would no doubt have been bewildering; but to those concerned with some measure of detail, irritation may have led to despair.

Most long-term planning models result in a considerable output of information when run in full. By giving minimum attention to print-out formats, we did not assist any subsequent analysis of the results.

Naturally, there were more errors in this first model, but a lengthy catalogue has an air of repetion. We feel the above to be a representative and possibly useful selection to anyone interested from a practical viewpoint.

Of design successes, (other than the fact that the model was capable of operation, however inflexibly) three are perhaps worth passing mention:

(1) The raw materials of importance in the manufacturing process were assumed to be key determinants of factory cost; all other materials and services were consolidated into two summary headings.

An obvious decision—though it would have been equally simple to make numerous additions in portraying an 'accurate' factory cost statement. But we felt that the model, when operational, should be able to display effectively possible future trends in the business over a maximum ten-year period. Consideration of detailed factory costs in this context simply yields a model with an excessive number of input forecasts, whose claims to greater accuracy are largely illusory.

(2) Calculation of working capital levels was also made on the basis of isolating key elements.

Another hardly less than obvious remark. So for the same reason outlined in (1)—that it is always tempting to err on the side of detail in pursuit of the 'most accurate' result—we isolated the major elements of the company's investment in working capital. The annual movement in each largely governed the movement in working capital as a whole. As may be expected, the analysis showed that stock (finished product, raw material only) and trade debt were the determining factors. The remaining assets and liabilities had either relatively static levels or fairly predictable cyclical movements.

(3) There was a page selection print out facility.

Item (4) also gave the major negative presentation error; this facility helped at least to minimize the discomfort. Thus, for example, to see the effects of an adjustment to sales prices (in terms of revenue, trading profit and cash flow) required only five of the more than forty pages to be printed. It was unfortunate that the construction of the model still necessitated operation of the complete program, despite the diminution in requested print-out volume.

Phase II

It was late in 1972, after a year of comparative inactivity in the model-building field, that serious thought was given to the development of our limited experience to date. This time we approached the problem in a rather less insular way. In conjunction with the data-processing manager, a report was prepared for the group financial controller which proposed a revised and expanded modelling system, for the eventual use of all companies in the group. It explained the proposals under four main headings:

objectives;
benefits;

outline structure;
implementation and costs;

with three accompanying appendices:

detailed structure;
key data elements;
a comparison of available modelling systems on the market.

It may be of interest to summarize the objectives and benefits of the system as they were seen at that time.

(a) Objectives

(1) Assist management in the evaluation of long-term plans, using inter-linked computer based models to evaluate, and where possible optimize, profits and cash flow.

(2) Enable subsidiary plans to be produced in local currencies prior to conversion and consolidation into sterling.

(3) Provide detailed evaluation of sales and production forecasts; profit and loss accounts, balance sheets, cash flows, operating ratios and statistics, to be the minimum financial statements.

(4) Show separately the effects of inflation.

(5) Allow for the optimization of certain specified functions.

(6) Either incorporate or have access to a minimum of ten (preferably 20) years' historical statistics, to enable regression analysis to be carried out where requested.

(7) Anticipate the necessity for new factories or extensions to those already in existence, and indicate where any increase in productive capacity could be undertaken, based on the available input data.

The remaining objectives were viewed in terms of implementation, running costs, and ease of operation.

(8) Assemble a flexible structure with at least a five-year life expectancy.

(9) Keep the installation costs to a minimum, but without compromising achievement of the objectives as a whole.

(10) Be easy to maintain and develop, yet fast and efficient in operation (i.e. extensive use of disc storage).

(11) Enable alternative strategies to be evaluated without compromising original or basic data.

(12) Allow full acceptance and modification of data, with subsequent results displayed through computer terminals.

(13) Be capable of accepting as input data available information from other computer systems using the projected database.

(14) Incorporate alternative methods of data input through which the system may be activated.

(15) Ensure, if requested, that selected data and results be displayed through the various stages of operation.

(b) Benefits

(1) Would enable evaluation of long-term plans to be carried out throughout the year.

(2) Make more time available for detailed study of the results of alternative courses of action.

(3) Enable the present five-year view to be enhanced by a further five-year period, thus allowing the investigation and development of potentially more far-reaching strategies.

(4) The provision of individual self-contained subroutines to encourage greater participation by line management, in both the concept and formulation stages of the long-term planning process.

Heady stuff! And to be at all comprehensible a structural outline of the complete model was required.

In summary, the following were the important aspects contained in this part of the report.

(c) Outline Structure

(1) There were to be three major areas of operation which could broadly be classified as marketing, production and finance.

(2) The complete model was to be operational in five individual, but linked, levels:

    Level 1 Profit and loss accounts
                 Balance sheets
                 Cash flows
                 Ratios and statistics
    Level 2 Summarized sales and production forecasts (in the form of trading accounts).
    Level 3 Detailed marketing and production forecasts.
    Level 4 Optimization of marketing and production capacities.
    Level 5 Determination of world demand for the product.

(3) The model was to be designated as a hierarchical structure, level 1 being the 'highest' and level 5 the 'lowest'. But it was recognized that in the interests of flexibility, there had to be provision both to transmit data and forecasts from

one level to any other specified level (not necessarily in sequence) and to commence at any desired point. To be satisfactory, this effectively required that the upward sequence from level 5 to level 1 could be dispensed with if attention was to be directed to a particular planning area. It was therefore envisaged that a 'link data file' between each level and the next would give effect to these or any other operational circumstances requested.

An additional facility to be made available through these linking files was an overwrite option. In other words, as data progressed towards level 1, a user could make amendments to the result sequence by direct input of alterations or additions at each level. This was to ensure that the changed results or forecasts would be used thereafter in later levels of the model.

(4) There would be a similar set of submodels for each company in the group in levels 1–3. This was seen as simplifying the process of consolidation in levels 1 and 2, when programming commenced.

(5) Output data from all stages of the model would be available in either horizontal or vertical form, i.e. by function or company.

Although this completed the system in outline, some further amplification of the distinguishing characteristics in levels 2, 3 and 4 may assist clarification of the operational areas in the report.

(d) Level 2: Summarized Sales and Production Forecasts

(1) At this stage, a clear forecast relationship would have been established between sales and production functions throughout the group. The statistics could have been derived (through a logical operational sequence in the model, having commenced at level 5) or directly input at some intermediate stage through a a link data file.

(2) Level 2 would be the highest point in the structure where consideration of production and sales could be made in units of each (the profit and loss accounts in level 1 would assume a statutory accounts format). It therefore follows that this would also be the highest level wherein a contribution gap could be deduced from independent sets of data.

(3) Both sales revenues and production costs would be expressed in summary form.

(e) Level 3: Detailed Marketing and Production Forecasts

(1) Seen as an intermediate stage between the global supply/demand formulation at levels 4 and 5 and subsequent corporate trading results at level 2.

(2) This sub-routine would thus be primarily concerned with the evaluation of sales within group companies, by sales or marketing characteristics.

(3) The construction of a production cost forecast differentiating between variable and fixed costs would be made at this point.

(f) Level 4: Optimization of Marketing and Production Capacities

(1) Expected to be a marketing oriented subroutine where production capability would be a limiting factor. Thus, a marketing strategy (either directly input or developed at level 5) beyond productive capacity would be satisfied by the model automatically taking note of the shortfall, and suggesting a construction location/programme based on previously input parameters e.g. group strategy, cost of capital, availability of funds, production costs, etc.
(2) The marketing programme established, and feasible within the above constraints, maximization of group contribution would be attained by the distribution of sales and production targets to each manufacturing source, having regard to the appropriate costs and revenues existing at each.

The proposal was subsequently accepted and the project began early in 1973. We had thus progressed to

Phase III

(a) Output Specification

It was clear from the outset that with a (relatively) far more ambitious project under way, the original corporate model should be retired to the archives of experience. Clearly, to have attempted to amend the program would have taken more time than to write a new one.

This decision made, detailed output specifications were drawn up as a first step towards ultimate programming. During the course of this process, information gaps were discovered relating to the requirements of levels 4 and 5, such as to render their specification incomplete. As a result, and because each level would be programmed individually, it was decided to concentrate on levels 1–3 in the first instance.

(b) Flow Charts

Although we already had composite output specifications for these areas, we determined that detailed flow charts should be drawn from them before programming work commenced (an early lesson remembered!) This approach may not meet with the general approval of those experienced in data processing or corporate modelling activities. Nevertheless, we felt that the analysis had been worthwhile for the following reasons:

(1) The links to and from other levels and/or subroutines are clearly established.
(2) Forecast number usage is consequently restricted. The effects of providing for alternative courses of action and sources of input are properly evaluated.

(3) The programming function is simplified since objectives are clearly stated.
(4) Testing of programs and location of program errors is facilitated.
(5) Basic system design errors are readily evaluated, and the impact of their correction easily seen, prior to any program modification which may be necessary.

The original flow charts to the first three levels of the model are shown in Figures 21.1-21.6. Naturally, there have been some amendments, since they were drawn as a direct result of programming and operational experience (for example, see first comment under level 3 below). However, they did, and largely still do, represent a basis for the current system.

(c) Programming

Work commenced after certain fundamental program criteria had been established:

(1) We elected to dispose of the multiple instruction requirement (i.e. duplication of basic instructions and forecast number sequences for all companies in the group) by programming the first three levels for one company alone. The remaining companies' comparable models and subroutines would thereafter be installed either by total or selected duplication of this 'base' model.
(2) Level 3, containing much of the model's component detail, was the logical beginning.
(3) Provision for the use of trend and adjustment factors would be accommodated in the programs, but they would not be displayed in the subsequent printout. (This simply meant that if any part(s) of the output tabulations were required for publication in the ensuing group plan, presentation would not be affected by extraneous detail.)
(4) Where a company had more than one factory, the profitability of each would be assessed in addition to that of the company as a whole.

(d) Level 3

Almost immediately after commencement, some of the flowchart assumptions (Figure 21.5) were in question. During the early programming stages of major raw material (MRM) manufacturing cost, a problem had arisen concerning the evaluation of each material's usage. Originally, it had been the intention to calculate a weighted average price based upon the costs of opening stock and subsequent annual purchases.

Unfortunately, this involved the use of a considerable number of loops which, in operational terms, only served to slow the program down. Considered in the context of the model as a whole, a desirable solution appeared to be valuation

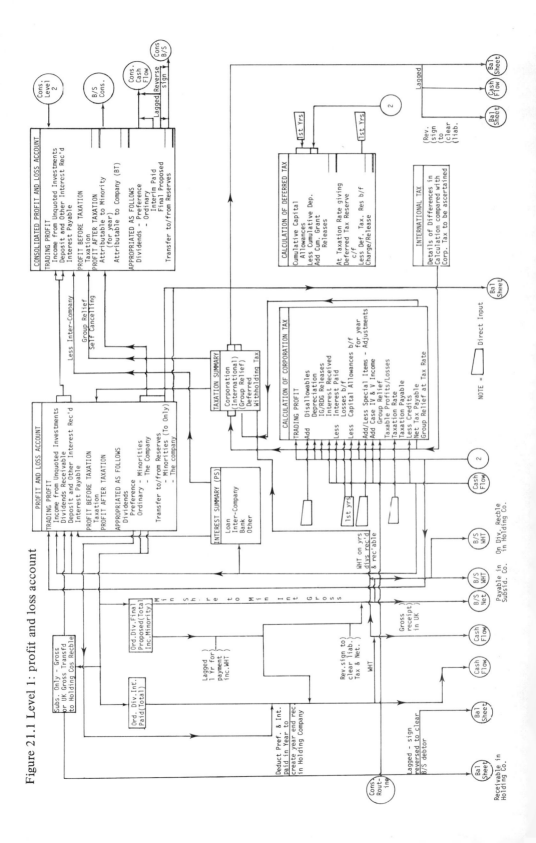

Figure 21.1 Level 1: profit and loss account

Figure 21.2 Level 1: balance sheet

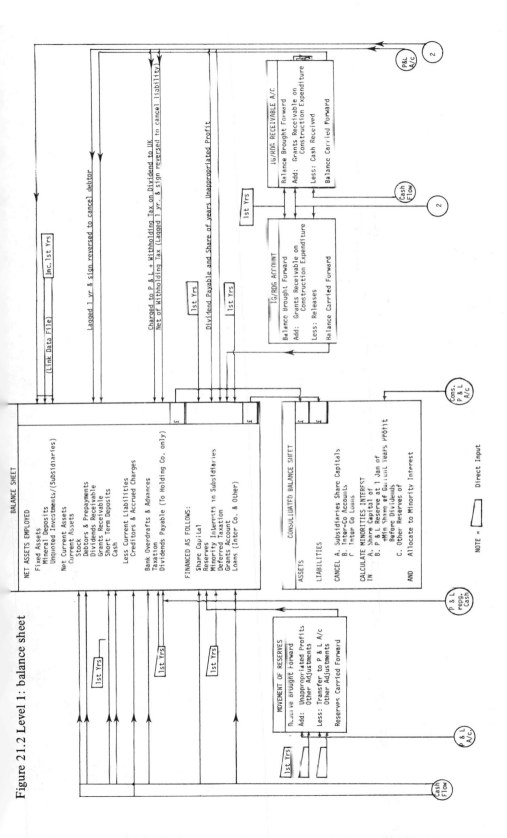

Figure 21.3 Level 1: cash flow

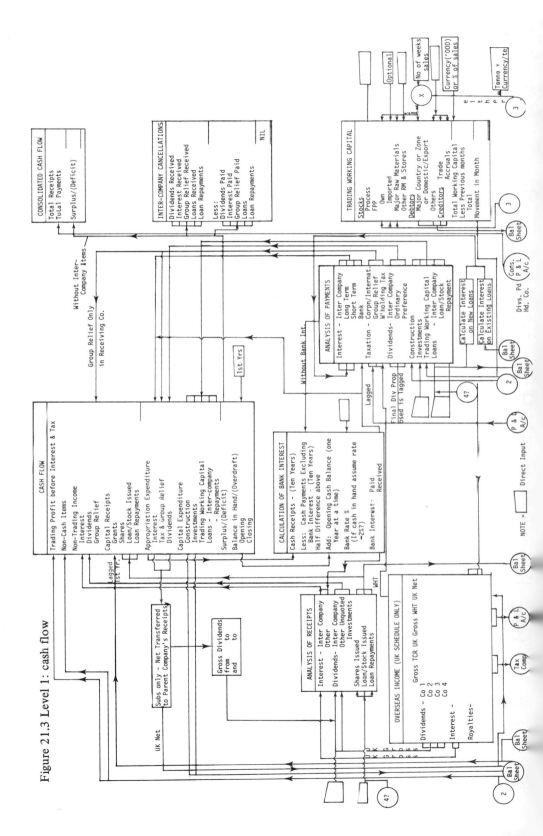

Figure 21.4 Level 2: trading

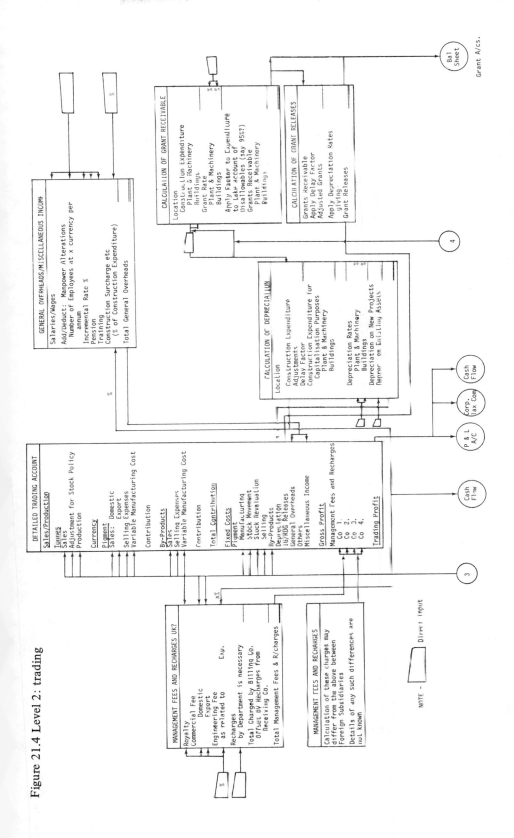

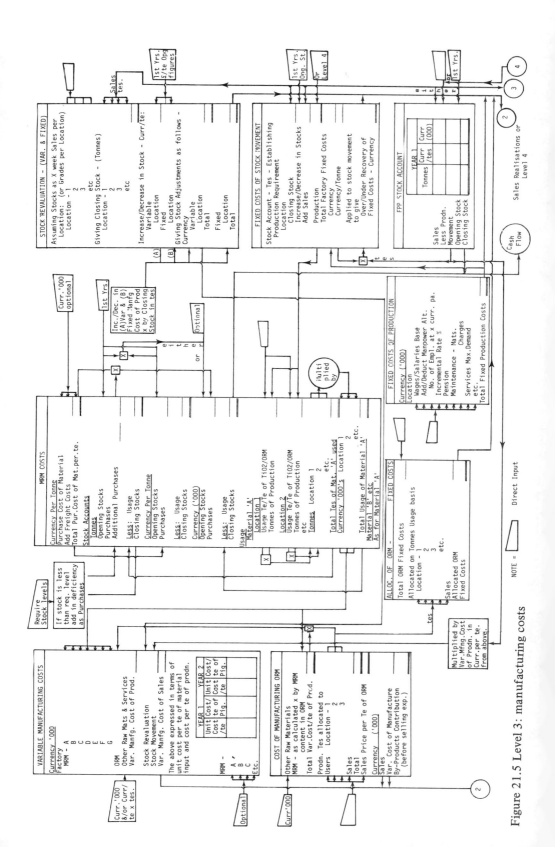

Figure 21.5 Level 3: manufacturing costs

Figure 21.6 Level 3: sales and related costs

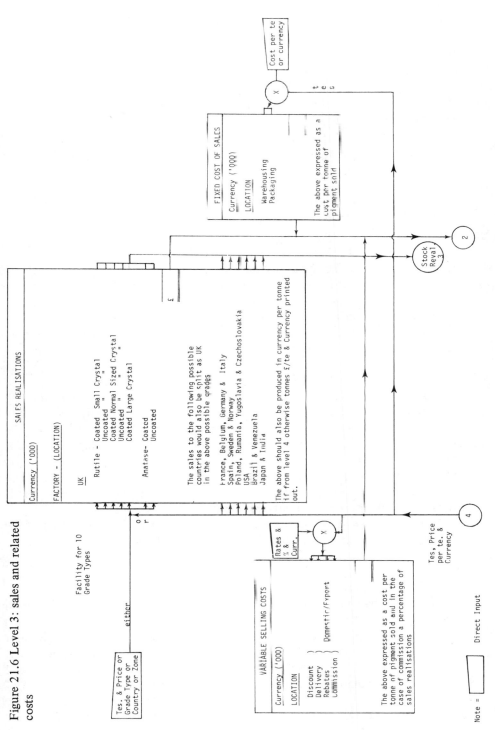

at the current year's purchase price: financially conservative in times of inflation and operationally faster.

The next contentious programming area which we encountered was also reminiscent of the original corporate model: calculation of sales, production and stock levels of finished product.

It will be recalled that one method only was previously available. Mindful of this serious shortcoming, we therefore proposed the following options for user consideration:

(1) Input: sales, production and first year's opening stock.
    Calculate: production.
(2) Input: sales, closing stock and first year's opening stock.
    Calculate: production
(3) Input: sales and first year's opening stock.
    Calculate: closing stock (as x weeks' sales) and production.

In all cases, input could be either direct or from level 4, (when completed).

The final reference to programming experience at this level of the structure concerns the assessment of fixed manufacturing costs, and in particular, a manpower planning facility.

As a result of time constraints, we were not able to conduct the background analysis which we felt the subject warranted: that is, a separate subroutine for each factory payroll. In these circumstances, we made provision for only one category of process labour, which therefore had to represent a weighted average of all relevant employee grades. Nevertheless, we suggested that a forecast compiled from this undesirable base at least recognized that costs of (salaries and) wages depend on numbers employed, as well as annual increments. Therefore, any proposed increase in production should display a sharp rise in the company's manpower investment if the resultant forecasts are to retain credibility.

During the first quarter of 1973, all programming and subsequent testing of the completed level 3 had been accomplished.

(e) Level 2

Once again, a flaw in the output specifications was quickly uncovered—this time in the calculation of depreciation and government grants.

We had presumed an instruction sequence operational here, immediately prior to compilation of the detailed trading account. But this overlooked the logical sequence which began in level 3 with the construction of individual factory and company profitabilities, where net depreciation is naturally a significant item of fixed cost.

We therefore had no alternative but to reopen level 3 and accommodate these amendments—a straightforward process which demonstrated (if demonstration was required) the inherent flexibility of a model comprising a series of individual subroutines.

Yet another departure from plan was also made when we determined that compilation of 'detailed' trading working capital was a more feasible proposition at this stage than the previously envisaged level 1.

The decision centred upon the degree of sophistication to be expected when considering certain strategies. For example, a ten-year assessment of outline data, which may be expected to take place within the boundaries of the first level, was thought unlikely to use anything more complex than an *ad hoc* estimation of total annual working capital movement. On the other hand, we reasoned that a view which began with summarized forecasts of sales and production units could well require a comparative assessment (at least) of the significant working capital elements.

Other than discovering an error in the PROSPER package itself, which was subsequently corrected by ICL, mid-year 1973 saw the completion of level 2.

All this enabled us to complete the programming for level 1 well before the end of the year.

Prior to their storage on disc, all three levels for the one company were run concurrently, and it was interesting to note that the total operational time of 26 minutes included 10 minutes for card input. The net effective 16 minutes comprised:

level 3   11 minutes
level 2   2 minutes
level 1   3 minutes

Up to Date and Beyond?

It is fortunate that continued development has not progressed as we expected. There have been a number of reasons for the slow down, but by far the most significant is the perennial complaint of many in commerce and industry: staff shortages. It is to our immediate benefit that within the recent past, steps have been taken to alleviate the situation, and we anticipate that much (if not all) of the backlog will have been eliminated before the end of this year (1975).

However, the above slightly despondent air is not to imply cessation of progress since June 1973; that would be far from true. We have managed to complete almost all the programming and subsequent testing of programs for other group companies, including the modifications which were necessary from the basic model described above. Disc storage space has been allocated for each, and the models are expected to be installed within the next two months.

To complete the first major segment of this second corporate modelling system therefore only requires the establishment of a consolidation routine at level 1; level 2 consolidation is already operational.

With an enlarged availability of resources, the outstanding parts of level 1, 2 and 3 will be speedily assembled and tested. In conjunction with colleagues in the Planning, Marketing and Data Processing Departments, we would anticipate completion of level 4 before the end of 1975.

Of the original proposal, this would leave only level 5 to successfully conclude the project. However, it is now thought likely that work in this sphere will be deferred in favour of an additional submodel at level 1. A program written during the last few months has already been the subject of some development work directed towards the establishment of corporate financial returns and objectives for the future. Its successful completion and addition to the present structure would, we believe, usefully enhance the Group's assessment of its long-term objectives, and the strategy which might be employed in their achievement.

As in much work of a development nature, the end of a project may signal the beginning of new or related investigations. So with this company's appproach to corporate modelling. We feel that with the resources at hand, two years represents the long-term—the sort of timescale to be expected for completion of all the above outline proposals. It will be interesting to see, in 1976, if we managed to achieve our objectives.

21.3 . . . But Long-term Finance Forecasts are Usually Wrong

The last section described some four years' work in corporate financial model building, ostensibly aimed at simplifying and improving the group's long-term planning process. Paradoxically, in view of these preceding circumstances, a disinterested observer could well conclude that one form of purgatory had been exchanged for another. For here was a catalogue of almost unremitting gloom laced with a series of conspicuous failures. Nevertheless, a note of cautious optimism was struck towards the end of the review: Utopia appeared to be just around the corner; even the future was 'more readily discernible', at least within the organization.

But experienced corporate modellers would not have been deceived. The signs would have been recognized for what they were—another false dawn: within a year, the large U.K. model that was to form a prototype for the remainder of the structure had already gathered its first layer of dust on a shelf to which it had been ignominiously consigned. It was there for the same reason that any other development project will always fail—if the work becomes an end in itself to the exclusion of the needs of the market place or, as here, the end-users.

This second instalment in the department's experience also measures four years. Apart from the inauspicious beginning sketched above and some eighteen months of desolate aftermath it is actually possible to claim a first significant success.

After recording the practical experience to this point the earlier barren years will be contrasted with later more productive ones, drawing in the next section on published material for comparison, to see whether any satisfactory conclusions can be drawn to account for some of the bizarre results which have accrued.

It is not intended that the reader be denied a second opportunity to survey further modelling calamities at leisure. Indeed, the display must be candid if lessons are to be learnt. And if those new to—or less experienced in—the field can successfully avoid some of the traps, their work will be the better for it, and recounting the latest instalment in this particular saga will have served its purpose.

There are again three clearly defined phases through which the work has progressed. The aim is still to be practical, even though there are no flow charts, nor a particular model structure to focus upon. This is because the salutary lessons are in the reasons for eventual success—and in particular, why the vision of so many years ago should have taken so long to materialize.

Phase IV

In early 1976 there was an expectant air amongst those building—or merely waiting upon—the second large-scale group financial model. At least, that was the impression gained by the two staff members in the North of England responsible for its development. Indeed, when one-half of the team was given a permanent position in the London-based Group Finance Department (of the recently renamed Tioxide Group Ltd) it was not even then immediately apparent that the department had lost any enthusiasm for the project which it had first requested. Of more pressing need—or so it seemed at the time—was how to successfully complete the development work with an enforced geographical separation of staff to contend with. The only answer seemed to be to continue as before. Why should distance be anything other than a minor practical irritant?

However, as the year wore on, it became clear that its earlier promise had been evanescent. Progress was ever more difficult to achieve. Other priorities both in London and the North were encountered; and modelling lost. The workload of the Group Finance Department was increasing, and though completion of the model was an accepted part of the new environment at the outset, its importance relative to other tasks steadily declined.

There were two principal reasons for this regrettable but ineluctable development: first, the group's management accounting system was materially changed; and second, when viewed from the centre, the model-building progress to date was by no means as succcesful as it had seemed to be from the subsidiary, only a few months before.

Ironically, the preceding progress report had correctly—but quite unwittingly—noted this development in its penultimate paragraph. For at the time (mid-1975) it was observed that:

> . . . it is now thought likely that work in this sphere will be deferred in favour of an additional sub-model at level 1. A program written during the last few months has already been the subject of some development work directed towards the establishment of corporate financial returns

> and objectives for the future. Its successful completion and addition to
> the present structure would, we believe, usefully enhance the Group's
> assessment of its long term objectives, and the strategy which might be
> employed in their achievement.

Stripped of all sentiment, this simply meant that the package in course of preparation was not going to meet user requirements. Consequently, work had begun separately in London on a model which would do so. The matter of user involvement in the model-building process—one of the key requirements for success—had in effect been blithely ignored by the modelling team for at least the previous two years.

Shortly after this realization had dawned, it required no great sense of prescience to conclude that further work on the model structure would be futile. Its own size had eventually ensured its technological and practical downfall. It had been difficult enough to accept the almost imperceptible progress since mid-1975 on a second ambitious project. But this was as nothing to the feeling of desolation which followed the inescapable conclusion that here was another spectacular and resounding failure. Which would probably have been a suitable point to have closed this whole, sorry financial model-building story, had it not been for a series of events—unconnected with the modelling process—which occurred during that same year of 1976. For they ushered in the era of third-generation long-term financial-planning models.

Phase V

The first development of significance was another change in the Group's planning systems. The previous annual process of compiling a long-term plan—a financially orientated document of some complexity and considerable detail—was to be replaced by a strategic plan. The difference lay not in the choice of words—the old ways merely refurbished—but in fundamental concept. Detail was recognized for what it often is at the top of a planning hierarchy: spurious accuracy to fill a void left by the absence of realistic assumptions or any feasible alternatives.

This strategic plan would comprise a series of statements resulting from the assessment of perceived alternative course of action. Its compilation was to focus on four main areas of the business: marketing, production, finance and personnel. And the emphasis would be placed on a careful review of the past and current environments, before the underlying assumptions for the forecast period were selected.

The second and most significant development in this context was a task for the Group Finance Department from the Board: to prepare, at three levels of confidence, ten-year projections for the pigment-producing companies, and the Group, showing forecast profit and loss accounts, cash flows, balance sheets and resultant ratio analyses. Quickly.

Without prior warning, this request had the instantaneous effect of concentrating departmental minds on an objective, output reports and timescale which

allowed no margin for failure. So the first problem was fundamental: how to begin?
There appeared to be only three alternative approaches:

(1) By hand—with full potential for a clerical exercise in which both content and
consumption of time were awesome to contemplate. Or,
(2) Use the (unfinished) Prosper model. The portents here were no less awesome,
since the model had to be finished (in areas where work had not even begun)
and tested, before the process of feeding in base data could begin. The previous
two years' work hardly suggested that a successful final outcome could be fore-
seen with confidence.

Which left only,

(3) Try another modelling language, better suited to the particular task. But which
one? At that time, Grinyer and Wooler (1975) listed 38 financial modelling
systems in their survey. How could they be ranked to satisfy Tioxide's criteria?

After a good deal of thought and outside consultation, the field was narrowed
down to two languages: Planmaster and FCS. The choice was difficult, because
both had competing attributes. But eventually it was apparent that Planmaster had
the edge in this particular application for the following reasons:

(1) Quick initial comprehension and ease of use thereafter
The given circumstances placed a high premium on time. It was important that
the operating principles of the chosen language could be easily grasped, and
that its subsequent use should be comparatively straightforward—even for the
relative novice. Designing and building the model was clearly going to be difficult enough. But to have saddled this process with an unwieldy (or low-level)
language would almost certainly have courted failure. This language had re-
markably few rules to learn, which thus ensured speedy development. (If it is
suggested that there is an analogy here with building a house—which may be
completed slowly by traditional means, using several different skills acquired
over the years; or quickly by use of prefabrication, which requires fewer skills
acquired in much less time—then the analogy is solely concerned with relative
completion times. There is no implied suggestion of better or worse structural
permanence.)
(2) Rule changes automatically resorted and validated before model updates
An efficiency advantage. Certain languages required specific editing, i.e. direct
replacement of logic or commands by the user within a model structure. Furthermore, it could not always be taken for granted that the other systems
would generate automatic error reports if changes were incorrectly programmed.
(3) Structural changes made with ease
It does not necessarily follow that a fundamental change in a model's structure—for example, the installation of a new company or product line—will be

accomplished with ease. Indeed, it is possible that the reverse circumstances may apply. At the very least, this could mean a considerable loss of time whilst a model is being built, and it would certainly affect the efficiency of maintenance and development work which must inevitably follow.

(4) Built-in consolidation facility

(5) Automatic currency conversion

Both factors simplified the construction process and made for ease of use thereafter. The initial directive required that full consolidated results be included in the presentation. These attributes of the language strongly— and correctly—influenced the final decision.

But the process of analysis and comparison also revealed some disadvantages which, though considered of minor importance at the time—since accomplishment of the task in hand was the overriding criterion—would not have been ignored under any other circumstances.

(1) Costly to run

This derived partly from the fact that the language was (and is still) only available through a time-sharing bureau, and partly from its mode of operation. The end result of the combination meant that any forecast of design and running costs had to be speculative—in fact, a guess—and it must be admitted that none was ever made.

(2) Static rules

Which meant that a total re-sort was necessary whenever changes were made. Though arguably inefficient, there was no doubt that this meant a greater use of computer time. In other words, the model was going to cost more to build and run.

(3) Less flexible report format compared with FCS

But the (exclusively financial) output requirements meant that this was of negligible importance. Within a small group of similar operating companies, the format for one profit and loss account or balance sheet almost certainly satisfies the remainder, with minor modifications.

So, the advantages of Planmaster outweighed its disadvantages, and the whole package was considered superior to FCS. (But it is essential to remember this record is portraying the respective attributes and drawbacks—as seen at the time—of two competing modelling languages, for a particular task, about to be attempted by a particular company. It did not follow that the same decision would necessarily be taken by another company in the same or differing circumstances. Nor even that the same decision would be made by this company today.)

However, in 1977, after a short period of training which followed system selection, the way was clear to flowchart the required structure; and thereafter to begin programming the model itself.

As with all previous experience to date in the company, there was only one person deputed to the project on a day-to-day basis. But this time, an attempt was made to secure effective insulation from the rest of the department's responsibilities; and of course, there was no geographical separation of staff to contend with. Needless to say, this did not work to perfection in practice, but a good deal of application and week-end work soon saw considerable progress being made.

It would not be unduly cynical to ask *how* this 'considerable progress' came to be made, in view of what had gone before. The main reason was force of circumstance: apart from the fact that this was a much higher-level language than the ICL-based Prosper of earlier days, it was clear from the start that there could be no concession to detail in the model structure. The built-in variables would have to be fewer than in either of the two previous model attempts—provided always that this criterion could be reasonably substantiated—if only to shorten the odds on success. In the event, statistical research of the recent past suggested that there were five variables which mattered more than any others in providing a satisfactory financial explanation for the results which had been posted by the manufacturing companies. Subsequent confirmation of these relationships and their quantification for each company meant that this latest suite of models had an excellent fundamental core on which the whole structure could be built. And with rather more confidence than had previously been the case.

From this point onwards, the only question of significance was whether the remaining time available would be sufficient to ensure completion of the models and their adequate testing, whilst still allowing for the assembly of live data for final report generation. Surprisingly enough, the target was achieved with time to spare. But even now, more than three years later, the day can still be savoured which first saw the production of a complete set of reports to the original specification—if only because there had been times during the years of failure when success was a word whose very existence had seemed in doubt.

Whilst reflecting that any financial modelling system which not only worked but was also in use in the company either gave cause for some celebration, or else served only to confirm the law of averages—depending upon the observer's viewpoint—there can be little doubt that completion of this project within three months was meritorious in its own right.

To the surprise of many—not least those directly concerned—this was all the time that was required from beginning to end. In fact, the Board's request which began the whole process in 1976 had arisen from its last meeting of the year in mid-December; system reviews culminated in selection of the Planmaster package in the first week of January, 1977; and the first complete print-out of results was produced in the middle of March.

21.4 The Years in Retrospect

It is always tempting to allow success to blind failures, and never more so than in the case of Tioxide's financial modelling experience. But this would do less than justice to the earlier misguided years of honest endeavour. Besides, if a change of approach can have such a fundamental effect on system building expectations, then it must be possible to discern reasons for the interest of others contemplating use of the technique for the first time. Indeed, if there are none, who could confront a learning curve of these proportions with equanimity?

In fact, there are some very clear conclusions to be drawn. But before doing so, it would perhaps be instructive to take account of the views of others. Whilst so doing, a consensus of opinion may be discerned on how to build models successfully —or at least how to lessen the likelihood of failure.

As Mann (1978) noted, models are not new, and to some may even be thought prolific, so there has been an increasing amount of literature devoted to the topic in recent years. Whilst the references which follow are claimed to be illustrative in a Tioxide context, their selection is strictly subjective. Nevertheless, the reader is invited to conclude that where there is a sufficient similarity in content or emphasis, then the opinions are not to be lightly ignored.

Mann observed that the effective use of practical models in a company's long-term planning process was rare, but suspected that this was only partly a function of the lack of success.

> Nor are models always useful. Over the years many have been constructed merely to satisfy the desires and aspirations of the model-builder, or to enhance the power of the computer. Problems were chosen where a solution was not necessarily of benefit to management

He then cited two golden rules:

(1) The model must be related to the real needs of the managers who are responsible for the running of the business. The model-builder must work closely *with* the manager, to understand his problems, to find a solution for use *within* the existing planning processes.

(2) The model must be simple, it must avoid the pit of size. This can be achieved by constructing a system on the modular approach, building a step at a time.

The same general lack of successful integration of models into the planning process, despite dramatic increases in usage of computer-based planning models since the beginning of the last decade, was noted by Naylor (1977). These failures severely limited the usefulness of models as planning tools. Yet little attention had been given to the problem of tailoring the model to the company's specific planning requirements. Naylor suggested that there were six steps to ensure successful integration:

(1) Review the planning environment. Begin with the organizational structure (of the company); then its management philosophy (management's attitude towards formal planning and the use of models in the process); and finally, the business environment and the planning process itself.
(2) Specify the planning requirements of individuals in the company: the type of report required and the questions to be answered; the business strategies to be followed in future years.
(3) Define the goals and objectives for planning—as required by management.
(4) Evaluate the existing planning resources. Only when a company has reviewed its planning environment requirements and resources could,
(5) Design of an integrated planning and modelling system, and,
(6) Strategy for integration of the planning model into the planning process,

be successfully accomplished. And in considering the latter, Naylor warned that a management education programme in the system's use would be necessary, whilst recommending that a modular building approach be taken, which tied performance to specific timetable dates.

In concluding their survey, Grinyer and Wooller (1975) remarked that

> our visits to companies with corporate models showed us again and again that the crucial factor is enthusiasm for the corporate model among top management (and especially senior financial management). Other conditions for success exist . . . but this is the one of overriding importance

However, their own experience and published literature suggested that there were six main interrelated conditions for successful modelling. (The absence of any three tended to produce failure):

(1) Sponsorship and continued support given by top management.
(2) Top management understands and has confidence in the model, and places at least some reliance on its results.
(3) The model meets specific management decision-making needs.
(4) Input data are readily available and not voluminous.
(5) The model is embedded in the planning process—used as a matter of course.
(6) Proper documentation has been kept throughout development.

If the past is to be examined before the future is contemplated, Hammond (1974) cautions against undue reliance upon empirical evidence—at least in model-building— if it is assumed that historical relationships or data would be maintained in future. (This point had in fact been taken in the Tioxide experience described above. Analysis of past results were certainly undertaken to *identify* the five variables and their inter-relationship within each company; but it was not henceforth assumed that they would remain at constant levels during the ensuing forecast time periods.)

Hammond elicits a ten-step process in the conception, creation and use of models in the planning process. In the first instance, it is necessary to decide where a model may be useful and only then whether to use it. Given that there will probably be a need for the release of significant resources in the company—both time and money—then a formal proposal should follow definition of the input and output specifications. It is then almost inevitable that program testing will require data collection, the results of which may question the program logic or even the fundamental concept that the model seeks to reproduce. Users have two important roles throughout: first, they must be educated and their acceptance of the model obtained, preferably to include contribution in its design; and second, they must be responsible for program validation prior to use. Finally, use of the model or passage of time must create the need for maintenance, whether of error correction or development to suit the needs of the business.

Several factors are noted to help the model-builder ensure success. The following selection is from a comprehensive list:

(1) Keep to established company procedures (at first) and use familiar input/output formats.
(2) Start and stay simple in concept. 'Companies should beware of channelling effort to the development of a mammoth model before understanding has been firmly established by both managers and modellers and scope and feasibility have been made clear!
(3) Beware of optimistic delivery dates—plan for the fact that programs always take longer than expected.
(4) Aim to produce some managerially useful results as soon as possible.
(5) Ensure continuous update of the model once it has been built, and maintain high standards of documentation throughout.

In a recently published book Higgins (1980) lists a number of practical aspects which must be heeded in developing and implementing corporate models. Noting that the prospects for successful innovation and continued use of the model are enhanced if the project has been commissioned by top management, he considers that a relatively simple structure is usually preferable at first to gain full comprehension. Then managers could be expected to have sufficient belief in the model to use its results and ensure that it becomes an integral part of the planning process. Indeed 'senior managers should be encouraged to use real-time corporate models directly. . .'

Higgins also observes that

> as an organisation gains experience in model-building, it will be well advised to develop a suite of models rather than a unique, large model. A modular structure illustrates the general issue of flexibility or versatility

of corporate models. . . Flexibility of logic implies that the model can accommodate major changes in organisational structure, e.g. the creation of new divisions or subsidiaries, without the need for reprogramming.

And finally, whilst reviewing the progress of management information networks in a marketing context, Schewe (1974) defined a few key directives for a successful system:

(1) 'Gain top management support.
    First and perhaps foremost, top management must be given *tangible* evidence of the value of the . . . system. There must be total commitment from top executives within the firm and this should be obtained by provision of immediate and tangible returns on the firm's system investment.
(2) 'Set reasonable system objectives.'
    The degree of technical sophistication should be related to the needs of the company;
(3) 'Build the system over time, not over night.'
    Begin simply and work slowly towards greater complexity.
(4) 'Gain user involvement'
    The system must be user-orientated; it should begin with the manager's perception of the decision environment and related information needs. There must be user involvement in the building process: participation throughout the design and implementation stages should facilitate both knowledge of the system and its early acceptance.
(5) 'Provide system users with sufficient training.'
    And to this end, avoid jargon so that communication is at the user's level and thus fully comprehensible.

Although this last article is concerned with an information system for marketing, on the same subjective basis which governed selection of all quoted references within this Tioxide review, Schewe's pithy statements can be seen to encapsulate most of the recommendations for success noted by the other authors.

It should by now be reasonably clear to the reader why failure resulted from the earlier Tioxide attempts before an operationally satisfactory and usable structure was eventually devised. The first model simply broke every one of Schewe's system-building principles.

Sadly, the second effort fared little better. Its early stages flattered to deceive: the top management support gained by acceptance of the initial comprehensive report specification was clearly forfeited when there were no early tangible returns once modelling had begun. Eventually, the users lost interest in the project. Why? Because in retrospect, it can be seen that the crucial decision was the very first programming step: in choosing to begin at level 3 (the area of most component detail in that particular model) all possible hopes for retention of user goodwill were lost on two counts. First, the amount of detail involved was of no interest to them and second, it was inevitable that they would have to wait for *any* tangible return.

In contrast, the third attempt scored because the principles *were* observed. Certainly, the restrictive time allowance was in this sense a benefit—there had to be a reasonably early return if the task was to be completed in time. But the reader should not be misled: this success did not accrue following discovery and careful assimilation of all the above quoted material. With the exception of the book of Grinyer and Wooller (1975), none of the other sources were then known to exist! Which probably only goes to show that a final vital ingredient in any successful modelling venture is a substantial portion of luck.

Phase VI

In the opening paragraphs of this second corporate progress review, no mention was made of events following completion of the successful model. Until recently, from an innovative or design point of view, there has been virtually no further progress—other than routine maintenance and development of the model program. However, it has long been apparent in Tioxide that a relatively small Group finance function convinced of the virtues of modelling must look to the technique to increase its departmental efficiency and effectiveness.

To this end, a good deal of time was spent in 1979 surveying the available modelling systems. For it was certain that a greater investment of computer time could only mean much greater expenditure of money. Since an ambitious programme had been planned—covering almost every aspect of the department's responsibilities from exchange exposure to statutory accounting—there was little doubt that a two- to three-year programme of modelling work could be expected. This in turn suggested that all models should be programmed in the same language, to enhance operational efficiency and prepare the way for an integrated Group management information system. For no matter how far in the future this latter eventuality might be, it is a reasonable assumption that many other international businesses will see it as an ultimate goal.

The time which has passed since selection of the Planmaster package has seen many changes in the available systems. So perhaps there is a certain amount of poetic justice in disclosing that the result of this latest review has recommended another change: away from Planmaster—to FCS. In the department's view, all the previous substantive drawbacks of FCS have been more than made good during the last three years. Added to which the FCS software house gives an excellent service, and has a staff of some forty persons almost all of whom are concerned with further development of the language.

When a programme of this magnitude is being contemplated, covering tasks not previously attempted, management would expect to be given realistic cost estimates of both development and later model usage. However, since the time involved is largely unpredictable and future bureaux costs unknown, no realistic assessment could possible be made on a time-sharing format.

The language is therefore ultimately preferred overall because it can be bought outright for in-house installation (Planmaster cannot) which limits the department's cash outlay without impeding its operational flexibility.

It would be tempting providence a second time to close this commentary on a euphoric note. So whilst recognizing that the narrative has been devoted to the description of a model-building programme whose avowed aim has always been directed towards assisting the strategic planning process—no matter how implausible the results—it is well to remember that a successful model can never be a surrogate for selection of feasible alternatives, or indeed the conception of planning. Nor can it predict or state best answers, whatever they might be. Management must weigh and ultimately decide upon the available opinions, facts and forecasts within its own business environment. A successful model can only be a useful tool in the entire process; no more, no less.

Last words, then, to Drucker (1979) who had the following observations to make whilst considering what strategic planning is *not*:

> It is not a box of tricks, a bundle of techniques. Many techniques may be used in the process—but, then again, none may be needed. Strategic planning may require a computer, but the most important question— 'what *is* our business?' or 'what *should* it be?'—cannot be quantified and programmed for the computer. Model building or simulation may be helpful but they are not strategic planning; they are tools for specific purposes and may or may not apply in a given case.
>
> Quantification is not planning. To be sure, one uses rigorous logical methods as far as possible if only to make sure that one does not deceive oneself. But some of the most important questions in strategic planning can be phrased only in terms such as 'larger' or 'smaller', 'sooner', or 'later'. These terms cannot easily be manipulated by quantitative techniques. And some equally important areas: such as those of political climate, social responsibilities, or human (including managerial) resources, cannot be quantified at all. They can be handled only as restraints, or boundaries but not as factors in the equation itself.
>
> Strategic planning is *not* 'the application of scientific methods to business decision . . .' It is the application of thought, analysis, imagination, and judgement. It is responsibility rather than technique.

You have been warned!

References

Drucker, P. F. (1979). *Management: Tasks, Responsibilties, Practices,* Pan, London.

Grinyer, P. H. and Wooller, J. (1975). *Corporate Models Today,* Institute of Chartered Accountants in England and Wales, London.

Hammond, J. S. (1974). 'Do's and dont's of computer models for planning', *Harvard Business Review,* **52**(2), 110–123.

Higgins, J. C. (1980). *Strategic and Operational Planning Systems,* Prentice-Hall, London.

Linneman, R. E. and Kennell, J. D. (1977). 'Shirt-sleeve approach to long-range plans', *Harvard Business Review,* **55**(2), 141–50.

Mann, C. W. (1978). 'The use of a model in long term planning—a case history', *Long Range Planning,* **11**(5), 55–62.

Naylor, T. H. (1977). 'Integrating models into the planning process', *Long Range Planning,* **10**(6), 11–15.

Precious, J. R. and Wood, D. R. (1975). 'Corporate modelling: when success can be a long-term forecast', *Accounting and Business Research (20), 254–72.*

Schewe, C. D. (1974). 'Management information systems in marketing—a promise not yet realised', *Management Informatics,* **3**(5), 251–5.

Financial Modelling in Corporate Management
Edited by J. W. Bryant
© 1982 John Wiley & Sons Ltd.

22

A Model Development and Evolution Strategy: A Case Study

JOHN HOLLAND

22.1 Introduction

In this chapter a detailed case study of financial model development and evolution in one company is presented. The approach used in this company was a managerial strategy designed to enable managers to understand and avoid the pitfalls involved in financial model building. This strategy for financial model development and evolution is outlined and its implications for managers and academics discussed.

The remainder of the chapter is divided into four sections. First, in Section 22.2, financial modelling by managers and academics is briefly discussed. Managerial financial modelling is generally referred to as corporate modelling and has been extensively researched by Grinyer and Wooller (1975) in the U.K., and by Naylor and Jeffress (1975) in the U.S.A. Major limitations of these models are identified. A further discussion on financial modelling by academics indicates problems, in particular in the implementation of such models in practical decision situations.

In the Section 22.3 the author draws from his research experience (Holland, 1978) in financial modelling, to outline a strategy for managers to develop their corporate models.

In Section 22.4 the implementation of this strategy in one company is outlined. This detailed case study traces the development from one simple budgetary model through to a sophisticated suite of linked investment, financing, and accounting models.

Section 22.5 summarizes the strategy for financial model development and evolution, and its implications for managers and academics.

22.2 Financial Modelling

In the world of financial practice, managers have a tendency to use a pragmatic approach to decision-making. Such an approach concentrates on the search for rules of thumb which work with regard to planning problems and readily available data (Cooley and Copeland, 1975). Both Grinyer and Wooller (1975) in the U.K. and Naylor and Jeffress (1975) in the U.S.A. found that models generally used with this pragmatic mode of decision-making are normally deterministic report simulators, e.g. balance sheets, profit and loss, or flow of funds statements. These corporate models are simple data-processing models using the company's accounting conventions.

Such accounting-based deterministic models give the manager little guidance in making important decisions and most of the work is done by the manager outside of the model in establishing the various unwritten relationships. These models are used to speed up routine aspects of data processing as the manager moves between problem specification and possible solutions. Such movement is iterative in nature, as the manager moves by successive approximations, towards a 'satisfactory' solution. These models are, therefore, limited as financial planning tools because of their concentration on detail and use of accounting frameworks.

These problems in managerial model building have been recognized by academic observers for some time (Carleton, Dick, and Downes, 1972). However, the response of academics in the field of financial model building has itself been beset by problems of implementation.

This area of financial model building generally consists of a 'marriage' between the theory of business finance, and sophisticated management-science techniques such as linear programming and Monte Carlo simulation.

For example, Carleton, (1970) has built a model for long-range financial planning. This model simultaneously chooses values for amounts invested, dividends paid, and debt/equity structure, within accounting, economic, institutional and corporate policy constraints, such that common stock price is maximized. This model is of interest because of the way in which the authors have tied together the theory of corporate finance and microeconomic theory of the firm into a mathematical framework and model that seeks optimal financial plans.

Myers and Pogue (1974) have updated this modelling approach to financial planning incorporating recent advances in capital market theory. Pogue and Lall (1974) suggested that: 'Models of this type are clearly going to play an increasingly important role in the formulation of corporate financial plans.' However, linear programming has been used sparingly by management. Some companies report starting with linear programming only to switch to simple report generators. Thus L.P. financial planning models have been mainly developed by financial theorists to develop and investigate theory, even through Carleton, Pogue, Myers and others may have initially wished to aid practitioners directly. Grinyer and Wooller (1974) recently suggested some reasons for the low success rate of this approach, and the predominance of simulation models:

Managers seem to find simulation models more intelligible. Complex relationships can be represented more easily in simulation than in optimisation models. Top managers often find it difficult, or politically inexpedient, to make objectives explicit, preferring instead to leave them implicit in the alternatives shown.

But optimisation models require an explicit statement of objectives, whilst simulation models do not. Moreover, because estimates on which strategic decisions are based are liable to such wide errors, there is doubt as to the significance of a mathematical optimum based on them.

Many authors argue that the reasons why L.P. and other sophisticated O.R. techniques have proved unsuccessful in the past is because managers have not been sufficiently involved in building the model. (Gershefski, 1969; Hall, 1973). Further reasons have been the independence of the model from the manager, and the fact that often the manager does not consider decisions simultaneously. Hence the manager believes that the L.P. model is taking major decisions without reference to him. He may understand relationships build into the model developed from his own ideas but because he is not part of the simultaneous process he finds it hard to accept the result. This is the case with all models of business situations but the paradox of the L.P. method is that its strength is also its weakness. i.e. the capacity to consider *many* decision alternatives simultaneously is beyond the manager and hence increases his scepticisim.

Similarly the manager may believe and understand the logical structure and solution search procedure of an L.P. model. However, he may object to the solution on the basis that he will often make or be forced to make single financial decisions without being able to change other major financial decisions. He would, therefore, like a capacity to 'behave', i.e. order the major decisions, in a way in which they may occur but which may not be logical vis-a-vis the theory of finance. This is essentially a simulation exercise.

Another management-science approach which has proved popular in the academic financial modelling literature is risk analysis. This is normally seen as an embellishment of simulation modelling. However, as Grinyer and Wooller noted (1974) this modelling approach has also experienced problems:

> Quite a large number of modellers spoke of early attempts to introduce probabilistic models. These had almost invariably failed to get management support. Risk analysis may become more acceptable to management as they become more familiar with models. For the present, though, most modellers would be unwise to build probabilistic models until their management are fully conversant with simple, deterministic ones.

Therefore, the problem at the moment with the L.P. model of Carleton, Dick, and Downes (1970), and with risk analysis and other similar normative models, is that they give *too* much guidance. The mathematical and financial theory is likely to be embedded in the model and the significant interaction between decision variables hidden from the manager.

22.3 A Managerial Strategy for Financial Model Development

There are, therefore, problems in financial model building in both the practical and theoretical context.

(1) Financial planning models based on financial theory and management science have proved too complex for managers to use.
(2) Simulation models currently in use are very simple and give little guidance to the decision-maker.

These problems have arisen in part because of the differing goals managers and academics have pursued in model building (Cooley and Copeland, 1975). Essentially managers are interested in improving the quality of decision-making through immediate application of financial models. Academics' immediate concern in the short term is to build financial models that are internally consistent *vis-à-vis* the theory of finance. Academics are generally interested in improving the quality of managerial decision-making in the long term through the development of fruitful theory and associated decision models. This has meant that most of the energies of academics have been employed in refining the theoretical constructs, and little attention has been given to implementation problems. Managers, in turn, have made little effort to pierce this abstract world of mathematical and economic thought.

The situation is a serious problem for both the 'state of the art' of financial model building and the advancement of a theory of financial decision-making. This is because within these abstractions lie extensive frameworks for thinking about financial decision-making. In particular these can provide useful decision guidelines when using and developing deterministic simulation models.

For example, in linear programming for capital budgeting, the following elements in the decision area are made explicit:

(1) Within a potential set of investment projects, there may be competition for resources in a period, and over many periods.
(2) Investment projects may themselves be a source of resources.
(3) The objective to be achieved is explicit and quantified.
(4) Other secondary objectives are expressed through non-violation of constraints.
(5) There is a valuation problem in the last period of the capital budget plan.
(6) The solution procedure finds the 'best' solution given the objective and constraints.

In risk analysis for a single investment project the manager has to identify:

(1) key variables which affect cash flow that are random from the company's viewpoint;
(2) dependencies between these variables over time.

These lists of ideas implicit in each 'package' are but small samples of the store of concepts actually held. The problem for the manager is that in using normative *models* developed from the 'packages', he receives the *whole* 'package' at a time. In the author's view, managers appear to learn on a marginal basis. Thus a manager will choose and use that element of a package that is currently useful. The author would agree with criticisms of normative models, but would argue that the decision framework implicit in such models can be useful to managers, and influence the design of financial models in practice. Therefore, a key requirement is how to encourage managerial access to such frameworks, without their having to accept whole 'packages'.

To encourage this access, managers require a strategy to learn how to use and develop financial models over time, by drawing from management science experience and financial theory; and thus ultimately improve their 'state of the art' (Holland, 1978).

The major elements of this strategy include the use of:

(1) model design guidelines derived from the 'state of the art' of corporate modelling;
(2) a local theory of financial decision-making;
(3) guidelines from the general theory of business finance to guide the use of models.

Design Guidelines from the 'State of the Art'

Research on corporate modelling indicates that successful corporate models contain many common design features and implementation characteristics (Grinyer and Wooller, 1975; Naylor and Jeffress, 1975; Power, 1975; Gershefski, 1969; Hall, 1973, 1975). Models considered most useful are those that:

(1) are sponsored by top management;
(2) form part of existing decision processes;
(3) use simple data processing;
(4) can be used as research and learning tools by management;
(5) respond quickly to environmental uncertainty;
(6) enhance creative problem capacity;
(7) are tailor made for a company;
(8) contain separate sub-models for investment, financing and dividend decisions with the sub-models easily linked for data flows;
(9) are thoroughly documented throughout their development and use.

A 'Local Theory' of Financial Decision-making

A local theory of financial decision-making includes detailed studies at company or industry level of:

(1) The unique nature of the investment decision and its cash flow patterns. This covers existing decision rules including 'rules of thumb'.
(2) Similar studies of the financing and dividend decisions, and the relationships between these areas.
(3) Management science techniques currently in use, and areas with likely applications.

This concept of a local theory of financial decision-making emerged as a result of the observation that financial decision-making was poorly documented within companies and industries. Existing documentation generally amounted to a statement of accounting principles and the investment appraisal method used. Financing and dividend decisions were not based upon an explicit statement of underlying principles. Clearly such decisions are made but the analysis involved, especially the trading-off of the interdependencies between the investment, financing and dividend decisions, do not generally appear to be explicit formalized procedures. The development of a local theory is designed to bridge this gap. Finally, to ensure ease of communication this 'local' theory should use the terminology common in the industry for financial decision-making.

Guidelines from the General Theory of Business Finance

An important ingredient of this local theory would be an input from the general theory of finance which is simple and flexible enough to be used in a practical decision process to guide the use of financial submodels. For example, Sihler (1971) has attempted to systematize in easily understood fashion the insights provided by research in corporate finance by directly considering management needs.

The result is a compendium of suggested procedures which if followed will produce sensible financial plans (Carleton, 1972). These procedures are:

(1) assume projected capital requirements of the company;
(2) tentatively settle the debit/equity question;
(3) make the dividend growth analysis within the framework of the debt/equity choice;
(4) investigate the impact of the last two steps on the capital costs, and the impact of the capital costs on the investment volume.

This approach has considerable merit because it focuses on the key financial decision areas and allows the manager to explore possible inter-relationships which exist in his company's specific situation. It also provides a direct, if simple, link from theory to practice, and it can be used to guide the way in which the financial sub-models are used in relation to each other

22.4 A Case Study of Model Development and Evolution

Introduction

In the following case study the use of the model design guidelines, local theory, and guidelines from business finance theory, are demonstrated in the development of a suite of models is an instalment credit financial intermediary (i.e. a 'finance house').

The author was involved in several such model-building exercises as part of a research project (Holland, 1978). The strategy for model development and evolution emerged from early model-building experiences and was then tested in the companies. This case study therefore reflects a typical experience in model building during the research.

(a) The Context of the Study

The company was a medium-sized finance house with hire purchase and similar instalment credit balances outstanding of approximately £6 million, and an annual turnover of approximately £7.5 million (turnover is the aggregate of new business financed, excluding finance charges).

The company was a subsidiary of a large financial corporation, and had 15 branches in the U.K. The branches were mostly located in the major regional centres and the company was moving towards nationwide coverage. Sources of finance were initially loans from the parent group, but arrangements existed between the company and the banks for deposits, and the public were invited to make deposits. Consideration was being given at the time to the raising of short and long-term debt in the London money markets. The senior manager of this company was an accountant and his company title was controller. He had responsibility for:

(1) overall control of operations, through his head office, and branch management;
(2) policy-making for medium and long-term decisions (e.g. growth rate, composition of asset and liability portfolios).

This wide range of roles performed by one decision-maker was due to the firm being at an early stage in its development. A subdivision of these roles was expected as the company grew. The manager had a strong interest in corporate modelling and some ideas on applications in the policy-making areas.

(b) Initial Problem Definition

Early discussions between the manager and researcher indicated that there was:

(1) immediate need for a simple budgetary model to replace tedious manual calculations;
(2) medium-to-long-term need for a model capacity to jointly manage the asset/liability portfolios.

The strategy proposed was as follows:

(1) Develop the simple budgetary model to satisfy the immediate need, and to gain some experience and insight into model building.
(2) At the same time, develop a framework to analyse asset/liability decision-making, i.e. an initial statement of local theory of investment/financing decision-making was required.
(3) The experience gained from the above was expected to point towards the kind of model capacity required for joint asset/liability decision-making.

The actual development of models occurred in four major stages:

Stage 1:   Initial budgetary (accounting) model
Stage 2:   Adapted accounting model, and the initial asset (investment) portfolio model.
Stage 3:   Final accounting model, the adapted asset model, and the initial liability (financing) portfolio model.
Stage 4:   Establishment of links between the models.

These four stages are described below.

Stage 1

(a) Manual Budgetary Process

The existing budget, prior to the introduction of the budgetary model, was hand-calculated as follows:

(1) Branch managers prepared budgets for advances of new business. This was done one year ahead in quarters, and for the following two years on an annual basis, and budget estimates were single-point expected values.
(2) Branch values could be amended by Head Office.
(3) Head Office prepared budgets for expenses both for Head Office and branches.
(4) Branch and Head Office figures were aggregated to develop a company budget.

(5) The income and cash flows expected as a result of these new business advances were laboriously hand-calculated using the accounting method and cash-flow calculation rules.

The final step involved a very tedious calculation, even with very limited budget data, e.g. three months' budget data containing four classes of business. Thus the initial role of the computer model was to calculate quickly these income and cash flows for company profit and cash plans

(b) Purpose of Initial Budgetary Model

The manager's view of the required uses of the budgetary model was as follows:

(1) To help make policy decisions, i.e. ask 'What if' questions, about such policy variables as:
   the growth rate of advances;
   pricing (per annum flat rates);
   asset mix;
   commission and handling costs and their effect on cash flow and income.
(2) Given decisions in these policy areas, to help to establish a budget or a set of flexible budgets which could subsequently form a basis for control and analysis of variance at company level.
(3) To amend new business targets for branches, and give branches guidelines for the setting of per annum flat rates (P.A.F.).

A longer-term use envisaged was that as the branches grew into larger operations, the model could be used to develop branch budgets. This could be done either by Head Office or by the branches, using an approach which took initial branch estimates amended where necessary by Head Office. To summarize, the manager saw the model as:

(1) a data-processing aid for *part* of his existing budgetary process;
(2) a tool for the investigation of policy variables.

(c) Structure of Initial Budgetary Model

Using the model design guidelines outlined earlier in this chapter the budgetary model was developed with the structure shown in Figure 22.1. The accounting logic was based on the conventional 'Rule of 78' employed in instalment credit revenue recognition. The model itself was written in the Basic computer language and developed on a commercial time-sharing system. This language was chosen primarily because:

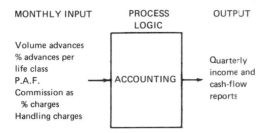

Figure 22.1 Budgetary model

(1) it is widely available.
(2) programs in Basic can be easily transformed between commercial systems.
(3) it is easy to use, is an interactive language, and permits flexible input/output formatting.

The budget model was successfully incorporated into the existing budgetary process with few problems. This success was not surprising, given that it merely automated a well-tried calculation procedure. However, after six months of frequent use the manager began to see major limitations in the model.

Stage 2

(a) Budgetary Model Limitations

At this point, the manager and the author investigated the limitations of this budgetary model by assessing it against:

(1) the manager's expanding decision requirement;
(2) the initial statement of local theory of investment, and financing decision-making for finance houses;
(3) the theory of business finance;
(4) the set of design guidelines for financial modelling.

The results of these influences can be summarized as follows:

(1) The manager was aware that the model was based on the original manual calculations. These included many approximations and short cuts to reduce the calculation load. These were now seen as constraints on model usefulness. It was therefore thought possible to disaggregate key policy variables and look at the output in greater detail. Thus the use of the model had not only eliminated computational constraints but also relaxed their associated perceptual constraints, and the manager was beginning to investigate his problem situation in greater depth. Two specific variables were considered in more detail: the per annum rate and the costs.

The pricing policy had initially been assumed to be the same for all classes of data per input month. However, in practice different P.A.F.s were applied for different classes of business. Thus P.A.F. generally increased with the life of business to ensure that the true interest rate increased as the time risk increased. Also, certain categories of goods were considered riskier than others (e.g. second-hand cars were riskier than new cars) and thus a higher P.A.F. was charged.

Costs previously developed in the model were commission and handling charges (acquisition charges). Commission was estimated as a percentage of total charges per class, and handling charges were input as monthly totals to be divided using the asset composition data. Key cost variables omitted from the model were bad debts, operating costs and the cost of money. By assuming a cost structure in which all these variables are simply estimated as a percentage of earned charges, a wider analysis was deemed feasible.

(2) Output by quarters over several years was suitable for a longer-term outlook, but for shorter-term profit and cash planning, monthly figures were more suitable. In the long run an option in the model to allow various levels of output (period) aggregation was necessary.

(3) Further developments were also indicated in the collection and storage of input data for the model. Crude links could be initially established with the data processing and reporting system by inputting the unearned charges schedule developed from the latter into the model. This could be linked to new business calculations in the model to develop an updated unearned charges schedule. This in turn provides the basis for calculating earned charges taken from new and old business for a month. Finally these data could be used with the cost structure to develop a budget.

Another change considered useful was the storage (in the program, or in data files) of several years new business data. This was essentially to consider the accounting consequences of the longer-term investment decision.

(4) It was also considered useful to have the capacity easily to redefine the accounting method, and thus the ability to assess the 'best' method.

(b) Other Modelling Needs Perceived

The manager was also becoming increasingly aware of the inadequacies of the budgetary model as a tool for analysing the asset portfolio, especially with regard to the sole use of the accounting framework for investment appraisal and cash planning. Investment appraisal was done on an aggregate portfolio profit basis. Further, cash output from the model was only in the form of contractual payments. Such contractual payments were an unlikely outcome given the number of contracts settled early.

Thus the manager felt that a separate asset portfolio model should be developed with a capacity for producing:

(1) a detailed analysis of the effect of variables such as arrears and early settle-ments, which distributed cash and income flows;
(2) an analysis over different segments of the portfolio, and over the whole port-folio, of return and of the margin over the cost of capital;
(3) assessments of the risk/return characteristics of asset portfolios of varying composition.

These extra decision needs had been mentioned at the start of the research; they had now been emphasized by the limitations of the existing budgetary model and the influences of local and general business finance theory. They indicated the development of a separate asset portfolio cash-flow model, using a present-value cash-flow frame of analysis, suitably adapted to the unique nature of the decision to invest in instalment credit financial assets. The manager also became interested in the possible development of a financing model. Its role was seen as:

(1) Providing useful input information in the form of interest costs to the account-ing model. The accounting model was at the time using subjectively determined estimates for the cost of money.
(2) Providing data to calculate the cost of capital for use with asset portfolio decision-making.
(3) Complementing the asset portfolio model by providing comprehensive cash-flow data covering both asset and liability portfolios.
(4) Investigating the long-term financing decisions.

Limited resources were available for model development and therefore the manager had to set priorities for the next stage of development. He made the following assessments of the urgency, relevance and feasibility of the identified requirements:

(1) All of the proposed adaptations to the accounting models were simple to imple-ment and from the manager's position offered the most immediate return.
(2) The asset portfolio model shared many structural similarities, and much common input data, with the accounting model. It therefore seemed a straight-forward model to flowchart and program. It was also a much-needed model for the manager. This was because he was relatively new to this business and he felt a strong need to understand the phenomena affecting asset cash flows. He therefore hoped to improve his cash-forecasting skills and his general manage-ment of the existing portfolio.
(3) The financing model was not considered an urgent priority because funds were at the time available from the parent banking group and were fairly predictable. However it was expected that as the company grew it would borrow more

funds from the conventional money markets and thus the need for a financing model would increase.

(c) The Adapted Accounting Model

Adaptation of the existing budgetary model to satisfy the new decision needs was a straightforward task. This was partially due to the minor nature of the programming changes, and also because of the segmental nature of the original design. This latter feature allowed easy addition of new segments to input, process, and output logic. There was therefore little fundamental change in the structure of model, but major changes occurred in its capacity to satisfy managerial decision needs. This can be demonstrated by the following applications of the adapted model:

(1) It was used to ask 'what if' questions about the following short-term profit planning issues:
  (a) Varying levels of business for the overall asset portfolio and segments of the portfolios; thus it was used to assess the effect of seasonality on profit and other output.
  (b) Changes in elements of the cost structure per class.
  (c) Changes in the pricing policy.
  (d) Changes in the product classes analysed, including: changes in transaction life classes; changes in transaction value classes; changes in goods financed classes; and combinations of these changes.
  (e) Changes in estimates of early settlement refunds as a percentage of charges. This was a very simple approach to the prediction of this variable.
  (f) Any combination of the above changes, and their joint effects on any of the output variables.
(2) It was used in the medium (12 months) to long-term (3 years) within the context of the strategic and financial planning cycle. Thus it was used as the accounting model in a longer-term planning exercise. The input options in the model were such that it was possible to proceed quickly through twelve months of input.
(3) It was used throughout the hierarchy to produce company, regional and some branch budgets.

(d) Initial Asset Portfolio Model

Given the expanded investment decision needs and the limitations of the accounting model, a simple working version of an asset portfolio model was also built. This model had the basic structure shown in Figure 22.2. The model was also written in Basic, using the same commercial time-sharing system. This ensured consistency and common standards for the existing models. This principle was also adopted for all subsequent models in the company.

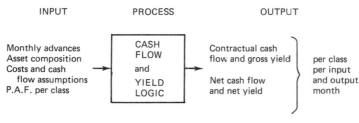

Figure 22.2 Asset portfolio model

Some problems were encountered in implementing this model because the manager was unfamiliar with the discounting logic at the heart of the model. The problems were circumvented by programming and implementing the model in simple, confidence-building stages. Thus, the model was firstly built to analyse the cash flow and yield (internal rate of return) of a single transaction. The model was then extended through many classes of input data, then many months of input data, and finally included the required cost cash-flow variables. From demonstration runs it was clear to the manager that this simple asset portfolio model needed the following improvements.

(1) The ability to work towards a target percentage composition of asset portfolio at the end of each year
(2) The ability to assess the effects of

   (a) changing *many* cost cash flow assumptions;
   (b) arrears and bad debts;
   (c) early settlements on cash flow and yields.

   This was seen as essential for short-term (1 to 6 months) cash management and for long-term cash projections.

Each of these improvements, with the exception of early settlements, was found to be feasible over a three-month period. However, the early-settlements variable proved to be intractable during this stage of model development. This considerably reduced the usefulness of the asset portfolio model because this variable was by then proving to be an important influence on cash-flow volatility. In a similar fashion, income flows were also becoming difficult to predict, and so this problem was now affecting the usefulness of the accounting model. At the same time, the company was beginning to expand its operations in the money markets, and the manager was developing a need for a financing model.

Stage 3

(a) Revised Accounting and Asset Portfolio Models

These models have common limitations which centred around the early settlement variables, i.e.:

(1) volume of early settlements per month per class;
(2) rebate policy.

The required output information was,

(1) earned charges taken (after settlement) by the finance house per month;
(2) charges rebated or refunded to customers per month.

The manager had always seen early settlements as a 'problem' in that although higher profits were produced in the period of settlement, income and cash flows were distributed in a manner that was difficult to predict. This problem had recently become acute. He was aware that if he could estimate the effects of this variable, and given that he had some control over the volume of early settlements per month (through offering favourable rates), he would have an important control over income and liquidity.

Thus new design specifications for the accounting and asset portfolio models were developed. These included the following:

(1) the generation of early settlements distribution per input month from historical records, or through the manager subjectively developing the data;
(2) random sampling of these distributions in order to simulate the effect of this variable (i.e. risk analysis).

The specifications suggested:

(1) a long programming effort which would result in very large asset portfolio and accounting models requiring extensive input of data by the manager;
(2) final models of dubious value because of time spent developing input data, and actually inputting it.

The manager did not want the model-building effort to develop into a large and expensive programming activity focused around one variable, and he therefore indicated that 'cut-down' versions would probably prove adequate. Thus simpler risk-estimating procedures were adopted. These had the potential to develop into an extended risk analysis if needed, and proved fairly easy to program.

Other information output now seen as useful was asset capital balances outstanding resulting from new business decisions over several periods. Given an investment decision, and the accounting method, the valuation of these asset balances was defined, and it proved fairly easy to adjust the accounting model for this output to balance-sheet calculations. Finally, it was required that all output data could be aggregated into monthly, quarterly, or annual values, and that monthly earned charges could be disaggregated to show the estimated monthly interest charges for tax calculations.

These changes in both models took over six months to implement. This was due to a problem of data collection for the early settlement estimation procedures. However, once this variable was included, albeit using a very crude form of risk analysis, the manager expressed considerable satisfaction with the models and considered them fairly complete for the existing decision needs.

(b) The Financing Model

The manager's interest in this model grew considerably during this period due to:

(1) the company's increased dependence on the money markets for funds;
(2) a higher than usual level of volatility in the money markets.

The author had also investigated the financing decision for the company as part of the development of a statement of local theory. From these two sources it was clear that a financing model was required to help in the following areas:

(1) decisions relating to the financing of capital requirements for each period;
(2) projection of liabilities in the balance sheet;
(3) liability maturity analysis;
(4) liability mix analysis;
(5) risk analysis of the liability portfolio;
(6) updating of the source of funds budget;
(7) development of data for calculation of liquidity rates and cost of capital.

This was an extensive initial list of decision requirements and clearly involved much programming effort. The central logic of the program was expected to be the calculation of balances and interest charges for each liability type. This was relatively straightforward, with the major programming effort expected in designing flexible input and output software to cope with specific decision needs taken from the list above, or with groups of such needs.

The basic structure of the initial design of the financing model was as shown in Figure 22.3. Once again, the model was programmed in Basic, and was implemented in a number of steps:

(1) Submodels were built for each liability type and these were validated using manual calculations from historical liabilities with known data.
(2) These sub-models were aggregated into a portfolio model which could calculate balances and interest charges, for each liability, and for the whole portfolio.
(3) Further adjustments included many months of input and years of output data.
(4) At this point a variety of financing rules were built into the model with options open to the manager to choose sets of rules.
(5) Finally, considerable effort was expended in adding flexible input and output software to the model.

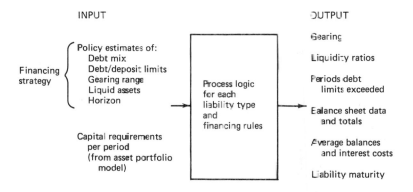

Figure 22.3 Financing model

This incremental approach to validation and implementation was essential in ensuring that the manager fully understood and had confidence in the wholly new model. Thus few problems were encountered in using this model during the financing decision process. Its major value proved to be in allowing the manager to understand the implications of various financing rules generally employed in the industry, and to devise suitable rules for his company. However, the model was considered to have a major limitation, in that the capital requirements data was manually transferred from the asset portfolio model. It was this limitation that led to the final stage of model development involving physical links between models.

Stage 4

(a) Liquidity Planning

The increased need to analyse the financing decision increased the manager's awareness of the range of issues which existed with respect to joint/asset liability decision-making. In particular, problems were emerging in assessing the risk of insolvency and in analysing the liquidities (maturities) of asset and liability portfolios. These suggested that the manager should consider in detail the joint effects of the investment and financing decisions. In Figure 22.4 the sources of liquidity from the asset and liability portfolio are identified and their influence on insolvency pinpointed.

In the figure, asset liquidity is divided into four major components:

(1) Liquid assets; these are the 'cushion' against insolvency.
(2) Block discounting, which with the liquidation values of segments of the asset portfolio, can be considered sources of liquidity.

   If a regular market exists for sale of segments of the portfolio under discount, either under duress (liquidation) or as a normal transaction (block discounting), then the company can rely on this to some degree as a source of concealed asset liquidity.

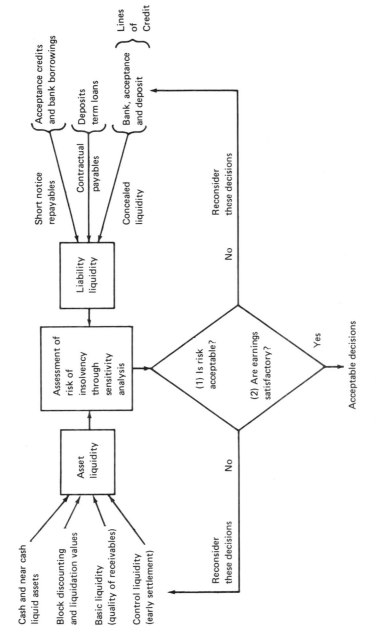

Figure 22.4 Liquidity and the risk of insolvency

(3) Basic liquidity, which is the liquidity resulting from the investment decision of the firm, and its associated business risk (i.e. bad debts, arrears, dealer defaults, etc.).
(4) Control liquidity, which is the extra liquidity the firm can generate by making terms for early settlement more attractive, and so is therefore the concealed asset portfolio liquidity.

Liability liquidity is divided into three categories:

(1) Short notice repayables, such as Bank overdraft and acceptance credits.
(2) Contractual repayables, such as short-term deposits or long-term loans.
(3) Concealed liability liquidity, which consists of bank and acceptances lines of credits, and possible roll-overs of deposits. Also, some finance houses have links with major financial institutions who will ultimately guarantee them funds.

The figure indicates that joint asset and liability portfolio liquidity can be assessed if the asset and liability portfolio models are made to run in sequence.

This proved to be a very easy adaptation of the models, and only involved the setting up of output files from one model to be used as an input file to the other.

Thus the joint asset/liability models were used to assess the risk of insolvency by sensitivity analysis of these liquidity components of joint investment-financing plans under various assumptions of uncertainty. These were:

(1) Pessimistic outcomes for joint investment-financing plans. For example, arrears and bad debts were expected to be high, early settlements late in agreements and very uncertain. On the liability side, shrinkage in deposit markets was expected. Thus the manager was interested in finding values for gearing, debt structure, levels of liquid assets, and asset composition which would stand up to these severe financial problems.
(2) Expected (or the most likely) cash-flow outcomes of joint investment-financing plans were simulated, and their risk of insolvency assessed. The level of liquid assets required to keep this risk at acceptable levels was compared with the pessimistic value developed above. This allowed the manager to assess the cost of his risk attitudes and therefore aid his choice of what was an appropriate level of liquid assets.

Given this understanding of the firm's insolvency risk, 'rule of thumb' liquidity ratios relevant to the firm were developed. These were used to aid operational decision-making and to influence lenders.

(b) Financial Planning

Having established and tested the physical link between the asset portfolio and liability portfolio for this one major decision need, (i.e. liquidity planning) the models were now available for a whole range of joint uses.

These included:

(1) variance analysis of the sources and use of funds budget;
(2) long-term (up to five years) financial planning;
(3) investigation of the interdependencies between the investment, financing and dividend decisions.

The financial planning and interdependencies issues required the development of a minor model to calculate the cost of capital for the company. Figure 22.5 summarizes the use of the models in financial planning.

(c) Further Development

The models had essentially reached a stage where they were recognizable *vis-à-vis* the theory of business finance. The next major development envisaged was to use the model to assess the impact of the investment, financing, and dividend decision on the value of the company. However, the development never materialized because the manager was more interested in developing 'satisfactory' (to him!) plans, and using these plans to argue for more long-term funds from the parent corporation.

Summary

The major steps in implementing the strategy in the case study were as follows:

(1) Initial statements of local theory and the accounting methods used in the budgetary process were developed.
(2) The first model built was the model which promised the most immediate impact and highest return. In this case it was the accounting model.
(3) The other financial models were based on the decision rules embodied in local theory, and the model design guidelines. These were built in order of managerial priority,
(4) The guiding procedure from the general theory of business finance was used to link the submodels in developing comprehensive financial plans, and investigating joint investment/financing issues.
(5) The local theory was expanded by documenting the use and effectiveness of the models.
(6) The models were continuously adapted from changes occurring in local theory.

This approach was initially sequential through steps (1)–(6). However, in the long run, steps (4)–(6) interacted in a continuous manner, as the firm expanded its knowledge base.

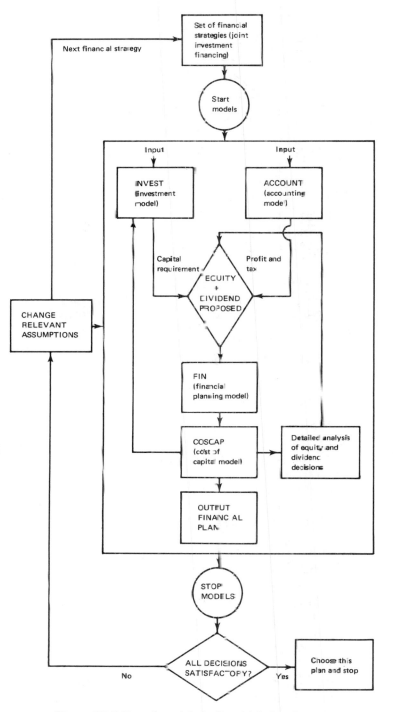

Figure 22.5 Use of models in financial planning

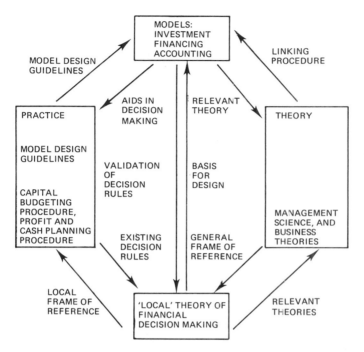

Figure 22.6 Theory and practice in financial planning

22.5 Appraisal of the Methodology

The role of models and local theory mediating between theory and practice can be summarized diagrammatically as shown in Figure 22.6. Thus the 'local' theory, expressed in the language of the industry but influenced by general theory, provides an important communication medium between theory and practice. The models developed in the context of the local theory are guided and influenced by theory, and have potential as research tools. For example, a manager can blend existing rules of thumb with the guiding procedure as follows:

(1) Use the rules of thumb, based on a historical understanding of the inter-relationships between the investment, financing and dividend decisions, to develop the 'scale' or size of these expected decisions.
(2) Use the submodels and linking framework to investigate many alternatives in much greater detail.

This approach is rational in that it is based on sound finance. Also, by speeding up the process, managers have the opportunity to learn how the decisions inter-act. They can therefore develop a 'feel' for the linked nature of these decisions, and hopefully extend both local and general theories of decision-making.

Hence, one is attempting to benefit from the theory of finance by trying to approach the simultaneous ideal in a practical interactive manner. This is also done in the context of a decision process in which the skills, judgments, biases, and personal goals of the key actors are present. This allows the role of the financial planning models in the decision process and procedure to be made explicit. Such a perspective is a key ingredient in modelling to aid financial decision-making. It also gives the opportunity for an eventual feedback to theory from practical observations.

In this learning experience managers may develop linear programming and risk-analysis models as aids for decision-making. The financial submodels, guided by simple theory, are therefore seen as a first step in developing a financial planning model, which may eventually include elements of stochastic processes and programming (e.g. stochastic cash generation models, or L.P. for financing decision with debt only).

Academics are in a key position in starting such a communication process between existing decision theory and practice. Academic studies of 'local' theories and their use as a basis for financial model-building will provide useful stimuli for the managers concerned. More significantly, they will influence the long-term development of theoretical models for decision-making. In the author's view such models normally start from a theoretical base and build on this, rather than continuously interacting with practice. Thus, these two roles for academic model builders are necessary complements, with the former role now emerging in response to the problems identified in model building.

Another change of role may occur for the manager by moving from being predominantly involved in deterministic model building to extra involvement in local theory building and eventually general theory building.

Hence, this philosophy of modelling to learn, learning through modelling, and further modelling through experience, is a deliberate attempt to release managers from the constraint of abstract decision theory, both financial and mathematical, while eventually benefitting from these by selecting those tools of direct and proven use.

I believe that this approach recognizes that the qualitative benefits of a modelling research effort will come from giving managers a capacity to research their decision behaviour. Also by making the investigation of decision-making as important as taking the decision, one hopes to improve the quality of the decision eventually taken.

References

Carleton, W. T. (1970). 'An Analytical Model for Financial Planning', *Journal of Finance,* 25(2), 291–315.

Carleton, W. T. Dick, C. L., and Downes, D. H. (1972). *Converting Finance Theory into Practice*, Working Paper, Amos Tuck School, Dartmouth College, Massachusetts.

Cooley, P. and Copeland, R. (1975). 'Contrasting Roles of Financial Theories and Practice', *Business Horizons,* 18(4), 25–31.

Gershefski, G. (1969). 'Building a Corporate Financial Model', *Harvard Business Review,* **47**(4), 61–72.

Grinyer, P. H. and Wooller, J. (1974). 'Cash in on Corporate Planning', *Computer Management,* **9**(10), 31–4.

Grinyer, P. H. and Wooller, J. (1975). *Corporate Models Today,* Institute of Chartered Accountants in England and Wales, London.

Hall, W. K. (1973). 'Strategic Planning Models: are top managers really finding them useful', *Journal of Business Policy,* **3**(2), 33–42.

Hall, W. K. (1975). 'Why Risk analysis Isn't Working', *Long Range Planning,* **8**(6), 25–9.

Holland, J. B. (1978). *Financial Models For Finance Houses,* Ph.D. thesis, C.N.A.A., London.

Myers, S. C. and Pogue, G. A. (1974). 'A Programming Approach to Corporate Financial Management', *Journal of Finance,* **29**(2), 579–99.

Naylor, T. H. and Jeffress, C. (1975). 'Corporate Simulation Models—a Survey', *Simulation,* **24**(6), 171–6.

Pogue, G. A. and Lall, K. (1974). 'Corporate Finance: an Overview', *Sloan Management Review,* **15**(3), 19–38.

Power, P. D. (1975). 'Computers and Financial Planning', *Long Range Planning,* **8**(6), 53–9.

Robichek, A. A. and Myers, S. C. (1965). *Optimal Financing Decisions,* Prentice-Hall, Englewood Cliffs, New Jersey.

Sihler, W. M. (1971). 'Framework for Financial Decisions', *Harvard Business Review,* **49**(2), 123–35.

PART 6
THE PRACTICE OF FINANCIAL MODELLING

As for most new products or technologies, the take-up of financial modelling, after a hesitant start in the mid 1960s, has been quite striking, so that today it forms an accepted part of financial management. With a slight lag this progress is being followed by the inclusion of financial modelling as an essential element in the education of those entering the accounting profession and related management careers. This will help to ensure the continued use and development of financial modelling in policy analysis. At the same time new technologies are improving the ease with which information can be accessed and manipulated and this will also encourage a wider interest and application of financial modelling methods.

The history of financial modelling, as revealed by surveys, is described in Chapter 23. This account concludes with a brief look into the future, a topic that is taken up in more detail in Chapter 24, which considers various aspects of likely developments.

Financial Modelling in Corporate Management
Edited by J. W. Bryant
© 1982 John Wiley & Sons Ltd.

23

The Historical Development and Current Practice of Corporate Modelling in the U.K.

Peter Grinyer

23.1 The Growth of Modelling

Since the late 1960s corporate modelling has grown rapidly, even when defined somewhat narrowly as the development and use of computer-operated routines that map the financial logic of a company and produce financial reports such as balance sheets, profit and loss accounts, and statements of sources and uses of funds.

In 1969 Gershefski (1970) was able to identify only 63 out of 1900 American companies which he approached, which had or were developing corporate models. At that time corporate modelling was even less widespread in the U.K. Companies developing models, like those whose experience is reported in Grinyer and Batt (1974), regarded themselves as pioneers. Despite their feeling of isolation however, the rate of introduction quickened markedly in 1968. This is shown in Figure 23.1 by the start dates for corporate models in the 65 companies visited by Grinyer and Wooller (1975a). Nonetheless, in a second survey, Grinyer and Wooller (1975b) found that only 8% of the largest U.K. companies, the 'Times 1000', had such models in 1974.

Unfortunately, no comparable survey has been carried out for the years since 1974, although subjective estimates by consultants and other informed observers suggest an even more rapid growth of modelling. A rough index of the growth in modelling in the U.K. between 1974 and 1978 is the increase in the number of U.K. users claimed by computer bureaus in surveys of those years (Grinyer and Wooller 1975a) . Even allowing for the fact that some companies had used more than one

*This chapter is based upon P. H. Grinyer and J. Wooller, An overview of a decade of corporate modelling in the U.K., published in *Accountancy and Business Research.*

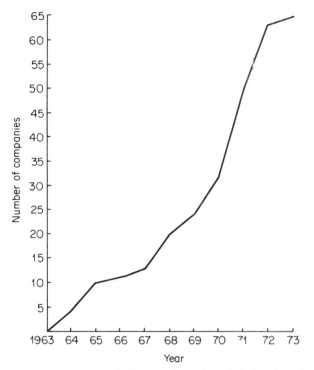

Figure 23.1 Cumulative number of models developed

bureau, either in turn or at the same time, the number was already high by 1974. In total the bureaus claimed just under 1000 users. By 1978 the figures had risen by about 50% to just over 1500. This difference understates the real increase however, for the maximum number recorded for any one bureau is 100 (as when the number of users exceeded 100 they were shown in the surveys as 'in excess of 100'). The rate of increase is perhaps more evident from that fact that in 1974 only three bureaus claimed more than 100 users for their modelling system whilst in 1978 as many as ten did so. Whilst some bureaus advanced but little, others increased their numbers of customers tenfold over the four years. Allowing for these factors it would be not unreasonable to guess that the number of corporate modellers had at least doubled and possibly trebled in the U.K. during the four years.

23.2 Reasons for Growth

In the absence of statistical analyses, one can only speculate on the reasons for this rapid spread of corporate models, drawing upon both personal experience and the views of others. These suggest a number of inter-related causes. Models became cheaper, more quickly produced, more flexible, more easily understood by managers and consequently more readily accepted, as the lessons of the failure of some of the early, large-scale, general-purpose models became assimilated. This change in type of model was assisted by the development of new high-level planning languages designed specifically to aid corporate modelling. Vigorous promotion of these languages by the computer bureaus not only led to substitution of these for general-purpose languages, like FORTRAN and PL/1, but also sold the concept of modelling to senior management. Moreover, because of the relative ease with which they could be learnt and used, these new languages opened a new era of modelling by users, primarily accountants, which led to easier acceptance of corporate models as legitimate tools. The growth of modelling was not, however, unrelated to changing applications. Initially, use of corporate models spread because they were found to permit speedy evaluation and exploration of a wider range of alternatives in a wider range of possible future conditions. Then the adverse economic conditions of the mid-1970s led to recognition of their potential as aids to control. This gave a further fillip to their development. Finally, in addition to such good reasons, it is probable that corporate modelling was introduced into some companies because it became fashionable. In one company known to the author a corporate model was developed without a clear idea of the costs, benefits, or even applications.

Together these factors are intertwined in the evolving experience of modelling over the last decade to which we turn more fully in subsequent sections.

23.3 Types of Model in Use

One of the most conspicuous changes in corporate modelling between 1968 and 1980 has been in their type. Grinyer and Wooller (1975a) found that, by 1974, the simple, deterministic, financial simulation model was already dominant as Figure 23.2 shows. Moreover, their inspection of type of model by year of start revealed a strong trend away from optimizing and probabilistic models towards this simpler type. Some of the modellers interviewed had actually substituted smaller deterministic simulation models for optimizing and probabilistic ones. They said that optimizing models often failed to reflect adequately the complex and changing mix of company objectives, sometimes suggested 'optimal solutions' which were not credible to managers, and were mostly ill-understood by managers outside the oil industry. Probabilistic models, too, mystified managers, who were often unable to estimate subjective inputs or to interpret output. Moreover, some modellers thought them technically suspect because of the apparent impossibility of adequately representing interdependencies. In addition, they involved high costs of development and excessive running costs, this being consistent with Flower's reference (Flower, 1973) to them as 'gold-plated'. Perhaps for these reasons, the trend towards simpler, deterministic corporate models has continued strongly. Experience of corporate modellers consulted suggests that the vast majority of models developed since 1974 have been relatively simple, deterministic, financial simulation models.

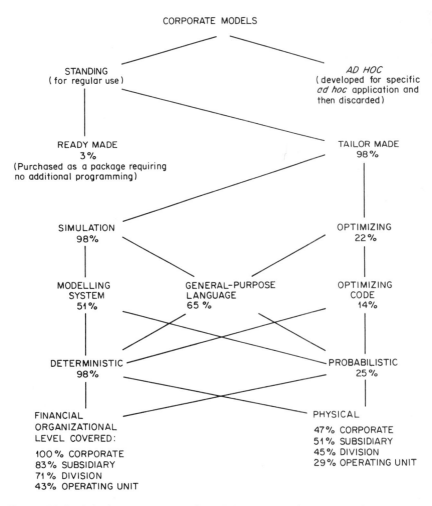

CORPORATE MODELS

STANDING
(for regular use)

AD HOC
(developed for specific
ad hoc application and
then discarded)

READY MADE
3 %
(Purchased as a package requiring
no additional programming)

TAILOR MADE
98 %

SIMULATION
98 %

OPTIMIZING
22 %

MODELLING
SYSTEM
51 %

GENERAL–PURPOSE
LANGUAGE
65 %

OPTIMIZING
CODE
14 %

DETERMINISTIC
98 %

PROBABILISTIC
25 %

FINANCIAL
ORGANIZATIONAL
LEVEL COVERED :

100 % CORPORATE
83 % SUBSIDIARY
71 % DIVISION
43 % OPERATING UNIT

PHYSICAL

47 % CORPORATE
51 % SUBSIDIARY
45 % DIVISION
29 % OPERATING UNIT

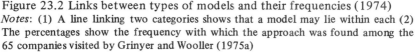

Figure 23.2 Links between types of models and their frequencies (1974)
Notes: (1) A line linking two categories shows that a model may lie within each (2)
The percentages show the frequency with which the approach was found among the
65 companies visited by Grinyer and Wooller (1975a)

At the same time there was a move away from the huge models of the entire
operations of the company, like Gershefski's (1969) renowned but apprently ill-
starred model of the Sun Oil company or the massive linear-programming model
of British Petroleum (Deam, Bennet and Leather, 1975), towards a modular
approach within which smaller, more application specific, models are linked, often
by disc-held files. Large, 'monolithic' models which mapped production and marketing processes as well as financial logic took too long to develop, were too frequently seen to be of no particular value to any group of managers because they

had been designed as general-purpose tools and required too many input data. Also they were often expensive to run, because the detailed data was aggregated from operational level to successively higher hierarchical levels, despite the fact that such operational data were often thought irrelevant to strategic decision taking. For instance, it is possible to question the importance to long-term capacity decisions of optimizing the material mix, as in the model of Van der Burghs (Cooper and Jones, 1972), on the basis of estimates of distant prices, when such predictions are so liable to error.

Moreover, because of their complexity such models were time consuming to modify or update, yet many of the strategic options that decision-makers wish to explore involve structural changes in the company and hence the model. Where the model builder anticipated at least some of these, the options could be represented by subroutines programmed into the model, and called by choice of appropriate control parameters. The control parameters input at the start of each run thus determined which of alternative routines would be followed. But use of such devices increased the size of the model, its complexity, the difficulty of understanding it and learning how to operate it, development time and cost, and cost of running, yet were unlikely to cover all feasible structural changes.

Perhaps for these reasons, a number of companies like Unilever, British Petroleum, Shell, and Pearson Longman have chosen a modular approach. Small, application-specific models, linked via disc-held files when appropriate, have considerable advantages over large, integrated ones. An earlier pay-off is achieved after relatively little expenditure of time and money; managers can identify more closely with specific models clearly designed to meet their particular decision-making needs; the models are more comprehensible to managers; they have lower, more readily satisfied appetites for data, and can be more easily integrated into the existing planning process; data may be inspected and amended before transfer between models; and the individual model can be more easily updated to meet changing circumstances.

Grinyer and Wooller (1975a) found that the trend towards simple, deterministic, financial simulation models, interlinked where appropriate, coincided with entry of a new breed of modeller. During the 1960s most models were developed by computer or operational research specialists, who saw corporate models as a means of extending their activities beyond the constraints of marketing and production studies. By 1974 there had been such a large influx of accountants, planners and other users that the dominance of the earlier, 'professional' modeller was already challenged. The trend has continued strongly since, with accountants now doing the lion's share of corporate modelling, and operational researchers entering when more complex marketing or mathematical relationships are involved. Whilst clearly associated with adoption of the modular approach, which permitted the inexperienced modeller to learn on small, simple models, without high cost or disastrous results, this entry of the accountant was above all related to a changed approach to programming.

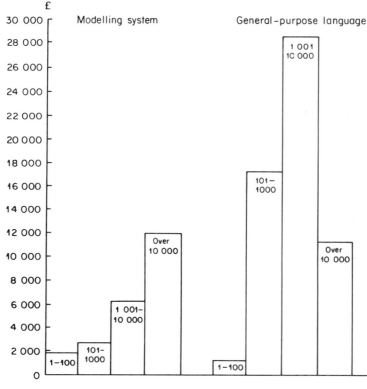

Figure 23.3 Average costs of model development

In the 1960s corporate models in the UK, as in the USA (Gershefski, 1970), were largely programmed in FORTRAN and batch run. Frequently large, processing a mass of data, and with voluminous reports, they were often time-consuming and expensive to produce. Gershefski (1969) calculated that 23 man-years had been spent on the Sun Oil model. Grinyer and Wooller (1975a) found that eight of their sample of 65 companies had spent over two man-years on programming alone, and had also incurred total costs of over £50 000 on their models. Such effort and cost was largely associated with size of model and use of a general-purpose language like FORTRAN as Figure 23.3 shows. The time and cost of programming in FORTRAN, with sometimes poor file-handling facilities, reinforced the weaknesses of the large, monolithic models already mentioned. Recognition of this led to development of high-level languages orientated towards planning applications, and with associated file handling, editing and report-generating routines, that have become called 'modelling systems' in the U.K.

Some of the earliest modelling systems were developed within companies for their own use. Schrieber (1970) includes a description of such a development in Xerox, in the U.S.A., but in the U.K. there were parallel developments in, for instance, Unilever, RTZ and Wiggins Teape. In each of these cases, to spread the considerable cost of development the company concerned offered its modelling system for sale to others. At the same time, modelling systems were becoming available from computer mainframe suppliers, in particular IBM and ICL. The ICL modelling system, PROSPER, developed in the early 1960s mainly for its own internal planning purposes, now began to be used more widely, largely because it was available free of charge to owners of ICL computers. Realizing the potential, an increasing number of computer bureaus climbed onto the bandwagon, including IBM's CALL system (STRATPLAN/AS) and ICL's Computel system (PROSPER), and made available modelling systems on a time-sharing interactive basis. Modelling systems became an important part of their sales thrust and quickly began to overtake FORTRAN as the preferred method of programming. Those bureaus which had not developed their own modelling systems, or which decided that their early products had been superseded by those of competitors, then entered the fray, often with software developed by specialists such as EPS (FCS) in the U.K. and SSI (SIMPLAN) in the U.S.A. (Naylor, 1979) or by companies such as Unilever and Wiggins Teape. The clear advantages of modelling systems, combined with the considerable marketing effort put behind them by the bureaus, led not only to their dominance as an approach to modelling but also to the more rapid introduction of corporate models *per se*.

By using a constant planning horizon set at the start of a run, the concept of a common file format with time on one axis of a two-dimensional matrix and variables on the other, and standard report-generating routines, the modelling systems were able to reduce input and output statements to a minimum, and handle the time dimension automatically, so removing the need to program the 'DO' loops necessary in FORTRAN. Programming was further facilitated by introduction of special functions and subroutines, called by simple instructions, for dealing with depreciation, taxation, net present value and other financial calculations, as well as aggregation of financial results to successively higher levels of a corporate organizational hierarchy. When added to the software already available for setting up permanent and temporary files, editing data, and statistical analysis (which were operated as standard features of time-sharing interactive systems), this planning-orientated software provided an easily learnt but powerful aid to financial planning.

Throughout the 1970s the modelling systems have been developed continuously and a wide range of sophisticated, yet cost effective, software packages are now available, many but not all tied to use of a computer bureau. Indeed, as many as 35 modelling systems currently available in the U.K. were analysed by Grinyer and Wooller (1975a). Some of these still have limitations, in terms for instance of somewhat restrictive constraints on the numbers of time periods, inputs, or program statements handled, or through being confined to performing only row operations (as opposed to column operations), but quite a number now offer the user more facilities than he is likely to need. He may use row or column operations, optimizing techniques, risk analysis, automatic sensitivity analysis, backward iteration, (routines for iteratively determining the value of any specificed input variable, values of the others being given, which would yield a desired value of any particular output variable), as well as a wide range of statistical techniques, mathematical and financial functions.

The better modelling systems now permit the user considerable flexibility in his modelling and some allow routines programmed in FORTRAN to be imbedded within the model. One at least, TABOL (described by Bhaskar (1978)), allows the programmer to write in FORTRAN at any point within the modelling system program without even needing to signal the change in language, a facility which some value but others inevitably claim to be of doubtful advantage. Similarly, an appropriate choice of modelling language can give access to powerful data-management systems, highly efficient editing routines, and flexible report-generating facilities which will aggregate rows or columns, and produce percentages, subtotals, underlinings, pagination, and titles desired with comparative ease.

These advances have led to significant reductions in programming costs. Informed sources estimate that the cost of programming using a good modelling system is no more than about a fifth of that of using FORTRAN. In the early 1970s, this cost advantage was, to some extent, offset by considerably higher running costs when frequent use and large volumes of data were involved. As many of the modelling systems used interpretative routines to convert their high-level language into FORTRAN, which was in turn compiled into machine code, this meant increased core-store requirement and additional use of the central processing unit. As improvements have occurred, however, this differential in running costs has narrowed, and is now claimed by some to be under 1.5 of that of running a FORTRAN program. It would be unwise to rely on this figure for any particular bureau though, for their file storage and other bases of charging differ widely, and costs for running a similar model seem to vary quite considerably.

In addition to faster programming, and hence lower development cost, modelling systems also offer ease of updating and above all of learning. Programming has become so greatly simplified, in some cases by the use of mnemonics, that the uninitiated can be taught to develop and run their own simple models within less than a week.

Hayes and Nolan (1974), in detecting similar trends within the U.S.A., suggested that modelling systems would become associated with *ad hoc* modelling of specific problems by the ultimate users themselves. Such a tendency is not apparent in the U.K. Most models are still 'standing' as opposed to *ad hoc*; in other words a model is developed for regular use, is held on a permanent file, but may be dumped onto a temporary file for modification as appropriate in particular runs. Such an approach has considerable advantages in terms of speed and economy of use, and is appropriate insofar as large parts of many corporate models are basically generators of financial reports. Again, Grinyer and Wooller (1975a) found only one finance director using corporate models who developed his own, and even he now leaves the task to younger, more junior accountants on his staff. Moreover, very few

	Ad hoc	Regular, scheduled
Evaluation of alternatives	Appraisal of specific problems or projects of an *ad hoc* nature	Regular annual corporate planning
Aid to control	Appraisal of financial implications of external events, such as changes in rates of tax or exchange rates, and of alternative responses open to management	1. Aggregation and analysis of monthly or quarterly financial reports of subsidiaries 2. Preparation of weekly or monthly reports on liquidity

Figure 23.4 Application classification matrix

senior managers access the computer directly themselves, preferring to leave this to supporting staff. Hence the concept of senior managers undertaking *ad hoc* modelling and using the computer via terminals as an extension of their minds is, in the U.K. at least, unrealized and, I suspect, will be unrealizable for some years to come.

Nonetheless, the rapid growth of corporate models, the development and widespread use of modelling systems, and the influx of the accounting fraternity have led to a complete transformation of the corporate modelling scene in the U.K. in the last decade.

23.4 Changing Applications

Corporate modelling applications may be divided along two dimensions, into *ad hoc* or regular (scheduled) on the one hand, and evaluation of alternatives or control on the other, the resulting four-cell matrix being shown in Figure 23.4. Within each cell, applications may be analyzed according to the hierarchical level and function within a company using the model. Grinyer and Wooller's survey (1975a) provides a snap-shot of applications in the mid-1970s: 83% of companies had models extending to the subsidiaries, and as many as 43% to operating unit level. This reflects, to a large measure, the early tendency to develop large, integrated models representing the detailed operations of the company. The major uses and outputs of the models are shown in Tables 23.1–23.4. One feature of these results from 1974 is very evident. The emphasis is on evaluation of alternatives on an *ad hoc* or regular basis, the latter within a planning framework. Gershefski (1970) noted that development of corporate models lagged corporate planning by about three years. Similarly, in the U.K., corporate modelling was introduced in the early years as an aid to plan-

Table 23.1 Planning applications of models

Application	Number	%
(1) As *ad hoc* devices only (e.g. for merger proposals)	5	8
(2) In regular corporate and divisional planning only	29	44
(3) Both (1) and (2) above	30	46
(4) As a research tool	1	1

Table 23.2 Model users

User	Number	%
Planners	21	32
Accountants	20	31
Operational researchers	9	14
Actuaries	2	3
Computer specialists	4	6
Others	9	14

Table 23.3 Major uses of models

Application	Number	%
Financial planning (up to 1 year)	25	38
Financial planning (1 to 5 years)	51	78
Financial planning (over 5 years)	29	45
Cash-flow analysis	49	75
Aid marketing decisions	42	65
Aid production decisions	39	60
Project evaluation	29	45
Aid distribution decisions	25	38
Financing	9	14
New venture evaluation	9	14
Acquisition studies	8	12
Manpower	8	12
Aid purchasing decisions	7	11
Market share forecasting	5	8
Computer evaluation (purchase/rent)	3	5

ning, a means of evaluating alternatives and extrapolating financial results on the basis of a variety of assumptions.

In 1974 and 1975, as the world economy entered perhaps its worst recession since the Second World War, the emphasis in many U.K. companies switched abruptly from long-term planning to survival as their liquidity ratios deteriorated.

Table 23.4 Output reports generated by models

Report	Total company	Subsidi-aries	Divisions	Operating units
Profit and loss	64	28	26	14
Balance sheet	51	24	16	8
Cash flow	50	24	18	10
Financial ratio analysis	44	20	15	12
Source and use of funds statement	36	18	13	7
Marketing operations	22	16	20	15
Project evaluation	22	16	8	10
Production	22	14	18	14
Distribution	19	11	13	11
Purchasing	7	5	5	4
Manpower	6	4	6	4
Financing	5	1	1	1
New venture	2	1	2	1

Planners had often to devote their energies to liquidity planning. Short- and medium-term control became more important than evaluating long-term alternatives. Within this climate, the emphasis switched to use of corporate modelling to aid the control of cash flows. This change of emphasis was further reinforced by the impact of exchange-rate changes, price-control decisions and the like on company performance. Access to a standing model permitted companies to calculate the effect of the latest uncontrollable fiscal, price, or other changes in a matter of minutes rather than hours, and so allowed speedy response.

At the same time, a number of conglomerates began to turn to corporate models as a means of processing financial data submitted by their subsidiaries as both a means of control and an aid to planning. All in all, while planning applications did continue, the mid-1970s saw a growing emphasis on the application of corporate models for control purposes.

The upswing in the economy in 1977 and 1978, which terminated in 1979, witnessed a return to planning applications but associated with continued use for control purposes.

23.5 A Prognostication

Looking into the future, I would predict a continuation of existing trends, but with some major changes.

First, now that accountants have learnt to model, their dominance of the field of financial modelling is likely to continue. Indeed, in a number of companies they have already begun to extend their modelling beyond the financial domain, and their entry to an activity undertaken historically by mathematically orientated operational researchers may enrich it.

Second, accountants and others will continue to use modelling systems. These in turn will be further developed but in a manner to compensate for existing deficiencies. The modelling systems of the market leaders already include a plethora of routines suitable for financial modelling, and the marginal return to additional routines must be very small. Indeed further sophistication, by adding to learning time as well as the core-store requirement, could deter potential users. Yet improvement of editing, data management, programs, and output routines is still desirable in some of these cases. Similarly, some bureaus have placed heavy emphasis on development of excellent input, output, data management, and editing software, but still have some way to go incorporating financial routines for, say, tax calculations into their modelling systems. Further development is likely, then, to be a matter of market leaders matching the strengths of their competitors. It is difficult to see much scope in pressing further along the lines emphasized in the past.

Third, the modular approach to modelling has such advantages that it is likely to remain with us. However, it is probable that a 'standing' aggregative financial model will receive inputs from more *ad hoc* as well as other standing models. As accountants and planners with modelling skills move up the management hierarchy, they may well turn to more *ad hoc* modelling of particular problems, and then input their results into the report-generating corporate model. Input to models may also come direct from the routine files supported by an accounting system. Certainly more extensive use of data-management systems will permit an effective interface between corporate models and management information systems.

Fourth, this trend towards *ad hoc* modelling is likely to accelerate because of the rapid spread of minicomputers. Packages such as FCS and FINAR have been available for use on minicomputers for some time, and others are expected to move in the same direction. With increasingly cheap, and more widely used, minicomputers it is probable that *ad hoc* modelling and generation of standard reports will be undertaken more and more on hardware in the user's own offices and that the use of computer bureaus for small *ad hoc* models will decline.

Fifth, the use of corporate models for financial control of subsidiaries is likely to spread, and computer bureaus may well be used as a medium for rapid transfer of data. A subsidiary can use its own model to prepare a monthly statement of performance against budget, which once released can be accessed by head office, printed out and questioned, or aggregated directly into higher-level figures. Indeed explanations of variations from budget can also be held on file. Most of the leading bureaus offer extensive networks which can be accessed by local telephone. For example, the Honeywell system allows access, by such a call, from within the U.S.A., U.K., Continental Europe, or Australia to any file within minutes of its creation, given use of the appropriate user numbers, passwords, and file name. The potential for centralizing financial control are obvious, the dangers perhaps less so, and care must clearly be taken when planning the system to protect to a reasonable degree the security and autonomy of managers below the corporate level.

Finally, ten years ago those just entering the field of corporate modelling, with brave and grandiose visions, were very much pioneers. During the last decade, they have learnt that simplicity, low-cost, rapid development, and solution of specific problems, rather than sophistication, mathematical complexity and general decision making aids, are what management wants. Consequently, they have moved to modular, simple deterministic, financial simulation models, and have been strengthened in this change of direction by the entry to modelling of pragmatic but often mathematically limited accountants. Somehow acceptance by the accountancy fraternity has given corporate models a legitimacy, and they are becoming integrated into the fabric of financial planning procedures. In the process, corporate models have become practical tools, rather than intellectual toys, and for this reason are likely to continue as widely used but rarely talked about aids.

If the 1960s was the decade of critical path analysis, which is now used as a matter of course where appropriate but is no longer the subject of high-level seminars, the 1970s has been that of the corporate model. It is perhaps a sign of maturity that the frequency of seminars on corporate modelling is already beginning to decline in the U.K. In 1989 we will perhaps be talking about environmental models instead.

References

Bhaskar, K. (1978). *Building Financial Models: a Simulation Approach*, Associated Book Publishers, London.

Cooper, J. and Jones, P. (1972). 'The Corporate Decision', *Data Processing*, 14(2), 84-90.

Deam, R. J., Bennet, J. W., and Leather, J. (1975). *Firm: A Computer Model of a Growth Company*, Research Committee Paper No. 5, Institute of Chartered Accountants in England and Wales, London.

Flower, J. (1973). *Computer Models for Accountants*, Accountancy Age, Haymarket Press, London.

Gershefski, G. W., (1969). 'Building a Corporate Financial Model , *Harvard Business Review*, 47(4), 61-72.

Gershefski, G. W. (1970). 'Corporate Models: the State of the Art', *Management Science*, B, 16(6), 303-12.

Grinyer, P. H. and Batt, C. D. (1974). 'Some Tentative Findings on Corporate Financial Simulation Models', *Operational Research Quarterly*, 25(1), 148-67.

Grinyer, P. H. and Wooller, J. (1975a). *Corporate Models Today*, Institute of Chartered Accountants in England and Wales, London.

Grinyer, P. H. and Wooller, J. (1975b). 'Computer models for corporate planning', *Long Range Planning*, 8(1), 14-25.

Hayes, R. H. and Nolan, R. L. (1974). 'What Kind of Corporate Modelling Functions Best?', *Harvard Business Review*, 52(3), 102-12.

Naylor, T. H. (1979). *Corporate Planning Models*, Addison-Wesley. Reading, Massachussetts.

Schrieber, A. N. (ed.) (1970). *Corporate Simulation Models*, University of Washington, Washington.

24

Future Developments in Financial Modelling

JAMES BRYANT

24.1 Introduction

It seems improbable that the years ahead will simply be a period of consolidation in the application of modelling approaches to financial management. In this field, as in many others, computer-based techniques will inevitably proliferate, and it is likely that the lack of up-to-date information which currently hampers so many management decisions will largely disappear, to be replaced by difficulties of a more intractable nature relating to the forecasting of events in a far more uncertain and volatile environment. This future business environment will almost certainly stimulate advances in the theory and practice of financial control, and new techniques will develop to bring these ideas to bear on practical management problems.

Three main areas of future development in financial modelling will be examined briefly in this chapter. Firstly, new information requirements for financial decision-making and control will be considered. These stem largely from the growing complexity of the context in which management must operate. In the following section, new methodologies which may emerge to help meet these needs are suggested. Some specific recent theoretical developments which appear to have considerable potential are mentioned here. Finally, the supporting advances in computing technology, which will certainly occur during the remainder of this century, and their implications for financial modelling in the short- to medium-term, are discussed.

24.2 New Requirements

Two major areas of change seem likely to alter the requirements for financially related information in organizations of all sizes. The first is associated with the growing tendency to consider explicitly many more variables than have hitherto been used when financial decisions are taken. The second is linked with the acceptance of a wider responsibility by corporate management, both to employees and to the community at large. These two areas will now be examined in turn.

The development of multidimensional accounting practice stems from the realization that the activities of any organization give rise not only to monetary or cash flows, but also to physical flows and to changes in the levels of non-financial variables. Thus a manufacturing company not only uses capital assets and personnel expertise to generate profits through the sale of processed raw materials, but also necessarily produces end products from physical resources and energy inputs. The uses of accounting-type methodologies to measure these flows has led to the development of such techniques as energy accounting (Watt Committee on Energy, 1979) in which a traditional accounting framework has been used to record energy flows within organizations with a view to the more effective management of these increasingly costly movements. Other, broader forms of physical resource flow accounting have been reported (Bryant, 1980), while the changes taking place in the nature of the work and its implications for employment point to the probable extension of manpower accounting methods. It might appear that the developments which have been referred to lie outside the domain of financial reporting, and in a sense this is true. However, I feel that in the future the historical demarcations between traditional areas of corporate management will become blurred, and the 'financial models' which will be used then will make reference to and inform other areas of organizational control.

A further aspect of multidimensional accounting which seems likely to attain greater prominence is that of the relationships between the increased portfolio of control variables over time. An inevitable complication of making reference to a wider range of financial and non-financial variables as part of the decision-making process is that the relative importance of each variable and their relative movements over time must be considered. By comparison the theoretical concept of an 'economic man' motivated solely and exclusively by profit is indeed a simple one.

The growing complexity and detail of corporate reporting which has been referred to above stems to a large extent from social changes and an altered view of the nature and responsibilities of business enterprises and government agencies. Organisations are experiencing such changes both internally and externally. Within, there is a growing demand for employee participation in decision-making at all levels, and indeed no organization can survive without that tacit consent of its employees—workers who are becoming increasingly aware of their influence on the corporate future. Without, the mood is one of a responsibility that extends beyond the nominal owners of the organization to all those on whom its activities impinge to any significant degree. In some countries aspects of these developments have been expressed in the form of statutory corporate restructuring and reporting requirements. Ackoff (1974) has indicated a possible direction for future change, and it appears highly probable that such developments will be a necessary basis for any degree of social stability.

The whole question of social stability both on a national and on an international scale is of course one which underlies any attempt at predicting the course of future information requirements. It seems probable that those responsible for financial management in the future will have to deal with a very much more rapidly changing environment and possibly with conflicts against similarly well-informed and technically competent protagonists—a daunting prospect indeed.

24.3 New Methodologies

Inflation accounting and new approaches to such hoary old problems as stock valuation are recent responses to the changed economic circumstances in which organizations now operate. It is likely that the management context sketched out in the last section will also lead to new theoretical advances in the subject of accounting. In particular the difficulty posed by the comparison of alternatives, each expressed in terms of a multiplicity of variables, is one which confronts many of the social sciences, and developments in accounting will undoubtedly be related to new ideas used elsewhere. As yet, the area of multicriteria decision making is little explored except by theoreticians and it remains to be seen how practical implementation will advance.

One of the central problems of contemporary management is that of management education. It has been pointed out many times how such conceptually simple methodologies as risk analysis and optimization methods have failed to gain credence with managers, who regard them as abstruse and practically irrelevant techniques. Undoubtedly there has been a lamentable lack of communication between academics and managers in this as in other areas, the former possibly overselling their product, the latter regarding new ideas with undue scepticism. New techniques can play an important supporting role in aiding and informing managerial decisions without abrogating management skills and judgment.

A theory which may do much to bridge the gap between the inexact and unpredictable world in which a manager operates and the precise and rational models which he may use to help him, is the recently developed concept of fuzzy sets (Zadeh, 1965). This makes it possible to handle vague data in a mathematically rigorous way. Thus, for example, in the classic capital rationing problem of selecting a set of projects yiedling the maximum N.P.V., a fuzzy formulation would allow the user to employ vague estimates of future cash flows or the budget available, and yet still find an attractive (if not 'optimal' in a more limited sense) solution.

Other methodologies which have still to realize their full potential in financial modelling include systems dynamics which Shehata (1977) has applied to cash-flow planning, and advanced forecasting techniques. The latter have been used extensively in planning various aspects of corporate operation, but have rarely been used in conjunction with financial models, although the value of any such modelling exercise depends crucially on the quality of the forecasts of input variables which have to be provided.

Other developments in the area of methodology which may be hoped for, relate to the presentation of information to the user, and the provision of a relevant and useful database for decision-making. Such futuristic visions as the 'control room' suggested by Beer (1975) and actually implemented, albeit for a very brief period, in the government of a country, may not lie in the immediate future, but the basic idea of a readily accessed bank of information from which selected features can be drawn out and their probable consequences explored is a sound one. The importance of effective methods of presenting complex information to management without thereby distorting or simplifying away essential features cannot be over-stated and it is to be hoped that new visual techniques derived from the arts and from the skills of the media business may be drawn upon to provide assistance here.

24.4 New Faciltities

None of the developments in financial modelling which have been described in this book would have been practicable without the dramatic advances in computing technology over the past thirty years. Future changes in this area will have equally far-reaching repercussions.

The essential features of the computer revolution are concerned with information handling: compact methods of storage; rapid techniques for manipulation; and vastly improved capabilities of transmission. This has led to the setting up of computerized databases on a national, regional, company, and in some instances on even a household or personal level. Communication between these databases through improved telecommunication systems is rapdily developing and is no longer confined, for instance, to the simple transmission of data from company subsidiaries to head offices or from retail outlets to a central sales monitoring facility, but also links providing organizations with sales intelligence data, government-compiled statistics and environmental data such as share prices. The further integration of such methods into the management process will be a major influence on financial modelling which has hitherto often been hampered by the burden imposed by the need to provide adequate input data for model validation and use.

A succinct statement of future developments in computer hardware and software might be that there will be a democratization of information handling. The use of computers need no longer be the prerogative of large organizations, and the availability of small, cheap microcomputers is already making inroads on such traditional areas of historical accounting as sales, purchase and nominal ledgers within relatively small companies. Hundreds of off-the-shelf, low-priced systems are on the market from which small businesses can choose and so the cost of development, apart from minimal tailoring to individual requirements, is slight for any single user. More relevant to the subject of financial modelling are signs that the application of microcomputers to problems of financial decision-making is now developing and a variety of uses of this sort has recently been reported covering such subjects as managing a share portfolio (Hayman, 1980), currency trading (Taylor, 1980) and betting-shop management (Knight, 1979). Not all users of microcomputers are individuals or small businesses, however, and Carreras Rothmans, one of the leading U.K. tobacco manufacturers, is using a micro-based system in marketing planning to produce financial reports in response to 'what if' questions (Floyd, 1980). Such developments bring computing power very much closer to the individuals responsible for decision-making and may well encourage a more adventurous and innovative management approach, as a wider range of options may be considered and explored without any need to make them known to a wider audience.

Specific developments which may be expected which are relevant to the financial modelling field include the growth of a new generation of modelling languages which will provide the user with more conversational interactive facilities, and the formation of computer/telecommunications networks giving vastly improved access to databases (and also to other models, rather in the manner that the Treasury model of the U.K. economy is currently available to other users). However, even if the dream of the management team routinely using their desk-top computer is realized, it will be management, however defined, who still bear the lonely responsibility for decision-making.

References

Ackoff, R. L. (1974). *Redesigning the Future*, Wiley, New York.

Beer, S. (1975) *Platform for Change*, Wiley, Chichester, Sussex.

Bryant, J. W. (1980). 'Flow Models for Assessing Human Activities', *European Journal of Operational Research*, 4, 73–83.

Floyd, K. (1980). 'Playing with money', *Practical Computing*, 2(11), 84.

Hayman, M. (1980). 'Directing a Large Investment Portfolio from his Armchair', *Practical Computing*, 3(9), 82–3.

Knight, M. (1979). 'Betting on PET', *Personal Computer World*, 2(6), 48–9.

Shehata, H. (1977). 'Systems Dynamics and Cash Flow Planning' *Management Decision*, 15(1), 19–36.

Taylor, S. J. (1980). 'Identifying that Profitable Moment for Buying Currency', *Practical Computing*, 2(11), 74–8.

Watt Committee on Energy (1979). *Evaluation of Energy Use*, Report No. 6, The Watt Committee on Energy, London.

Zadeh, L. A. (1965). 'Fuzzy sets' *Information Control*, 8, 338–53.

Additional Bibliography

Part 1 Fundamentals

Bhaskar, K. (1978). *Building Financial Models,* Associated Book Programmes, London.

Flower, J. (1973). *Computer Models for Accountants,* Haymarket, London.

McRae, T. W. (1977). 'Financial Computer Models', *Management Decision,* **15**(1), 2–18.

Meyer, H. I. (1977). *Corporate Financial Planning Models,* Wiley, New York.

Myers, S. C. (1976). *Modern Developments in Financial Management,* Dryden, Hinsdale, Illinois.

Naylor, T. H. (1970). *Corporate Planning Models,* Addison-Wesley, Reading, Massachusetts.

Wheelwright, S. C. and Makridakis, S. G. (1972). *Computer-Aided Modeling for Managers,* Addison-Wesley, Reading, Massachusetts.

Part 2 Operational Planning Models

Archer, W. R. V. (1971). 'The R.T.Z. Financial Modelling Programme', *Long Range Planning,* **3**(4), 32–8.

Bell, J. A. (1970). 'Production Strategy Decisions—a Simulation Model Approach', *Long Range Planning,* **2**(4), 62–73.

Franks, J. R., Bunton, C J., and Broyles, J. E. (1974). 'A Decision Analysis Approach to Cash Flow Management', *Operational Research Quarterly,* **25**(4), 573–87.

Gregory, G. (1976). 'Cash Flow Models: a Review', *Omega,* **4**(6), 643–56.

Grimmelman, F. J. (1979). 'Managing Construction Funds and Investments with a Computer Model', *Hospital Financial Management,* February, 34–40.

Kingshott, A. L. (1968). 'Financial Forecasting for Corporate Planning', *Long Range Planning,* **1**(2), 28–36.

Lieberman, G. (1978). 'A Systems Approach to Foreign Exchange Risk', *Harvard Business Review,* **56**(6), 14–19.

Mallinson, A. H. (1974). 'A Risk Analysis Approach to Profits Forecasts', *Accounting and Business Research* (4), 83–95.

Murphy, R. C. (1975). 'A Computer Model Approach to Budgeting', *Management Accounting,* June, 34–6.

Packer, J. J. L. (1971). 'The Projection of Financial Results', *Long Range Planning,* **3**(3), 49–53.

Rivers, R. and Oxner, T. H. (1980). 'A Network Simulation for Budgeting' paper presented at Joint National Meeting of The Institute of Management Science and Operations Research Society of America, Washington D.C., May 1980.
Shehata, H. (1977). 'Systems Dynamics and Cash Flow Planning', *Management Decision,* **15**(1), 19–36.

Part 3 Strategic Planning Models

Ashton, D. J. and Atkins, D. R. (1970). 'Multicriteria Planning for Financial Planning', *Journal of the Operational Research Society,* **30**(3), 259–70.
Cooper, I. and Hodges, S. (1979). *A Portfolio Simulation Model–U.K. Pension Funds,* London Business School, London.
Deam, R. J., Bennet, J. W., and Leather, J. (1975). *Firm: A Computer Model For Financial Planning,* Institute of Chartered Accountants in England and Wales.
Hertz, D. B. (1979). 'Risk Analysis in Capital Investment', *Harvard Business Review,* **57**(5), 169–81.
Palma, F. (1972). 'Computerized Analysis of Capital Projects by DCF Techniques', *Long Range Planning,* **5**(4), 53–60.
Spronk, J. (1979). *Interactive Multiple Goal Programming as an Aid for Capital Budgeting and Financial Planning with Multiple Goals,* Erasmus University, Rotterdam.
Zettergren, L. (1975). 'Financial Issues in Strategic Planning', *Long Range Planning,* **8**(3), 23–32.

Part 4 Models in Corporate Planning

Baynes, P. (ed.) (1973). *Case Studies in Corporate Planning,* Pitman, London.
Gardiner, C. and Ward, P. W. (1974). 'A Long Range Financial Resource Planning Model for a Local Authority', *Operational Research Quarterly,* **25**(1), 55–64.
Ishikawa, A. (1975). *Corporate Planning and Control Model Systems,* New York University Press, New York.
Roper, D. A. (1978). 'Planning Developments in British Nuclear Fuels Ltd.', *Long Range Planning,* **11**(5), 32–40.
Sprague, R. H. and Watson, H. J. (1976). 'A Decision Support System for Banks', *Omega,* **4**(6), 657–71.
Welter, P. (1971). 'Financial Aspects of Company Planning', *Long Range Planning,* **6**(1), 36–41.

Part 5 Financial Modelling Case Histories

Ashcroft, K. (1979). 'Selecting Modelling Packages', *Accountancy,* April, 107–10.
Chartered Institute of Public Finance and Accountancy (1979). *Financial Modelling,* C.I.P.F.A., London.
Hammond, J. S. (1974). 'Do's and don'ts of computer models for planning', *Harvard Business Review,* **52**(2), 110–23.
Higgins, J. C. and Finn, R. (1976). 'Managerial Attitudes towards Computer Models for Planning and Control', *Long Range Planning,* **9**(6), 107–12.
Mann, C. W. (1978). 'The Use of a Model in Long Term Planning—a Case History', *Long Range Planning,* **11**(5), 55–62.
Mulvaney, J. E. and Mann, C. W. (1976). *Practical Business Models,* Heinemann, London.
Naylor, T. H. and Mansfield, M. J. (1977). 'The Design of Computer-based Planning and Modelling systems', *Long Range Planning,* **10**(1), 16–25.

Rowe, P. and Basson, P. (1973). 'Implementing Financial Modelling', *Data Processing,* **20**(5), 17–19.

Part 6 The Practice of Financial Modelling

Boulden, J. B. (1971). 'Computerised Corporate Planning', *Long Range Planning,* 3(4), 2–9.
Faus, D. J. (1974). 'Financial Models: a European Survey', *Journal of General Management,* 1(3), 48–59.
Financial Executives' Research Foundation (1975). *The Use of Financial Models in Business,* FERF, New York.
Naylor, T. H. and Schauland, H. (1976). 'Experience with corporate simulation models—a survey', *Long Range Planning,* 9(2), 94–100.
Power, P. D. (1975). 'Computers and Financial Planning', *Long Range Planning,* 8(6), 53–9.

Index

See also the detailed list of Contents for further information

Academic/managerial interface, 443
Accounting, control, 10, 23
    decision, 9, 23
    financial, 9, 23
    inflation, 13, 443
    management, 9, 10, 23
    multidimensional, 442
Accounting conventions, 12, 13
Acquisitions, analysis, 205, 261
    capital structure, 276, 277
    cash price, 273–278
    feasibility, 275, 276
    financed by cash, 266–277
    financed by stock, 277–280
    rate of return, 275
    valuation, 264–266
Adaptive forecasting, 38
Allowances, model of capital, 49, 52,
    179–181, 208, 217, 361
Asset portfolio model, 412–416

Backward iteration, 433, 434
Balance sheet, 11
    model, 55, 59, 209, 348, 381
Bank interest model, 49, 54
Beer costing application, 104, 105, 109,
    110, 112–115
Bottom up models, 32
Box-Jenkins forecasting, 39
Budget, 18
    model, 32, 86–89, 99–115, 149–173,
    324–335, 361–364, 409–411,
    413, 415
    variances, 18, 150, 409
Budget/actual, comparisons, 18, 166,
    172, 228, 330, 331, 358
    ratios, 19, 20

Budgetary control system, 149, 150
Budgeting process, 150, 408, 409

Capital allowances model, 49, 52,
    179–181, 208, 217, 266, 273, 361
Capital cycle, 4, 5, 49
Capital expenditure model, 324–326
Capital rationing, 252–258
Cardboard box costs application, 98, 99,
    104–108
Cash budget, 122, 123, 143, 144
Cash budgeting, heuristic methods,
    122–140, 143, 145
    optimizing methods, 145–147
Cash flow, control of, 121, 122
    forecasting, 124
    in acquisitions, 265, 268, 270, 271
    model, 131–134, 208, 289, 353–357
Cash flow cycle, capital, 4, 5, 49
    trading, 4, 5, 48, 67
Cash management, 121, 122, 141, 142,
    250
Cash purchase, 176, 273–278
Causal regression models, 39, 42
Cement industry application, 203
Central/unit matching, 163, 356, 357
Chemical industry application, 345
Choice environment, 6
Cigar costing application, 98, 99,
    100–103
Closed loop models, 35
Coal industry application, 81, 82
Column processing, 207, 208, 433
Compound growth model, 37
Computer, hardware, 24
    language, 25, 30, 31
    mini/micro, 139, 363–367, 438, 444

451

networks, 445
program, 24, 25
software, 25, 30–32
Consolidation, 35
    model, 152–160, 332, 333, 353, 362
Construction materials industry
    application, 149
Control accounting, 10, 23
Control chart, cashflow, 124
    variance, 18, 19
Control ratios, 18–21
Control variables, choice of, 13, 442
Conventions of accounting, 12, 13
Cost of capital, 266, 273
Costing models, 49–51, 73, 74, 86–89,
    97–119, 189
Corporate expansion, 204, 205, 261,
    262
Corporate modelling, future trends,
    437–439
    historical development, 427–429
Corporate objectives, 3, 4, 45, 245, 246
Corporate planning, developmental,
    290–293
    model, 86, 89–92, 294–315, 321–340
    operational, 319–321, 336–339
Corporate responsibility, 246, 442
Corporate self, evaluation, 263, 264
Corporate trajectory, 10, 11, 23
Current assets model, 49, 53
Current cost accounting (CCA),
    convention, 13
    model, 55, 61, 354–356
Curve-fitting methods, 38, 40
Cycles, financial, 4, 5, 49

Data, 35
    collection, 79, 92, 132, 133, 157,
        172, 355
    files, 152, 153, 298, 300, 301, 350,
        354
    influence on model structure, 133
    input forms, 156, 159–162
    level of aggregation, 240
    links to datafiles, 65, 172, 411
    storage, 444
    transmission, 444
Database communication, 444, 445
Debtors model, 126, 127
Debugging programs, 209
Decision accounting, 9, 23
Decision-making cycle, 5–8

Delays in financial flows, 129–132
Dependency relationships, 44
Depreciation model, 52, 61, 225
Deterministic models, 29, 429, 431
Discount rate, 14, 178
Discounted cash flow (DCF), 15, 175,
    178–181, 208, 238
Discounting methods, 14–17
Dividend, model, 49
    policy, 231, 234, 235, 248
Double entry system, 12

Explanatory models, 39

FCS, calculation, 349, 351
    data files, 152
    files, 151
    hierarchy files, 152, 353–356
    input data, 349, 350
    logic files, 151, 349, 350
    reports, 349, 350
    sensitivity analysis, 349, 352
Finance house application, 407
Financial accounting, 9, 23
Financial decision-making, 5–8
    choice environment, 6
    constraints, 8
    evaluative comparisons, 7, 13–17
    local theory, 405, 406
    measurement scales, 7
    problem recognition, 6
    solution generation, 7
Financial model, 24
Financial model, example of, 47–65
    balance sheet, 55, 59
    bank interest, 49, 54
    current assets, 49, 53
    dividends, 49
    finished products, 49, 51
    fixed assets, 49, 52
    flow of funds, 55, 57
    implementation, 65
    inflation accounting, 55, 61
    investments, 49, 53
    profit and loss, 55, 56
    program structure, 60, 63, 64
    raw materials, 49, 50
    taxation, 49, 55, 58
    value added, 55, 60
Financial modelling, computerized, 25
Financial models, bottom up, 32
    closed loop, 35

diagrammatic representation, 26
flow diagram, 26
middle up, 32
open loop, 35, 37
operations tree, 25, 26
output facilities, 32, 444
size, 31
top down, 32
variables, 26
Financial objectives, 3, 4, 17, 442
Financial planning process, 294, 295
Financial relationships, 29
Financial reports, 10–13
Financial trajectory, 10, 35
constraints on, 45
optimal, 45
Financing policy, 175–178, 225,
231–233, 416, 417, 419–421
Finished products model, 49, 52
Fit of model, 37
Fixed assets model, 49, 52, 412–416
Flow diagram, 26
Flow of funds, statement, 11
model, 55, 57
Food pricing application, 111, 112,
116–118
Forecasting, 35–40
cycles, 38
trends, 38
Forecasting models, adaptive, 38
Box-Jenkins, 39
causal regression, 39, 42
choice of, 39, 40
compound growth, 37
curve fitting, 38, 40
explanatory, 39
fit of, 37
linear growth, 37
quadratic, 38
sigmoid, 38
smoothing techniques, 38, 39
subjective estimates, 36, 37, 42
Fuzzy sets, 443

General theory of finance, 405, 406
Graphical reports, 310, 311, 367–369

Hardware, 24
configuration, 362, 364–367
installation, 365, 366
Health care system, description of,
285–288

Health maintenance organization (HMO),
288–290
Hierarchy structure (FCS), 153, 154
High-level language, 30
Hire purchase, 176, 177
Historical cost convention, 12

Inflation, effects in project evaluation,
13, 186
testing alternative rates of, 307, 310,
311
Inflation accounting, 13, 443
model, 55, 61, 354–356
In-house modelling, 30, 433
transfer to, 347, 348
Input variables, selection of, 187, 188
Interactive sequence, examples of,
74–76, 160, 161, 195, 196,
332–335
Internal rate of return (IRR), 15, 191,
193
Investment appraisal model, 32,
204–229, 243
Investment criteria, 15–17
Investment policy, timing, 238–240
Investments model 53

Language, computer, 25, 30, 31
see also Programming languages
Leasing, 177, 178
Linear growth model, 37
Linear programming, 46, 143–147, 404,
430, 431
Liquidity planning, 417–419
Loan purchase, 176
Loans model, 222, 223, 225, 327, 328
Local authority system, description of,
318, 319
Local theory of financial decision-
making, 405, 406
Logic structure (FCS), 153
Long-range planning, 402
Low level language, 31

Macrostructure, model, 26
Management accounting, 9, 10, 23
Managerial/academic interface, 443
Manufacturing overheads model, 117
Marketing/production, conflict, 70
interface, 377, 378
Mathematical programming, 46,
143–147, 404, 430, 431

Microcomputers, 139, 363–367, 438, 444
Microstructure, model, 26
Middle up models, 32
Minicomputers, 139, 363–367, 438, 444
Model, role in planning, 336–339
Model benefits, 93–94, 111, 135–139, 150, 172, 199–201, 376
Model consolidation, 110, 332, 333
Model debugging, 209
Model design, 77, 78, 132, 133
  guidelines, 405
Model development, approach, 71, 104, 126–128, 150–151, 187, 204, 205
  effort, 94, 240, 312, 314, 323, 349, 361
  pitfalls, 372, 373
  team, 77, 78, 323
Model implementation, 77, 104, 311, 312
Model objectives, 71, 152, 296, 375, 390, 391, 435–437
Model operating requirements, 340
Model philosophy, 71, 205, 423
Model programming, 78, 126, 127, 134, 379
Model structure, 86–88, 98, 99, 104, 105, 152–156, 197, 198, 206, 296–298, 323, 324, 376–385
Model use, 76, 77, 84–86, 92, 93, 99, 104, 128, 129, 160, 198, 226–228, 312–314, 335, 336
  resources consumed, 89, 105, 229, 312, 347, 387
Model users, 77, 228, 229, 340
Model validation, 209
Modellers, 431, 439
Modelling, reasons for, 82, 83, 150, 186
  successful, 395–399
Modelling languages, 30, 430, 434, 445
Modelling systems, 30, 432, 439,438
  advantages, 434, 435
  facilities, 352, 433
Modular structure, 29, 31, 125, 126, 208, 209, 323, 324, 431, 438
Monte Carlo method, 42

Net present value (NPV), 15, 178
Networks, computer, 445
New project evaluation, 185
Non-optimizing models, 29

Objective function, 45
Open-loop models, 35–37
Operations tree, 25–29
  conventions, 27
  evaluation, 29
Optimization, 45, 46, 403
  constraints, 45
  mathematical programming, 46
  objective function, 45
Optimizing models, 30, 429, 433
Organization responsibility, 442
Output, facilities, 32
  graphical, 367
Output reports, 437
  balance sheet, 209, 212, 213, 216, 217, 348, 381
  budget, 102, 103, 152, 158
  cashflow, 136–139, 198, 210, 211, 252–258, 269, 382
  depreciation, 220, 221, 225
  financial ratios, 209, 224
  income, 73
  loans, 221, 223
  manufacturing costs, 384
  material costs, 112–115
  planning summaries, 298, 302–306
  prices, 100, 101, 106–108
  profit and loss, 90, 209, 214, 215, 309, 311, 348, 361–363, 380
  sales, 385
  trading, 155, 156, 162–171, 383

Paper industry application, 69, 70
Payback period, 15
Performance ratio, 20, 21
Pigment industry application, 371, 372
Planning, developmental, 290–293
  model, 86, 89–92, 294–315, 328–340
  operational, 319–321, 336–339
  requirements for model, 321, 322
Plant budget model, 84–89
Plant planning, 81
Port authority activities, description of, 185
Probabilistic models, 30, 429
  interpretation of, 44
Probability, 40
  assigning, 187
  density function, 40, 41
  distribution, 40, 41
Processing, column, 207, 208, 433

row, 207, 208
Product-line decisions, 69, 70
Product map, 71
Production/marketing, conflict, 70
  interface, 377, 378
Profit and loss account, 12
  model, 55, 56
Profit maximization, 3
Profitability ratio, 15, 20, 21
Program, computer, 24, 25
  debugging, 209
Programming languages, Basic, 65, 409,
    410
  COMPOSIT, 77, 346
  DATAFORM, 346
  FCS, 151, 347, 391, 392, 398, 433,
    438
  FORTRAN, 206, 429, 432–434
  PL/1, 429
  PLANMASTER, 346, 391, 392, 398,
    399
  PROSPER, 104, 150, 372, 393, 433
  SIMPLAN, 433
  STRATPLAN, 433
  TABOL, 434
Programming personnel, 31
Purchase for cash, 176, 273–278

Quadratic growth model, 38

Rate, discount, 14, 178
Rate of return, 15
  estimation of, 271
Ratios, budget/actual, 19–20
  control, 18–21
Raw materials supply model, 50, 84
Resource recovery, description of, 194,
  195
Revenue model, 327–329, 331
Revenue/cost ratio, 190, 192
Risk analysis, 40–44, 191, 192, 403,
  404, 473

advantages, 44
Row processing, 207, 208, 356, 433

Sales reports, 361, 362, 364
Sensitivity analysis, 167, 191, 194, 299,
  307, 310, 311
Share capital model, 53
Shareholder benefit, 4, 246–249
Sigmoid growth model, 38
Simulation, 42–44, 429, 431
  applications, 135, 188, 189
  appraisal, 200, 201
  dependency in, 44
  dividend growth models, 250–252
Smoothing techniques in forecasting, 38,
  39
Software, 25
  choices of, 30–32
Solvency ratio, 20, 21
Stakeholder benefit, 4
State space, 10
State variables, 10
Stochastic models, 10
Stock valuation, 13
Subjective forecasts, 36, 37, 42
Systems dynamics, 443

Taxation, allowances, 225
  models, 49, 55, 58, 357–361
Time value of money, 14
Time valued payback year, 191
Top down models, 32
Trading cycle, 48
Trajectory, 10, 35

Unit/central matching, 163, 356, 357

Validation, 209
Value added model, 55, 60
Variance, 18
  control chart, 18, 19
  quantity, 150

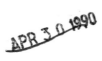